HOLLYWOOD KILLS

HOLLYWOOD KILLS

Edited by the Staff of *Mystery Scene*

Introduction by John Jakes

Carroll & Graf Publishers, Inc.
New York

Short Story Index
<u>1989-1993</u>

First Carroll & Graf edition 1993

Carroll & Graf Publishers, Inc.
260 Fifth Avenue
New York, NY 10001

Library of Congress Cataloging-in-Publication Data
Hollywood kills / edited by the staff of Mystery scene ;
    introduction by John Jakes. — 1st Carroll & Graf ed.
        p.   cm.
    ISBN 0-88184-879-4 : $21.00
    1. Detective and mystery stories, American.   2. Motion
picture industry—California—Los Angeles—Fiction.
3. Hollywood (Los Angeles, Calif.)—Fiction.   I. Mystery
scene.
PS648.D4H65   1993
813'.087208—dc20   93-21932
                                                                       CIP

Manufactured in the United States of America

Contents

Introduction

Hollywood Is a Story Town

But it wasn't always.

For years, while San Francisco boomed, the pueblo of Los Angeles remained a dusty adobe cowtown. Then, in the 1880s, the Southern Pacific Railroad began to offer excursion fares from the Midwest, hoping to attract settlers, and more business.

The settlers who came during the first land boom were quite unlike San Francisco's rainbow population. Southern California attracted chiefly midwestern WASPs; the demographic difference is evident to this day.

Two of these WASP immigrants, H. H. Wilcox and his wife Daeida, spotted a promising tract for development, in the shadow of the Cahuenga Mountains about a half day's buggyride from downtown Los Angeles. There was little growth on the tract of flatland except fig trees. Wilcox bought the acreage for three hundred dollars. His wife, allegedly in honor of a fond remembrance of holly trees at her family home in Illinois, christened it Hollywood.

Growth was slow and life was placid, not to say dull, until early in the twentieth century, when two things happened. To stimulate sales, the developers of Hollywood persuaded the Cahuenga Valley Railroad to extend a line out Western Avenue to Hollywood Boulevard; and certain raffish individuals from the East discovered Southern California's year-round sunshine. These of course were the early movie-makers from Biograph, Vitagraph, and other studios on Manhattan, Long Island, and the cliffs of New Jersey.

The first so-called studio opened in some rundown railroad buildings in 1909. In 1913, young Cecil B. DeMille turned out the first picture filmed entirely in the Hollywood area, "The Squaw Man." The established residents didn't like this new crowd of loose-living thespians, or the East European cloak-and-suit merchants and scrap iron dealers who financed the pictures. Nasty real estate advertisements appeared. "No dogs, Jews or actors." But the tide was coming in, and it would never go out again. Goodbye, 14th Street; goodbye, Fort Lee; Hollywood was forever the movie town.

A spicy stew of money, glamour, and often-unstable artistic temperament was destined to heat up and bubble over from time to time. There were drug deaths, crimes of passion, and other assorted scandals. An industry so exotic and lucrative was also bound to attract individuals who lived outside the law, and that, too, came to pass. Greed, gangsters, sudden fame, equally sudden failure, sex, sunshine—what a combination. Sure to generate great true-crime stories.

And it did. Think of the famous "wild party" precipitating the trial and fall from grace of Roscoe ("Fatty") Arbuckle. The unsolved murder of director William Desmond Taylor. The assassination of Las Vegas dream merchant Bugsy Siegel. The Charles Manson slaughter. The clouds of suspicion still surrounding the death of Marilyn Monroe.

It's a story town in other ways. For instance, every other person in Hollywood has an unproduced script. I realized this a few years ago during a taxi ride from LAX to Westwood, where I was to meet producer David L. Wolper at his Olympic Committee office. The cabbie actually carried a copy of his masterwork beside him on the front seat. He was a nice enough gent, pumped up with the Hollywood dream of instant success. He was a retiree and—guess what—a WASP transplant from mid-America.

But many besides cabbies and professional screen writers have been drawn to Hollywood because of the dynamite story material it generates. A list of novelists would include Nathanael West, Budd Schulberg, and the author some consider the best of our century, F. Scott Fitzgerald. His unfinished masterwork, "The Last Tycoon," has as its central character a studio genius named Monroe Stahr (read Irving Thalberg).

Harold Robbins was a motion picture executive before he turned to writing books. And we mustn't overlook the works of Jackie Collins, Judith Krantz, and other, lesser mistresses of shopping-

and-*shtupping* fiction more often than not involving movies and movie stars.

Hollywood fictions that are particular favorites of mine include Joseph Wambaugh's "The Glitter Dome," Michael Tolkin's "The Player," and Robert Campbell's *noir* novels of La-la Land; with unsparing honesty, all picture the Hollywood where dreams are more often nightmares.

This entertaining collection of shorter fiction likewise draws its inspiration from the darker, less savory side of the town. The editors have assembled talents as fine and diverse as Ross Macdonald, F. Paul Wilson, Robert Bloch, Fritz Leiber, and William Campbell Gault to bring you a group of tales ranging from realistic private-eye yarns to spooky supernatural stories.

Proving, simply, one more time, that Hollywood is indeed a place that we can't get enough of . . . a fabulous story town where some of the best stories are written outside, not inside, studio gates.

—JOHN JAKES
Hilton Head Island
September 1993

Robert Bloch's fiction is unique in the way it uses irony as a counterpoint to terror. *Psycho*, for all its grisliness, is not without its humorous moments, and his neglected small masterpiece *The Cunning* is one of the most grimly humorous takes on death and dying ever written.

Here, however, is a different side of Bob Bloch, the nostalgic Midwestern Bob Bloch, caught up in the melancholy many of us feel for the movies of yesteryear.

The Movie People

Robert Bloch

Two thousand stars.

Two thousand stars, maybe more, set in the sidewalks along Hollywood Boulevard, each metal slab inscribed with the name of someone in the movie industry. They go way back, those names; from Broncho Billy Anderson to Adolph Zukor, everybody's there.

Everybody but Jimmy Rogers.

You won't find Jimmy's name because he wasn't a star, not even a bit player—just an extra.

"But I deserve it," he told me. "I'm entitled, if anybody is. Started out here in 1920 when I was just a punk kid. You look close, you'll spot me in the crowd shots in *The Mark of Zorro*. Been in over 450 pictures since, and still going strong. Ain't many left who can beat that record. You'd think it would entitle a fella to something."

Maybe it did, but there was no star for Jimmy Rogers, and that bit about still going strong was just a crock. Nowadays Jimmy was lucky if he got a casting call once or twice a year; there just isn't any spot for an old-timer with a white muff except in a western barroom scene.

Most of the time Jimmy just strolled the boulevard; a tall, soldierly-erect incongruity in the crowd of tourists, fags and freakouts. His home address was on Las Palmas, somewhere south of Sunset. I'd never been there but I could guess what it was—one of those old

frame bungalow-court sweatboxes put up about the time he crashed
the movies and still standing somehow by the grace of God and the
disgrace of the housing authorities. That's the sort of place Jimmy
stayed at, but he didn't really *live* there.

Jimmy Rogers lived at the Silent Movie.

The Silent Movie is over on Fairfax, and it's the only place in
town where you can still go and see *The Mark of Zorro*. There's
always a Chaplin comedy, and usually Laurel and Hardy, along with
a serial starring Pearl White, Elmo Lincoln, or Houdini. And the
features are great—early Griffith and DeMille, Barrymore in *Dr.
Jekyll and Mr. Hyde,* Lon Chaney in *The Hunchback of Notre Dame,*
Valentino in *Blood and Sand,* and a hundred more.

The bill changes every Wednesday, and every Wednesday night
Jimmy Rogers was there, plunking down his ninety cents at the box
office to watch *The Black Pirate* or *Son of the Shiek* or *Orphans of
the Storm.*

To live again.

Because Jimmy didn't go there to see Doug and Mary or Rudy or
Clara or Gloria or the Gish sisters. He went there to see himself, in
the crowd shots.

At least that's the way I figured it, the first time I met him. They
were playing *The Phantom of the Opera* that night, and afterward I
spent the intermission with a cigarette outside the theatre, studying
the display of stills.

If you asked me under oath, I couldn't tell you how our conversation started, but that's where I first heard Jimmy's routine about the
450 pictures and still going strong.

"Did you see me in there tonight?" he asked.

I stared at him and shook my head; even with the shabby hand-
me-down suit and the white beard, Jimmy Rogers wasn't the kind
you'd spot in an audience.

"Guess it was too dark for me to notice," I said.

"But there were torches," Jimmy told me. "I carried one."

Then I got the message. He was in the picture.

Jimmy smiled and shrugged. "Hell, I keep forgetting. You
wouldn't recognize me. We did *The Phantom* way back in 'twenty-
five. I looked so young they slapped a mustache on me in Make-up
and a black wig. Hard to spot me in the catacombs scenes—all long
shots. But there at the end, where Chaney is holding back the mob,
I show up pretty good in the background, just left of Charley Zim-

mer. He's the one shaking his fist. I'm waving my torch. Had a lot of trouble with that picture, but we did this shot in one take."

In weeks to come I saw more of Jimmy Rogers. Sometimes he was up there on the screen, though truth to tell, I never did recognize him; he was a young man in those films of the twenties, and his appearances were limited to a flickering flash, a blurred face glimpsed in a crowd.

But always Jimmy was in the audience, even though he hadn't played in the picture. And one night I found out why.

Again it was intermission time and we were standing outside. By now Jimmy had gotten into the habit of talking to me and tonight we'd been seated together during the showing of *The Covered Wagon.*

We stood outside and Jimmy blinked at me. "Wasn't she beautiful?" he asked. "They don't look like that any more."

I nodded. "Lois Wilson? Very attractive."

"I'm talking about June."

I stared at Jimmy and then I realized he wasn't blinking. He was crying.

"June Logan. My girl. This was her first bit, the Indian attack scene. Must have been seventeen—I didn't know her then, it was two years later we met over at First National. But you must have noticed her. She was the one with the long blond curls."

"Oh, *that* one." I nodded again. "You're right. She was lovely."

And I was a liar, because I didn't remember seeing her at all, but I wanted to make the old man feel good.

"Junie's in a lot of the pictures they show here. And from 'twenty-five on, we played in a flock of 'em together. For a while we talked about getting hitched, but she started working her way up, doing bits—maids and such—and I never broke out of extra work. Both of us had been in the business long enough to know it was no go, not when one of you stays small and the other is headed for a big career."

Jimmy managed a grin as he wiped his eyes with something which might once have been a handkerchief. "You think I'm kidding, don't you? About the career, I mean. But she was going great, she would have been playing second leads pretty soon."

"What happened?" I asked.

The grin dissolved and the blinking returned. "Sound killed her."

"She didn't have a voice for talkies?"

Jimmy shook his head. "She had a great voice. I told you she was all set for second leads—by nineteen thirty she'd been in a dozen talkies. Then sound killed her."

I'd heard the expression a thousand times, but never like this. Because the way Jimmy told the story, that's exactly what had happened. June Logan, his girl Junie, was on the set during the shooting of one of those early ALL TALKING—ALL SINGING—ALL DANCING epics. The director and camera crew, seeking to break away from the tyranny of the stationary microphone, rigged up one of the first traveling mikes on a boom. Such items weren't standard equipment yet, and this was an experiment. Somehow, during a take, it broke loose and the boom crashed, crushing June Logan's skull.

It never made the papers, not even the trades; the studio hushed it up and June Logan had a quiet funeral.

"Damn near forty years ago," Jimmy said. "And here I am, crying like it was yesterday. But she was my girl—"

And that was the other reason why Jimmy Rogers went to the Silent Movie. To visit his girl.

"Don't you see?" he told me. "She's still alive up there on the screen, in all those pictures. Just the way she was when we were together. Five years we had, the best years for me."

I could see that. The two of them in love, with each other and with the movies. Because in those days, people *did* love the movies. And to actually be *in* them, even in tiny roles, was the average person's idea of seventh heaven.

Seventh Heaven, that's another film we saw with June Logan playing a crowd scene. In the following weeks, with Jimmy's help, I got so I could spot his girl. And he'd told the truth—she was a beauty. Once you noticed her, really saw her, you wouldn't forget. Those blond ringlets, that smile, identified her immediately.

One Wednesday night Jimmy and I were sitting together watching *The Birth of a Nation.* During a street shot Jimmy nudged my shoulder. "Look, there's June."

I peered up at the screen, then shook my head. "I don't see her."

"Wait a second—there she is again. See, off to the left, behind Walthall's shoulder?"

There was a blurred image and then the camera followed Henry B. Walthall as he moved away.

I glanced at Jimmy. He was rising from his seat.

"Where you going?"

He didn't answer me, just marched outside.

When I followed I found him leaning against the wall under the marquee and breathing hard; his skin was the color of his whiskers.

"Junie," he murmured. "I saw her—"

I took a deep breath. "Listen to me. You told me her first picture was *The Covered Wagon.* That was made in 1923. And Griffith shot *The Birth of a Nation* in 1914."

Jimmy didn't say anything. There was nothing to say. We both knew what we were going to do—march back into the theatre and see the second show.

When the scene screened again we were watching and waiting. I looked at the screen, then glanced at Jimmy.

"She's gone," he whispered. "She's not in the picture."

"She never was," I told him. "You know that."

"Yeah." Jimmy got up and drifted out into the night, and I didn't see him again until the following week.

That's when they showed the short feature with Charles Ray— I've forgotten the title, but he played his usual country-boy role, and there was a baseball game in the climax with Ray coming through to win.

The camera panned across the crowd sitting in the bleachers and I caught a momentary glimpse of a smiling girl with long blond curls.

"Did you see her?" Jimmy grabbed my arm.

"That girl—"

"It was Junie. She winked at me!"

This time I was the one who got up and walked out. He followed, and I was waiting in front of the theatre, right next to the display poster.

"See for yourself." I nodded at the poster. "This picture was made in 1917." I forced a smile. "You forget, there were thousands of pretty blond extras in pictures and most of them wore curls."

He stood there shaking, not listening to me at all, and I put my hand on his shoulder. "Now look here—"

"I *been* looking here," Jimmy said. "Week after week, year after year. And you might as well know the truth. This ain't the first time it's happened. Junie keeps turning up in picture after picture I know she never made. Not just the early ones, before her time, but later, during the twenties when I knew her, when I knew exactly what she was playing in. Sometimes it's only a quick flash, but I see her—then she's gone again. And the next running, she doesn't come back.

"It got so that for a while I was almost afraid to go see a show—figured I was cracking up. But now you've seen her too—"

I shook my head slowly. "Sorry, Jimmy. I never said that." I glanced at him, then gestured toward my car at the curb. "You look tired. Come on, I'll drive you home."

He looked worse than tired; he looked lost and lonely and infinitely old. But there was a stubborn glint in his eyes, and he stood his ground.

"No, thanks. I'm gonna stick around for the second show."

As I slid behind the wheel I saw him turn and move into the theatre, into the place where the present becomes the past and the past becomes the present. Up above in the booth they call it a projection machine, but it's really a time machine; it can take you back, play tricks with your imagination and your memory. A girl dead forty years comes alive again, and an old man relives his vanished youth—

But I belonged in the real world, and that's where I stayed. I didn't go to the Silent Movie the next week or the week following.

And the next time I saw Jimmy was almost a month later, on the set.

They were shooting a western, one of my scripts, and the director wanted some additional dialogue to stretch a sequence. So they called me in, and I drove all the way out to location, at the ranch.

Most of the studios have a ranch spread for western action sequences, and this was one of the oldest; it had been in use since the silent days. What fascinated me was the wooden fort where they were doing the crowd scene—I could swear I remembered it from one of the first Tim McCoy pictures. So after I huddled with the director and scribbled a few extra lines for the principals, I began nosing around behind the fort, just out of curiosity, while they set up for the new shots.

Out front was the usual organized confusion; cast and crew milling around the trailers, extras sprawled on the grass drinking coffee. But here in the back I was all alone, prowling around in musty, log-lined rooms built for use in forgotten features. Hoot Gibson had stood at this bar, and Jack Hoxie had swung from this dance-hall chandelier. Here was a dust-covered table where Fred Thomson sat, and around the corner, in the cut-away bunkhouse—

Around the corner, in the cut-away bunkhouse, Jimmy Rogers sat on the edge of a mildewed mattress and stared up at me, startled, as I moved forward.

"You—?"

Quickly I explained my presence. There was no need for him to explain his; casting had called and given him a day's work here in the crowd shots.

"They been stalling all day, and it's hot out there. I figured maybe I could sneak back here and catch me a little nap in the shade."

"How'd you know where to go?" I asked. "Ever been here before?"

"Sure. Forty years ago in this very bunkhouse. Junie and I, we used to come here during lunch break and—"

He stopped.

"What's wrong?"

Something *was* wrong. On the pan make-up face of it, Jimmy Rogers was the perfect picture of the grizzled western old-timer; buckskin britches, fringed shirt, white whiskers and all. But under the make-up was pallor, and the hands holding the envelope were trembling.

The envelope—

He held it out to me. "Here. Mebbe you better read this."

The envelope was unsealed, unstamped, unaddressed. It contained four folded pages covered with fine handwriting. I removed them slowly. Jimmy stared at me.

"Found it lying here on the mattress when I came in," he murmured. "Just waiting for me."

"But what is it? Where'd it come from?"

"Read it and see."

As I started to unfold the pages the whistle blew. We both knew the signal; the scene was set up, they were ready to roll, principals and extras were wanted out there before the cameras.

Jimmy Rogers stood up and moved off, a tired old man shuffling out into the hot sun. I waved at him, then sat down on the moldering mattress and opened the letter. The handwriting was faded, and there was a thin film of dust on the pages. But I could still read it, every word. . . .

> Darling:
>   I've been trying to reach you so long and in so many ways. Of course I've seen you, but it's so dark out there I can't always be sure, and then too you've changed a lot through the years.

But I *do* see you, quite often, even though it's only for a moment. And I hope you've seen me, because I always try to wink or make some kind of motion to attract your attention.

The only thing is, I can't do too much or show myself too long or it would make trouble. That's the big secret— keeping in the background, so the others won't notice me. It wouldn't do to frighten anybody, or even to get anyone wondering why there are more people in the background of a shot than there should be.

That's something for you to remember, darling, just in case. You're always safe, as long as you stay clear of closeups. Costume pictures are the best—about all you have to do is wave your arms once in a while and shout, "On to the Bastille," or something like that. It really doesn't matter except to lip-readers, because it's silent, of course.

Oh, there's a lot to watch out for. Being a dress extra has its points, but not in ballroom sequences—too much dancing. That goes for parties, too, particularly in a DeMille production where they're "making whoopee" or one of von Stroheim's orgies. Besides, von Stroheim's scenes are always cut.

It doesn't hurt to be cut, don't misunderstand about that. It's no different than an ordinary fadeout at the end of a scene, and then you're free to go into another picture. Anything that was ever made, as long as there's still a print available for running somewhere. It's like falling asleep and then having one dream after another. The dreams are the scenes, of course, but while the scenes are playing, they're real.

I'm not the only one, either. There's no telling how many others do the same thing; maybe hundreds for all I know, but I've recognized a few I'm sure of and I think some of them have recognized me. We never let on to each other that we know, because it wouldn't do to make anybody suspicious.

Sometimes I think that if we could talk it over, we might come up with a better understanding of just how it happens, and why. But the point is, you *can't* talk, every-thing is silent; all you do is move your lips and if you tried to communicate such a difficult thing in pantomime you'd surely attract attention.

I guess the closest I can come to explaining it is to say it's like reincarnation—you can play a thousand roles, take or reject any part you want, as long as you don't make yourself conspicuous or do something that would change the plot.

Naturally you get used to certain things. The silence, of course. And if you're in a bad print there's flickering; sometimes even the air seems grainy, and for a few frames you may be faded or out of focus.

Which reminds me—another thing to stay away from, the slapstick comedies. Sennett's early stuff is the worst, but Larry Semon and some of the others are just as bad; all that speeded-up camera action makes you dizzy.

Once, you can learn to adjust, it's all right, even when you're looking off the screen into the audience. At first the darkness is a little frightening—you have to remind yourself it's only a theatre and there are just people out there, ordinary people watching a show. They don't know you can see them. They don't know that as long as your scene runs, you're just as real as they are, only in a different way. You walk, run, smile, frown, drink, eat—

That's another thing to remember, about the eating. Stay out of those Poverty Row quickies where everything is cheap and faked. Go where there's real set-dressing, big productions with banquet scenes and real food. If you work fast you can grab enough in a few minutes, while you're off-camera, to last you.

The big rule is, always be careful. Don't get caught. There's so little time, and you seldom get an opportunity to do anything on your own, even in a long sequence. It's taken me forever to get this chance to write you—I've planned it for so long, my darling, but it just wasn't possible until now.

This scene is playing outside the fort, but there's quite a large crowd of settlers and wagon-train people, and I had a chance to slip away inside here to the rooms in back—they're on camera in the background all during the action. I found this stationery and a pen, and I'm scribbling just as fast as I can. Hope you can read it. That is, if you ever get the chance!

Naturally, I can't mail it—but I have a funny hunch. You see, I noticed that standing set back here, the bunkhouse, where you and I used to come in the old days. I'm going to leave this letter under the mattress, and pray.

Yes, darling, I pray. Someone or something *knows* about us, and about how we feel. How we felt about being in the movies. That's why I'm here, I'm sure of that; because I've always loved pictures so. Someone who knows *that* must also know how I loved you. And still do.

I think there must be many heavens and many hells, each of us making his own, and—

The letter broke off there.

No signature, but of course I didn't need one. And it wouldn't have proved anything. A lonely old man, nursing his love for forty years, keeping her alive inside himself somewhere until she broke out in the form of a visual hallucination up there on the screen—such a man could conceivably go all the way into a schizoid split, even to the point where he could imitate a woman's handwriting as he set down the rationalization of his obsession.

I started to fold the letter, then dropped it on the mattress as the shrill scream of an ambulance siren startled me into sudden movement.

Even as I ran out the doorway I seemed to know what I'd find; the crowd huddling around the figure sprawled in the dust under the hot sun. Old men tire easily in such heat, and once the heart goes—

Jimmy Rogers looked very much as though he were smiling in his sleep as they lifted him into the ambulance. And I was glad of that; at least he'd died with his illusions intact.

"Just keeled over during the scene—one minute he was standing there, and the next—"

They were still chattering and gabbling when I walked away, walked back behind the fort and into the bunkhouse.

The letter was gone.

I'd dropped it on the mattress, and it was gone. That's all I can say about it. Maybe somebody else happened by while I was out front, watching them take Jimmy away. Maybe a gust of wind carried it through the doorway, blew it across the desert in a hot Santa Ana gust. Maybe there *was* no letter. You can take your choice—all I can do is state the facts.

And there aren't very many more facts to state.

I didn't go to Jimmy Rogers' funeral, if indeed he had one. I don't even know where he was buried; probably the Motion Picture Fund took care of him. Whatever *those* facts may be, they aren't important.

For a few days I wasn't too interested in facts. I was trying to answer a few abstract questions about metaphysics—reincarnation, heaven and hell, the difference between real life and reel life. I kept thinking about those images of actual people indulging in make-believe. But even after they die, the make-believe goes on, and that's a form of reality too. I mean, where's the borderline? And if there *is* a borderline—is it possible to cross over? *Life's but a walking shadow—*

Shakespeare said that, but I wasn't sure what he meant.

I'm still not sure, but there's just one more fact I must state.

The other night, for the first time in all the months since Jimmy Rogers died, I went back to the Silent Movie.

They were playing *Intolerance,* one of Griffith's greatest. Way back in 1916 he built the biggest set ever shown on the screen—the huge temple in the Babylonian sequence.

One shot never fails to impress me, and it did so now; a wide angle on the towering temple, with thousands of people moving antlike amid the gigantic carvings and colossal statues. In the distance, beyond the steps guarded by rows of stone elephants, looms a mighty wall, its top covered with tiny figures. You really have to look closely to make them out. But I did look closely, and this time I can swear to what I saw.

One of the extras, way up there on the wall in the background, was a smiling girl with long blond curls. And standing right beside her, one arm around her shoulder, was a tall old man with white whiskers. I wouldn't have noticed either of them, except for one thing.

They were waving at me . . .

Long ago and far away—on the other side of the generation gap—the silent movies were important. To people like myself, who grew up in an era before radio, television, and air transportation brought us into contact with the far corners of the earth, movies were our window on the world. We attended regularly, and the stars and players we saw on the screen frequently became more familiar to us than our own cousins, uncles, and aunts. We learned to love the films and the actors featured in them. And for some of us, first loves last forever.

Luckily for me, I got to Hollywood just in time to meet some of the people who'd represented romance to me in my childhood. Names like Monte Blue, Francis McDonald, Chester Conklin, and Julia Faye may not mean anything to youngsters today, but I remembered them fondly. And I'll always be grateful for the opportunity to reminisce with Boris Karloff and play baseball with Buster Keaton. In 1964, when Elly and I were married, our wedding cake was the gift of Joan Crawford. No sense denying it; I'm hung up on silent films and those who made them. And I think some of that feeling comes through in "The Movie People."

The idea itself occurred to me because I'd seen some of my favorite films repeatedly in revivals—and each time I discovered something new, something I'd overlooked before. One day I got to wondering. What if that "something new" turned out to be *people?*

After that, the story wrote itself. To those who find it difficult to reconcile it with the sort of thing I'm usually associated with, I can only say that it must have been written on an off day.

But those who believe that "God is love" will have no doubt as to just where this particular story came from.

Fritz Leiber died recently and with him took a myriad of sad, funny, violent, terrifying and wholly original worlds. Few people have ever witten so many different kinds of fiction so well. We all have our favorites but high on every Leiber list must be the following story, which is all the more pertinent today than it was even when first written back in the forties.

The Girl with the Hungry Eyes

Fritz Leiber

All right, I'll tell you why the Girl gives me the creeps. Why I can't stand to go down and see the mob slavering up at her on the tower, with that pop bottle or pack of cigarettes or whatever it is beside her. Why I hate to look at magazines any more because I know she'll turn up somewhere in a brassière or a bubble bath. Why I don't like to think of millions of Americans drinking in that poisonous half-smile. It's quite a story—more story than you're expecting.

No, I haven't suddenly developed any long-haired indignation at the evils of advertising and the national glamor-girl complex. That'd be a laugh for a man in my racket, wouldn't it? Though I think you'll agree there's something a little perverted about trying to capitalize on sex that way. But it's okay with me. And I know we've had the Face and the Body and the Look and what not else, so why shouldn't someone come along who sums it all up so completely, that we have to call her the Girl and blazon her on all the billboards from Times Square to Telegraph Hill?

But the Girl isn't like any of the others. She's unnatural. She's morbid. She's unholy.

Oh, these are modern times, you say, and the sort of thing I'm hinting at went out with witchcraft. But you see I'm not altogether sure myself what I'm hinting at, beyond a certain point. There are vampires and vampires, and not all of them suck blood.

And there were the murders, if they were murders. Besides, let me ask you this. Why, when America is obsessed with the Girl, don't we find out more about her? Why doesn't she rate a *Time* cover with a droll biography inside? Why hasn't there been a feature in *Life* or *The Post?* A profile in the *New Yorker?* Why hasn't *Charm* or *Mademoiselle* done her career saga? Not ready for it? Nuts!

Why haven't the movies snapped her up? Why hasn't she been on "Information, Please?" Why don't we see her kissing candidates at political rallies? Why isn't she chosen queen of some sort of junk or other at a convention?

Why don't we read about her tastes and hobbies, her views of the Russian situation? Why haven't the columnists interviewed her in a kimono on the top floor of the tallest hotel in Manhattan and told us who her boy friends are?

Finally—and this is the real killer—why hasn't she ever been drawn or painted?

Oh, no she hasn't. If you knew anything about commercial art you'd know that. Every blessed one of those pictures was worked up from a photograph. Expertly? Of course. They've got the top artists on it. But that's how it's done.

And now I'll tell you the why of all that. It's because from the top to the bottom of the whole world of advertising, news and business, there isn't a solitary soul who knows where the Girl came from, where she lives, what she does, who she is, even what her name is.

You heard me. What's more, not a single solitary soul ever sees her—except one poor damned photographer, who's making more money off her than he ever hoped to in his life and who's scared and miserable as hell every minute of the day.

No, I haven't the faintest idea who he is or where he has his studio. But I know there has to be such a man and I'm morally certain he feels just like I said.

Yes, I might be able to find her, if I tried. I'm not sure though— by now she probably has other safeguards. Besides, I don't want to.

Oh, I'm off my rocker, am I? That sort of thing can't happen in the Era of the Atom? People can't keep out of sight that way, not even Garbo?

Well I happen to know they can, because last year I was that poor damned photographer I was telling you about. Yes, last year, when the Girl made her first poisonous splash right here in this big little city of ours.

Yes, I know you weren't here last year and you don't know about it. Even the Girl had to start small. But if you hunted through the files of the local newspapers, you'd find some ads, and I might be able to locate you some of the old displays—I think Lovelybelt is still using one of them. I used to have a mountain of photos myself, until I burned them.

Yes, I made my cut off her. Nothing like what that other photographer must be making, but enough so it still bought this whiskey. She was funny about money. I'll tell you about that.

But first picture me then. I had a fourth-floor studio in that rathole the Hauser Building, not far from Ardleigh Park.

I'd been working at the Marsh-Mason studios until I'd gotten my bellyful of it and decided to start in for myself. The Hauser Building was awful—I'll never forget how the stairs creaked—but it was cheap and there was a skylight.

Business was lousy. I kept making the rounds of all the advertisers and agencies, and some of them didn't object to me too much personally, but my stuff never clicked. I was pretty near broke. I was behind on my rent. Hell, I didn't even have enough money to have a girl.

It was one of those dark, gray afternoons. The building was very quiet—I'd just finished developing some pix I was doing on speculation for Lovelybelt Girdles and Budford's Pool and Playground. My model had left. A Miss Leon. She was a civics teacher at one of the high schools and modeled for me on the side, just lately on speculation, too. After one look at the prints, I decided that Miss Leon probably wasn't just what Lovelybelt was looking for—or my photography either. I was about to call it a day.

And then the street door slammed four stories down and there were steps on the stairs and she came in.

She was wearing a cheap, shiny black dress. Black pumps. No stockings. And except that she had a gray cloth coat over one of them, those skinny arms of hers were bare. Her arms are pretty skinny, you know, or can't you see things like that any more?

And then the thin neck, the slightly gaunt, almost prim face, the tumbling mass of dark hair, and looking out from under it the hungriest eyes in the world.

That's the real reason she's plastered all over the country today, you know—those eyes. Nothing vulgar, but just the same they're looking at you with a hunger that's all sex and something more than sex. That's what everybody's been looking for since the Year One— something a little more than sex.

Well, boys, there I was, alone with the Girl, in an office that was getting shadowy, in a nearly empty building. A situation that a million male Americans have undoubtedly pictured to themselves with various lush details. How was I feeling? Scared.

I know sex can be frightening. That cold heart-thumping when you're alone with a girl and feel you're going to touch her. But if it was sex this time, it was overlaid with something else.

At least I wasn't thinking about sex.

I remember that I took a backward step and that my hand jerked so that the photos I was looking at sailed to the floor.

There was the faintest dizzy feeling like something was being drawn out of me. Just a little bit.

That was all. Then she opened her mouth and everything was back to normal for a while.

"I see you're a photographer, mister," she said. "Could you use a model?"

Her voice wasn't very cultivated.

"I doubt it," I told her, picking up the pix. You see, I wasn't impressed. The commercial possibilities of her eyes hadn't registered on me yet, by a long shot. "What have you done?"

Well, she gave me a vague sort of story and I began to check her knowledge of model agencies and studios and rates and what not and pretty soon I said to her, "Look here, you never modeled for a photographer in your life. You just walked in here cold."

Well, she admitted that was more or less so.

All along through our talk I got the idea she was feeling her way, like someone in a strange place. Not that she was uncertain of herself, or of me, but just of the general situation.

"And you think anyone can model?" I asked her pityingly.

"Sure," she said.

"Look," I said, "a photographer can waste a dozen negatives trying to get one halfway human photo of an average woman. How many do you think he'd have to waste before he got a real catchy, glamourous photo of her?"

"I think I could do it," she said.

Well, I should have kicked her out right then. Maybe I admired the cool way she stuck to her dumb little guns. Maybe I was touched by her underfed look. More likely I was feeling mean on account of the way my pictures had been snubbed by everybody and I wanted to take it out on her by showing her up.

"Okay, I'm going to put you on the spot," I told her. "I'm going to try a couple of shots of you. Understand it's strictly on spec. If somebody should ever want to use a photo of you, which is about one chance in two million, I'll pay you regular rates for your time. Not otherwise."

She gave me a smile. The first. "That's swell by me," she said.

Well, I took three or four shots, close-ups of her face since I didn't fancy her cheap dress, and at least she stood up to my sarcasm. Then I remembered I still had the Lovelybelt stuff and I guess the meanness was still working in me because I handed her a girdle and told her to go behind the screen and get into it and she did, without getting flustered as I'd expected, and since we'd gone that far, I figured we might as well shoot the beach scene to round it out, and that was that.

All this time I wasn't feeling anything particular one way or the other, except every once in a while I'd get one of those faint dizzy flashes and wonder if there was something wrong with my stomach or if I could have been a bit careless with my chemicals.

Still, you know, I think the uneasiness was in me all the while.

I tossed her a card and pencil. "Write your name and address and phone," I told her and made for the darkroom.

A little later she walked out. I didn't call any good-bys. I was irked because she hadn't fussed around or seemed anxious about her poses, or even thanked me, except for that one smile.

I finished developing the negatives, made some prints, glanced at them, decided they weren't a great deal worse than Miss Leon. On an impulse I slipped them in with the pictures I was going to take on the rounds next morning.

By now I'd worked long enough, so I was a bit fagged and nervous, but I didn't dare waste enough money on liquor to help that. I wasn't very hungry. I think I went to a cheap movie.

I didn't think of the Girl at all, except maybe to wonder faintly why in my present womanless state I hadn't made a pass at her. She had seemed to belong to a—well, distinctly more approachable social strata than Miss Leon. But then, of course, there were all sorts of arguable reasons for my not doing that.

Next morning I made the rounds. My first step was Munsch's Brewery. They were looking for a "Munsch Girl." Papa Munsch had a sort of affection for me, though he razzed my photography. He had a good natural judgment about that, too. Fifty years ago he might have been one of the shoe-string boys who made Hollywood.

Right now he was out in the plant pursuing his favorite occupation. He put down the beaded schooner, smacked his lips, gabbled something technical to someone about hops, wiped his fat hands on the big apron he was wearing, and grabbed my thin stack of pictures.

He was about halfway through, making noises with his tongue and teeth, when he came to her. I kicked myself for even having stuck her in.

"That's her," he said. "The photography's not so hot, but that's the girl."

It was all decided. I wonder now why Papa Munsch sensed what the Girl had right away, while I didn't. I think it was because I saw her first in the flesh, if that's the right word.

At the time I just felt faint.

"Who is she?" he said.

"One of my new models." I tried to make it casual.

"Bring her out tomorrow morning," he told me. "And your stuff. We'll photograph her here.

"Here, don't look so sick," he added. "Have some beer."

Well, I went away telling myself it was just a fluke, so that she'd probably blow it tomorrow with her inexperience, and so on.

Just the same, when I reverently laid my next stack of pictures on Mr. Fitch's, of Lovelybelt's, rose-colored blotter, I had hers on top.

Mr. Fitch went through the motions of being an art critic. He leaned over backwards, squinted his eyes, waved his long fingers, and said, "Hmm. What do you think, Miss Willow? Here, in this light, of course, the photograph doesn't show the bias cut. And perhaps we should use the Lovelybelt Imp instead of the Angel. Still, the girl . . . Come over here, Binns." More finger-waving. "I want a married man's reaction."

He couldn't hide the fact that he was hooked.

Exactly the same thing happened at Budford's Pool and Playground, except that Da Costa didn't need a married man's say-so.

"Hot stuff," he said, sucking his lips. "Oh boy, you photographers!"

I hot-footed it back to the office and grabbed up the card I'd given her to put down her name and address.

It was blank.

I don't mind telling you that the next five days were about the worst I ever went through, in an ordinary way. When next morning rolled around and I still hadn't got hold of her, I had to start stalling.

"She's sick," I told Papa Munsch over the phone.

"She's at a hospital?" he asked me.

"Nothing that serious," I told him.

"Get her out here then. What's a little headache?"

"Sorry, I can't."

Papa Munsch got suspicious. "You really got this girl?"

"Of course I have."

"Well, I don't know. I'd think it was some New York model, except I recognized your lousy photography."

I laughed.

"Well, look, you get her here tomorrow morning, you hear?"

"I'll try."

"Try nothing. You get her out here."

He didn't know half of what I tried. I went around to all the model and employment agencies. I did some slick detective work at the photographic and art studios. I used up some of my last dimes putting advertisements in all three papers. I looked at high school yearbooks and at employee photos in local house organs. I went to restaurants and drugstores, looking at waitresses, and to dime stores and department stores, looking at clerks. I watched the crowds coming out of movie theaters. I roamed the streets.

Evenings, I spent quite a bit of time along Pick-Up Row. Somehow that seemed the right place.

The fifth afternoon I knew I was licked. Papa Munsch's deadline —he'd given me several, but this was it—was due to run out at six o'clock. Mr. Fitch had already canceled.

I was at the studio window, looking out at Ardleigh Park.

She walked in.

I'd gone over this moment so often in my mind that I had no trouble putting on my act. Even the faint dizzy feeling didn't throw me off.

"Hello," I said, hardly looking at her.

"Hello," she said.

"Not discouraged yet?"

"No." It didn't sound uneasy or defiant. It was just a statement.

I snapped a look at my watch, got up and said curtly, "Look here, I'm going to give you a chance. There's a client of mine looking for a girl of your general type. If you do a real good job you might break into the modeling business.

"We can see him this afternoon if we hurry," I said. I picked up my stuff. "Come on. And next time if you expect favors, don't forget to leave your phone number."

"Uh, uh," she said, not moving.

"What do you mean?" I said.

"I'm not going out to see any client of yours."

"The hell you aren't," I said. "You little nut, I'm giving you a break."

She shook her head slowly. "You're not fooling me, baby, you're not fooling me at all. They want me." And she gave me the second smile.

At the time I thought she must have seen my newspaper ad. Now I'm not so sure.

"And now I'll tell you how we're going to work," she went on. "You aren't going to have my name or address or phone number. Nobody is. And we're going to do all the pictures right here. Just you and me."

You can imagine the roar I raised at that. I was everything—angry, sarcastic, patiently explanatory, off my nut, threatening, pleading.

I would have slapped her face off, except it was photographic capital.

In the end all I could do was phone Papa Munsch and tell him her conditions. I knew I didn't have a chance, but I had to take it.

He gave me a really angry bawling out, said "no" several times and hung up.

It didn't worry her. "We'll start shooting at ten o'clock tomorrow," she said.

It was just like her, using that corny line from the movie magazines.

About midnight Papa Munsch called me up.

"I don't know what insane asylum you're renting this girl from," he said, "but I'll take her. Come round tomorrow morning and I'll try to get it through your head just how I want the pictures. And I'm glad I got you out of bed!"

After that it was a breeze. Even Mr. Fitch reconsidered and after taking two days to tell me it was quite impossible, he accepted the conditions too.

Of course you're all under the spell of the Girl, so you can't understand how much self-sacrifice it represented on Mr. Fitch's part when he agreed to forego supervising the photography of my model in the Lovelybelt Imp or Vixen or whatever it was we finally used.

Next morning she turned up on time according to her schedule, and we went to work. I'll say one thing for her, she never got tired and she never kicked at the way I fussed over shots. I got along okay, except I still had that feeling of something being shoved away gently. Maybe you've felt it just a little, looking at her picture.

When we finished I found out there were still more rules. It was about the middle of the afternoon. I started with her to get a sandwich and coffee.

"Uh, uh," she said. "I'm going down alone. And look, baby, if you ever try to follow me, if you ever so much as stick your head out of that window when I go, you can hire yourself another model."

You can imagine how all this crazy stuff strained my temper—and my imagination. I remember opening the window after she was gone—I waited a few minutes first—and standing there getting some fresh air and trying to figure out what could be behind it, whether she was hiding from the police, or was somebody's ruined daughter, or maybe had got the idea it was smart to be temperamental, or more likely Papa Munsch was right and she was partly nuts.

But I had my pictures to finish up.

Looking back it's amazing to think how fast her magic began to take hold of the city after that. Remembering what came after, I'm frightened of what's happening to the whole country—and maybe the world. Yesterday I read something in *Time* about the Girl's picture turning up on billboards in Egypt.

The rest of my story will help show you why I'm frightened in that big, general way. But I have a theory, too, that helps explain, though it's one of those things that's beyond that "certain point." It's about the Girl. I'll give it to you in a few words.

You know how modern advertising gets everybody's mind set in the same direction, wanting the same things, imagining the same things. And you know the psychologists aren't so skeptical of telepathy as they used to be.

Add up the two ideas. Suppose the identical desires of millions of people focused on one telepathic person. Say a girl. Shaped her in their image.

Imagine her knowing the hiddenmost hungers of millions of men. Imagine her seeing deeper into those hungers than the people that had them, seeing the hatred and the wish for death behind the lust.

Imagine her shaping herself in that complete image, keeping herself as aloof as marble. Yet imagine the hunger she might feel in answer to their hunger.

But that's getting a long way from the facts of my story. And some of those facts are darn solid. Like money. We made money.

That was the funny thing I was going to tell you. I was afraid the Girl was going to hold me up. She really had me over a barrel, you know.

But she didn't ask for anything but the regular rates. Later on I insisted on pushing more money at her, a whole lot. But she always took it with that same contemptuous look, as if she were going to toss it down the first drain when she got outside.

Maybe she did.

At any rate, I had money. For the first time in months I had money enough to get drunk, buy new clothes, take taxicabs. I could make a play for any girl I wanted to. I only had to pick.

And so of course I had to go and pick . . .

But first let me tell you about Papa Munsch.

Papa Munsch wasn't the first of the boys to try to meet my model but I think he was the first to really go soft on her. I could watch the change in his eyes as he looked at her pictures. They began to get sentimental, reverent. Mama Munsch had been dead for two years.

He was smart about the way he planned it. He got me to drop some information which told him when she came to work, and then one morning he came pounding up the stairs a few minutes before.

"I've got to see her, Dave," he told me.

I argued with him, I kidded him, I explained he didn't know just how serious she was about her crazy ideas. I even pointed out he was cutting both our throats. I even amazed myself by bawling him out.

He didn't take any of it in his usual way. He just kept repeating, "But, Dave, I've got to see her."

The street door slammed.

"That's her," I said, lowering my voice. "You've got to get out."

He wouldn't, so I shoved him in the darkroom. "And keep quiet," I whispered. "I'll tell her I can't work today."

I knew he'd try to look at her and probably come bustling in, but there wasn't anything else I could do.

The footsteps came to the fourth floor. But she never showed at the door. I got uneasy.

"Get that bum out of there!" she yelled suddenly from beyond the door. Not very loud, but in her commonest voice.

"I'm going up to the next landing," she said. "And if that fat-bellied bum doesn't march straight down to the street, he'll never get another picture of me except spitting in his lousy beer."

Papa Munsch came out of the darkroom. He was white. He didn't look at me as he went out. He never looked at her pictures in front of me again.

That was Papa Munsch. Now it's me I'm telling about. I talked around the subject with her, I hinted, eventually I made my pass.

She lifted my hand off her as if it were a damp rag.

"No, baby," she said. "This is working time."

"But afterwards . . ." I pressed.

"The rules still hold." And I got what I think was the fifth smile.

It's hard to believe, but she never budged an inch from that crazy line. I mustn't make a pass at her in the office, because our work was very important and she loved it and there mustn't be any distractions. And I couldn't see her anywhere else, because if I tried to, I'd never snap another picture of her—and all this with more money coming in all the time and me never so stupid as to think my photography had anything to do with it.

Of course I wouldn't have been human if I hadn't made more passes. But they always got the wet-rag treatment and there weren't any more smiles.

I changed. I went sort of crazy and light-headed—only sometimes I felt my head was going to burst. And I started to talk to her all the time. About myself.

It was like being in a constant delirium that never interfered with business. I didn't pay any attention to the dizzy feeling. It seemed natural.

I'd walk around and for a moment the reflector would look like a sheet of white-hot steel, or the shadows would seem like armies of moths, or the camera would be a big black coal car. But the next instant they'd come all right again.

I think sometimes I was scared to death of her. She'd seem the strangest, most horrible person in the world. But other times . . .

And I talked. It didn't matter what I was doing—lighting her, posing her, fussing with props, snapping my pictures—or where she was—on the platform, behind the screen, relaxing with a magazine —I kept up a steady gab.

I told her everything I knew about myself. I told her about my first girl. I told her about my brother Bob's bicycle. I told her about running away on a freight, and the licking Pa gave me when I came home. I told her about shipping to South America and the blue sky at night. I told her about Betty. I told her about my mother dying of cancer. I told her about being beaten up in a fight in an alley behind a bar. I told her about Mildred. I told her about the first picture I ever sold. I told her how Chicago looked from a sailboat. I told her about the longest drunk I was ever on. I told her about Marsh-Mason. I told her about Gwen. I told her about how I met Papa Munsch. I told her about hunting her. I told her about how I felt now.

She never paid the slightest attention to what I said. I couldn't even tell if she heard me.

It was when we were getting our first nibble from national advertisers that I decided to follow her when she went home.

Wait, I can place it better than that. Something you'll remember from the out-of-town papers—those maybe murders I mentioned. I think there were six.

I say "maybe" because the police could never be sure they weren't heart attacks. But there's bound to be suspicion when attacks happen to people whose hearts have been okay, and always at night when they're alone and away from home and there's a question of what they were doing.

The six deaths created one of those "mystery poisoner" scares. And afterwards there was a feeling that they hadn't really stopped, but were being continued in a less suspicious way.

That's one of the things that scares me now.

But at that time my only feeling was relief that I'd decided to follow her.

I made her work until dark one afternoon. I didn't need any excuses, we were snowed under with orders. I waited until the street door slammed, then I ran down. I was wearing rubber-soled shoes. I'd slipped on a dark coat she'd never seen me in, and a dark hat.

I stood in the doorway until I spotted her. She was walking by Ardleigh Park towards the heart of town. It was one of those warm fall nights. I followed her on the other side of the street. My idea for tonight was just to find out where she lived. That would give me a hold on her.

She stopped in front of a display window, of Everley's department store, standing back from the flow. She stood there looking in.

I remembered we'd done a big photograph of her for Everley's, to make a flat model for a lingerie display. That was what she was looking at.

At the time it seemed all right to me that she should adore herself, if that was what she was doing.

When people passed she'd turn away a little or drift back further into the shadows.

Then a man came by alone. I couldn't see his face very well, but he looked middle-aged. He stopped and stood looking in the window.

She came out of the shadows and stepped up beside him.

How would you boys feel if you were looking at a poster of the Girl and suddenly she was there beside you, her arm linked with yours?

This fellow's reaction showed plain as day. A crazy dream had come to life for him.

They talked for a moment. Then he waved a taxi to the curb. They got in and drove off.

I got drunk that night. It was almost as if she'd known I was following her and had picked that way to hurt me. Maybe she had. Maybe this was the finish.

But the next morning she turned up at the usual time and I was back in the delirium, only now with some new angles added.

That night when I followed her she picked a spot under a streetlamp, opposite one of the Munsch Girl billboards.

Now it frightens me to think of her lurking that way.

After about twenty minutes a convertible slowed down going past her, backed up, swung into the curb.

I was closer this time. I got a good look at the fellow's face. He was a little younger, about my age.

Next morning the same face looked up at me from the front page of the paper. The convertible had been found parked on a sidestreet. He had been in it. As in the other maybe-murders, the cause of death was uncertain.

All kinds of thoughts were spinning in my head that day, but there were only two things I knew for sure. That I'd got the first real offer from a national advertiser, and that I was going to take the Girl's arm and walk down the stairs with her when we quit work.

She didn't seem surprised. "You know what you're doing?" she said.

"I know."

She smiled. "I was wondering when you'd get around to it."

I began to feel good. I was kissing everything good-by, but I had my arm around hers.

It was another of those warm fall evenings. We cut across into Ardleigh Park. It was dark there, but all around the sky was a sallow pink from the advertising signs.

We walked for a long time in the park. She didn't say anything and she didn't look at me, but I could see her lips twitching and after a while her hand tightened on my arm.

We stopped. We'd been walking across the grass. She dropped down and pulled me after her. She put her hands on my shoulders. I was looking down at her face. It was the faintest sallow pink from the glow in the sky. The hungry eyes were dark smudges.

I was fumbling with her blouse. She took my hand away, not like she had in the studio. "I don't want that," she said.

First I'll tell you what I did afterwards. Then I'll tell you why I did it. Then I'll tell you what she said.

What I did was run away. I don't remember all of that because I was dizzy, and the pink sky was swinging against the dark trees. But after a while I staggered into the lights of the street. The next day I closed up the studio. The telephone was ringing when I locked the door and there were unopened letters on the floor. I never saw the Girl again in the flesh, if that's the right word.

I did it because I didn't want to die. I didn't want the life drawn out of me. There are vampires and vampires, and the ones that suck blood aren't the worst. If it hadn't been for the warning of those dizzy flashes, and Papa Munsch and the face in the morning paper, I'd have gone the way the others did. But I realized what I was up against while there was still time to tear myself away. I realized that wherever she came from, whatever shaped her, she's the quintessence of the horror behind the bright billboard. She's the smile that tricks you into throwing away your money and your life. She's the eyes that lead you on and on, and then show you death. She's the creature you give everything for and never really get. She's the being that takes everything you've got and gives nothing in return. When you yearn towards her face on the billboards, remember that. She's the lure. She's the bait. She's the Girl.

And this is what she said, "I want you. I want your high spots. I want everything that's made you happy and everything that's hurt you bad. I want your first girl. I want that shiny bicycle. I want that licking. I want that pinhole camera. I want Betty's legs. I want the blue sky filled with stars. I want your mother's death. I want your blood on the cobblestones. I want Mildred's mouth. I want the first picture you sold. I want the lights of Chicago. I want the gin. I want Gwen's hands. I want your wanting me. I want your life. Feed me, baby, feed me."

Whenever one mentions Tom Reamy, one hears of his early death, and of his unfulfilled promise. And yet when one reads his stories, one sees that nothing was left unfulfilled—he packed a powerful lot of living and perception into his slender body of work, and left us a real testament to his gnarly affectionate soul. They just don't get much better than "Under the Hollywood Sign."

Under the Hollywood Sign

Tom Reamy

For Pat Cadigan

I can't pinpoint the exact moment I noticed him. I suppose I had been subliminally aware of him for some time, though he was just standing there with the rest of the crowd. Anyway, I had other things on my mind: a Pinto and a Buick were wrapped around each other like lettuce leaves. The paramedics had two of them out, wrapped in plastic sheets waiting for the meat wagon, and were cutting out a third with a torch. He appeared to be in the Buick, but you couldn't really tell.

My partner Carnehan and I were holding back the crowd of gawkers. A couple of bike cops in their gestapo uniforms were keeping the traffic moving on Cahuenga, not letting any of them stop and get out. But there were still twenty or twenty-five of them standing there—eyes bright, noses crinkled, mouths disapproving.

All except him.

That's one of the reasons I noticed him in particular. He wasn't wearing that horrified, fascinated expression they all seem to have. He might have been watching anything—or nothing. His face was smooth and placid. I think that's the first time I ever saw a face totally without expression. It wasn't dull or blank or lifeless. No, there was vitality there. It just simply wasn't doing anything at the moment.

And he was . . . Don't get the wrong idea—my crotch doesn't get tight at the sight of an attractive young man. But there's only one word to describe him—beautiful!

I've seen my share of pretty boys—the ones that flutter and the ones that don't. It seems the prettier they are, the more trouble they get into. But he wasn't that *kind* of beautiful.

Even though the word is used these days to describe practically everything, it was the only one that fitted. I thought at first he was very young: nineteen, twenty, not more than twenty-one. But then I got the impression he was much older, though I don't know why, because he still looked twenty. He was about five-ten, a hundred and sixty-seven pounds—one of those bodies the hero of the book always has but that you never see in real life.

His hair was red, or it might have just been the light from the flashers. There were no peculiarities of feature; just a neutral perfection. I've heard it said that perfect beauty is dull, that it takes an imperfection to make a face interesting. Whoever said it had never seen this kid.

He was standing with his hands in his pockets, watching the guys with the torch, neither interested nor uninterested. I guess I was staring at him, because his head turned and he looked directly at me.

I could smell the rusty odor of the antifreeze dribbling from the busted radiators and the sharp ozone of the acetylene and the always remembered smell of blood. A coyote began yipping somewhere in the darkness.

Then a couple of kids got too close and I had to hustle them out of the way. When I looked back, he was no longer there.

They finally got the third one out of the Buick. When they pulled him out I could see the wet brown stain all over the seat of his pants where his bowels had relaxed in death. The ambulance picked up all three of them and the wrecker hauled off the two cars still merged as one. Part of the mess was dragging on the street and I could hear the scraping for a long time. The bike cops did a few flashy turns and roared away. The crowd started to wander off, and Carnehan and I began sweeping the broken glass from the pavement.

But there was only one thing I could think of: I couldn't remember the color of his eyes.

Nothing much happened the rest of the night. We cruised the Boulevard a few times, but there wasn't anything going on. A few hustlers still lounged around the Gold Cup and the Egyptian, never giving up hope. There was no point in hassling them—they'd just say they were waiting for a bus, and we couldn't prove they weren't. It was a pretty scruffy-looking bunch this late in the morning. The presentable ones had scored a long time ago. You could probably get most of these with an offer of breakfast.

Carnehan reached behind the seat and pulled an apple from the paper sack he always kept back there. He took a bite that sounded like a rifle shot and then offered me one. "No, thanks."

"An apple a day keeps the doctor away." He grinned and took another bite.

"You're keeping the entire AMA at bay."

He laughed; partly chewed apple dribbled down his chin. He wiped it off with the back of his hand. I kept my eyes on the street. "Why don't you eat soft apples? They're quiet."

"I like the hard ones."

We stopped a car with only one taillight and gave the guy a warning ticket.

Then the sun was coming up. It was hitting the tops of the Hollywood Hills and illuminating the Hollywood sign. It looked decent from this far away. You couldn't tell it was made of rotting timbers and sagging sheet metal clinging in the wind. From here you couldn't see the obscenities scrawled on it.

We went back to the station, reported, and then into the locker room. The rest of the graveyard shift were wandering in, showering, and changing out of their uniforms. Cunningham has the locker next to mine. He had been on the Pansy Patrol and was wearing a shirt unbuttoned to the waist, no underwear, and pants so tight you could count every hair on his ass.

Wharton, one of the police psychiatrists, was leaning against the lockers talking to him. Doc was on his favorite theme again. He was telling Cunningham why he, Cunningham, was so successful on the Pansy Patrol. The fags recognized a kindred spirit; the fags always knew one of their own kind; if Cunningham would only stop fooling himself, just stop deluding himself that he was straight, just know himself, just start living a conscious life, he would be a happier, more fulfilled person.

I had been on the Pansy Patrol with Cunningham a few times and had seen him operate. I wasn't completely sure Doc was wrong.

Cunningham was peeling off the tight pants and I watched in fascination, although I'd seen it before, as the sizable bulge in his crotch stayed with the pants.

Poor Cunningham.

He was standing there naked with a slight smile on his face, putting the pants neatly on a hanger, listening to Doc's clarinet voice. He looked a lot like the cop on "Adam-12," whatever his name is, the kid. The boys had even called him "Adam-12" for a while until they got tired of it. I couldn't keep from comparing him to the guy I had seen at the wreck, but Cunningham didn't compare at all. He was just a good-looking kid with a slim muscular body, and not much equipment. But it didn't seem to bother him. He always grinned and said it wasn't size that counted, it was technique.

I took off my own pants and looked at myself. I wasn't as young or as good-looking as Cunningham, but I did all right on the Pansy Patrol. I was bulkier and more heavily muscled and hairier; I guess I appealed to the rough trade crowd. I was never very comfortable without underwear, and thank God I didn't have to wear padding.

Wharton finished his catalogue of Cunningham's emotional failings. Cunningham looked at me and winked. "I don't really know anything about it, Doc, but maybe the reason I'm not interested in sex with another man is because I'm just *not interested* in sex with another man."

Doc's lips got a little tight and his face was slightly flushed. I knew Cunningham had been reading Kingsley Amis again and had probably maneuvered Doc into the whole conversation—and Doc was eminently maneuverable. I'd heard most of it before, so I got a towel and started for the showers. Cunningham followed me and Wharton followed him.

"You're right, Cunningham, you don't know anything about it!"

I turned on the water and began soaping. Cunningham got next to me and Doc stood at the door, still talking. Cunningham looked at me and grinned and said loudly, "Sorry, Doc, I can't hear you with the water running!"

There were about ten other guys in the shower, grinning at each other. Cunningham leaned toward me. "Hey, Rankin, you notice how Doc always manages to look in the showers?"

I shrugged.

"According to him everyone is either a fag or a closet queen."

"What about himself?" I asked.

He rolled his eyes and laughed. "Getting him to talk about himself is like catching fairies in a saucepan."

Carnehan came in, pitching an apple core into the wastebasket. I could see why he had never been on the Pansy Patrol. Then . . . I don't know why I thought of it, but the thought crossed my mind. I wondered what the guy at the wreck looked like naked.

I left the station and got into my five-year-old Dart. It looked like a nice day. There was enough wind from the ocean to clear away the smog. Of course, the wind was packing it into the San Gabriel Valley, but that was their problem, not mine. I went straight home and went to bed.

I was scrambling some eggs and watching *The Price is Right* when the phone rang. They were doing the one where the screaming dame has to zero in on the prices of two objects within thirty seconds. When she names a price, the MC says "Higher" or "Lower." This keeps up until she guesses the price. You can get it in ten guesses maximum. She started at a hundred on a color TV and worked up ten dollars at a time.

"Hundred and ten!"

"Higher!"

"Hundred and twenty!"

"Higher!"

"Hundred and thirty!"

"Higher!"

She got to three-seventy before her time ran out. Dumb dame!

It was Carnehan on the phone. "Hey, Lou, Margaret wants you to come over for dinner tonight."

"Hell, Carnehan, I wish you'd said something this morning. I've already made other plans." You stupid jerk! Don't you ever wonder why your wife is always inviting me to dinner?

"Got a heavy date, Lou?"

"Something like that. Some other time, Carnehan." No other time, Carnehan. Margaret's a pretty good-looking dame for her age, but not good enough to take chances with. You didn't even notice how her hand stayed under the table all through dinner last time.

"Margaret says how about Wednesday?"

"I'll have to let you know later." And you never even had a suspicion about what goes on after you fall asleep in front of the TV, Carnehan. If you ever found out . . .

"Okay, Lou. I'll remind you Tuesday night."

"You do that." And I'll have a good excuse ready. Not that I give a good goddamn if you do find out, but you could make a stink in the department. I don't want to lose my job, Carnehan. I like being a cop.

" 'Bye, Lou. See you later."

" 'Bye, Carnehan." I hung up the phone in time to see a granny-lady have an orgasm over winning a dune buggy.

I usually eat dinner about eight o'clock at David's. I know it's a fag hangout but the food's good and, since I let it be known I was a cop, the service is even better. I spotted him as I was leaving about nine. He went into the gay bar next to David's. It was called Goli-ath's, of course. I only glimpsed him from behind but I was sure of the red hair and body. Wouldn't you know he'd be a queer!

I paid my dollar and a quarter cover charge and went through the black curtains after him. I don't know what I was planning to do, but I hadn't been able to get him out of my mind. I stood for a moment, waiting for my eyes to adjust to the gloom and my ears to the plaster-cracking music. There were three small stages with na-ked boys dancing on them, wiggling their little round butts for all they were worth. There were also five screens showing movies of naked boys doing everything it's physically possible for naked boys to do and a few things I would have thought impossible before I joined the force.

Then there were the customers. A few were at the bar and a few were scattered around but most of them were packed like Vienna sausages against one wall. There was plenty of room and no need for the press of bodies—no need but one, and the busy hands told what that was. A few watched the movies but mostly they watched each other. One of the dancers was waving around a hardon and was getting some attention but not much. A couple of dykes at the bar watched him. I guess this is the only chance they have to see one.

I spotted the back of the red head in the middle of the mass, so I waded in. There's no way to move through something like that. No one can move out of your way; they're just as trapped as you are. You just wait and move with the current because the pack is in constant eddy as they move from one body to the next, trying to touch everything.

It was no more than thirty seconds before I felt feather touches on my ass. I thought about my wallet, but I knew that wasn't what they were after. I pushed away the first hand that closed on my crotch and saw a pout of disappointment flicker across a face in front of mine. I put my wallet in my shirt pocket anyway.

After five minutes and fifty gropes, I finally reached the redhead but he was turned the other way. I was pressed against him and could feel his hard body. By pushing with determination, I managed to get to the side of him. He was standing face to face with another guy. Both of them had their eyes closed and their mouths slightly open, occasionally coming together in a lazy kiss. Their hands were out of sight but I could feel the movement.

It wasn't him.

This was one of the pretty ones. I might even have said beautiful if I hadn't seen the other one. But, like Cunningham, he was ordinary in comparison.

He opened his eyes and saw me watching him and he smiled dreamily. I felt a hand massaging my crotch but I couldn't tell for sure if it was him. I was so disappointed I didn't push it away. Then my zipper went down and fingers expertly scooped everything out. The press was so tight I couldn't even get my arms down, much less move away. Whoever was working on me was very good and I couldn't help getting it up.

Jesus Christ!

I had a wild urge to take out my badge and shove it in every face in sight. I enjoyed my mental image of the panic it would create. But I didn't do it. I forced my arms down, pushed the clutching hands away, closed my pants, and got the hell out of there.

When I went into the locker room about eleven thirty, Carnehan already had his uniform on, sitting there reading a copy of the *Advocate* and eating an apple. He looked up when I rattled my locker.

"Hey, Lou! You missed a great dinner."

"It couldn't be helped, Carnehan."

"Don't forget about Wednesday."

"I won't."

I took off my shirt and remembered my wallet was still in the pocket. I put it on the shelf and took off my pants. I grabbed a towel and headed for the shower. I felt clammy. I must have sweated off a pound in that damn bar. Those groping bodies can generate a lot of heat.

Carnehan laughed out loud. He came toward me waving the newspaper. "Hey, Lou! Did you see this cartoon in the *Advocate?*"

"Why in hell would I be reading the *Advocate?*"

"Look, there's these two cops standing before a judge with a handcuffed fag and a hooker. One of the cops is saying, 'But Your Honor, you can get *hurt* chasing robbers and murderers.' Isn't that a scream?"

"Ha ha," I said and went on to the showers. He started rushing around the room showing it to everyone else.

I was almost finished when Cunningham came in. He turned on the water and stood under it leaning against the wall with his eyes closed and a sappy grin on his face.

"You look like the cat that swallowed the aviary," I said.

He sighed. "I am *exhausted!*"

"Let me guess from what."

"I met the most fan*tas*tic girl! A waitress at the Hamburger Hamlet on the Strip. I'm gonna give it two weeks and, if I'm *still* alive, I'm gonna propose." He rubbed his hand between his legs. "I tell you, Rankin, I didn't know I had it in me. Boy, I'd like to see Wharton try to convince *her* I'm a repressed homosexual."

I laughed dutifully. He began soaping and glanced down at me.

"You look a little shriveled up yourself. Have a big night?" He grinned goodnaturedly, wanting to share his sexual excitement.

"Yeah. Some women are just as happy with size as they are with technique."

He looked a little wistful for a moment, then the grin returned. "Shit! If I had your size and my technique, I'd quit the force, put an ad in the *Free Press,* and open a screwing service."

And I wondered about *him* again. With that face and that body, did he worry about size and technique? How did women react to him? Were they intimidated by his beauty? Was he as beautiful in bed?

I saw him going into the Vogue Record Shop on the Boulevard. This time there was no mistake. I told Carnehan to park the car and meet me at the entrance. When I went through the turnstiles, I saw him leaning against the end of the counter. I walked into the book department and watched him from behind a rack of paperbacks.

He had his back to me and it took me a moment to figure out what he was doing. The cashier was playing the *Symphonie Fantastique*—it was the passage where the two shepherds are calling to each other on their flutes and, at the end, one doesn't answer—and he was standing there listening to the music. Then he turned slightly and I could see his face.

I could feel the skin crawling on the back of my neck.

It wasn't the same one!

It was all there: the red hair, the magnificent body, the neutral beauty of the bland face. But the features were different. He had to be the other one's brother, they were so alike.

The lights in the store were very bright. No one else was in the place but the cashier and she had her nose in a paperback volume of Toynbee. His clothes were clean and neatly pressed but they were old and hadn't cost much when they were new. His hair was neat and not very long. His face was so smooth I doubted that he shaved. And his eyes were gray—just as beautiful and as neutral as the rest of him.

Finally the record ended and he left. I glanced at the book I had been holding. The cover was a photograph of Burt Reynolds standing with his back to the camera looking over his shoulder. He was wearing nothing but a football jersey, with his bare ass hanging out. I closed the book, put it back on the rack, and for some reason thought of Betty Grable.

The cashier never even looked up when he went out. Carnehan, standing on the sidewalk looking confused, never glanced at him as he walked by. The girl was watching me. She smiled but her eyes were guarded.

"Did you know the man who just went out?" I asked, trying to sound casual.

She glanced out the door, but he had turned left toward Las Palmas. She looked back at me. "I don't think so, officer. Did he do something?"

"No. I just thought I'd seen him before. Maybe in the movies or on television."

She shrugged. "Movie stars come in here all the time. Joanne Worley was in yesterday. Wendall Burton comes in every once in a while."

"Thanks." I left before she could give me a complete catalogue of the celebrities she'd seen. She raised her voice as I went out the door.

"Chad Everett was in a couple of weeks ago but I was off that day."

I looked down the Boulevard but didn't see him. I told Carnehan to wait for me and went after him. At Las Palmas I looked in every direction but there was no sign of him. The hustlers standing around the Gold Cup pretended to ignore me, but a couple of drag queens gave me defiant looks.

There was another bad one that night on the off-ramp at Western. Four cars were scattered half a block. There were seven dead and two others who probably wouldn't see morning. And there were two of *them* in the crowd. Two different ones.

I motioned Carnehan over.

"Yeah, Lou?"

"Carnehan. See those two guys over there, the ones with red hair?"

He looked confused. "Where?"

"You see the black dame in the yellow dress? The one with pigtails all over her head that make her look like an upside-down johnny brush?"

He snickered. "Sure."

"One of them is standing right beside her. On her left. You see him?"

Slowly: "Yeah."

"What does he look like?"

He looked up at me. "What d'ya mean?"

"No! Keep looking at him!" He looked back. "You still see him?"

"Yeah."

"Describe him to me."

He thought for a moment. "Don't forget. Tomorrow's Wednesday. Margaret's expecting you for dinner."

"Carnehan! Concentrate on the redheaded guy. Don't think about anything else. What does he look like?"

"I don't know. He's just a guy."

"How old is he?"

"It's hard to tell. The light's not too good."

"Is he under thirty?"

He considered. "Yeah."

"Under twenty-five?"

"Yeah. Yeah, I'd say so."

"Under twenty?"

He was silent for a moment. Good old Carnehan. His little pea brain was doing its best. "Maybe . . . but probably not."

"What about his face?"

"What about it?"

"Is it an ugly face?"

"No."

"Is it a handsome face?"

"Yeah, I guess so."

"How handsome?"

"Golly, Lou."

"Very handsome?"

"Yeah."

"Better-looking than Cunningham?"

"Yeah." His voice suddenly got excited. "Hey, Lou, is that a movie star or something?"

We went through the whole thing again with the other one. Carnehan finally saw them the same way I did, but he couldn't remember the one at the record shop. Later I asked him if he remembered the two good-looking redheaded guys.

"Sure. How could you forget somebody who looks like that? Especially when there's two of 'em. Hey, you suppose they're twins?"

"Are they still there?"

"Naw. They musta left," he said, looking right at them. "Don't forget about dinner Wednesday night."

Then they both turned and looked at me with their expressionless eyes. Or were they expressionless? I thought I saw recognition and speculation, but I wasn't sure. Carnehan was right. The light *was* bad.

They kept us hopping the rest of the night. We'd barely get through with one before we were sent to another.

An old hotel on Vermont burned to the ground. Half the department was there, keeping the curious out from underfoot, rerouting traffic. My eyes were burning and watery from the smoke, but it didn't keep me from seeing them.

I counted seven. Seven beautiful redheaded young men with perfect bodies.

I leaned against my locker in pure exhaustion, wondering if I should take a shower. I was grimy from smoke and dust but I was so tired I only wanted to go to bed. Cunningham came in, looking as beat as I felt.

He looked at me and sighed, shaking his head.

"What are you doing in uniform?" I asked, not really caring. "You off the Pansy Patrol?"

He started undressing. "Yeah. They called us in about three. What got into people last night, anyway? Seems like everybody was trying to get themselves killed."

The same thought had crossed my mind, but not seriously. I had other things to think about.

Margaret called herself the next afternoon to remind me about dinner. But I'd already laid out my plan of action.

"I'm sorry, Margaret. I was just about to call you. I'm leaving for Texas in about two hours. My father is very ill and I've taken a leave of absence from the department."

"Oh, Lou, I'm so sorry. Is there anything I can do?"

"No, thank you, Margaret. Everything's taken care of."

"At least let me drive you to the airport."

"I'm not flying. I'll need my car when I get there."

"How long will you be gone?"

"I don't know. My father isn't expected to live . . ." I let my voice break a little. "Say so long to Carnehan for me."

"Of course, Lou. You're sure there's nothing I can do?"

"No. Nothing. Good-bye, Margaret."

" 'Bye, Lou, dear."

Well, it wasn't *all* a lie. My father had taken three months to die seventeen years ago when I was in high school, but nobody out here knew that. The Lieutenant hadn't much liked the idea of giving me an indefinite leave of absence, but what could he do? I packed enough supplies in the Dart to last two people six weeks, paid my landlady two months in advance, drove up La Brea to the Boulevard, and put my car in the underground garage near Graumann's Chinese. I walked down to the Vogue and caught a double feature.

It was dark when I came out. I could hear sirens in several directions. I got in the car and drove to David's for something to eat. All I had to do was get in one place and wait, no driving around, no taking extra chances of being seen.

I had almost finished eating when I heard the sirens. I didn't pay much attention because there would be plenty of time and plenty of sirens, if tonight was anything like last night. When I came out of the restaurant there were little bunches of people standing on the corners looking south down La Brea. I walked over and saw a crowd around the Gordon, standing in that tense way they do when somebody's had it. This was going to be a lot easier than I'd thought.

I crossed over Melrose past the camera store, and eased my way through the press of bodies. The colored neon of the marquee made the blood look black. The guy was under a blanket, flat on his back on the sidewalk, one brown hand poking out from under the edge. The hand had blood on it and a spot had soaked through the blanket. More of it was smeared around on the concrete.

One of the cops talking to a couple of people was named Henderson. I only knew him vaguely, so he probably wouldn't know I was supposed to be on my way to Texas. I began sorting through a number of excuses for my delay just in case.

He saw me and waved. The patrol car was behind him at the curb, the flashers turning hypnotically, but losing out to the bright marquee. A young Chicano sat in the back seat looking dazed and surly. He wiped at his mouth with the back of his hand and I saw the glint of cuffs. A girl was hunched in the front seat weeping.

Henderson finished with his witnesses and started toward me. "Hello, Rankin. Don't you get enough of this on duty?"

"Just passing by. What happened?"

He groaned and shook his head. "Couple of kids in a knife fight over a senorita. Wonder if she was worth it."

"The way she's carrying on, the wrong one musta lost."

"Yeah." Another siren approached. "Here's the ambulance. See you around, Rankin." He walked away, being very official, moving the onlookers back another inch.

I looked over the crowd and saw him almost immediately. He was about twelve feet from me, his eyes on the blanket. As usual no one was paying him the slightest attention. I edged toward him as they put the body in the ambulance. The crowd began drifting away but I kept my eyes on that beautiful boy. I wasn't sure if I had seen him before, they all looked so much alike.

He turned and walked north on La Brea. I followed him across Melrose. A few people were still milling around the intersection, but I couldn't let him get too far away from my car.

I overtook him, touched his arm, and said, "Excuse me." I had my badge in my hand when he turned with a startled look.

My face was only a foot from his. I saw the clear, healthy skin and the bewildered gray eyes that looked at me with recognition. All the artists for the last thousand years have been trying to paint that face on angels, but their poor fumbling attempts never came close. It was only for an instant but I had to look away or be overwhelmed.

The traffic on La Brea moved by us silently, like a movie with the sound turned off. But, oddly enough, I could hear the hum and click of the traffic lights as they changed. I realized I was still stupidly holding my badge in my hand, and put it away. I forced myself to look at him again.

"Will you please come down to the station with me . . ." My voice cracked. Come on, Rankin, get hold of yourself! "It's purely a routine matter."

"What do you want?"

It was only four words, but I realized I'd never heard one of them speak. How can you describe music to a deaf person? Any actor in the world would trade his prick for that voice. My own words stopped and we looked at each other. Get your shit together! You're acting like some poor fairy who's just been propositioned by Robert Redford.

"I can make . . . this official if you refuse to cooperate."

His shoulders sagged slightly. He nodded.

He followed me to the Dart without protest. I had been a little worried because I wasn't in uniform and wasn't in a squad car, but he didn't seem to notice. I had my revolver handy when I handcuffed him to the door handle, but he sat slumped in the seat looking at nothing.

I took the Hollywood Freeway to the Pasadena Freeway. I was going down Colorado Boulevard when he said, "Why are you doing this to me?"

I glanced at him but he was still looking at nothing. I almost turned the car around. I wish I had, but I didn't.

He didn't say anything else as I got on the Foothill Freeway and headed east through the San Gabriel Valley. It was almost dawn when I pulled off the pavement winding up Mt. Baldy. I opened the gate to the gravel road down the canyon. I drove through and put on the padlock I had brought with me. I drove up the canyon a couple of miles until the road ended at a cabin. It belonged to a director friend of mine who was on location in Jamaica and would be for several months. He'd let me use it before. Besides, what he didn't know wouldn't hurt him.

I had to break a window to get in, but that could be fixed. I'd brought a pane of glass and a cutter. I turned on the electricity at the meter box and took him in. I took the chain I had brought, handcuffed one end to his ankle and the other end around the commode. Now he could use the bathroom and the bed, but the chain wasn't long enough to reach the bedroom door or the window. He didn't complain through any of this. He acted as if he didn't even know I was there.

I unloaded the car, put on a pot of coffee, scrambled some eggs, and tried to get him to eat something but he wouldn't. I finished eating, unpacked my clothes, took a shower in the other bathroom and went to sleep in the other bedroom.

He still wouldn't eat when I woke up. I took another shower and shaved. I moved a chair just out of the limit of the chain—he hadn't given me any trouble but I wasn't taking chances—and sat down to watch him.

He was still sitting on the side of the bed, where he'd been when I put on the chain, his magnificent body relaxed and his beautiful face calm. His cheeks were as smooth as ever. I knew for sure he didn't have to shave. His hands were folded in his lap and his eyes seemed to be on them. For two hours he didn't move except for gentle breathing. I didn't realize so much time had passed until the room began to get dark.

I turned on the lights and went to him, holding out my hand. "Give me your wallet." He acted as if he hadn't heard me. "Give me your wallet," I said again, louder.

He looked up at me then, puzzlement in his eyes. "I don't have one."

"Stand up," I said. He hesitated for a moment, then stood. I went over him quickly. He was telling the truth. He had no wallet; nothing but empty pockets.

I returned to my chair and sat, watching him. He stood where I had left him, stood as calmly as he had sat. "How many of you are there?" I said. He didn't seem to hear. "Look, we might as well get a few things straight. You're gonna tell me everything I want to know. We can do it easy or we can do it hard. It's up to you."

He stood for a moment in the same position, then looked at me. "I don't know." His voice still made the hair on my arms stand up.

"You must have some idea. A hundred? A thousand? Ten thousand? A million?" He shook his head. Maybe he wasn't going to let it be easy after all. I let it go; there was plenty of time. "I can fix you something to eat if you want. I'm not trying to starve you to death. Aren't you hungry?"

He said nothing.

"Look! It won't do any good to go on a hunger strike. Not one damn bit of good!" No response. I used my buddy voice. "You can have anything you want. Just name it."

He looked at me quickly. "I want to leave."

I laughed. "Anything but that."

He looked back at his hands. "I would like to bathe."

"Sure. Go ahead."

He moved his foot; the chain rattled. I dug the key out of my pocket and pitched it to him. "Unlock the cuff and throw the key back." I picked up the revolver. He unlocked the chain and tossed me the key. He started for the bathroom.

"Wait!" My heart was beating too hard. "Undress in here and leave the clothes." My mouth was dry and I swallowed. He took off his shirt and hung it on the back of the chair. He took off the shoes and socks and the pants and jockey shorts. His back was toward me but it wasn't modesty. He just happened to be standing that way. Michelangelo, you bumbling incompetent! If you could see this, you'd take a hammer to all those misshapen pieces of rock you spent so much time on.

He took a step toward the bathroom. I made a croaking sound in my throat. I tried again.

"Stop!" He stopped. "Turn around." He turned. I felt the blood singing in my ears. I don't know how long I looked at him. He stood unselfconsciously, totally unconcerned by my staring or his own nakedness. There wasn't a blemish on him. Light reddish-gold hair was scattered on his arms, legs, and chest. You could hardly see it until it caught the light. There was a darker, thicker patch of pubic hair, and he was uncircumcised. He wasn't as large as me, or as small as Cunningham. Either way would have been wrong, out of proportion, a staggering flaw. My own that I'd always been so proud of—it seemed now gross and mutilated. I felt the pressure of it and realized I had a hardon.

The gun was pointing at him. What would he look like with a bullet there? Nothing between those perfect thighs but blood. Would he writhe screaming? Would that inhumanly placid face show human agony? "Get out of here," I said.

While he showered, I put the clothes in a grocery sack and stuck them in the closet of my bedroom. When he came out of the bathroom, he looked at the empty chair, then at me.

"You won't need them. Put the cuff back on." He sat in the chair, snapped the cuff around his ankle. I could take it only for an hour. I got my bathrobe and tossed it to him. He put it on but only because I told him to. It didn't seem to matter to him one way or the other.

I wondered if he had ever smiled. What would those perfect lips look like with a big happy grin on them? I could feel goosebumps popping out on my arms.

*   *   *

For three weeks I watched him do nothing. He sat in the chair and sometimes lay on the bed, but I never saw him sleep. I watched him and asked questions, but the only things I learned for sure were: he didn't eat or use the toilet. He ignored me except when I forced him to answer a question. And the answers were usually meaningless.

Some days neither of us said a word. I would just watch his face and never tire of it, the way you never tire of looking at a perfect piece of art. Then, suddenly, it would be night again. He bathed every day, but I never let him remove the robe until he was in the bathroom. I didn't want to go through that again.

Sometimes I would force him to speak—not because I expected to learn anything, but because I wanted to hear his voice again. I was trying to find out what he did when he wasn't siren-chasing. I said something inane like: "Why aren't you in the movies? You wouldn't even need talent; with your looks you could make a fortune. The movies or television would eat you up."

He turned his head toward me. "My looks?"

"Don't you know how beautiful you are?"

"I'm ugly." His fantastic voice colored the words with subtle shades of despair. "Everything is ugly."

I studied him closely. I think he believed what he said. "Don't you want to be rich? Don't you want the luxuries of life?"

"There's no point."

"Why not?"

"We're here such a short time. There's no point in gathering possessions. There's no point in anything. And there's not enough time."

"Not enough time?"

He had drifted off in a reverie. "A very short time—but it seems like forever." Impatience, hope, futility, expectation, anticipation; the voice showed it all.

"But how do you pass the time? What do you do?"

I think he sighed. "We wait," he said. "We wait."

"What are you waiting for?" I yelled in exasperation. He didn't answer. I knew better than to continue with a frontal attack. I backed up and started in at a different angle. "You said, 'We wait.' Are the others like you?"

"Yes."

A thought occurred to me. "Do they know you're here?"

"Yes."

"Why don't they try to rescue you?"

"They're afraid."

"Afraid? Of me?"

"Yes."

"Why?"

"You're dangerous."

"Dangerous?"

"Yes. They would do anything to prevent premature interruption of the cycle."

I started to ask what the hell he was talking about, but I knew it wouldn't do any good. "How am I dangerous?"

"You can see us."

"Do you know why I can see you?"

"No."

"Am I the only one?"

"The only one we know of now."

"Now?"

"It's happened before."

I changed directions again. "Are you afraid of me?"

"Yes."

"Why? I haven't hurt you."

"There is danger that you will interrupt the cycle."

"Why did you come with me so passively?"

"I couldn't believe you would do this to me." Again subtle shadings of accusation, hopelessness, and sadness in the beautiful voice. He turned his head to look at me. For an instant, the barest instant, I felt like a real son of a bitch. Then he looked away. He sat on the side of the bed, my bathrobe too big for him, the chain snaking into the bathroom.

Don't get the idea that he had become an unexpected chatterbox. That conversation is a distillation of three weeks' questions and silences.

About a week later, I went during the night to check on him. I hadn't been sleeping very well. My mind was full of wild, impossible speculations. I won't go into them but they consisted of men from Mars and other equally incredible flights of fancy. I started to put on my bathrobe but remembered he was wearing it. I tiptoed down the hall stark naked hoping to catch him doing something—doing *anything*.

The door to his room was always left open. I looked in cautiously.

I couldn't see him anywhere. I turned on the light. He was pressed against the outside wall of the room, my bathrobe crumpled at his feet. His arms were outstretched to bring as much of him against the wall as possible. He didn't seem to notice me, but then, he never did. I went to him and saw his face, the side of it flat against the wall. It was no longer expressionless. It was filled with the most overpowering hopelessness I had ever seen. I felt my throat constrict.

"What's wrong?" I whispered.

He didn't answer for a moment—not because he was ignoring me as he usually did, but because he was preoccupied. Then he said, very softly, in a voice caressed by a cold, bleak wind: "The small creatures in the forest; their deaths are so tiny and insignificant. There's hardly any life energy at all."

Then he really was aware of me. I saw him retreat until the eyes and face were neutral. I bellowed and slapped him as hard as I could. I remembered them standing around the wrecks. He fell to his knees, the crimson print of my hand on his face. I pulled him up by his armpits and looked into his empty face.

"Stop hiding from me!" I screamed and slapped him again. He slumped against me and my arms were around him, holding him up. Our naked bodies were together, exciting me. The blood rushed to my groin and my erection was painful. He was there, in the eyes, not completely, but there. I put my mouth over his. He neither drew away nor responded but his bruised lips were sweet and I didn't want to stop.

I had been looking at his placid face for a month. I knew he was capable of emotion if he would let it show. He hadn't uttered a sound or responded in any way to physical blows. He had to have a breaking point somewhere. I pushed him onto the bed on his stomach. The chain rattled. I rammed into him, trying to hurt him. He was tight, very tight. It must have been painful, but he didn't cry out or even moan. It had been a long time since the last time—a month —too long. It only took a dozen strokes, my pelvis pounding against the flawless flesh of his buttocks, before I came. I shouldn't have waited so long. It burned.

I lay on him for a moment, then reached and pulled his face around. It was vacant. I withdrew, still hard. I pulled him into a sitting position facing me. That beautiful face. That beautiful bland, bruised face. I put my hands on either side of it.

"Don't hide from me. It doesn't do any good. I can see you. I can see you!" He swam to the surface and looked at me. "Did you enjoy it? Did you even feel it?"

"Yes."

"Did it feel good? Did it hurt?"

"Yes."

"Why didn't you groan? Why didn't you scream? Why didn't you beg me to stop? Why don't you get mad? Why don't you curse me? What's inside you?" I put my hand on his breast and felt the hard nipple against my palm. "Do you have a heart? I can feel something in there. Is it a heart? What would I find if I got a knife and slit you open? Do you have sexual feelings at all?" I grabbed his penis and squeezed. It was soft but firm. "Has it ever been hard? You don't piss with it. What do you use it for?"

I put his hand on my tingling erection. He didn't pull away. It just lay there. "That's what it's for. That's how a human uses it!" He started going away again. I slapped him. "Stay with me. Stay with me every second." I pushed him on his back. The chain clattered on the floor. I hooked his knees over my shoulders, watching his eyes the whole time. He tried to go away a few times but I slapped him back. I took a very long, slow time and I enjoyed the hell out of it.

The next morning I drove down the mountain to the village and phoned the Department. With direct dialing you can't tell where a long-distance call is coming from. My father was worse and not expected to live much longer. Yeah, too bad. I shouldn't be away much longer. Good-bye.

I started going to him every night. I hadn't meant to but I couldn't sleep without him. He didn't go away anymore and I didn't have to slap him. The bruises on his face faded finally. He was there all right, but that was all. I never succeeded in bringing emotion to his face.

Finally I began sleeping in the same bed with him, touching him all night, feeling his hard nipples under the palms of my hands.

He woke me one morning, moaning. The window was gray with light and I could see his mouth moving. I touched his face. It was hot and dry. He spoke and the music in his voice was muted. "Why have you done this to me? I never harmed you. I've never harmed anyone. All we ever want is to survive until the birth."

"What's wrong with you?"

"It's time. The end of the cycle. The birth."

"Isn't that what you've been waiting for?"

"I'm not strong enough. I haven't collected enough life energy."

"I'll let you go. I'll take you back to L.A."

"It's too late. Too late."

He never said anything again. I watched him for three days. His fever got worse and the life went from his vibrant flesh. His skin flaked away in gray scales. He was struggling with all his might against something. I don't know what. But in the end he failed. His moans were so piteous that I had to put my hands over my ears. But I couldn't take my eyes off the disintegration of that magnificent creature.

And that's all he was, wasn't he? A creature. Something not human. It wasn't my fault that, by some fluke, I could see them. I didn't know this would happen. He never told me.

On the second day a hump began forming on his back. He was curling more and more into a fetal position as the hump forced him over. He began bleeding at the mouth. I put the shower curtain under him. When I rolled him over, my hands got covered with something like ashes.

On the third day he began to quieten and I knew it was almost over. He hadn't moved in several hours except for ragged breathing. There was a sharp cracking sound, like Carnehan biting into a new apple, only louder. The now ugly body trembled violently for a few moments, and then nothing. He lay facing me, his eyes open, the color of clay.

The breathing stopped.

It was finished.

I got out of the chair and walked around to the other side of the bed. The hump on his back had split and something white was sticking out. I reached down and pulled on it. It was a wing, a large, white wing covered with feathers. No, not feathers. Soft, white silky hair.

There was a second wing but it was twisted and not properly developed. I pulled away all of the body and exposed what was inside it.

I cleaned up the cabin so no one would know it had been occupied. I packed everything back in the Dart. I buried them both in the woods, the body of the dead winged thing, and the husk that had held it. I drove back to Hollywood. It seemed as if I passed a wreck every half mile. I went into my apartment without noticing the apple cores in the yard. I unlocked the door, went straight to the toilet, and vomited.

I was splashing cold water on my face when I heard her.

"Lou? Is that you?" She walked in wearing a slip, her eyes red from sleep, and her hair sticking out on one side where she'd been lying on it.

"Margaret! What the hell are you doing here?"

"Oh, Lou!" She pressed against me. "It's been *awful!* Alfred found out about us!"

My head was spinning. "Who the shit is Alfred?"

She looked puzzled. "My husband!"

Jesus Christ! I'd forgotten Carnehan's first name. She was right. It was awful. "What'd he do? Do they know at the Department?"

"He hit me!" She began to blubber on my shoulder. "I was afraid. I've been hiding here for three *days!* He keeps pounding on the door but I stay quiet. He doesn't know for sure I'm here."

"How did he find out?"

"I don't *know!* He came home from work three days ago, screaming at me and hitting me. Oh, Lou. I was so frightened." She kissed me and her breath was bad. *His* breath had had no odor at all. "Come to bed with me, Lou. It's been so long," she whined.

I felt her doughy flesh through the thin slip. But it was woman flesh and I had to forget about him. I led her to the bed and began undressing. I was sticky. I hadn't bathed or shaved since he started . . . Stop it!

She pulled the slip over her head, unhooked her bra, and peeled down her pantyhose. Her tits were beginning to sag, her thighs were puffy, and there was a small roll of fat around her waist. Her skin looked muddy, not clear like . . . Stop it!

She walked toward me, smiling coyly. I wish I had been able to see . . . Stop it!

I pushed her roughly onto the bed and she squealed. Margaret liked it rough. I was about to make her very happy. She gasped deep in her throat every time my pelvis slammed against her flabby flesh. It was good—but . . . Stop it!

I lay on my back, half asleep. Margaret lay on top of me, licking my nipples and trying to coax it back up again. It hadn't lasted long enough for her, but she was wasting her time and she was heavy. I closed my eyes, trying to stay awake. I felt her hair on my face. There was a noise and her head hit mine. Her breath rushed out in one stale puff and I felt something dripping on my cheek.

I focused my eyes. Carnehan was standing over us, his nightstick raised. I couldn't move Margaret's dead weight. "Carnehan!

Don't!" I yelled. The stick came down. I remembered I hadn't locked the door.

When I came out of it, it was dark. I was in a moving car. My head hurt and the car sounded as if it were driving in the bottom of a well. I could feel dried blood in my left eye; maybe mine or maybe Margaret's. I tried to wipe it away but my hands wouldn't move. I heard the clink of handcuffs and felt the door handle. My head was leaning against the glass. It felt cool. I opened my eyes and saw brush going past and a sea of lights spread out below. I could see a dozen fires burning. We must be somewhere in the Hollywood Hills.

I turned my head and looked at Carnehan driving the car. He stared straight ahead. "Carnehan, what do you think you're doing?" The words didn't come out as forcefully as I had intended. He ignored me. "Carnehan, Margaret doesn't mean anything to me." That was the wrong thing to say. Think straight! "She's not worth it, Carnehan. I'm not worth it. Neither of us is worth destroying your-self."

He wasn't listening. "You can't hope to get away with this." Of course he didn't. "Why don't you just write it off as a mistake?"

The car had been bouncing around for a while. We must not have been on a main road. I couldn't raise myself high enough to see ahead. After a bit Carnehan stopped the car and got out. He opened the back door on my side and began dragging out Marga-ret's naked body. She must have been already dead, the way she flopped around like a rubber dummy. He dragged her a few feet from the car and rolled her down a hill. I could hear her crackling the brush, then silence.

Carnehan opened my door and the handcuffs pulled me out. I felt sharp rocks digging into my butt and realized I was naked too. He pulled out his revolver.

"Carnehan! Don't be a fool!"

He shot me in the stomach. Good old Carnehan. He remembered what we'd been taught: always aim for the gut.

He unlocked the handcuffs and pulled me to the edge. All I had to do was overpower him and get away, but I decided to wait be-cause I was very tired. I rolled down the hill like a sack of potatoes. I didn't feel the prickly pears and sharp brush. The pain in my belly was too fierce. I hit something hard and I think my shoulder broke.

I was lying on my back, my head leaning against whatever I'd hit, looking back up the hill. The car drove away. Carnehan, you bungler! I'm not dead! You wasted it all!

The sound of the car died away. It was very quiet, just crickets and the faroff rumble of traffic. You couldn't get away from that sound anywhere in Los Angeles County. A slight wind was blowing, making some loose sheet metal creak and groan somewhere near by.

I couldn't just lie here. I was bound to die if I didn't get help. I tried to move and looked up. An immense "Y" loomed over me. I was under the Hollywood sign. I couldn't see Margaret anywhere. Let me rest a moment more and get my breath back. Damn fuckin' Carnehan. Are you gonna be surprised when they haul you in and I'm there to point the finger. I looked down at my stomach. A mistake. But it doesn't hurt so much anymore. I must be in shock. I've heard that happens.

I can see my prick. It looks wrinkled and shrunken, even smaller than Cunningham's. This is a hell of a time to be thinking about pricks! My shoulder hurts worse than my gut. I can feel blood on the ground under my back. I've rested long enough.

What's that noise? Sounded like a twig cracking somewhere in the darkness. What if it's a coyote? I wonder if it will attack me. Probably not. Do coyotes react to the smell of blood the way sharks do?

Footsteps. Not a coyote. People. More than one. I'm saved! Up yours, Carnehan!

There are four of them: four redheaded young men who don't look a day over twenty. Four perfect faces that I used to think were overwhelmingly beautiful—until I saw the face of that dead winged thing. But I did see it. And I had to cover it because the beauty was too painful to look at.

Four magnificent bodies that only a few days ago would have sent the blood rushing to my penis—if I hadn't seen the pale body of the winged creature, all the more beautiful because it was sexless. A body I knew would have gleamed had it been alive.

Now these four faces seem drab and plain and the four bodies might belong to trolls.

But the eyes! They stand around me, watching me with eyes I still think beautiful because the winged creature's eyes were closed in death.

Those four pairs of beautiful, bland eyes look at me the same way Carnehan looks at an apple he's been saving for a special occasion.

F. Paul Wilson sits now on the cusp of best-sellerdom. Deservedly so. But in the rush to rediscover his older novels, which invariably happens when an author achieves prominent note, one hopes that his short stories aren't forgotten. He's a masterful short story writer as he proves here, in this wry dark look at the real nature of movie making.

Cuts

F. Paul Wilson

It started in Milo's right foot. He awoke in the dark of his bedroom with a pins-and-needles sensation from the lower part of his calf to the tips of his toes. He sat up, massaged it, walked around the bedroom. Nothing helped. Finally, he took a Darvocet and went back to bed. He managed to get to sleep but was awake again by dawn, this time with both feet tingling. In the wan light, he inspected his lower legs.

A thin, faintly red line around each leg about three inches up from the ankle. Milo snapped on the night table light for a closer look. He touched the line. It was more than a line—an indentation, actually, like something left after wearing a pair of socks too tight at the top. But it felt as if the constricting band were still there.

He got up and walked around. It felt a little funny to stand on partially numb feet but he couldn't worry about it now. In just a couple of hours he was doing a power breakfast at the Polo with Regenstein from TriStar and he had to be sharp. He padded into the kitchen to put on the coffee.

As he wove through L.A.'s morning commuter traffic, Milo envied the drivers with their tops down. He would have loved to have his 380 SL opened up to the bright early morning sun. Truthfully, he would have been glad for an open window. But for the sake of his hair he stayed bottled up with the a-c on. He couldn't afford to let the breeze blow his toupe around. It had been especially stubborn about blending in with his natural hair this morning and he didn't have any more time to fuss with it. And this was his good piece. His back-up had been stolen during a robbery of his house last week, an occurrence that still baffled the hell out of him. He wished he didn't have to worry about wearing a rug. He had heard about a new experimental lotion that was supposed to start hair growing again. If that ever panned out, he'd be first on line to—

His right hand started tingling. He removed it from the wheel and fluttered it in the air. Still it tingled. The sleeve of his sports coat slipped back and he saw a faint indentation running around his forearm, just above the wrist. For a few heartbeats he studied it in horrid fascination.

What's happening to me?

Then he glanced up and saw the looming rear of a truck rushing toward his windshield. He slammed on the brakes and slewed to a screeching stop inches from the tailgate. Gasping and sweating, Milo slumped in the seat and tried to get a grip. Bad enough he was developing mysterious little constricting bands on his legs and now his arm, he had almost wrecked the new Mercedes. This sucker cost more than his first house back in the seventies.

When traffic started up again, he drove cautiously, keeping his eyes on the road and working the fingers of his right hand. He had some weirdshit disease, he just knew it, but he couldn't let anything get between him and this breakfast with Regenstein.

"Look, Milo," Howard Regenstein said through the smoke from his third cigarette in the last twenty minutes. "You know that if it was up to me the picture would be all yours. You know that, man."

Milo nodded, not knowing that at all. He had used that same line himself a million times—maybe *two* million times. *If it was up to me* . . . Yeah, right. The great cop-out: I'm a nice guy and I have all the faith in the world in you but those money guys, those faithless, faceless Philistines who hold the purse strings, won't let guys with vision like you and me get together and make a great film.

"Well, what's the problem, Howie? I mean, give it to me straight."

"All right," Howie said, showing his chiclet caps between his thin lips. He was deeply tanned, wore thick horn-rimmed glasses; his close-cropped curly hair was sandy-colored and lightly bleached. "Despite my strong—and, Milo, I do mean *strong*—recommendation, the money boys looked at the grosses for *The Hut* and got scared away."

Well. That explained a lot of things, especially this crummy table half hidden in an inside corner. The real power players, the ones who wanted everybody else in the place to see who they were doing breakfast with, were out in the middle or along the windows. Regenstein probably had three breakfasts scheduled for this morning. Milo was wondering what tables had been reserved for the others when a sharp pain stabbed his right leg. He winced and reached down.

"Something wrong?" Regenstein said.

"No. Just a muscle cramp." He lifted his trouser leg and saw that the indentation above his ankle was deeper. It was actually a cut now. Blood oozed slowly, seeping into his sock. He straightened up and forced a smile at Regenstein.

"*The Hut,* Howie? Is *that* all?" Milo said with a laugh. "Don't they know that project was a loser from the start? The book was a bad property, a piece of clichéd garbage. Don't they know that?"

Howie smiled, too. "Afraid not, Milo. You know their kind. They look at the bottom line and see that Universal's going to be twenty mill in the hole on *The Hut,* and in their world that means something. And maybe they remember those P.R. pieces you did a month or so before it opened. You never even mentioned that the film was based on a book. Had me convinced the story was all yours, whole cloth."

Milo clenched his teeth. That had been when he had thought the movie was going to be a smash.

"I had a *concept,* Howie, one that cut through the bounds and limitations of the novel. I wanted to raise the level of the material but the producers stymied me at every level."

Actually, he had been pretty much on his own down there in Haiti. He had changed the book a lot, made loads of cuts and condensations. He had made it "A Milo Gherl Film" but somewhere along the way he had lost it. Unanimously hostile one-star reviews with leads like, "Shut 'The Hut'" and "New Gherl Pix the Pits" hadn't helped. Twentieth had been pushing an offer in its television division and he had been holding them off—who wanted to do tv when you could do theatricals? But as the bad reviews piled up and the daily grosses plummeted, he grabbed the tv offer. It was good money, had plenty of prestige, but it was still television.

Milo wanted to do films, and very badly wanted in on the new package Regenstein was putting together for TriStar. Howie had Jack Nicholson, Bobby De Niro, and Kathy Turner firm, and was looking for a director. More than anything else in his career, Milo wanted to be that director. But he wasn't going to be. He knew that now.

Well, at least he could use the tv job to pay the bills and keep his name before the public until *The Hut* was forgotten. That wouldn't be long. A year or two at most and he'd be back directing another theatrical. Not a package like Regenstein's, but something with a decent budget where he could do the screenplay and direct. That was the way he liked it—full control on paper and on film.

He shrugged at Regenstein and put on his best good-natured smile. "What can I say, Howie? The world wasn't ready for *The Hut.* Someday, they'll appreciate it."

Yeah, right, he thought as Regenstein nodded noncommittally. At least Howie was letting him down easy, letting him keep his dignity here. That was important. All he had to do now was—

Milo screamed as pain tore into his left eye like a bolt of lightning. He lurched to his feet, upsetting the table as he clamped his hands over his eye in a vain attempt to stop the agony. *Pain!* Oh, Christ, pain as he had never known it was shooting from his eye straight into his brain. This had to be a stroke! What else could hurt like this?

Through his good eye he had a whirling glimpse of everybody in the dining room standing and staring at him as he staggered around. He pulled one hand away from his eye and reached out to steady himself. He saw a smear of blood on his fingers. He took the other hand away. His left eye was blind, but with his right he saw the dripping red on his palm. A woman screamed.

"My God, Milo!" Regenstein said, his chalky face swimming into view. "Your eye! What did you do to your *eye?*" He turned to a gaping waiter. "Get a doctor! Get a fucking ambulance!"

Milo was groggy from the Demerol they had given him. In the blur of hours since breakfast he'd been wheeled in and out of the emergency room so many times, poked with so many needles, examined by so many doctors, X-rayed so many times, his head was spinning.

At least the pain had eased off.

"I'm admitting you onto the vascular surgery service, Mr. Gherl," said the bearded doctor as he pushed back one of the white curtains that shielded Milo's gurney from the rest of the emergency room.

His badge said, *Edward Jansen, M.D.,* and he looked tired and irritable.

Milo struggled up the Demerol downgrade. "Vascular surgery? But my eye—!"

"As Dr. Burch told you, Mr. Gherl, your eye can't be saved. It's ruined beyond repair. But maybe we can save your feet and your hand if it's not too late already."

"Save them?"

"If we're lucky. I don't know what kind of games you've been into, but getting yourself tied up with piano wire is about the dumbest thing I've ever heard of."

Milo was growing more alert by the second now. Over Dr. Jansen's shoulder he saw the bustle of the emergency room personnel, saw an old black mopping the floor in slow, rhythmic strokes. But he was only seeing it with his right eye. He reached up to the bandage over his left. *Ruined?* He wanted to cry, but Dr. Jansen's piano wire remark suddenly filtered through to his consciousness.

"Piano wire? What are you talking about?"

"Don't play dumb. Look at your feet." Dr. Edwards pulled the sheet free from the far end of the gurney.

Milo looked. The nail beds were white and the skin below the indentations was a dusky blue. And the indentations had all become clean, straight, bloody cuts right through the skin and into the meat below. His right hand was the same.

"See that color?" Jansen was saying. "That means the tissues below the wire cuts aren't getting enough blood. You're going to have gangrene for sure if we don't restore circulation soon."

Gangrene! Milo levered up on the gurney and felt his toes with his good hand. *Cold!* "No! That's impossible!"

"I'd almost agree with you," Dr. Jansen said, his voice softening for a moment as he seemed to be talking to himself. Behind him, Milo noticed the old black moving closer with his mop. "When we did X rays, I thought we'd see the wire embedded in the flesh there, but there was nothing. Tried Xero soft-tissue technique in case you had used fishing line or something, but that came up negative, too. Even probed the cuts myself but there's nothing in there. Yet the arteriograms clearly show that the arteries in your lower legs and right forearm are compressed to the point where very little blood is getting through. The tissues are starving. The vascular boys may have to do bypasses."

"I'm getting out of here!" Milo said. "I'll see my own doctor!"

"I'm afraid I can't allow that."

"You can't stop me! I can walk out of here anytime I want!"

"I can keep you seventy-two hours for purposes of emergency psychiatric intervention."

"Psychiatric!"

"Yeah. Self-mutilation. Your mind worries me almost as much as your arteries, Mr. Gherl. I'd like to make sure you don't poke out your other eye before you get treatment."

"But I didn't—!"

"Please, Mr. Gherl. There were witnesses. Your breakfast companion said he had just finished giving you some disappointing news when you screamed and rammed something into your eye."

Milo touched the bandage over his eye again. How could they think he had done this to himself?

"My God, I swear I didn't do this!"

"That kind of trauma doesn't happen spontaneously, Mr. Gherl, and according to your companion, no one was within reach of you. So one way or the other, you're staying. Make it easy on both of us and do it voluntarily."

Milo didn't see that he had a choice. "I'll stay," he said. "Just answer me one thing: You ever seen anything like this before?"

Jansen shook his head. "Never. Never *heard* of anything like it either." He took a sudden deep breath and smiled through his beard with what Milo guessed was supposed to be doctorly reassurance. "But, hey. I'm only an ER doc. The vascular boys will know what to do."

With that, he turned and left, leaving Milo staring into the wide-eyed black face of the janitor.

"What are you staring at?" Milo said.

"A man in *big* trouble," the janitor said in a deep, faintly accented voice. He was pudgy with a round face, watery eyes, and two days' worth of silvery growth on his jowls. With a front tooth missing on the top, he looked like Leon Spinks gone to seed for thirty years. "These doctors can't be helpin' what you got. You got a *Bocor* mad at you and only a *Houngon* can fix you."

"Get lost!" Milo said.

He lay back on the gurney and closed his good eye to shut out the old man and the emergency room. He hunted for sleep as an escape from the pain and the gut-roiling terror, praying he'd wake up and learn that this was all just a horrible dream. But those words wouldn't go away. *Bocor* and *Houngon* . . . he knew them some-how. Where?

And then it hit him like a blow—*The Hut!* They were voodoo terms from the novel *The Hut!* He hadn't used them in the film—he'd scoured all mention of voodoo from his screenplay—but the author had used them in the book. If Milo remembered correctly, a *Bocor* was an evil voodoo priest and a *Houngon* was a good one. Or was it the other way around? Didn't matter. They were all part of Bill Franklin's bullshit novel.

Franklin! Wouldn't he like to see me now! Milo thought. Their last meeting had been anything but pleasant. Unforgettable, yes. His mind did a slow dissolve to his new office at Twentieth two weeks ago . . .

"Some conference!"

The angry voice startled Milo and he spilled hot coffee down the front of his shirt. He leaped up from behind his desk and bent forward, pulling the steaming fabric away from his chest. "Jesus H.—"

But then he looked up and saw Bill Franklin standing there and his anger cooled like fresh blood in an arctic breeze. Maggie's anxious face peered over Franklin's narrow shoulder.

"I tried to stop him, Mr. Gherl, honest I did, but he wouldn't listen!"

"You've been ducking me for a month, Gherl!" Franklin said in his nasal voice. "No more tricks!"

Maggie said, "Shall I call security?"

"I don't think that will be necessary, Maggs," he said quickly, grabbing a Kleenex from the oak tissue holder on his desk and blotting at his stained shirt front. Milo had moved into this office only a few weeks ago, and the last thing he needed today was an ugly scene with an irate writer. He could tell from Franklin's expression that he was ready to cause a doozy. Better to bite the bullet and get this over with. "I'll talk to Mr. Franklin. You can leave him here." She hesitated and he waved her toward the door. "Go ahead. It's all right."

When she had closed the door behind her, he picked up the insulated brass coffee urn and looked at Franklin. "Coffee, Billy-boy?"

"I don't want coffee, Gherl! I want to know why you've been ducking me!"

"But I haven't been ducking you, Billy!" he said, refreshing his own cup. He would have to change this shirt before he did lunch later. "I'm not with Universal anymore. I'm with Twentieth now, so naturally my offices are here." He swept an arm around him. "Not bad, ay?"

Milo sat down and tried his best to look confident, at ease. Inside, he was anything but. Right now he was a little afraid of the writer stalking back and forth before the desk like a caged tiger. Nothing about Franklin's physical appearance was the least bit intimidating. He was fair-haired and tall with big hands and feet attached to a slight, gangly frame. He had a big nose, a small chin, and a big adam's apple—Milo had noticed on their first meeting two years ago that he could slant a perfectly straight line along the tips of those three protuberances. A moderate overbite did not help the picture. Milo's impression of Franklin had always been that of a patient, retiring, rational man who never raised his voice.

But today he was barging about with a wild look in his eyes, shouting, gesticulating, accusing. Milo remembered an old saying his father used to quote to him when he was a boy: *Beware the wrath of a patient man.*

Franklin had paused and was looking around the spacious room with its indirect lighting, its silver-gray floor-to-ceiling louvered blinds and matching carpet, the chrome and onyx wet bar, the free-form couches, the abstract sculptures on the Lucite coffee table and on Milo's oversized desk.

"How did you ever rate this after perpetrating a turkey like *The Hut?*"

"Twentieth recognizes talent when it sees it, Billy."

"My question stands," Franklin said.

Milo ignored the remark. "Sit down, Billy-boy. What's got you so upset?"

Franklin didn't sit. He resumed his stalking. "You know damn well what! My book!"

"You've got a new one?" Milo said, perfectly aware of which book he meant.

"No! I mean the only book I've ever written—*The Hut!*—and the mess you made out of it!"

Milo had heard quite enough nasty criticism of that particular film to last him a lifetime. He felt his anger flare but suppressed it. Why get into a shouting match?

"I'm sorry you feel that way, Billy, but let's face facts." He spread his hands in a consoling gesture. "It's a dead issue. There's nothing more to be done. The film has been shot, edited, released, and—"

"—and withdrawn!" Franklin shouted. "Two weeks in general release and the theatre owners sent it back! It's not just a flop, it's a catastrophe!"

"The critics killed it."

"Bullshit! The critics blasted it, just like they blasted other 'flops' like *Flashdance* and *Top Gun* and *Ernest Goes to Camp*. What killed it, Gherl, was word of mouth. Now I know why you wouldn't screen it until a week before it opened: You knew you'd botched it!"

"I had trouble with the final cut. I couldn't—"

"You couldn't get it to make sense! As I walked out of that screening I kept telling myself that my negative feelings were due to all the things you'd cut out of my book, that maybe I was too close to it all and that the public would somehow find my story in your mass of pretentions. Then I heard a guy in his early twenties say, 'What the hell was *that* all about?' and his girlfriend say, 'What a boring waste of time!' and I knew it wasn't just me." Franklin's long bony finger stabbed through the air. "It was you! You raped my book!"

Milo had had just about enough of this. "You novelists are all alike!" he said with genuine disdain. "You do fine on the printed page so you think you're experts at writing for the screen. But you're not. You don't know the first goddamn thing about visual writing!"

"You cut the heart out of my story! *The Hut*'s was about the nature of evil and how it can seduce even the strongest among us. The plot was like a house of cards, Gherl, built with my sweat. Your windbag script blew it all down! And after I saw the first draft of the script, you were suddenly unavailable for conference!"

Milo recalled Franklin's endless stream of nit-picking letters, his deluge of time-wasting phone calls. "I was busy, dammit! I was writer-director! The whole thing was on my shoulders!"

"I warned you that the house of cards was falling due to the cuts you made. I mean, why did you remove all mention of voodoo and zombiism from the script? They were the two red herrings that held the plot together."

"Voodoo! Zombies! That's old hat! Nobody would pay to see a voodoo movie!"

"Then why set the movie in Haiti, f'Christsake? Might as well have been in Pasadena! And that monster you threw in at the end.

Where in hell did you come up with that? It looked like the Incredible Hulk in drag! I spent years in research. I slaved to fill that book with terror and dread—all you brought to the screen were cheap shocks!"

"If that's your true opinion—and I disagree with it absolutely— you should be glad the film was a flop. No one will see it!"

Franklin nodded slowly. "That gave me comfort for a while, until I realized that the movie isn't dead. When it reaches the video stores and the cable services, tens of millions of people will see it— not because it's good, but simply because it's there and it's something they've never heard of before and certainly have never seen. And they'll be directing their rapt attention at your corruption of my story, and they'll see 'Based on the Novel by William Franklin' and think that the pretentious, incomprehensible mishmash they're watching represents my work. And that makes me *mad,* Gherl! Fucking-A crazy *mad!"*

The ferocity that flashed across Franklin's face was truly frightening. Milo rushed to calm him. "Billy, look: Despite our artistic differences and despite the fact that *The Hut* will never turn a profit, you were paid well into six figures for the screen rights. What's you're beef?"

Franklin seemed to shrink a little. His shoulders slumped and his voice softened. "I didn't write it for money. I live off a trust fund that provides me with more than I can spend. *The Hut* was my first novel—maybe my only novel ever. I gave it everything. I don't think I have any more in me."

"Of course you do!" Milo said, rising and moving around the desk toward the subdued writer. Here was his chance to ease Franklin out of here. "It's just that you've never had to suffer for your art! You've had it too soft, too cushy for too long. Things came too easy on that first book. First time at bat you got a major studio film offer that actually made it to the screen. That hardly ever happens. Now you've got to prove it wasn't just a fluke. You've got to get out there and slog away on that new book! Deprive yourself a little! *Suffer!"*

"Suffer?" Franklin said, a weird light starting to glow in his eyes. "I should suffer?"

"Yes!" Milo said, guiding him toward the office door. "All great artists suffer."

"You ever suffer, Milo Gherl?"

"Of course." *Especially this morning, listening to you!*

"Look at this office. You don't look like you're suffering for what you did to *The Hut.*"

"I did my suffering years ago. The anger you feel about *The Hut* is small change compared to the dues I've had to pay." He finally had Franklin across the threshold. "I'm through suffering," he said as he slammed the door and locked it.

From the other side of the thick oak door he thought he heard Franklin say, "No, you're not."

"Missing any personal items lately, mister?" said a voice.

Milo opened his good eye and saw the big black guy standing over him, leaning on his mop handle. What was *wrong* with this old fart? What was his angle?

"If you don't leave me alone I'm gonna call—" He paused. "What do you mean, 'personal items'?"

"You know—clothing, nail clippings, a brush or comb that might hold some of your hair. That kinda stuff."

A chill swept over Milo's skin like an icy breeze in July. *The robbery!* Such a bizarre thing—a pried-open window, a few cheap rings gone, his drawers and closets ransacked, an old pair of pajamas missing. And his toupe, the second-string hairpiece . . . gone. Who could figure it? But he had been shaken up enough to go out and buy a .38 for his night table.

Milo laughed. This was so ludicrous. "You're talking about a voodoo doll, aren't you?"

The old guy nodded. "It got other names, but that'll do."

"Who the hell *are* you?"

"Name's André but folks call me Andy. I got connections you gonna need."

"You need your head examined!"

"Maybe. But that doctor said he was lookin' for the wires that was cuttin' into your legs and your arm but he couldn't find them. That's because the wires are somewheres else. They around the legs and arm of a doll somebody made on you."

Milo tried to laugh again but found he couldn't. He managed a weak "Bullshit."

"You'll believe me soon enough. And when you do, I'll take you to a *Houngon* who can help you out."

"Yeah," Milo said. "Like you really care about me."

The old black showed his gap-tooth smile. "Oh, I won't be doin'

you a favor, and neither will the *Houngon*. He'll be wantin' money
for pullin' you' fat out the fire."

"And you'll get a finder's fee."

The smile broadened. "Tha's right."

That made a little more sense to Milo, but still he wasn't buying.
"Forget it!"

"I be around till three. I'll keep checkin' up on you case you
change you' mind. I can get you out here when you want to go."

"Don't hold your breath."

Milo rolled on his side and closed his eyes. The old fart had some
nerve trying to run that corny scam on him, and in a hospital yet!
He'd report him, have him fired. This was no joke. He'd lost his eye
already. He could be losing his feet, his hand! He needed top medi-
cal-center care, not some voodoo mumbo-jumbo . . .

. . . but no one seemed to know what was going on, and everyone seemed to think he'd put his own eye out. God, who could do
something like that to himself? And his hand and his feet—the doc
had said they were going to start rotting off if blood didn't get
flowing back into them. What on earth was happening to him?

And what about that weird robbery last week? Only personal
articles had been stolen. All the high-ticket stereo and video stuff
had been left untouched.

God, it couldn't be voodoo, could it? Who'd even—

Shit! Bill Franklin! He was an expert on it after all those years of
research for *The Hut*. But he wouldn't . . . he couldn't . . .

Franklin's faintly heard words echoed in Milo's brain: *No, you're
not.*

Agony suddenly lanced through Milo's groin, doubling him over
on the gurney. Gasping with the pain, he tore at the clumsy stupid
nightshirt they'd dressed him in and pulled it up to his waist. He
held back the scream that rose in his throat when he saw the thin
red line running around the base of his penis. Instead, he called out
a name.

"Andy! *Andy!*"

Milo coughed and peered through the dim little room. It smelled of
dust and sweat and charcoal smoke and something else—something
rancid. He wondered what the hell he was doing here. He knew if
he had any sense he'd get out now, but he didn't know where to go
from here. He wasn't even sure he could find his way home from
here.

The setting sun had been a bloody blob in Milo's rearview mirror as he'd hunched over the steering wheel of his Mercedes and followed Andy's rusty red pick-up into one of L.A.'s seamier districts. Andy had been true to his word: He'd spirited Milo out of the hospital, back to the house for some cash and some real clothes, then down to the garage near the Polo where his car was parked. After that it was on to Andy's *Houngon* and maybe end this agony.

It *had* to end soon. Milo's feet were so swollen he was wearing old slippers. He had barely been able to turn the ignition key with his right hand. And his dick—God, his dick felt like it was going to explode!

After what seemed like a ten-mile succession of left and right turns during which he saw not a single white face, they had pulled to a stop before a dilapidated storefront office. On the cracked glass was painted:

M. Trieste
Houngon

Andy had stayed outside with the car while Milo went in.

"Mr. Gherl?"

Milo started at the sound and turned toward the voice. A balding, wizened old black, six-two at least, stood next to him. His face was a mass of wrinkles. He was dressed in a black suit, white shirt, and thin black tie.

Milo heard his own voice quaver: "Yes. That's me."

"You are the victim of the *Bocor?*" His voice was cultured, and accented in some strange way.

Milo pushed back the sleeve of his shirt to expose his right wrist. "I don't know what I'm the victim of, but Andy says you can help me. You've *got* to help me!"

He stared at the patch over Milo's eye. "May I see?"

Milo leaned away from him. "Don't touch that!" It had finally stopped hurting. He held his arm higher.

M. Trieste examined Milo's hand, tracing a cool dry finger around the clotted circumferential cut at the wrist. "This is all?"

Milo showed him his legs, then, reluctantly, opened his fly.

"You have a powerful enemy in this *Bocor,*" M. Trieste said finally. "But I can reverse the effects of his doll. It will cost you five hundred dollars. Do you have it with you?"

Milo hesitated. "Let's not be too hasty here. I want to see some results before I fork over any money." He was hurting, but he wasn't going to be a sucker for this clown.

M. Trieste smiled. He had all his teeth. "I have no wish to steal from you, Mr. Gherl. I shall accept no money from you unless I can effect a cure. However, I do not wish to be cheated either. Do you have the money with you?"

Milo nodded. "Yes."

"Very well." M. Trieste struck a match and lit a candle on a table Milo hadn't realized was there. "Please be seated," he said and disappeared into the darkness.

Milo complied and looked around. The wan candlelight picked up an odd assortment of objects around the room: African ceremonial masks hung side by side with crucifixes on the wall; a long conga drum sat in a corner to the right, and a statue of the Virgin Mary, her small plaster foot treading a writhing snake, occupied the one on his left. He wondered when the drums would start and the dancers appear. When would they begin chanting and daubing him with paint and splattering him with chicken blood? God, he must have been crazy to come here. Maybe the pain was affecting his mind. If he had any smarts he'd—

"Hold out your wrist," M. Trieste said, suddenly appearing in the candlelight opposite him. He held what looked like a plaster coffee mug in his hand. He was stirring its contents with a wooden stick.

Milo held back. "What are you going to do?"

"Help you, Mr. Gherl. You are the victim of a very traditional and particularly nasty form of voodoo. You have greatly angered a *Bocor* and he is using a powerful *loa,* via a doll, to lop off your hands and your feet and your manhood."

"My left hand's okay," Milo said, gratefully working the fingers in the air.

"So I have noticed," M. Trieste said with a frown. "It is odd for one extremity to be spared, but perhaps there is a certain symbolism at work here that we do not understand. No matter. The remedy is the same. Hold your arm out on the table."

Milo did as he was told. His swollen hand looked black in the candlelight. "Is . . . is this going to hurt?"

"When the pressure is released, there will be considerable pain as the fresh blood rushes into the starved tissues."

That kind of pain Milo could handle. "Do it."

M. Trieste stirred the contents of the cup and lifted the wooden handle. Instead of the spoon he had expected, Milo saw that the man was holding a brush. It gleamed redly.

Here comes the blood, he thought. But he didn't care what was in the cup as long as it worked.

"André told me about your problem before he brought you here. I made this up in advance. I will paint it on the constrictions and it will nullify the influence of the *loa* of the doll. After that, it will be up to you to make peace with this *Bocor* before he visits other afflictions on you."

"Sure, sure," Milo said, thrusting his wrist toward M. Trieste. "Let's just get on with it!"

M. Trieste daubed the bloody solution onto the incision line. It beaded up like water on a freshly waxed car and slid off onto the table. Milo glanced up and saw a look of consternation flit across the wrinkled black face towering above him. He watched as the red stuff was applied again, only to run off as before.

"Most unusual," M. Trieste muttered as he tried a third time with no better luck. "I've never . . ." He put the cup down and began painting his own right hand with the solution. "This will do it. Hold up your hand."

As Milo raised his arm, M. Trieste encircled the wrist with his long dripping fingers and squeezed. There was an instant of heat, and then M. Trieste cried out. He released Milo's wrist and dropped to his knees cradling his right hand against his breast.

"The poisons!" he cried. "Oh, the poisons!"

Milo trembled as he looked at his dusky hand. The bloody solution had run off as before. "What poisons?"

"Between you and this *Bocor!* Get out of here!"

"But the doll! You said you could—!"

"There is no doll!" M. Trieste said. He turned away and retched. "There *is* no doll!"

With his heart clattering against his chest wall, Milo pushed himself away from the table and staggered to the door. Andy was leaning on his truck at the curb.

"Wassamatter?" he said, straightening off the fender as he saw Milo. "Didn't he—?"

"He's a phony, just like you!" Milo screamed, letting his rage and fear focus on the old Black. "Just another goddamn phony!"

As Andy hurried into the store, Milo started up his Mercedes and roared down the street. He'd drive until he found a sign for one of the freeways. From there he could get home.

And from home, he knew where he wanted to go . . . where he *had* to go.

"Franklin! Where are you, Franklin?"

Milo had finally found Bill Franklin's home in the Hollywood Hills. Even though he knew the neighborhood fairly well, Milo had never been on this particular street, and so it had taken him a while to track it down. The lights had been on inside and the door had been unlocked. No one had answered his knocking, so he'd let himself in.

"Franklin, goddammit!" he called, standing in the middle of the cathedral-ceilinged living room. His voice echoed off the stucco walls and hardwood floor. "Where are you?"

In the ensuing silence, he heard a faint voice say, "Milo? Is that you?"

Milo tensed. Where had that come from? "Yeah, it's me! Where are you?"

Again, ever so faintly: "Down here . . . in the basement!"

Milo searched for the cellar door, found it, saw the lights ablaze from below, and began his descent. His slippered feet were completely numb now and he had to watch where he put them. It was as if his feet had been removed and replaced with giant sponges.

"That you, Milo?" said a voice from somewhere around the corner from the stairwell. It was Franklin's voice, but it sounded slurred, strained.

"Yeah, it's me."

As he neared the last step, he pulled the .38 from his pocket. He had picked it up at the house along with a pair of wire cutters. He had never fired it, and he didn't expect to have to tonight. But it was good to know it was loaded and ready if he needed it. He tried to transfer it to his right hand but his numb, swollen fingers couldn't keep hold of the grip. He kept it in his left and stepped onto the cellar floor—

—and felt his foot start to roll away from him. Only by throwing himself against the wall and hugging it did he save himself from falling. He looked around the unfinished cellar. Bright, reflective objects were scattered all along the naked concrete floor. He sucked in a breath as he saw the hundreds of sharp curved angles of green glass poking up at the exposed ceiling beams. They looked like shattered wine bottles—big, green, four-liter wine bottles smashed all over the place. And in among the shards were scattered thousands of marbles.

"Be careful," said Franklin's voice. "The basement's mined." The voice was there, but Franklin was nowhere in sight.

"Where the hell are you, Franklin?"

"Back here in the bathroom. I thought you'd never get here."

Milo began to move toward the rear of the cellar where brighter light poured from an open door. He slid his slippered feet slowly along the floor, pushing the green glass spears ahead of him, rolling the marbles out of the way.

"I've come for the doll, Franklin."

Milo heard a hollow laugh. "Doll? What doll, Milo? There's just me and you, ol' buddy."

Milo shuffled around the corner into view of the bathroom. And froze. The gun dropped from his fingers and further shattered some of the glass at his feet. "Oh, my God, Franklin! Oh, my *God!*"

William Franklin sat on the toilet wearing Milo's rings, his old slippers, his stolen pajamas, and his other hairpiece. His left eye was patched and his feet and his right hand were as black and swollen as Milo's. There was a maniacal look in his remaining eye as he grinned drunkenly and sipped from a four-liter green-glass bottle of white wine. The cuts in his flesh were identical to Milo's except that a short length of twisted copper wire protruded from each. A screwdriver and a pair of pliers lay in his lap.

M. Trieste's parting words screamed through his brain: *There is no doll!*

"See?" Franklin said in a slurred voice. "You said I had to suffer."

Milo wanted to be sick. "Christ! What have you done?"

"I decided to suffer. But I didn't think I should suffer alone. So I brought you along for company. Sure took you long enough to figure it out."

Milo bent and picked up the pistol. His left hand wavered and trembled as he pointed it at Franklin. "You . . . you . . ." He couldn't think of anything to say.

Franklin casually tossed the wine bottle out onto the floor where it shattered and added to the spikes of glass. Then he pulled open the pajama top. "Right here, Milo, old buddy!" he said, pointing to his heart. "Do you really think you want to put a slug into me?"

Milo thought about that. It might be like putting a bullet into his own heart. He felt his arm drop. "Why . . . how . . . I don't deserve . . ."

Franklin closed his eye and grimaced. He looked as if he were about to cry. "I know," he said. "It's gone too far. Maybe you really don't deserve all this. I've always known I was a little bit crazy, but maybe I'm a lot crazier than I ever thought I was."

"Then for God's sake, man, loosen the wires!"

"No!" Franklin's eye snapped open. The madness was still there. "I entrusted my work to you. That's a sacred trust. You were responsible for *The Hut*'s integrity when you took on the job of adapting it to the screen."

"But *I'm* an artist, too!" Why was he arguing with this nut? He slipped the pistol into his front pocket and reached around back for the wire cutters.

"All the more reason to respect another man's work! You didn't own it—it was only on loan to you!"

"The contract—"

"Means nothing! You had a moral obligation to protect my work, one artist to another."

"You're overreacting!"

"Am I? Imagine yourself a parent who has sent his only child to a reputable nursery school only to learn that the child has been raped by the faculty—then you will understand *some* of what I feel! I've come to see it as my sacred duty to see to it that you don't molest anyone else's work!"

Enough of this bullshit! If Franklin wouldn't loosen the wires, Milo would cut them off! He pulled the wire cutters from his rear pocket and began to shuffle toward Franklin, sweeping the marbles and daggers of glass ahead of him.

"Stay back!" Franklin cried. He grabbed the pliers and pushed them down toward his lap, grinning maliciously. "Didn't know I was left-handed, did you?" He twisted something.

Searing pain knifed into Milo's groin. He doubled over but kept moving toward Franklin. Less than a dozen feet to go. If he could just—

He saw Franklin drop the pliers and pick up the screwdriver, saw him raise it toward his right eye, the good eye. Milo screamed,

"No!"

And then agony exploded in his eye, in his head, robbing him of the light, sending him reeling back in sudden impenetrable blackness. As he felt his feet roll across the marbles, he reached out wildly. His legs slid from under him and despite the most desperate flailings and contortions, there was nothing to grasp on the way down but empty air.

Jon L. Breen is equally good at writing fiction and criticising it. A very good novelist and story writer, and a regular book columnist for *Ellery Queen's Magazine*, Breen is one of the most influential mystery figures of his generation. The ironic grace of the following tale shows you why.

Starstruck

Jon L. Breen

Quite a few people had seen the tall, bent figure in the gray raincoat staggering along Hollywood Boulevard that April morning. Police were able to glean quite a complete description of his activites. He'd crossed to the north side of the street at Cherokee and staggered eastward, past Whitley. As the figure lurched along, witnesses agreed, he was looking down at the sidewalk, muttering the names of the show-business personalities immortalized on the Hollywood Chamber of Commerce's Walk of Fame. "Clem McCarthy . . . Danny Kaye . . . Ruth Etting . . . Toby Wing . . . David Butler . . . Ozzie Nelson . . ."

But why didn't anybody help him? He obviously was in pain, he obviously was in trouble, yet no one had come to his aid.

"I thought he was just drunk or on drugs," said one of the passersby.

"Half the people you pass on Hollywood Boulevard are talking to themselves," said another.

"I was just glad he didn't stop in front of my window," a merchant admitted.

You see all kinds of weird people on Hollywood Boulevard. Gaudily dressed prostitutes of both sexes, plus hustlers of every other variety; street preachers, bag women, and discharged mental patients; drunks, derelicts, and beggars; adolescents dressed, dyed, and clipped in punk style, earphones shutting out the world; aging

hippies in army fatigues; and an occasional nattily dressed octoge-
narian who might have belonged to the old Hollywood. And some
disillusioned tourists who, once they've had a look at the footprints
in front of Mann's Chinese Theatre and a walk around the third-
rate wax museum, have trouble finding much glamour in the tacky
souvenir shops, junk-food stands, video parlors, barber college,
empty store fronts, and—unless they are bibliophiles—bookshops.

The figure in the raincoat had lurched along another half block
after crossing Whitley and finally fallen on one of the stars, a star
shinier than the others, having been dedicated only a few weeks
before. When the man fell, his raincoat came open, and passersby
could see the red bloodstain spreading on his chest. Then they
called the police.

The man on the street had been shot, dying slowly with every
painful step he took, and soon actor Trent Gordon's glittering new
star was roped off as a crime scene.

"Who are all these people?" Detective Gary Holmes asked his
partner. "Clem McCarthy?"

"Used to call the Kentucky Derby on the radio," said Detective
Manny Gonzales.

"And Toby Wing? Who was he?"

"No idea." Manny wished his partner didn't have such an appe-
tite for nonessentials.

Holmes read on. "James Dunn . . . Reed Hadley . . . John
Forsythe . . . Helen Hayes . . . Basil Rathbone . . . Penny Sin-
gleton . . . Martha Raye." There the trail of occasional blood
spatters stopped. Beyond Trent Gordon's star, the stars of Jack
Warner, Bob Hope, Mickey Rooney, and others were half covered
by a building-site fence.

"We've got ID," one of the technicians said. "His wallet says he
was Howard Achitty. And look what else he was carrying. Isn't this
a friend of yours?" He handed over a business card.

Rachel Hennings was relieved when Manny Gonzales told her,
somewhat regretfully, that his visit to Vermilion's Bookshop consti-
tuted official business. She led him through her extensive stock of
used and rare books to the easy chairs in the back of the shop. She
offered a smile that tried to be warm and friendly without encouraging romantic advances. As Manny spoke, the smile faded.

"To put it simply, Rachel, we found a dead man on Hollywood

Boulevard who had your business card in his pocket. Fellow named Howard Achitty." He briefly outlined the significant details.

"Yes, he was here yesterday," she confirmed. "A tall man? Late fifties? Distinguished-looking?"

"Tall, yes, and the age is about right, maybe a little older than that. He didn't look too distinguished when I saw him, though. He'd taken a slug in the chest from a distance of a few feet. After it happened, he managed to stumble along the boulevard at least a block and a half. We're not sure just where he collected the slug. Tell me about his visit here."

"He came at the height of the rainstorm, a little after four, I think. I remember him well, because I didn't have another customer all afternoon. When he came in, I thought he looked a little familiar. Maybe one of the regular customers Uncle Oscar had when I used to visit the shop as a child. And he had that look in his eye, as if Vermilion's once meant something important to him. Finally he walked up to the desk in front and said he was looking for a book. Then he looked at me for a long moment and didn't say anything."

"I can see his point."

She shrugged off the flattery. "Finally he asked me if I was old Oscar's niece, the one who inherited the store. I said I was. He said, 'We all used to come to Oscar's to get out of the sun and keep this damned climate from drying out our brains.' I told him, 'Los Angeles never did that to anybody. It's just a nice place to live.' And he said, 'Don't tell me that. I need an explanation for why I never managed to rival Thomas Wolfe.' 'You were a writer?' I said. 'Sure, I was a writer. Weren't all of Oscar's customers writers?' " She shook her head sadly. "He was a nice guy."

"What book was he looking for?"

"It was the autobiography of Burton François, the director. I didn't have one in stock—I'd just sold one a few weeks ago, in fact. It was published only about fifteen years ago but has gotten to be a pretty scarce item. I asked him if he'd tried any of the public libraries or other bookshops, and he said nobody seemed to have a copy available. I even asked him if he knew François, if he might be able to get a copy from him personally. He sort of snorted at that and said, 'I don't trust any of those guys.' I wondered what he meant. Then I remembered that François was best known as a science-fiction director, and I thought my friend Blast-Off Meagher, who specializes in sf, might have the book. I gave him a call, and he did, said he'd hold it for my customer. Blast-Off asked me the customer's name, and that was when he told me he was Howard Achitty."

"Blast-Off Meagher," Manny said. "His shop's on Cherokee, just off Hollywood, right?" Rachel nodded. "Achitty might have been there just before he died. He came from that direction. But he sure didn't have a book on him. . . . Did he say anything else?"

"No—once I'd told him about Blast-Off, he went out in that rain with such enthusiasm you'd have thought he was Gene Kelly."

"Would he have been able to buy the book from Meagher yesterday after leaving here?"

Rachel thought a moment. "I doubt it. This was late afternoon, and I think Blast-Off closes at five."

"Then I'll bet that's where he was this morning. You've been a big help, Rachel. Uh, how about dinner tonight? We could talk some more about the case. You could be a kind of unofficial consultant."

She grinned at him, suspicious as always of any invitation from Manny Gonzales to be an "unofficial consultant." "The LAPD always has time to entertain gifted amateur detectives, huh? Why wait for tonight? I have more for you now. After he left, I took down one of my movie references to find out what the connection was between Howard Achitty and Burton François. Let me show you." She stretched to pull a large book down from a high shelf, giving Manny a pleasurable view of a few inches of skin between blouse and jeans. She opened the book on the round table between them and showed Manny the credits for a film called *Menace of the Solar System,* released in 1952.

"It was François's first feature, and Achitty wrote the screenplay," Rachel said. "Look who the male lead was."

"Sure enough, Trent Gordon," said Manny. "And now Achitty dies a day after he was looking for François's autobiography . . ."

"And chooses to fall on Gordon's star."

"Chooses? Maybe he just couldn't go any farther."

"It would be quite a coincidence, though, wouldn't it?"

"They do happen. What do you think, it's Ellery Queen time? A dying message? Rachel, in all the time I've worked homicide, *nobody* has given me a dying message."

"So you've been deprived. You said the witnesses thought he was reading the stars. Maybe he was looking for the right one to flop down on. Maybe Gordon killed him."

"Maybe Bob Hope killed him, but he couldn't get that far."

Rachel made a face. "Don't tease your unofficial consultant."

"I just can't buy the dying-message bit," Manny said. "But we'll look into it. Was this a major picture? Gordon was a pretty big star at one time, wasn't he?"

"Not in movies," Rachel said. "In the early fifties, Trent Gordon was strictly a B star. He only became really famous when he made that TV western series."

"I thought he was a private eye."

"That was later. He had a cowboy show first."

"I never saw it. Never liked westerns, even as a kid. Did you ever see a smart Mexican in a western, Rachel? Truthfully now."

Rachel ignored the question. "What was the symbol on Gordon's Walk of Fame star?"

"Symbol?"

"They identify them according to what branch of show business they became famous in. There's a microphone, a movie camera, a record, a TV set . . ."

Manny nodded. "It was a TV set all right." He looked back at the credits. "Who else was in this picture? Audrey Vance . . ."

"I think she later married Burton François, but it didn't last."

"How cozy. You seem to know Hollywood gossip as well as you know books."

Rachel shrugged. "Can I help it if things stick in my mind?"

"Billy Hook," Manny read. "Song-and-dance man, wasn't he?"

"He'd have been a big star if they'd kept making musicals."

"And Guy Wheatley. He goes back a long way."

"He was in silents. You going to talk to all these people, Manny?"

Manny snorted. "If they're still alive, I may have Holmes do it. He's the one that's starstruck. No reason to think any of the others have any connection to Achitty's death, but I guess I have to follow up on Trent Gordon and Burton François. Had Achitty done anything since the sci-fi epic?"

"Don't let Blast-Off hear you call it sci-fi," Rachel said. She reached down another reference tome, this one on screenwriters, found the Achitty entry, and handed the book across to Manny. "Mostly B movies through the late fifties, then lots of TV scripts into the middle seventies. Then his career seems to have petered out. I noticed he talked about his writing in the past tense."

"You didn't give me an answer about dinner," Manny said.

"Well—"

"Look, why don't you come with me to see Blast-Off Meagher? I mean, you know books and all this movie lore, and it's looking pretty important."

"I'm in business here, Manny. I can't just leave the shop."

The UCLA library school student Rachel had recently hired as a relief clerk chose that moment to enter through the front door and roar in a theatrical bass, "Your slave is here, Rachel. What is it today, shelve or study my cataloguing? Say shelve, please."

Rachel wasn't sorry her excuse for not accompanying Manny had disappeared. But she'd have to make it clear to him their relationship would be strictly professional.

Blast-Off Meagher greeted them amid a seeming chaos of hardbacks and paperbacks, pulps and digests, scripts and souvenirs, nearly all with some science-fictional connection. The seeming disorder contrasted sharply with the neatness of Vermilion's, but the elderly, bushy-bearded bookseller seemed to know where everything was, despite a visual handicap that seemed insurmountable for somone in the book business.

"Sure, he was here this morning, and I sold him the book."

"Are you sure it was Achitty?" Manny asked.

"He said he was, but you have to realize, I'm legally blind, so I can't describe the guy."

"What did his voice sound like?" Rachel asked.

Blast-Off considered for a moment. "He sounded a little like Johnny Carson. Under sedation."

Rachel nodded. "That's the same man."

"Was he alone?" Manny asked.

"No. I heard him talking to somebody as he entered the shop. The other person stayed near the doorway, and as Achitty left, he started talking again."

"Did the other person say anything?"

"Not a word."

"Do you know if it was a man or a woman?"

"Can't help you there. Wasn't close enough to smell anything, and to tell somebody's sex, I have to be very, very close." Blast-Off chuckled.

"What time was this?"

"I don't make the effort to look at my watch until near closing time. I guess it was ten-thirty or so. I hadn't been open for long."

"Did you hear anything after he left the shop?"

"Yeah. For what seemed like a half hour, somebody was playing rock music outside—a tape, I guess, or a car radio—loud enough to make the building shake. I was afraid if they didn't quit soon, I'd be legally deaf, too."

"You didn't hear a shot?"

"No, and I wouldn't have. That music would have drowned anything out."

Rachel said, "Blast-Off, what do you remember about a movie called *Menace of the Solar System?*"

"Interesting picture. Sort of a cult item. Some people in the sf field think it was one of the classic films of the 1950s. You have to realize that you can find sf fans who will make a case for every bug-eyed-monster movie made before 1960, so you can't take what all of them say too seriously. But I think *Menace of the Solar System* was probably a pretty good flick. It had one of the great movie robots in it, right up there with Robbie and C3PO. They called it Ishmael—a little pretentious, don't you think? Of course, Burton François at that time was your basic Hollywood boy wonder, and he was under a great deal of pressure to come up with a movie to justify his advance billing. He put together a great crew of technicians and special-effects people and a cast that was straight out of a B-movie stock company. But as I recall, there was some problem with the studio about his finished product, and I think they took it out of his hands and did some recutting on it. Of course, the picture did make a little bit of money, and Burton François went on to become a pretty successful director, if not quite the *Wunderkind* people expected back then."

"What do you know about that vacant store next to you?" Manny asked.

Blast-Off laughed. "There's been everything in there from a hair salon to a hamburger stand to an old-record store. Place is jinxed. Bad location, I guess."

"Do they often leave the door unlocked?"

"They've been careless about that, yes. You have to realize there's nothing in there to steal, but the boulevard freaks have all sorts of unsavory uses for an empty store—flophouse, needle academy, stolen-goods exchange, coed brothel—"

"If somebody fired a shot in that empty store, would you have heard it?"

Blast-Off shook his head. "Not with that rock music going, I wouldn't."

As they left, Rachel looked at the empty shop on the Hollywood Boulevard side of Blast-Off's. The doorway was slightly recessed into the building, and there was only enough window space to show no one was doing business there.

"The scene of the crime?" she asked.

Manny nodded. "I think so. It all figures. Achitty and his companion come out of Meagher's. He's anxious to have a look at the book. They duck into the doorway, see it's unlocked, go into the empty store to examine their treasure. Once they're out of public view, Achitty finds out his friend is not so friendly. The other guy—"

"It could have been a woman," Rachel pointed out. "Blast-Off said—"

"Sure, it could have been a woman. The other person shoots him, takes the book—"

"And Achitty goes lurching down toward the Boulevard. Why didn't the killer finish him off, make sure he was dead?"

Manny agreed that was a good point. "It doesn't look like a pro. Maybe once the shot was fired, the killer got so scared he—or she— just bolted. Well, we'll find out."

"What's next?" Rachel asked.

"How about some lunch? It's after one o'clock, and I was going to meet Gary Holmes at my uncle's place."

Manny's uncle's place served some of the best Mexican food in Los Angeles, so Rachel found herself readily agreeing. It should get her off the hook for dinner.

Joining them at their table, Detective Gary Holmes roared, "Hey, I didn't know they let Mexicans in here!"

Manny winced at his partner's heavy-handed humor, but he knew it was benignly intended. "I didn't know they allowed WASPs either," he said in a lower voice. "Sit down and try to behave yourself." Thanks to its location on Fairfax Avenue, Tio Pedro's perhaps had the largest Jewish clientele of any Mexican restaurant in the world.

Holmes picked up the menu, knowing he could ignore the prices. "You're sure this stuff is all kosher?" he said, winking at Rachel.

"Shut up," Manny said. "We know where the crime was committed and a little bit of why. What have you got to show for the last couple hours?"

"I've identified most of the stars. Reed Hadley played Zorro in a serial and used to have a TV show called *Racket Squad.* But I still don't know who Toby Wing—"

"Can it, Gary. Did you get to talk with Trent Gordon?"

"Sure I did. Just caught him going out the door, on the way to the library, he said, to study his art. Quite a character. All the acting talent of Tab Hunter, but to talk to him you'd think he was Laurence Olivier or something. The guy does have a connection to Howard Achitty. Ever heard of a sci-fi flick called *Menace of the Solar System?*"

Manny glanced at Rachel. "I think I've heard of it, yeah."

"Well, the guy that directed it was Burton François. It was his first picture, and now he's a big-shot director. In the last couple of weeks, François has gotten the idea he wants to reshoot the ending of the flick."

"Reshoot the ending?" Rachel said. "But it was over thirty years ago."

"I know. But it seems the studio screwed up the picture, didn't release it the way François wanted it. I guess in those days the director didn't have diddly-squat to say about what they did with his flick. Now François is rich and does what he wants. He bought up all the rights to the flick from the studio. All the main actors are still alive. He wants to reshoot a new finish, with all the characters thirty years later, then rerelease the picture the way he wants it. Some idea, huh?"

"Yeah," said Manny. "Has anybody ever done that before?"

Rachel said, "I remember hearing that Orson Welles wanted to do something like that with *The Magnificent Ambersons,* but it never happened."

"Anyway," Gary Holmes continued, "François had scheduled a meeting of the main actors at his home in Beverly Hills tonight."

"Is the meeting still on?" Manny asked.

"As far as Gordon knows it is."

"Was Howard Achitty one of the people invited?"

"I asked, and Gordon wasn't sure. It seems likely."

"I wonder if Mr. Burton François would mind if we dropped in on this little meeting."

Realizing the hounds were on the scent and the unofficial consultant would only be in the way, Rachel begged off the reiterated dinner invitation and left the two policemen to their investigations. But she had a busy afternoon planned for herself. Back at Vermil-

ion's, she first made a quick call to the Hollywood Chamber of
Commerce. She had an idea of the possible significance of Achitty's
falling on Gordon's bright new star.

She asked if any of the principals in *Menace of the Solar System* or
director François had stars in the sidewalk. François did, she was
told, but his star was well up Vine Street, near the Huntington
Hartford Theatre, quite a distance from the scene of Achitty's
death. Guy Wheatley also rated a star, one of the first to be im-
planted back in 1961, but it, too, was blocks away from where
Achitty had been found. Audrey Vance and Billy Hook had never
been honored.

Next she drove down to the Los Angeles Public Library, an ornately imposing building dating from 1926. It was soon to be vacated for a long-needed expansion and remodeling, for now the old
library was little changed, a historic landmark bursting its bounds.

The library's film book collection was located in the Art and
Music department on the second floor. As she'd expected, the cir-
culating copy of François's autobiography was not there, but there
was a reference copy she could peruse on the premises. She
scanned through it quickly, looking for references to *Menace of the
Solar System* and its cast.

François had been born in 1925, which made him just over sixty
now and in his middle to late twenties at the time of *Menace of the
Solar System.* The most recent of the volume's selection of photographs showed a mildly boyish-looking man in his mid-forties. People had always said François seemed too shy and retiring a person
to be a successful director, and the photographs seemed to bear
that illusion out. It was difficult to imagine his controlling a movie
set.

"Most of us were kids when we made that picture," François had
written about *Menace of the Solar System,* "and we were positive it
was going to be the greatest science-fiction picture ever made. In
our original conception, it would have been. What most of the mov-
iemakers of the fifties (and later) forgot was that science fiction is a
literature of ideas, not of horrors, and that was what we were trying
to reflect in our film. But it was the time of the witch-hunt, and it's
hard for people looking back to realize just what the atmosphere of
Hollywood was like in those days. We were all afraid of our own
shadows. I was only a genius on Mondays, Wednesdays, and Fri-
days. On Tuesdays and Thursdays, I was a scared kid, afraid what
I'd achieved to that point would crumble under my feet like the

sand on the beach at Malibu. When I was told to make changes, lest I be thought a purveyor of Communist propaganda, which I absolutely was not, I made the changes readily like a good little studio hack."

There was disappointingly little detail about the making of the film and no elaboration on the reference to the Communist witch-hunt. What had anyone found Communistic in the original script of *Menace of the Solar System?* And what changes had been mandated? François was maddeningly silent on the point.

There was also little about the others involved in making the film.

"Howard Achitty was a gifted writer who knew what I wanted and could provide it, knew what the studio wanted and could provide that, too. We worked well together but never had the opportunity to do so again. . . .

"Trent Gordon seemed destined for a career as a B leading man along the lines of Kane Richmond or Robert Lowery. Television would bring him a popularity beyond anyone's wildest dreams—but maybe not beyond his own. . . .

"Billy Hook was a song-and-dance star that the gods of the studio, in their infinite wisdom, signed to a long-term contract just a week before they decided to shut down their musical unit. They put him in various projects, including our picture, and he wasn't happy. But he was going to a drama coach and did his best to bring himself up to snuff as a straight actor. He did a good job as the comic second lead in *Menace.* Later on he made a mint in real estate. . . .

"Guy Wheatley had long been one of the great movie villains, from a silent-picture career leering at Leatrice Joy and Lillian Gish. He'd been young then but always played middle-aged. Our *Menace* was one of the best parts he'd ever had, he said, and he played it to the hilt. . . .

"Audrey Vance was about the most beautiful creature I'd ever seen, and shortly after we finished *Menace* I married her. She'd been married before, and she loved to talk about her previous husband's habit of reading scripts in bed. Everything was funny to Audrey, both in bed and out, and we just didn't get along at all."

François had no more to say about his *Menace of the Solar System* coworkers. Discussing later films and actors, he was much more forthcoming.

The photo section was better than the text. It offered a picture of the film's most memorable set: the spaceship's improbably grand and roomy flight deck. Trent Gordon was startlingly handsome in his futuristic space uniform—when his private-eye show had gone off the air only ten or so years ago, he'd hardly looked any older. And yes, Audrey Vance had been a notable beauty, tall and blond, her long legs fully revealed in the standard fifties vision of feminine space attire. The diminutive Billy Hook, playing Gordon's sidekick, had the kind of face that would appeal to specialists in sad-clown portraits. And Guy Wheatley had a suitably evil countenance as the titular Menace.

The picture's renowned robot, Ishmael, not as cute as Robbie or C3PO but somehow more believable, was shown in one still with Trent Gordon. As Rachel was looking at it, a voice from over her shoulder said, "He was a terrible scene-stealer."

She nearly jumped a foot. Turning, she found herself looking into the face of Trent Gordon. The actor was still so matinee-idol handsome she immediately thought about facelifts.

"I'm sorry if I frightened you. Could I have a look at that book when you're finished with it, please?"

"Yes, certainly, I was nearly finished."

Gordon sat down. Some of the other readers, who had old-fashioned principles about silence in libraries, were glaring at him.

"It's terrible for the ego," he told her more softly. "I spend many afternoons among all these students of the film, and I'm rarely even asked for an autograph. I haven't seen you in here before."

The actor's knee had made tentative contact with Rachel's. She sensed he was more interested in her than in the book she was reading. She was a bit charmed in spite of herself, but not so charmed she wouldn't have made a swift exit if she hadn't had another motivation for cultivating him.

"That book's tough to track down these days. I didn't read it when it first came out, though I'm not one of those actors who never read books, only scripts. What's your interest in my old pal Burton François?"

The guy certainly had confidence in his irresistibility, quizzing a fellow library patron when it was clearly none of his damned business. Rachel could play along quite nicely. She manufactured a girlish blush.

"To be truthful, it's not Mr. François I'm interested in. I was really interested in you, Mr. Gordon. Professionally, I hasten to add," she said, not intending the disclaimer to be convincing. "I was doing research for an article I hoped to write for, uh, my college film journal about your career. That's why I was so startled to actually see you."

"Well, coincidences do happen. In fact, I'll let you in on another that I've been itching to tell somebody about. A man died today on Hollywood Boulevard. Murdered. And I may be the chief suspect."

Rachel widened her eyes like a Victorian ingenue. "Really?"

"Yes. And the reason I wanted to see the book . . ." He looked around. "We really shouldn't discuss this among all these serious students of the arts. That woman in the plaid looks as if she'd like to kill *me*. I presume you've read in there about the picture I made with François and that upstaging robot?"

"Of course. That's why I got the book."

"Then join me for a cup of coffee or a drink. If you're afraid of being in the company of a murder suspect, I assure you the itinerary is well-peopled and includes no dark alleys."

Rachel closed the book. "I'll be honored," she said.

At a little after four, Rachel was sipping a margarita with Trent Gordon in the bar of the newly refurbished Biltmore Hotel. On the short walk from the library, all his talk had been determinedly small and ingratiating. Rachel sensed the actor's interest was now about evenly divided between discussing the Achitty case and getting her into bed before the evening was over. Her own interest was concentrated in the first area.

"What I wanted to know," he said confidentially, "was whether François said anything in his book about the death of William Bingham."

"William Bingham? No, not a thing. Should he have?"

"That's debatable, but I'm not surprised he didn't. William Bingham was a very good actor. We were in a play together not far from here in the old Biltmore Theatre, years and years ago. Bingham had the misfortune of holding rather, um, advanced social views and signed his name to things a little too freely in the thirties and forties. To put it simply, he got himself blacklisted."

Rachel nodded. "I remember his name now. But why should François have mentioned his death?"

With the air of a magician producing a rabbit, Gordon said, "Bingham was found dead on the set of *Menace of the Solar System* one morning, that's why. He was lying at the controls of Burt's state-of-the-art movie spaceship. And he was murdered with a knife in his back. Don't look for that in the newspaper files, though—as far as they were concerned, he died in bed. The studios had a lot of influence in those days."

"It was covered up?"

"Quite successfully."

"Did the police . . . ?"

"Officially, the police knew nothing about it. Unofficially, well, I don't really know what strings the studio head might have pulled."

"What was Bingham doing on the set?"

"None of us knew. As a blacklisted Commie, he was a pariah on any movie lot. We'd all have been scared to death of any connection with him. Presumably, he got on the lot through some ruse, met somebody on our set, maybe threatened to blackmail him about something. That somebody killed him. Up until Bingham's death, the making of *Menace of the Solar System* had been pretty much left alone. After all, it was a B, a programmer, kids' matinee stuff, and the B directors had more freedom than the big guys as long as they stayed within schedule and budget. After Bingham died, a studio flunky was always there to watch the shooting. I think the studio head, who had built up an image of himself as a patriotic American compared to whom Howard Hughes was a fellow traveler, actually read the script and found some things that made him nervous. He demanded changes."

Gordon downed his drink and signaled for another. Rachel continued to nurse hers.

"Howard Achitty made the changes, but he wasn't happy about it any more than Burt François was. They weren't really political, either one of them, and there was no Commie propaganda in that script. Howard had a sort of obsession about what happened from then on. He used to mention it to me whenever I saw him, and I had to admit it made me nervous, though I was just as curious myself. I'm wondering if Howard might have found out something after all these years, something he shouldn't have." Trent Gordon paused reflectively. "The last time I saw him was just a few weeks ago. He showed up at the ceremonies when they dedicated my star on Hollywood Boulevard. And when he died this morning, he was lying on my star, almost as if he was fingering me for the murder, which I know he couldn't have been, because I didn't kill him."

Rachel was fighting back the urge to ask him questions about things she wasn't supposed to know, like Achitty's search for the François autobiography and tonight's scheduled meeting of the *Menace* cast. Was that still on? she wondered.

"It must be thrilling to have a star on Hollywood Boulevard," she said, still the starstruck college journalist.

Gordon smirked. "It came at a good time for me, because my career isn't exactly booming at the moment. Who knows what might help it?"

"What is your next project?"

Gordon looked at his watch and reacted stagily. Charming, but no great actor. "Well, look at the time! I'd love to talk to you some more, Rachel. How about some dinner later?"

"Well, I—"

"That's settled then. I have a little engagement first, though. I wonder if you might like to accompany me. You might find it interesting."

"Where are you—uh, we going?" she asked.

"To the Beverly Hills home of Mr. Burton François!"

Rachel considered swooning on the spot but decided that would be overdoing it.

Beverly Hills was one of the least-changed places in Southern California. As Gordon's car turned off Santa Monica Boulevard onto one of the tree-lined residential streets, Rachel saw an elderly black man in pristine white coat leading what looked like a purebred Pomeranian on a leash. He could have been Rochester, and the year 1940.

François's house was only slightly larger and more luxurious-looking than the Beverly Hills average. As they walked up the driveway to the front door, Gordon dropped the name of the silent-film star who had originally built it. "Screening room's bigger than those in some of these four-screens-in-one movie houses you see nowadays—that was one reason Burt bought it."

Sure enough, a butler let them into the living room. Posters and movie memorabilia were everywhere, recounting not just François's career but the whole history of Hollywood.

"Mr. François will be down in a few minutes," the butler said, and bowed his way out like a refugee from *Masterpiece Theatre.* A tall, still-blond Audrey Vance sprang from the sofa, and she and Trent Gordon greeted each other in the best effusive show-biz fashion. The former Mrs. François was heavier, a bit puffy-faced, and making no apparent effort to deny middle age, but her legs were fine as ever and shown to good advantage in her short loose-fitting dress.

Gordon introduced Rachel, and Audrey gave her a friendly greeting.

"I didn't know I could bring a date," Audrey said kiddingly.

"Rachel is my newly appointed official biographer. She goes with me everywhere."

"What, everywhere?" Audrey said with a leer.

Rachel practiced her girlish simper, while saying to herself, No, not everywhere, in fact hardly anywhere.

The two old costars halted their arch dialogue briefly to agree how tragic it was about poor old Howard.

"You and he were pretty good friends, weren't you?" Gordon said.

Audrey said sadly, "Used to be. I haven't seen him in years. Make yourself and Rachel a drink, why don't you?" Audrey gestured to a well-stocked bar. "I'm a couple ahead of you."

"I could tell," Gordon said. "I thought you'd gone on the wagon."

"No fun on the wagon."

"What's your pleasure, Rachel?" Gordon asked.

"Just some ginger ale." The margaritas at the Biltmore had been plenty.

"Funny idea remaking that movie," Audrey said. "I think I'll enjoy it, if Burt actually gets it off the ground. Take a little work to get myself in shape, of course. I know I'm supposed to be thirty years older, but I don't want to let myself look *too* ridiculous. Trent, you'll have to be heavily made up to look thirty years older."

"The hell I will, Audrey. You know cowboys and private eyes and space heroes never grow old. Or any older than they can help. Anybody else here yet?"

"Guy's here."

"Really? How is he?"

"All things considered, pretty good. Burt's chauffeur drove him down from the Motion Picture Country House in Woodland Hills, and he'll be staying over. He went up to his room to rest." She turned to Rachel. "The man's eighty-five, would you believe it? A little bit frail, but he's kept up his instrument—"

"You've already tested his instrument?" Gordon asked.

"His voice, you bastard. He says he's still capable of working, and I believe him. Next to George Burns, he's a kid. Give me a refill, will you?"

Trent Gordon delivered Rachel's glass and took Audrey's.

Audrey said to Rachel, "Don't mind our kidding, honey. You know, and he won't mind my saying this, kidding is why I'm not still married to Burt François. He always takes everything *sooo* seriously, and me, I'd make a joke out of anything. He and his work were too serious to kid about. My other husband was an income tax auditor, and even he had more humor about his job than Burt. Billy Hook was the same sort of guy, so you can imagine I made things kind of uncomfortable on the set. Trent and Guy like a good joke, but they know when to put a lid on it. I never knew when to put a lid on anything—and don't you make any filthy cracks, Trent." She took the drink. "Thanks, honey."

"What did Mr. François have to change in the film to begin with?" Rachel asked.

Audrey Vance laughed uproariously. "That was so damn funny, and nobody else seemed to see the humor of it at all. You know who was supposed to be mouthing the Communist propaganda in that movie? Ishmael the talking robot, that's who. This bucket of bolts was the one who was supposed to be giving you the Marxist-Leninist line. Basically, all Burt and poor old Howard had to do was change the lines of the robot. It was the funniest thing I ever heard —it was like in a cartoon, Mickey Mouse or Bugs Bunny's a Communist, you know? According to Burt, it changed the whole picture, the whole vision they had for it, and Howard was never the same again. But I don't know. I thought it was funny. Nobody else did."

"It seems funny now, Audrey, I have to admit," said Trent Gordon. "But those were the days of McCarthy, don't forget."

"Charlie McCarthy?"

A voice from the doorway said, "That's the McCarthy Howard Achitty said he felt like when he had to rewrite those lines."

"Why, Burt," said Audrey Vance, "did you just make a joke?"

"Sorry to disappoint you," said Burton François. "He didn't laugh when he said it." The director walked into the room, his face somber. He was clearly older but still oddly boyish-looking. His voice was soft. He dropped wearily into a chair. "I ought to have called this off."

"Why call it off?" Gordon replied. "You should go ahead with it as a memorial to Howard."

"I just meant for today. You really need the work, don't you, Trent?"

"Hell, no, but I insisted to my agent I had to fit this in. Out of respect for you, Burt, and film history."

Audrey's giggle spoiled the effect.

Burton François looked pointedly at Rachel. "I don't believe I know you."

"She's with me," Gordon said with wolfish pride. "Rachel Hennings."

"Are you in pictures?"

"No," said Rachel, praying her cover wouldn't be blown. "I'm a reporter," she said, trying for an air of sophomoric self-importance.

"You expect to write about tonight?"

"I'm not here professionally. I mean, I'm writing about Trent, but if you want anything kept off the record . . ."

"I want everything kept off the record," he said, still in soft and measured tones. She sensed he was angry at Gordon for bringing her but too concerned about keeping the peace to ask her to leave. "What paper are you with?"

Trent Gordon gave her a conspiratorial wink. "The *Times,* wasn't it?" he said.

"That's right, the *Times,*" she said, smiling at him gratefully.

The butler reappeared, escorting a little man who looked like a retired jockey who'd been catching up on his eating.

"Is that you in there, Billy?" Gordon said.

Billy Hook glared at him. "I can still do a back flip. Want to see me?"

"Please, no. I wouldn't want the responsibility."

The whole group performed the show-biz greeting rituals, but it didn't entirely clear the atmosphere.

"I remember now what a talent we all had for getting on one another's nerves," said Burton François. "In the interest of this project, maybe we should do our best to keep things friendly. Jacob, ask Mr. Wheatley if he's able to join us, will you?" The butler bowed out.

"We miss you out at the Colony, Burt," Billy Hook said.

"Malibu just isn't my style, I guess. I'm more a Beverly Hills person."

"I read a script about Malibu a while back," Gordon said. "It was called *Sandbags and Cocaine*. Great title, but it'll never get made."

A moment later, Guy Wheatley tottered into the room. He was as slow-moving and as fragile-looking as anyone Rachel had ever seen, and she would have estimated his life expectancy at five minutes. But when he spoke, it was in a booming baritone that could still project to the back row.

"You know when I worked last?" he roared. "It was a cigarette commercial. That'll tell you how long ago it was. There I was, a lifetime nonsmoker, sending young cowboys and beach bunnies to their deaths." He looked at Rachel. "What did you play in *Menace of the Solar System?* I don't remember any babes in arms in the picture, but you must have been awfully young."

Rachel smiled. "I'm not an actress. I'm just here on sufferance."

Wheatley peered at her. "You're lovely, you know that? Did you ever work for D. W. Griffith? Silly question, you couldn't have, but he'd have loved that face. Burt, isn't she a dead ringer for Miriam Cooper?"

"Who?" said Billy Hook.

"That's why I love you, Guy," said Audrey. "Only you refer to people I'm too young to remember."

"Then how do you know you're too young to remember her?" the old actor said slyly. "She could be somebody Burt and I met last week. How about it, Burt? Doesn't she?"

"A bit," said Burton François, who clearly knew Miriam Cooper at least from film, but was far less entranced by Rachel than Guy was. "Now that we're all here, why don't we get started? You all know why I wanted you to come, and I know you share my grief that Howard Achitty can't be here with us."

"What happened to him? Guy Wheatley demanded.

"He, uh, died this morning. But that sad event has nothing to do with our purpose here. As you know, I want to provide *Menace of the Solar System* with a new ending. And before we talk about it, there's something I want you to see."

François led the group out of the living room and along a corridor, decorated on both sides with movie posters, to a towering pair of ornately carved doors.

"The ballroom," said Gordon.

"It *was* the ballroom," said François, "but I have made another use of it, as you'll see." The director was more animated now, obviously eager for their reaction to what he was going to show them. He opened the double doors and directed them in with a flourish.

Filling most of the room was the memorable set from *Menace of the Solar System,* the deck of the spaceship, all steel and flashing lights, dials and screens, buttons and levers. In the center of it all, the main controls, facing a screen that showed a continuous pattern of whizzing asteroids, was the captain's chair. To one side, as if awaiting human orders, was Ishmael himself, one of moviedom's three or four most celebrated robots, who had narrowly escaped being the first blacklisted machine.

For a moment no one spoke. Rachel found the sight enormously impressive and strangely moving, and it didn't have the associations for her that it must have had for the others. Glancing at Audrey Vance, she was surprised to see tears in the actress's eyes.

Billy Hook was the first to speak. "I hated it when I worked here, Burt, but now it's like coming home."

"When do we shoot the new finish?" Gordon asked. "And are we all still on the space voyage or what?"

"These things take time," François said. "But it's going to happen, I assure you. This is still early stages."

"Better get on it fast," said Guy Wheatley. "I could pass away anytime, you know, and I don't want a coffin-nail spot for my last professional engagement."

Audrey had to cover her face, and François seemed close to weeping himself. "I'll do my best, Guy. I really will do my best."

Rachel walked over to the seat at the control board. Surely she wasn't the only one thinking about the death of a certain William Bingham in this very chair. "How long have you had this set, Mr. François?"

"Several years. I acquired it and the robot—and the rights to the film—when they tore down the old Apex studio in Culver City. At the time, my motives were strictly sentimental, but then I got the idea of shooting a new ending, and since all my principals were alive and well . . ."

"Was this the seat where William Bingham died?" Rachel asked softly.

François's mild face changed dramatically. It had been a dangerous thing to say, she knew. But surely there was safety in numbers—they weren't all going to murder her as a team effort.

"What the hell are you talking about? Who's been talking to you?"

"Do you know who killed Bingham? Did the same person kill Howard Achitty? You don't say much in your autobiography."

"I should have thrown you out of here as soon as I found out you were a reporter." François was talking in a low voice, as if to prevent anyone else from hearing their conversation, but it was no use.

"Who the hell is this dame, anyway?" said Billy Hook.

"She's a reporter," said François, "and she seems to want to stir up a lot of stuff better left unstirred."

Gordon said apologetically, "We've been kidding you, Burt. She's not with the *Times*—she's a college girl."

"And you told her all about William Bingham, did you, you stupid bastard?"

"That happened a long time ago, Burt. We don't have to be afraid of the witch-hunt anymore."

"Well, Howard Achitty just happened this morning. And there could be a connection."

"That's what I thought," Rachel said.

Trent Gordon stared at her. "What *you* thought? What do you know about it?"

"Right, Gordon," said Billy Hook. "Bring your latest piece of ass here and put us all in danger."

"Watch your language, Hook, or I'll roll you out of here like a beachball!" Gordon exploded. But the look he turned on Rachel wasn't friendly.

"You have more to lose than any of us, Trent," Burt said. "Howard died on your star. He could have been saying you killed him."

"I don't think so," said Rachel, anxious to defend Gordon and gain at least one ally. "I think Achitty was looking for Trent's star and picked that spot to fall. But he wasn't trying to tell the police you killed him, Trent. He was trying to establish a connection between his death and *Menace of the Solar System.* He knew where your star was, and he didn't know the location of anybody else's. Or if he did, he knew they were too far to get to."

Gordon shook his head. "You know more about all this than I do," he said.

"I wish we could come to some understanding here before the police arrive," François said.

"Police arrive?" Hook squeaked. "You're expecting the police?"

François shrugged. "A couple of L.A. detective asked permission to drop in. I could hardly refuse them. I thought it was just routine. But if there's some connection with Bingham . . ."

"Bingham died in bed," said Hook. "He had no connection to our picture, and he was never on the set."

"But he was," said Rachel.

"Only if somebody tells them so. The case is closed. Hell, it was never even open. Why bring up Bingham now?"

"I don't believe in coincidental murders," said Rachel.

"You don't believe—and who are you to believe or not believe?"

Billy Hook was turning red, and Audrey Vance put a hand on his arm to calm him down. He shook it off.

Rachel wondered why Hook was so much more wrought-up than the others. Was it just his nature, or was it something else?

"What did Bingham do for a living after he got blacklisted?" she asked.

Surprisingly, the answer came from Guy Wheatley. "The poor bastard did what a lot of the poor bastards did. Writers could write for less money under other names, but that wasn't open to actors. But he could teach. He became an acting coach. Gave private lessons, of course. Very secret."

"Who was your acting coach, Mr. Hook?" Rachel asked.

"I don't have to answer that," he said.

"No, you don't. But if Bingham was your acting coach, the information can't hurt you now as it could have then."

"Can't it?"

"Not unless you killed him."

"Well, I didn't."

"But if he was on the set to meet you, you couldn't have admitted it, could you? Your own career would disappear from under you. Guilt by association. Isn't that right?"

Billy Hook stared at her. "I didn't kill him. He helped me. He was a wonderful man. I had no reason to kill him. He turned me from an out-of-work hoofer into some sort of actor. I didn't make it big, but I made enough dough and invested it well enough to buy me a place in the Colony. I'd love to know who killed him." He shrugged. "At the time, I didn't have the luxury to wonder. I just wanted his blacklisted ass out of that studio like everybody else. That's the kind of egocentric son of a bitch I am."

Audrey had broken away from the group and had her arm around the robot. "Ishmael, you old bolshevik," she said, "I do believe you're the only human being in the room. Burt, any chance of another drink?"

François looked disgusted. "That won't always work, Audrey."

"Well, it's always worth a try," she said in a subdued voice, starting to sound weepy again.

The butler appeared at the door of the spaceship-deck set. "Two gentlemen from the police are here, sir. They're Los Angeles, though, not Beverly Hills. Should I call . . . ?"

"Let them come in, Jacob," François said dispiritedly.

When Rachel saw the look on Manny Gonzales's face, the un-

comfortable evening started to seem worth it. But she still had the
feeling everybody in the room wanted to murder her.

"Rachel, what the hell are you doing here?"

"She's a policewoman, right?" said Trent Gordon. "That meeting
at the library was no accident."

"She's Hollywood's own Miss Marple," Manny said icily.

That struck a nerve. Rachel said, "I'm the LAPD's unofficial
consultant, and I'm about to solve a couple of murders."

Gary Holmes was grinning, at both her chutzpah and his partner's embarrassment.

"I told you I didn't do it," said Billy Hook. Visibly trying to calm
himself, he said, "I'm ready to tell you everything I can, but I didn't
do it."

"I'm not accusing you, Mr. Hook. I don't need to accuse anybody. Trent, I'm not a policewoman, but I'm not a college student
either. I'm sorry I fooled you about that. I'm really a book dealer. I
have a friend, another book dealer, who has a wild sense of humor
that might appeal to you."

Manny was staring at her but said nothing.

Rachel took a deep breath and launched her bluff. "My friend
Blast-Off Meagher likes to pretend he's blind. But he's not. He can
see just as well as anybody here. He was the last person to see
Howard Achitty alive except his murderer. And he also saw
Achitty's companion. The one who stood waiting for him in the
doorway of the shop, the one who killed him." She turned to Audrey Vance. "Blast-Off can identify you."

Audrey seemed to go pale, but she managed to counterfeit a
laugh. "You're nuts. The old guy's blind as a bat."

"You do know him then?" said Manny softly.

"No, no, I never . . ." She started to slip, grabbed the robot for
support. "Tell 'em, Ishmael," she said. "Tell 'em the truth."

"You've had too much to drink," François said, leading her from
the robot.

"I haven't had enough," she retorted, still trying to laugh.

François tried to sit her in the captain's chair.

"No, not there," she said. "Please, not there."

Rachel felt drained. She'd been ready for Audrey to lunge at her
in murderous fury, but the woman had no kill left in her.

Manny touched her shoulder. "She did it?"

Rachel nodded.

"Can you prove it?"

"That's your department. I'm just the consultant. Consultants lay the groundwork and go away."

Rachel made Manny and Gary omelettes in the apartment over Vermilion's. They'd told her not to bother, but she was happier doing something. Audrey had come around and confessed, and they'd practically had to force her to consult a lawyer.

While they ate, Rachel explained. "Achitty was convinced the changes in *Menace of the Solar System* ruined his career. He became obsessed with the Bingham killing and spent years wanting to solve a murder no one else even admitted had taken place. With the ceremony planting Trent Gordon's star and François's plan to reshoot the end of the movie, things got stirred up again. And somebody Achitty confided in—we'll probably never know who, maybe somebody at the studio who had been involved with the cover-up—tipped him off that there was a clue to the truth in François's old autobiography. Maybe Achitty had never read it, or maybe he was convinced it was worth a fresh look. He started to look for a copy, and the harder it got to find, the more convinced he was.

"In the course of looking for the book, he told the wrong person, Audrey Vance, the only person in the *Menace* group he thought he could trust. Remember his remark to me that he couldn't trust any of those 'guys'? Well, how about a non-guy? After he talked to me yesterday, he must have called her and arranged to go to Blast-Off's with her. He'd probably already tried to get a copy of the book from her, and she'd put him off. She probably didn't really believe there was any clue in the book to implicate her, but she met Achitty armed just in case. She may have suggested that they duck into the store next to Blast-Off's. So just in case there *was* something, she could do—what she did. When she realized Achitty was getting the point, she drew her gun and shot him, knowing the noise from the rock band or whatever it was outside would muffle the sound. I think she was shocked when she'd done it. She'd murdered once before, but it had been years ago, and I don't think she was really a killer."

"Save the bleeding-heart stuff," said Gary.

"Leave it to her lawyer," Manny said. "He'll probably get her off on an insanity plea."

"That may be fair enough," Rachel said. "She fled, taking the book with her, not even waiting to see if Achitty was really dead. He lurched down the street in a semidaze, feeling good as dead, looking for the star that would at least connect his death with *Menace of the Solar System*. By the time we saw Audrey that night, she was her humorous self. But she was drinking, and Trent Gordon seemed surprised. He thought she'd given it up. But the events of the day had been enough to bring her back to it."

"The poor dear," said Gary.

"Look, I don't know how she could act that normal if she wasn't —sick!"

"Say that again. She couldn't act sane if she wasn't crazy? Is that it?"

Manny held up his hand. "Save the high school debate and tell me what clue Achitty was supposed to find in the autobiography."

"We know Audrey killed Bingham because she'd been married to him, unknown to anybody in Hollywood, and she knew her career could be ruined if it ever came out. When she saw him on the spaceship-deck set, she didn't know he'd come to see Billy Hook. She thought he'd come to blackmail her."

"Yeah, she told us that."

"She didn't deny she'd been married before, but her *official* ex-husband was a tax auditor. She told me that tonight. But there's a reference in François's book to a husband who liked to read scripts in bed. That doesn't fit a tax auditor, but it does fit an actor like William Bingham."

"That's it, the great clue?" said Manny in disbelief. "It also fits Clark Gable and Gary Cooper."

"Manny, to someone who knew all the circumstances—which only people on that picture did—it was enough to send him in the right direction."

"Why didn't anybody ever see it before?"

"It was the kind of thing you could miss if you weren't looking for it. There are all sorts of ways to investigate her background, given that clue, the same ones you'll be following."

They ate their omelettes in silence for a few moments. Then Gary Holmes said, "I guess they won't be finishing that movie now. Too bad for the old guy. He really wanted to work again. He's gay, you know."

Rachel looked up. The way Guy Wheatley had looked at her had struck her as decidedly, if inactively, heterosexual. "Why do you think he's gay?" she asked.

"Before we left, I asked if he could tell me who Toby Wing was, and he said Toby was one of the sexiest, most enchanting creatures he'd ever known. The old coot looked downright lustful when he talked about this guy Toby. Hey, what's so funny, Rachel?"

Rachel got up. "Oh, nothing. Excuse me while I go downstairs for one of my reference books. I think you deserve a look at Toby Wing, Gary. Besides, I want to look up Miriam Cooper."

Ross Macdonald loved and hated Hollywood and you get glimpses of both those feelings in this story. While Macdonald's first private-eye novels about Lew Archer owed an unseemly lot to Raymond Chandler, he ultimately developed his own voice and went on to write what some feel are the best private-eye novels ever published. This is early Macdonald, before he was at his very best, but already you can see the diffident soul of Archer trying to make some sense of Southern California's culture.

Find the Woman

Ross Macdonald

I sat in my brand-new office with the odor of paint in my nostrils and waited for something to happen. I had been back on the Boulevard for one day. This was the beginning of the second day. Below the window, flashing in the morning sun, the traffic raced and roared with a noise like battle. It made me nervous. It made me want to move. I was all dressed up in civilian clothes with no place to go and nobody to go with.

Till Millicent Dreen came in.

I had seen her before, on the Strip with various escorts, and knew who she was: publicity director for Tele-Pictures. Mrs. Dreen was over forty and looked it, but there was electricity in her, plugged in to a secret source that time could never wear out. Look how high and tight I carry my body, her movements said. My hair is hennaed but comely, said her coiffure, inviting not to conviction but to suspension of disbelief. Her eyes were green and inconstant like the sea. They said what the hell.

She sat down by my desk and told me that her daughter had disappeared the day before, which was September the seventh.

"I was in Hollywood all day. We keep an apartment here, and there was some work I had to get out fast. Una isn't working, so I left her at the beach house by herself."

"Where is it?"

"A few miles above Santa Barbara."

"That's a long way to commute."

"It's worth it to me. When I can maneuver a week end away from this town, I like to get *really* away."

"Maybe your daughter feels the same, only more so. When did she leave?"

"Sometime yesterday. When I drove home to the beach house last night she was gone."

"Did you call the police?"

"Hardly. She's twenty-two and knows what she's doing. I hope. Anyway, apron strings don't become me." She smiled like a cat and moved her scarlet-taloned fingers in her narrow lap. "It was very late and I was—tired. I went to bed. But when I woke up this morning it occurred to me that she might have drowned. I objected to it because she wasn't a strong swimmer, but she went in for solitary swimming. I think of the most dreadful things when I wake up in the morning."

"*Went* in for solitary swimming, Mrs. Dreen?"

" 'Went' slipped out, didn't it? I told you I think of dreadful things when I wake up in the morning."

"If she drowned you should be talking to the police. They can arrange for dragging and such things. All I can give you is my sympathy."

As if to estimate the value of that commodity, her eyes flickered from my shoulders to my waist and up again to my face. "Frankly, I don't know about the police. I do know about you, Mr. Archer. You just got out of the army, didn't you?"

"Last week." I failed to add that she was my first post-war client.

"And you don't belong to anybody, I've heard. You've never been bought. Is that right?"

"Not outright. You can take an option on a piece of me, though. A hundred dollars would do for a starter."

She nodded briskly. From a bright black bag she gave me five twenties. "Naturally, I'm conscious of publicity angles. My daughter retired a year ago when she married—"

"Twenty-one is a good age to retire."

"From pictures, maybe you're right. But she could want to go back if her marriage breaks up. And I have to look out for myself. It isn't true that there's no such thing as bad publicity. *I* don't know why Una went away."

"Is your daughter Una Sand?"

"Of course. I assumed you knew." My ignorance of the details of her life seemed to cause her pain. She didn't have to tell me that she had a feeling for publicity angles.

Though Una Sand meant less to me than Hecuba, I remembered the name and with it a glazed blonde who had had a year or two in the sun, but who'd made a better pin-up than an actress.

"Wasn't her marriage happy? I mean, isn't it?"

"You see how easy it is to slip into the past tense?" Mrs. Dreen smiled another fierce and purring smile, and her fingers fluttered in glee before her immobile body. "I suppose her marriage is happy enough. Her Ensign's quite a personable young man—handsome in a masculine way, and passionate she tells me, and naive enough."

"Naive enough for what?"

"To marry Una. Jack Rossiter was quite a catch in this woman's town. He was runner-up at Forest Hills the last year he played tennis. And now of course he's a flier. Una did right well by herself, even if it doesn't last."

What do you expect of a war marriage? she seemed to be saying. Permanence? Fidelity? The works?

"As a matter of fact," she went on, "it was thinking about Jack, more than anything else, that brought me here to you. He's due back this week, and naturally"—like many unnatural people, she overused that adverb—"he'll expect her to be waiting for him. It'll be rather embarrassing for me if he comes home and I can't tell him where she's gone, or why, or with whom. You'd really think she'd leave a note."

"I can't keep up with you," I said. "A minute ago Una was in the clutches of the cruel crawling foam. Now she's taken off with a romantic stranger."

"I consider possibilities, is all. When I was Una's age, married to Dreen, I had quite a time settling down. I still do."

Our gazes, mine as impassive as hers I hoped, met, struck no spark, and disengaged. The female spider who eats her mate held no attraction for me.

"I'm getting to know you pretty well," I said with the necessary smile, "but not the missing girl. Who's she been knocking around with?"

"I don't think we need to go into that. She doesn't confide in me, in any case."

"Whatever you say. Shall we look at the scene of the crime?"

"There isn't any *crime*."

"The scene of the accident, then, or the departure. Maybe the beach house will give me something to go on."

She glanced at the wafer-thin watch on her brown wrist. Its diamonds glittered coldly. "Do I have to drive all the way back?"

"If you can spare the time, it might help. We'll take my car."

She rose decisively but gracefully, as though she had practiced the movement in front of a mirror. An expert bitch, I thought as I followed her high slim shoulders and tight-sheathed hips down the stairs to the bright street. I felt a little sorry for the army of men who had warmed themselves, or been burned, at that secret electricity. And I wondered if her daughter Una was like her.

When I did get to see Una, the current had been cut off; I learned about it only by the marks it left. It left marks.

We drove down Sunset to the sea and north on 101 Alternate. All the way to Santa Barbara, she read a typescript whose manila cover was marked: "Temporary—This script is not final and is given to you for advance information only." It occurred to me that the warning might apply to Mrs. Dreen's own story.

As we left the Santa Barbara city limits, she tossed the script over her shoulder into the back seat. "It *really* smells. It's going to be a smash."

A few miles north of the city, a dirt road branched off to the left beside a filling station. It wound for a mile or more through broken country to her private beach. The beach house was set well back from the sea at the convergence of brown bluffs which huddled over it like scarred shoulders. To reach it we had to drive along the beach for a quarter of a mile, detouring to the very edge of the sea around the southern bluff.

The blue-white dazzle of sun, sand, and surf was like an arc-furnace. But I felt some breeze from the water when we got out of the car. A few languid clouds moved inland over our heads. A little high plane was gamboling among them like a terrier in a henyard.

"You have privacy," I said to Mrs. Dreen.

She stretched, and touched her varnished hair with her fingers. "One tires of the goldfish role. When I lie out there in the afternoons I—forget I have a name." She pointed to the middle of the cove beyond the breakers, where a white raft moved gently in the swells. "I simply take off my clothes and revert to protoplasm. *All* my clothes."

I looked up at the plane whose pilot was doodling in the sky. It dropped, turning like an early falling leaf, swooped like a hawk, climbed like an aspiration.

She said with a laugh: "If they come too low I cover my face, of course."

We had been moving away from the house towards the water. Nothing could have looked more innocent than the quiet cove held in the curve of the white beach like a benign blue eye in a tranquil brow. Then its colors shifted as a cloud passed over the sun. Cruel green and violent purple ran in the blue. I felt the old primitive terror and fascination. Mrs. Dreen shared the feeling and put it into words:

"It's got queer moods. I hate it sometimes as much as I love it." For an instant she looked old and uncertain. "I hope she isn't in there."

The tide had turned and was coming in, all the way from Hawaii and beyond, all the way from the shattered islands where bodies lay unburied in the burnt-out caves. The waves came up towards us, fumbling and gnawing at the beach like an immense soft mouth.

"Are there bad currents here, or anything like that?"

"No. It's deep, though. It must be twenty feet under the raft. I could never bottom it."

"I'd like to look at her room," I said. "It might tell us where she went, and even with whom. You'd know what clothes were missing?"

She laughed a little apologetically as she opened the door. "I used to dress my daughter, naturally. Not any more. Besides, more than half of her things must be in the Hollywood apartment. I'll try to help you, though."

It was good to step out of the vibrating brightness of the beach into shadowy stillness behind Venetian blinds. "I noticed that you unlocked the door," I said. "It's a big house with a lot of furniture in it. No servants?"

"I occasionally have to knuckle under to producers. But I won't to my employees. They'll be easier to get along with soon, now that the plane plants are shutting down."

We went to Una's room, which was light and airy in both atmosphere and furnishings. But it showed the lack of servants. Stockings, shoes, underwear, dresses, bathing suits, lipstick-smeared tissue littered the chairs and the floor. The bed was unmade. The framed photograph on the night table was obscured by two empty glasses which smelt of highball, and flanked by overflowing ash trays.

I moved the glasses and looked at the young man with the wings on his chest. Naive, handsome, passionate were words which suited the strong blunt nose, the full lips and square jaw, the wide proud eyes. For Mrs. Dreen he would have made a single healthy meal, and I wondered again if her daughter was a carnivore. At least the photograph of Jack Rossiter was the only sign of a man in her room. The two glasses could easily have been from separate nights. Or separate weeks, to judge by the condition of the room. Not that it wasn't an attractive room. It was like a pretty girl in disarray. But disarray.

We examined the room, the closets, the bathroom, and found nothing of importance, either positive or negative. When we had waded through the brilliant and muddled wardrobe which Una had shed, I turned to Mrs. Dreen.

"I guess I'll have to go back to Hollywood. It would help me if you'd come along. It would help me more if you'd tell me who your daughter knew. Or rather who she liked—I suppose she knew everybody. Remember you suggested yourself that there's a man in this."

"I take it you haven't found anything?"

"One thing I'm pretty sure of. She didn't intentionally go away for long. Her toilet articles and pills are still in her bathroom. She's got quite a collection of pills."

"Yes, Una's always been a hypochondriac. Also she left Jack's picture. She only had the one, because she liked it best."

"That isn't so conclusive," I said. "I don't suppose you'd know whether there's a bathing suit missing?"

"I really couldn't say, she had so many. She was at her best in them."

"Still *was?*"

"I guess so, as a working hypothesis. Unless you can find me evidence to the contrary."

"You didn't like your daughter much, did you?"

"No. I didn't like her father. And she was prettier than I."

"But not so intelligent?"

"Not as bitchy, you mean? She was bitchy enough. But I'm still worried about Jack. He loved her. Even if I didn't."

The telephone in the hall took the cue and began to ring. "This is Millicent Dreen," she said into it. "Yes, you may read it to me." A pause. " 'Kill the fatted calf, ice the champagne, turn down the sheets and break out the black silk nightie. Am coming home tomorrow.' Is that right?"

Then she said, "Hold it a minute. I wish to send an answer. To Ensign Jack Rossiter, USS *Guam,* CVE 173, Naval Air Station, Alameda—is that Ensign Rossiter's correct address? The text is: 'Dear Jack join me at the Hollywood apartment there is no one at the beach house. Millicent.' Repeat it, please. . . . Right. Thank you."

She turned from the phone and collapsed in the nearest chair, not forgetting to arrange her legs symmetrically.

"So Jack is coming home tomorrow?" I said. "All I had before was no evidence. Now I have no evidence and until tomorrow."

She leaned forward to look at me. "I've been wondering how far can I trust you."

"Not so far. But I'm not a blackmailer. I'm not a mind-reader, either, and it's sort of hard to play tennis with the invisible man."

"The invisible man has nothing to do with this. I called him when Una didn't come home. Just before I came to your office."

"All right," I said. "You're the one that wants to find Una. You'll get around to telling me. In the meantime, who else did you call?"

"Hilda Karp, Una's best friend—her *only* female friend."

"Where can I get hold of her?"

"She married Gray Karp, the agent. They live in Beverly Hills."

Their house, set high on a plateau of rolling lawn, was huge and fashionably grotesque: Spanish Mission with a dash of Paranoia. The room where I waited for Mrs. Karp was as big as a small barn and full of blue furniture. The bar had a brass rail.

Hilda Karp was a Dresden blonde with an athletic body and brains. By appearing in it, she made the room seem more real. "Mr. Archer, I believe?" She had my card in her hand, the one with "Private Investigator" on it.

"Una Sand disappeared yesterday. Her mother said you were her best friend."

"Millicent—Mrs. Dreen—called me early this morning. But, as I said then, I haven't seen Una for several days."

"Why would she go away?"

Hilda Karp sat down on the arm of a chair, and looked thoughtful. "I can't understand why her mother should be worried. She can take care of herself, and she's gone away before. I don't know why this time. I know her well enough to know that she's unpredict-able."

"Why did she go away before?"

"Why do girls leave home, Mr. Archer?"

"She picked a queer time to leave home. Her husband's coming home tomorrow."

"That's right, she told me he sent her a cable from Pearl. He's a nice boy."

"Did Una think so?"

She looked at me frigidly as only a pale blonde can look, and said nothing.

"Look," I said. "I'm trying to do a job for Mrs. Dreen. My job is laying skeletons to rest, not teaching them the choreography of the *Danse Macabre.*"

"Nicely put," she said. "Actually there's no skeleton. Una has played around, in a perfectly casual way I mean, with two or three men in the last year."

"Simultaneously, or one at a time?"

"One at a time. She's monandrous to that extent. The latest is Terry Neville."

"I thought he was married."

"In an interlocutory way only. For God's sake don't bring my name into it. My husband's in business in this town."

"He seems to be prosperous," I said, looking more at her than at the house. "Thank you very much, Mrs. Karp. Your name will never pass my lips."

"Hideous, isn't it? The name, I mean. But I couldn't help falling in love with the guy. I hope you find her. Jack will be terribly disappointed if you don't."

I had begun to turn towards the door, but turned back. "It couldn't be anything like this, could it? She heard he was coming home, she felt unworthy of him, unable to face him, so she decided to lam out?"

"Millicent said she didn't leave a letter. Women don't go in for all such drama and pathos without leaving a letter. Or at least a marked copy of Tolstoi's *Resurrection.*"

"I'll take your word for it." Her blue eyes were very bright in the great dim room. "How about this? She didn't like Jack at all. She went away for the sole purpose of letting him know that. A little sadism, maybe?"

"But she did like Jack. It's just that he was away for over a year.

Whenever the subject came up in a mixed gathering, she always insisted that he was a wonderful lover."

"Like that, eh? Did Mrs. Dreen say you were Una's best friend?"

Her eyes were brighter and her thin, pretty mouth twisted in amusement. "Certainly. You should have heard her talk about me."

"Maybe I will. Thanks. Good-bye."

A telephone call to a screen writer I knew, the suit for which I had paid a hundred and fifty dollars of separation money in a moment of euphoria, and a false air of assurance got me past the studio guards and as far as the door of Terry Neville's dressing room. He had a bungalow to himself, which meant that he was as important as the publicity claimed. I didn't know what I was going to say to him, but I knocked on the door and, when someone said, "Who is it?" showed him.

Only the blind had not seen Terry Neville. He was over six feet, colorful, shapely, and fragrant like a distant garden of flowers. For a minute he went on reading and smoking in his brocaded armchair, carefully refraining from raising his eyes to look at me. He even turned a page of his book.

"Who are you?" he said finally. "I don't know you."

"Una Sand—"

"I don't know her, either." Grammatical solecisms had been weeded out of his speech, but nothing had been put in their place. His voice was impersonal and lifeless.

"Millicent Dreen's daughter," I said, humoring him. "Una Rossiter."

"Naturally I know Millicent Dreen. But you haven't said anything. Good day."

"Una disappeared yesterday. I thought you might be willing to help me find out why."

"You still haven't said anything." He got up and took a step towards me, very tall and wide. "What I said was *good day.*"

But not tall and wide enough. I've always had an idea, probably incorrect, that I could handle any man who wears a scarlet silk bathrobe. He saw that idea on my face and changed his tune: "If you don't get out of here, my man, I'll call a guard."

"In the meantime I'd straighten out that marcel of yours. I might even be able to make a little trouble for you." I said that on the assumption that any man with his face and sexual opportunities would be on the brink of trouble most of the time.

It worked. "What do you mean by saying that?" he said. A sudden pallor made his carefully plucked black eyebrows stand out starkly. "You could get into a very great deal of hot water by standing there talking like that."

"What happened to Una?"

"I don't know. Get out of here."

"You're a liar."

Like one of the clean-cut young men in one of his own movies, he threw a punch at me. I let it go over my shoulder and while he was off balance placed the heel of my hand against his very flat solar plexus and pushed him down into his chair. Then I shut the door and walked fast to the front gate. I'd just as soon have gone on playing tennis with the invisible man.

"No luck, I take it?" Mrs. Dreen said when she opened the door of her apartment to me.

"I've got nothing to go on. If you really want to find your daughter you'd better go to Missing Persons. They've got the organization and the connections."

"I suppose Jack will be going to them. He's home already."

"I thought he was coming tomorrow."

"That telegram was sent yesterday. It was delayed somehow. His ship got in yesterday afternoon."

"Where is he now?"

"At the beach house by now, I guess. He flew down from Alameda in a Navy plane and called me from Santa Barbara."

"What did you tell him?"

"What could I tell him? That Una was gone. He's frantic. He thinks she may have drowned." It was late afternoon, and in spite of the whiskey which she was absorbing steadily, like an alcohol lamp, Mrs. Dreen's fires were burning low. Her hands and eyes were limp, and her voice was weary.

"Well," I said, "I might as well go back to Santa Barbara. I talked to Hilda Karp but she couldn't help me. Are you coming along?"

"Not again. I have to go to the studio tomorrow. Anyway, I don't want to see Jack just now. I'll stay here."

The sun was low over the sea, gold-leafing the water and bloodying the sky, when I got through Santa Barbara and back onto the coast highway. Not thinking it would do any good but by way of doing something or other to earn my keep, I stopped at the filling station where the road turned off to Mrs. Dreen's beach house.

"Fill her up," I said to the woman attendant. I needed gas anyway.

"I've got some friends who live around here," I said when she held out her hand for her money. "Do you know where Mrs. Dreen lives?"

She looked at me from behind disapproving spectacles. "You should know. You were down there with her today, weren't you?"

I covered my confusion by handing her a five and telling her: "Keep the change."

"No, thank you."

"Don't misunderstand me. All I want you to do is tell me who was there yesterday. You see all. Tell a little."

"Who are you?"

I showed her my card.

"Oh." Her lips moved unconsciously, computing the size of the tip. "There was a guy in a green convert, I think it was a Chrysler. He went down around noon and drove out again around four, I guess it was, like a bat out of hell."

"That's what I wanted to hear. You're wonderful. What did he look like?"

"Sort of dark and pretty good-looking. It's kind of hard to describe. Like the guy that took the part of the pilot in that picture last week—*you* know—only not so good-looking."

"Terry Neville."

"That's right, only not so good-looking. I've seen him go down there plenty of times."

"I don't know who that would be," I said, "but thanks anyway. There wasn't anybody with him, was there?"

"Not that I could see."

I went down the road to the beach house like a bat into hell. The sun, huge and angry red, was horizontal now, half-eclipsed by the sea and almost perceptibly sinking. It spread a red glow over the shore like a soft and creeping fire. After a long time, I thought, the cliffs would crumble, the sea would dry up, the whole earth would burn out. There'd be nothing left but bone-white cratered ashes like the moon.

When I rounded the bluff and came within sight of the beach I saw a man coming out of the sea. In the creeping fire which the sun shed he, too, seemed to be burning. The diving mask over his face made him look strange and inhuman. He walked out of the water as if he had never set foot on land before.

I walked towards him. "Mr. Rossiter?"

"Yes." He raised the glass mask from his face and with it the illusion of strangeness lifted. He was just a handsome young man, well-set-up, tanned, and worried-looking.

"My name is Archer."

He held out his hand, which was wet, after wiping it on his bathing trunks, which were also wet. "Oh, yes, Mr. Archer. My mother-in-law mentioned you over the phone."

"Are you enjoying your swim?"

"I am looking for the body of my wife." It sounded as if he meant it. I looked at him more closely. He was big and husky, but he was just a kid, twenty-two or -three at most. Out of school into the air, I thought. Probably met Una Sand at a party, fell hard for all that glamour, married her the week before he shipped out, and had dreamed bright dreams ever since. I remembered the brash telegram he had sent, as if life was like the people in slick magazine advertisements.

"What makes you think she drowned?"

"She wouldn't go away like this. She knew I was coming home this week. I cabled her from Pearl."

"Maybe she never got the cable."

After a pause he said: "Excuse me." He turned towards the waves which were breaking almost at his feet. The sun had disappeared, and the sea was turning gray and cold-looking, an anti-human element.

"Wait a minute. If she's in there, which I doubt, you should call the police. This is no way to look for her."

"If I don't find her before dark, I'll call them then," he said. "But if she's here, I want to find her myself." I could never have guessed his reason for that, but when I found it out it made sense. So far as anything in the situation made sense.

He walked a few steps into the surf, which was heavier now that the tide was coming in, plunged forward, and swam slowly towards the raft with his masked face under the water. His arms and legs beat the rhythm of the crawl as if his muscles took pleasure in it, but his face was downcast, searching the darkening sea floor. He swam in widening circles about the raft, raising his head about twice a minute for air.

He had completed several circles and I was beginning to feel that he wasn't really looking for anything, but expressing his sorrow, dancing a futile ritualistic water dance, when suddenly he took air and dived. For what seemed a long time but was probably about twenty seconds, the surface of the sea was empty except for the white raft. Then the masked head broke water, and Rossiter began to swim towards shore. He swam a laborious side stroke, with both arms submerged. It was twilight now, and I couldn't see him very well, but I could see that he was swimming very slowly. When he came nearer I saw a swirl of yellow hair.

He stood up, tore off his mask, and threw it away into the sea. He looked at me angrily, one arm holding the body of his wife against him. The white body half-floating in the shifting water was nude, a strange bright glistening catch from the sea floor.

"Go away," he said in a choked voice.

I went to get a blanket out of the car, and brought it to him where he laid her out on the beach. He huddled over her as if to protect her body from my gaze. He covered her and stroked her wet hair back from her face. Her face was not pretty. He covered that, too.

I said: "You'll have to call the police now."

After a time he answered: "I guess you're right. Will you help me carry her into the house?"

I helped him. Then I called the police in Santa Barbara, and told them that a woman had been drowned and where to find her. I left Jack Rossiter shivering in his wet trunks beside her blanketed body, and drove back to Hollywood for the second time.

Millicent Dreen was in her apartment in the Park-Wilshire. In the afternoon there had been a nearly full decanter of Scotch on her buffet. At ten o'clock it was on the coffee table beside her chair, and nearly empty. Her face and body had sagged. I wondered if every day she aged so many years, and every morning recreated herself through the power of her will.

She said: "I thought you were going back to Santa Barbara. I was just going to go to bed."

"I did go. Didn't Jack phone you?"

"No." She looked at me, and her green eyes were suddenly very much alive, almost fluorescent. "You found her," she said.

"Jack found her in the sea. She was drowned."

"I was afraid of that." But there was something like relief in her voice. As if worse things might have happened. As if at least she had lost no weapons and gained no foes in the daily battle to hold her position in the world's most competitive city.

"You hired me to find her," I said. "She's found, though I had nothing to do with finding her—and that's that. Unless you want me to find out who drowned her."

"What do you mean?"

"What I said. Perhaps it wasn't an accident. Or perhaps some-body stood by and watched her drown."

I had given her plenty of reason to be angry with me before, but for the first time that day she was angry. "I gave you a hundred dollars for doing nothing. Isn't that enough for you? Are you trying to drum up extra business?"

"I did one thing. I found out that Una wasn't by herself yester-day."

"Who was with her?" She stood up and walked quickly back and forth across the rug. As she walked her body was remolding itself into the forms of youth and vigor. She recreated herself before my eyes.

"The invisible man," I said. "My tennis partner."

Still she wouldn't speak the name. She was like the priestess of a cult whose tongue was forbidden to pronounce a secret word. But she said quickly and harshly: "If my daughter was killed I want to know who did it. I don't care who it was. But if you're giving me a line and if you make trouble for me and nothing comes of it, I'll have you kicked out of Southern California. I could do that."

Her eyes flashed, her breath came fast, and her sharp breast rose and fell with many of the appearances of genuine feeling. I liked her very much at that moment. So I went away, and instead of making trouble for her I made trouble for myself.

I found a booth in a drugstore on Wilshire and confirmed what I knew, that Terry Neville would have an unlisted number. I called a girl I knew who fed gossip to a movie columnist, and found out that Neville lived in Beverly Hills but spent most of his evenings around town. At this time of night he was usually at Ronald's or Chasen's, a little later at Ciro's. I went to Ronald's because it was nearer, and Terry Neville was there.

He was sitting in a booth for two in the long, low, smoke-filled room, eating smoked salmon and drinking stout. Across from him there was a sharp-faced terrier-like man who looked like his busi-ness manager and was drinking milk. Some Hollywood actors spend a lot of time with their managers, because they have a common interest.

I avoided the headwaiter and stepped up to Neville's table. He saw me and stood up, saying: "I warned you this afternoon. If you don't get out of here I'll call the police."

I said quietly: "I sort of am the police. Una is dead." He didn't answer and I went on: "This isn't a good place to talk. If you'll step outside for a minute I'd like to mention a couple of facts to you."

"You say you're a policeman," the sharp-faced man snapped, but quietly. "Where's your identification? Don't pay any attention to him, Terry."

Terry didn't say anything. I said: "I'm a private detective. I'm investigating the death of Una Rossiter. Shall we step outside, gentlemen?"

"We'll go out to the car," Terry Neville said tonelessly. "Come on, Ed," he added to the terrier-like man.

The car was not a green Chrysler convertible, but a black Packard limousine equipped with a uniformed chauffeur. When we entered the parking lot he got out of the car and opened the door. He was big and battered-looking.

I said: "I don't think I'll get in. I listen better standing up. I always stand up at concerts and confessions."

"You're not going to listen to anything," Ed said.

The parking lot was deserted and far back from the street, and I forgot to keep my eye on the chauffeur. He rabbit-punched me and a gush of pain surged into my head. He rabbit-punched me again and my eyes rattled in their sockets and my body became invertebrate. Two men moving in a maze of lights took hold of my upper arms and lifted me into the car. Unconsciousness was a big black limousine with a swiftly purring motor and the blinds down.

Though it leaves the neck sore for days, the effect of a rabbit punch on the centers of consciousness is sudden and brief. In two or three minutes I came out of it, to the sound of Ed's voice saying:

"We don't like hurting people and we aren't going to hurt you. But you've got to learn to understand, whatever your name is—"

"Sacher-Masoch," I said.

"A bright boy," said Ed. "But a bright boy can be too bright for his own good. You've got to learn to understand that you can't go around annoying people, especially very important people like Mr. Neville here."

Terry Neville was sitting in the far corner of the back seat, looking worried. Ed was between us. The car was in motion, and I could see lights moving beyond the chauffeur's shoulders hunched over the wheel. The blinds were down over the back windows.

"Mr. Neville should keep out of my cases," I said. "At the moment you'd better let me out of this car or I'll have you arrested for kidnaping."

Ed laughed, but not cheerfully. "You don't seem to realize what's happening to you. You're on your way to the police station, where Mr. Neville and I are going to charge you with attempted blackmail."

"Mr. Neville is a very brave little man," I said. "Inasmuch as he was seen leaving Una Sand's house shortly after she was killed. He was seen leaving in a great hurry and a green convertible."

"My God, Ed," Terry Neville said, "you're getting me in a frightful mess. You don't know what a frightful mess you're getting me in." His voice was high, with a ragged edge of hysteria.

"For God's sake, you're not afraid of this bum, are you?" Ed said in a terrier yap.

"You get out of here, Ed. This is a terrible thing, and you don't know how to handle it. I've got to talk to this man. Get out of this car."

He leaned forward to take the speaking tube, but Ed put a hand on his shoulder. "Play it your way, then, Terry. I still think I had the right play, but you spoiled it."

"Where are we going?" I said. I suspected that we were headed for Beverly Hills, where the police know who pays them their wages.

Neville said into the speaking tube: "Turn down a side street and park. Then take a walk around the block."

"That's better," I said when we had parked. Terry Neville looked frightened. Ed looked sulky and worried. For no good reason, I felt complacent.

"Spill it," I said to Terry Neville. "Did you kill the girl? Or did she accidentally drown—and you ran away so you wouldn't get mixed up in it? Or have you thought of a better one than that?"

"I'll tell you the truth," he said. "I didn't kill her. I didn't even know she was dead. But I was there yesterday afternoon. We were sunning ourselves on the raft, when a plane came over flying very low. I went away, because I didn't want to be seen there with her—"

"You mean you weren't exactly sunning yourselves?"

"Yes. That's right. This plane came over high at first, then he circled back and came down very low. I thought maybe he recognized me, and might be trying to take pictures or something."

"What kind of a plane was it?"

"I don't know. A military plane, I guess. A fighter plane. It was a single-seater painted blue. I don't know military planes."

"What did Una Sand do when you went away?"

"I don't know. I swam to shore, put on some clothes, and drove away. She stayed on the raft, I guess. But she was certainly all right when I left her. It would be a terrible thing for me if I was dragged into this thing, Mr.—"

"Archer."

"Mr. Archer. I'm terribly sorry if we hurt you. If I could make it right with you—" He pulled out a wallet.

His steady pallid whine bored me. Even his sheaf of bills bored me. The situation bored me.

I said: "I have no interest in messing up your brilliant career, Mr. Neville. I'd like to mess up your brilliant pan sometime, but that can wait. Until I have some reason to believe that you haven't told me the truth, I'll keep what you said under my hat. In the meantime, I want to hear what the coroner has to say."

They took me back to Ronald's, where my car was, and left me with many protestations of good fellowship. I said good night to them, rubbing the back of my neck with an exaggerated gesture. Certain other gestures occurred to me.

When I got back to Santa Barbara the coroner was working over Una. He said that there were no marks of violence on her body, and very little water in her lungs and stomach, but this condition was characteristic of about one drowning in ten.

I hadn't known that before, so I asked him to put it into sixty-four-dollar words. He was glad to.

"Sudden inhalation of water may result in a severe reflex spasm of the larynx, followed swiftly by asphyxia. Such a laryngeal spasm is more likely to occur if the victim's face is upward, allowing water to rush into the nostrils, and would be likely to be facilitated by emotional or nervous shock. It may have happened like that or it may not."

"Hell," I said, "she may not even be dead."

He gave me a sour look. "Thirty-six hours ago she wasn't."

I figured it out as I got in my car. Una couldn't have drowned much later than four o'clock in the afternoon on September the seventh.

It was three in the morning when I checked in at the Barbara Hotel. I got up at seven, had breakfast in a restaurant, and went to the beach house to talk to Jack Rossiter. It was only about eight o'clock when I got there, but Rossiter was sitting on the beach in a canvas chair watching the sea.

"You again?" he said when he saw me.

"I'd think you'd have had enough of the sea for a while. How long were you out?"

"A year." He seemed unwilling to talk.

"I hate bothering people," I said, "but my business is always making a nuisance out of me."

"Evidently. What exactly is your business?"

"I'm currently working for your mother-in-law. I'm still trying to find out what happened to her daughter."

"Are you trying to needle me?" He put his hands on the arms of the chair as if to get up. For a moment his knuckles were white. Then he relaxed. "You saw what happened, didn't you?"

"Yes. But do you mind my asking what time your ship got into San Francisco on September the seventh?"

"No. Four o'clock. Four o'clock in the afternoon."

"I suppose that could be checked?"

He didn't answer. There was a newspaper on the sand beside his chair and he leaned over and handed it to me. It was the Late Night Final of a San Francisco newspaper for the seventh.

"Turn to page four," he said.

I turned to page four and found an article describing the arrival of the USS *Guam* at the Golden Gate, at four o'clock in the afternoon. A contingent of Waves had greeted the returning heroes, and a band had played "California, Here I Come."

"If you want to see Mrs. Dreen, she's in the house," Jack Rossiter said. "But it looks to me as if your job is finished."

"Thanks," I said.

"And if I don't see you again, good-bye."

"Are you leaving?"

"A friend is coming out from Santa Barbara to pick me up in a few minutes. I'm flying up to Alameda with him to see about getting leave. I just had a forty-eight, and I've got to be here for the inquest tomorrow. And the funeral." His voice was hard. His whole personality had hardened overnight. The evening before his nature had been wide open. Now it was closed and invulnerable.

"Good-bye," I said, and plodded through the soft sand to the house. On the way I thought of something, and walked faster.

When I knocked, Mrs. Dreen came to the door holding a cup of coffee, not very steadily. She was wearing a heavy wool dressing robe with a silk rope around the waist, and a silk cap on her head. Her eyes were bleary.

"Hello," she said. "I came back last night after all. I couldn't work today anyway. And I didn't think Jack should be by himself."

"He seems to be doing all right."

"I'm glad you think so. Will you come in?"

I stepped inside. "You said last night that you wanted to know who killed Una no matter who it was."

"Well?"

"Does that still go?"

"Yes. Why? Did you find out something?"

"Not exactly. I thought of something, that's all."

"The coroner believes it was an accident. I talked to him on the phone this morning." She sipped her black coffee. Her hand vibrated steadily, like a leaf in the wind.

"He may be right," I said. "He may be wrong."

There was the sound of a car outside, and I moved to the window and looked out. A station wagon stopped on the beach, and a Navy officer got out and walked towards Jack Rossiter. Rossiter got up and they shook hands.

"Will you call Jack, Mrs. Dreen, and tell him to come into the house for a minute?"

"If you wish." She went to the door and called him.

Rossiter came to the door and said a little impatiently: "What is it?"

"Come in," I said. "And tell me what time you left the ship the day before yesterday."

"Let's see. We got in at four—"

"No, you didn't. The ship did, but not you. Am I right?"

"I don't know what you mean."

"You know what I mean. It's so simple that it couldn't fool anybody for a minute, not if he knew anything about carriers. You flew your plane off the ship a couple of hours before she got into port. My guess is that you gave that telegram to a buddy to send for you before you left the ship. You flew down here, caught your wife being made love to by another man, landed on the beach—and drowned her."

"You're insane!" After a moment he said less violently: "I admit I flew off the ship. You could easily find that out anyway. I flew around for a couple of hours, getting in some flying time—"

"Where did you fly?"

"Along the coast. I don't get down this far. I landed at Alameda at five-thirty, and I can prove it."

"Who's your friend?" I pointed through the open door to the other officer, who was standing on the beach looking out to sea.

"Lieutenant Harris. I'm going to fly up to Alameda with him. I warn you, don't make any ridiculous accusations in his presence, or you'll suffer for it."

"I want to ask him a question," I said. "What sort of plane were you flying?"

"FM-3."

I went out of the house and down the slope to Lieutenant Harris. He turned towards me and I saw the wings on his blouse.

"Good morning, Lieutenant," I said. "You've done a good deal of flying, I suppose?"

"Thirty-two months. Why?"

"I want to settle a bet. Could a plane land on this beach and take off again?"

"I think maybe a Piper Cub could. I'd try it anyway. Does that settle the bet?"

"It was a fighter I had in mind. An FM-3."

"Not an FM-3," he said. "Not possibly. It might just conceivably be able to land but it'd never get off again. Not enough room, and very poor surface. Ask Jack, he'll tell you the same."

I went back to the house and said to Jack: "I was wrong. I'm sorry. As you said, I guess I'm all washed up with this case."

"Good-bye, Millicent," Jack said, and kissed her cheek. "If I'm not back tonight I'll be back first thing in the morning. Keep a stiff upper lip."

"You do, too, Jack."

He went away without looking at me again. So the case was ending as it had begun, with me and Mrs. Dreen alone in a room wondering what had happened to her daughter.

"You shouldn't have said what you did to him," she said. "He's had enough to bear."

My mind was working very fast. I wondered whether it was producing anything. "I suppose Lieutenant Harris knows what he's talking about. He says a fighter couldn't land and take off from this beach. There's no other place around here he could have landed without being seen. So he didn't land.

"But I still don't believe that he wasn't here. No young husband flying along the coast within range of the house where his wife was —well, he'd fly low and dip his wings to her, wouldn't he? Terry Neville saw the plane come down."

"Terry Neville?"

"I talked to him last night. He was with Una before she died. The two of them were out on the raft together when Jack's plane came down. Jack saw them, and saw what they were doing. They saw him. Terry Neville went away. Then what?"

"You're making this up," Mrs. Dreen said, but her green eyes were intent on my face.

"I'm making it up, of course. I wasn't here. After Terry Neville ran away, there was no one here but Una, and Jack in a plane circling over her head. I'm trying to figure out why Una died. I *have* to make it up. But I think she died of fright. I think Jack dived at her and forced her into the water. I think he kept on diving at her until she was gone. Then he flew back to Alameda and chalked up his flying time."

"Fantasy," she said. "And very ugly. I don't believe it."

"You should. You've got that cable, haven't you?"

"I don't know what you're talking about."

"Jack sent Una a cable from Pearl, telling her what day he was arriving. Una mentioned it to Hilda Karp. Hilda Karp mentioned it to me. Its funny you didn't say anything about it."

"I didn't know about it," Millicent Dreen said. Her eyes were blank.

I went on, paying no attention to her denial: "My guess is that the cable said not only that Jack's ship was coming in on the seventh, but that he'd fly over the beach house that afternoon. Fortunately, I don't have to depend on guesswork. The cable will be on file at Western Union, and the police will be able to look at it. I'm going into town now."

"Wait," she said. "Don't go to the police about it. You'll only get Jack in trouble. I destroyed the cable to protect him, but I'll tell you what was in it. Your guess was right. He said he'd fly over on the seventh."

"When did you destroy it?"

"Yesterday, before I came to you. I was afraid it would implicate Jack."

"Why did you come to me at all, if you wanted to protect Jack? It seems that you knew what happened."

"I wasn't sure. I didn't know what had happened to her, and until I found out I didn't know what to do."

"You're still not sure," I said. "But I'm beginning to be. For one thing, it's certain that Una never got her cable, at least not as it was sent. Otherwise she wouldn't have been doing what she was doing on the afternoon that her husband was going to fly over and say hello. You changed the date on it, perhaps? So that Una expected Jack a day later? Then you arranged to be in Hollywood on the seventh, so that Una could spend a final afternoon with Terry Neville."

"Perhaps." Her face was completely alive, controlled but full of dangerous energy, like a cobra listening to music.

"Perhaps you wanted Jack for yourself," I said. "Perhaps you had another reason, I don't know. I think even a psychoanalyst would have a hard time working through your motivations, Mrs. Dreen, and I'm not one. All I know is that you precipitated a murder. Your plan worked even better than you expected."

"It was accidental death," she said hoarsely. "If you go to the police you'll only make a fool of yourself, and cause trouble for Jack."

"You care about Jack, don't you?"

"Why shouldn't I?" she said. "He was mine before he ever saw Una. She took him away from me."

"And now you think you've got him back." I got up to go. "I hope for your sake he doesn't figure out for himself what I've just figured out."

"Do you think he will?" Sudden terror had jerked her face apart.

I didn't answer her.

Death
Out of Focus

William Campbell Gault

For Richard Matheson whose idea it was.

William Campbell Gault's *Don't Cry For Me* is one of the best private-eye novels ever written. Just ask Raymond Chandler, who heaped on it rare and almost gaudy praise. In addition to his mystery writing, Gault spent a few decades writing Young Adult bestsellers. An entire generation of teenage readers grew up on his books.

The following novel is not only a good story, it is also a shrewd look at the television and movie business back in the late fifties. Here you'll see Gault's ability to create real people while advancing the action at almost relentless speed. You'll also see the sly way he always lets you know his opinion of certain subject, a trait he shared with his old friend John D. MacDonald.

Bill Pronzini is largely responsible for getting this novel back in print and the editors would like to thank him very much.

chapter one

He took the new script out to the sundeck and read it there. He had been in New York for six weeks of frustration; he needed the sun. He tried to blank from his mind all preconceptions, the connotations that a Harry Bergdahl script implied, and read this new one objectively, as a director should.

It was rough going. The script was cliché-ridden, pretentious, pseudo-arty. And yet, when he had finished, some vitality, some sense of truth born of the writer's intensity, stayed with him. A revision by a competent screenwriter could make a worth-while story out of this.

He would probably have to fight Harry on that. It would be logical to guess Bergdahl would want to strengthen the wrong elements and delete the worth-while ones in this tale of a young rebel.

There was a current and comparatively profitable twin tide running in the industry, science fiction stories and stories of adolescent revolt. Harry Bergdahl was a man who had maintained his solvency by never running against the tides. There was a rumor lately that his credit wasn't as sound as it had been, and Steve meant to investigate that rumor. If it weren't true, this call from the producer might well be the luckiest break for Steve in the past year.

It had been a bad year. He was thinking back on it when his housekeeper came out to tell him Mr. Bergdahl was calling. He didn't want to talk with Harry yet. But he took a deep breath and went into the house.

Before Bergdahl could ask, he said quickly, "I haven't had time to do any more than glance through the script, Harry. I've been tied with New York all morning."

A momentary silence, and "Oh . . . ? You want to ring me when you've read it? I'll be here most of the day."

"I'll do that." A pause. "Who is the writer? He's new to me."

"My nephew," Bergdahl said. "A very talented boy. He's got three credits."

"Story or screenplay?"

"Two story, one screenplay. Why, Steve?"

"I wondered. Just browsing through it, there seems to be a buried strength that doesn't quite come through. A little doctoring would bring it out, I'm sure."

"We can talk about that. And I've got the lead all lined up." A theatrical pause. "Hart Jameson."

Steve had never heard of Hart Jameson. But he said admiringly, "You *have* been busy, haven't you?"

Bergdahl chuckled. "You get to that script right away and then phone me, Steve. We're going to have a picture."

"I'll do that. Good-by, Harry."

He went back to the sundeck and picked up the script again. He read: "Story by David Louis Sidney." Was it Gabell who had said writers with three names are dead—or ought to be? What kind of a man was David Louis Sidney? Co-operative? He would need to be, or they would have a real lemon of a picture. And Steve couldn't afford any lemons this year.

He decided to have a talk with John Abbot before phoning Bergdahl again. He hadn't visited him for months, and today would be a good time. He was going out to his car, when the green Pontiac pulled into his driveway.

Steve stood in front of the garage door as the man behind the wheel got out and walked toward him. He was tall and slim, with black hair in a crew cut.

His voice was as soft as his brown eyes. "Mr. Leander, Steven Leander?"

"That's right?"

"My name is Tomkevic." He handed Steve a card. "Do you have a minute or two right now?"

Steve glanced at the card, saw the words "Veritable Insurance Company" and said, "I'm afraid I don't. My insurance needs are well taken care of, Mr. Tomkevic."

The tall man smiled. "You didn't read *all* of the card, Mr. Leander. I'm not a salesman. I'm an investigator."

"Oh . . . ? Checking one of the neighbors?"

Tomkevic shook his head. "Checking on a Mr. Harry Bergdahl."

Steve frowned, and stared at the man. "I don't understand."

"He's applied for insurance, the regular studio coverage, on a man named Hart Jameson. We handle a lot of this kind of insurance, you understand, Mr. Leander, but not usually to the tune of a quarter of a million on an *unknown* actor."

"Unknown?" Steve smiled. "Are you a movie fan, too, Mr. Tomkevic?"

"I am. I have to be, with the company I work for specializing in this kind of policy. Jameson's had some good reviews on the bits he's done, but he's still an unknown as far as the money people are concerned."

"I see. I thought it was Bergdahl you were investigating, not Jameson."

"It *is* Mr. Bergdahl. I'm going to be frank, Mr. Leander. He's never covered any of his other actors. Doesn't that seem strange, when you consider the money he's made on his pictures? And now, with rocky times in the industry, he comes up with this policy."

"I have a feeling," Steve said slowly, "that you're not being quite as frank as you promised. What's on your mind, Mr. Tomkevic?"

"First, he told us he had hired you as director. This morning I learned that wasn't true."

"It's true every way but technically," Steve said. "We had a rather firm oral agreement. Does my connection with the picture change the policy risk in any way?"

Tomkevic nodded. "My employers seem to think so. Your integrity is rather well known in the industry, Mr. Leander." His smile was thin. "You've—never worked with Mr. Bergdahl before, have you?"

"Never. Are you implying that Mr. Bergdahl's reputation isn't all it should be?"

"Do I need to?"

There was a long silence. Finally Steve said, "That was frank enough. But what can I tell you? As you've just said, I've never worked with Harry before. So what can I know about him?"

Tomkevic shrugged. "Not much, I suppose. This much you can tell me—are you going to direct the picture?"

"I think I am. Of course, terms would need to be worked out through my agent that will be acceptable to both of us, but the way it looks now, I'm going to do the picture."

Tomkevic nodded. "Well, I guess we can stall him until everything is signed. That's what I'll suggest to my firm, at any rate." He waved. "Thanks for your time, Mr. Leander." He went back to his car.

So Harry was insuring his young rebel. As a promotion gimmick undoubtedly. Harry didn't have enough regard for actors to consider any of them worth more than the trouble of replacing them. But why should that bother an insurance company that specialized in this unique kind of term coverage? Certainly, all of the policies of this kind were at least partially drawn for promotional reasons.

He got into his car and headed it for John Abbot's. Abbot lived in the hills above Hollywood and had lived there for forty years. He was distantly related to Steve's wife, Marcia, and had been influential in Steve's early success.

He had been a writer, director and producer but was now retired. He was, however, often consulted by those still active in the industry. He was in the front yard of his home, supervising the work of a Japanese gardener, when Steve drove up.

He came down to the car and said smilingly, "Trouble, I'll bet. I never see you otherwise. How's my Marcia?"

"She's fine," Steve said. "I'm sorry I haven't been around lately, John. I've been—scrambling."

Abbot nodded. "Everybody in the industry is. Stay for lunch and talk with an old man."

Steve got out of the car and came around it to walk toward the house with his host. "I had some New York work that looked as if it might lead somewhere. But it didn't. It's a rough time, isn't it?"

"Maybe we need some tough times," Abbot said "Maybe some good pictures will result."

"Maybe," Steve said. "But scared people don't usually make good pictures."

The house was dim and cool, as one came in from the glare of the day outside. From the living-room windows, the entire city was visible in three directions.

"Martini?" Abbot asked.

Steve nodded. "John, Harry Bergdahl wants me to direct a picture for him."

From the liquor cabinet Abbot chuckled. "No wonder you're all wound up. I hope you realize he needs you more than you need him."

Steve turned to stare at the older man. "Bergdahl . . . ? He's certainly solid enough. He never lost money on a picture, I've heard."

"Until his last two," Abbot said quietly. "Times have changed, and I don't think Harry has. He's a hangover from the days when the public would look at anything that moved."

"Lousy pictures are still being made, and some of them are making money," Steve argued.

Abbot brought him his drink. "Horror pictures, science fiction pictures, adolescent revolt pictures. How long will the public's stomach stand for those?"

Steve sipped his drink and said wryly, "I hope the public's stomach is stronger than you think, because the picture Harry plans is an adolescent revolt epic."

"But he's smart enough to know it needs the Leander touch. And I'm sure he'll promote the prestige value of that credit reading 'Directed by Steven Leander.' " Abbot sat down with his drink. "Steve, be careful."

"Of Harry?"

"That's right. He is going to survive. If you need him now, in order to continue functioning, work for him. These aren't times when a man can be choosy. *But be very damned careful.*"

"I'm not an innocent, John. I'm sure I can protect myself against any manipulations of Harry Bergdahl."

"Maybe. Where is he getting his money?"

Steve finished his drink. "It's Texas money, oil money." He looked at his empty glass.

"Mix your own," Abbot said. "Is the money actually committed?"

"I'm not sure." He went over to mix a drink.

"I asked," Abbot said quietly, "because I heard a silly rumor about Harry insuring Hart Jameson for some picture he'd planned."

Steve turned. "He's going to insure Jameson. Do you know anything about him?"

Abbot nodded. "He was in *Sunburst Alley.* He has all of Mr.

Brando's mannerisms and none of his talent. I can't believe an actor of his caliber is worth too much insuring."

He paused and continued. "You know, Steve, the sole purpose of a studio policy is to insure the picture against anything that might prevent its star from appearing. Injuries, loss of memory, death—whatever might affect shooting or cause expensive delays—are covered. The star happens to be the property involved, and his assessed value determines the need, even the amount of the policy.

"But times being what they are, just suppose—just suppose, you understand—that Bergdahl needing the money—an accident *should* happen to Jameson."

"You don't mean—" said Steve, "that Harry would . . . ?"

"I don't say so. I only raise the question."

"Oh, no, you're wrong. It's only a professional gimmick. It's not the first time that's been pulled, is it?"

"Of course not," Abbot said mildly. "It's just the first time it's been pulled by Harry Bergdahl."

Steve said irritatedly, "For heaven's sake, you make Harry sound like a—monster. He's not our first citizen, I'll grant you, but he's certainly not a—a murderer."

"Not unless he needs to be to survive," Abbot said blandly. "Let's eat and talk about something else."

It was a fine lunch and they didn't talk any more about Harry Bergdahl. Abbot dwelt, as was his habit lately, on his early days in the industry. Today, Steve listened absently, his mind on the picture.

Finally Abbot said, "All right, you may go now. You've been itching to, for half an hour."

"That's not true," Steve protested. "I enjoy your company and you know it."

"Not when you're ready to start a picture. You have Marcia phone me. Good luck, Steve. Keep in touch, won't you?"

"I certainly will," Steve said warmly and was conscious of half lying. He was at an age where the reminiscences of the old were discomforting. He was thirty-seven.

As he drove home, he reflected that a man of thirty-seven should be solidly established in his trade. At least he should know where his next dollar is coming from. He should be able to turn down offers from hacks like Harry Bergdahl.

He wasn't. So much for that.

He phoned Bergdahl as soon as he arrived home. He told him,

"I've read the script now." He took a careful breath. "Your nephew is going to need help on the screenplay."

"We're the boys who can give it to him," Bergdahl answered. "You—weren't suggesting another writer, were you, Steve?"

"Not if this one is co-operative. You know him better than I do, Harry."

"He's young and willing to learn," Bergdahl answered. "He'll make out. I suppose this means you're ready to talk terms?"

"That's my agent's headache," Steve said. "Is the money committed, Harry?"

"Half of it's firm and the other half should be firm in a day or two. Look, why don't you and me and David get together tonight and talk story? Bring Marcia and come over to the house."

"As soon as she gets home, I'll find out if she's free tonight. Shall I phone you then?"

"Not if you're free. If she is, bring her. If she isn't, bring yourself. Dotty would love to see her, though."

Dotty was Harry's latest, and fifth, wife, a bleached sex bomb who had been cultivating Marcia without success for months.

Steve said, "I'll be there. And Marcia probably will, too."

He would have preferred talking with David Louis Sidney alone, but perhaps he could do that later. He was making notes on a few of the script's more painful pretensions when Marcia came home.

She stood in the doorway to the study and said lightly, "I've some gossip for you. I got it from Ellen at lunch."

"I'm all ears."

"It's about Harry Bergdahl. He's found a pair of gullible Texans."

"I know that."

"But you don't know the funny part, I'll bet."

He said patiently, "Tell me the funny part."

"These—cowboys had never heard of any of the pictures Harry had produced. But they knew all the ones you had directed. And Harry told them he had you under contract." She came over to kiss him. "See? Harry needs you more than you need him."

Steve said, "As much, but not more, Marcia, I'm going to do the picture."

"On your terms?"

"On the best terms I can get."

"Why, Steve?"

"Because we have always lived beyond our means and I need the work. And Harry is the only one who has offered me a job out here in nine months."

She said, "Because you need the work, you are going to go crashing down into oblivion with Harry Bergdahl? That's where he's heading."

"No, he isn't. If anyone survives, Harry will. Now, kiss me again and go mix us a drink."

"In a second," she said. "Is it my fault we're in bad financial shape, Steve?"

"No, it's our fault." He stroked her hair. "I love you, Marcia Bishop Leander."

"I know it," she said. "Why don't we take a swim and then—well, kind of—loll around?"

He smiled at her as desire stirred in him. "I've lolled around with you before. But not in the afternoon, not lately. You're being compassionate."

"Let's go," she said. "Let's forget the future for a few hours."

chapter two

It was later, it was six o'clock when he told her. "Dotty Bergdahl is expecting you tonight. I'm going over there for a story conference with Harry and his nephew."

Marcia sighed and stretched on the big bed. "You do demand a lot of me, don't you? An evening with Dotty Bergdahl—ouch!"

"I didn't promise you'd come. I told Harry I wasn't sure if you were free tonight."

"I'll go, master," she whispered. "You have rendered me temporarily docile with your ministrations."

Later, as they drove over to Brentwood, Steve tried to frame words in his mind, words that would be tactful but not servile, words that would help to establish a working agreement for the salvation of that impossible script.

The knowledge that Bergdahl needed him would strengthen his

hand. The tradition that the director is king but the producer is God would help to strengthen Bergdahl's.

They were traveling along San Vicente when Marcia said quietly, "Go in there believing you don't *have* to direct this picture. Go in there feeling *big*, because you are."

"Were," he said.

"Are. And Harry knows it. Why else would he want you? Out of compassion? Think, Steve."

The house was rustic, board and batten, painted a dusty almond, a U-shaped structure with a circular drive serving the front door and a parking area leading off on the righthand side.

Dotty and Harry were sitting in the screened front patio having a drink as the Leanders came up the flagstone walk. Harry was in shorts and his thick legs were almost black from the sun.

Dotty was in pale yellow chiffon, looking appealingly summery, but neither chiffon nor a pinafore could disguise her essential and basic attraction.

Sex surged from her appraising eyes, her sinuous movements, her sultry voice. She was no brain, but before settling down with Harry she had attracted some of the gentlemen who passed for brains in this superficial town. She had been squired, also, by old, young and medium-aged male stars whose choice was wide and opportunities endless.

She had a reputation as a girl who truly enjoyed the bed, a rarity among those who used their bodies to aspire to high places. What she lacked in intellect, she more than made up in cunning.

Harry said, "Stop staring at my wife, Steve, and name your poison." He patted a portable bar, complete with mechanical refrigeration. "Dotty's anniversary present to me."

"I had no idea's it's been a year," Marcia said.

"It hasn't," Harry said. "Six months, it's been." He winked at Steve. "That's kind of a record for me."

Genial opening touch, Steve thought. *At least we're starting as friends.* He asked causally, "Where's our writer?"

"He'll be along," Harry answered. "I wanted to talk to you first, Steve. You see, Dave's young and kind of artistic and we're going to have to go easy on him."

"A Princeton boy," Dotty put in. "You know how it is with Princeton boys . . ."

Marcia said sweetly, "No. Tell us how it is, Dotty, with Princeton boys?"

For a moment Steve stood rigidly, shocked and frightened.

Then Harry's guffaw broke the tension. "That Marcia! She kills me. Oh, man, Steve, you've got one there!"

Steve looked at his wife appraisingly. He had one there, remarks for all occasions, personalities for all gatherings, an astute and daring darling. "She kills me, too, at times," he admitted and began to breathe again.

They talked about David Louis Sidney then and it was standard enough. David was still conscious of Princeton. He had published a few short stories and one slim novel before coming to work in Hollywood.

Harry said, "He admires you, Steve. I think it would be better, maybe, if you brought him around to our way of thinking. I'm just his dumb uncle, to him."

Steve nodded. He paused before saying, "Harry, how much leeway do I get with this picture?"

Bergdahl looked at his wife and back at Steve. He licked his lips. "I phoned you, didn't I? I know how independent you can be, but I called you. What can I promise? I never had a lemon, Steve; you got to remember that."

"I remember it. And I'm aware that there are a lot of directors currently unemployed. But if we're at cross-purposes, Harry, nothing good can come out of this for either of us."

Bergdahl's smile was purely facial. "You figure me for a dumb uncle, too, huh?"

Steve shook his head. "I find it hard to say what has to be said, Harry. I—want us to understand each other."

Dotty smiled vapidly. Marcia watched them intently. Bergdahl inclined his head back and his big jaw came up almost defiantly. "I can say it. You're the artist. I'm the cornball. That's where I built my reputation, on corn. Maybe today the market ain't so good for corn. Maybe I even need you more than you need me. But I raised the money and I'm still the producer. I'll give a lot of thought to every change you want and respect it. But I will still be the producer."

There was a static moment all around before Steve smiled and said, "Harry, I would be extremely uncomfortable any time I sensed that you weren't being *all* producer. I think we're going to get along."

"Sure we are," Bergdahl said jovially. "Hell, yes. Here, let me mix you a drink."

After that, the problem of David Louis Sidney turned out to be no problem at all. He was young and impressionable, and he was a Steven Leander fan. Every suggestion Steve made for a script change was eagerly agreed to by Sidney.

And then, to cap the evening, he told Steve, as he and Marcia were leaving, "I want to say that I consider it a great privilege to be able to work with you, Mr. Leander."

Steve smiled and winked at Harry. He said, "Dave, your uncle will agree with me, I'm sure, when I tell you it is a great privilege to be able to work at all in the industry today."

Harry laughed and Dotty giggled and the Leanders left them laughing.

In the car Marcia said, "You do have the cleverest exit lines. You soaped everyone with that last line, didn't you?"

"It was a bone for Harry. It was a winner's gesture, dear."

"I see. Did Harry tell you he had insured this Hart Jameson's life for a quarter of a million dollars?"

"Harry didn't tell me, but I knew he was trying to. The investigator for the insurance company came to see me this morning."

"Why? Why should he come to see you?"

"Because," Steve answered smugly, "he wanted to be sure I'd be connected with the picture. That way, he'd know there'd be no financial shenanigans. On account of my integrity, as he explained."

"Brother . . . !" Marcia said. "Aren't we something!" She took a deep breath. "Steve, you did come out on top, didn't you?"

"Temporarily."

"Is there any hope of making it a—worth-while picture?"

"More now than there was three hours ago. But, as I said, my dominance is only temporary." He paused. "Young Sidney told me that his friends at Princeton considered me one of the three great directors out here."

Marcia yawned. "Maybe he didn't have many friends at Princeton. Don't get smug. Young David may be a fan of yours—but he's Harry's *nephew.*"

"I'll never be able to get smug," he assured her. "Not while I'm married to you."

They rode the rest of the way in silence. At home, as the garage door opened and he drove into the lighted garage, Marcia said softly, "We could have saved money, couldn't we? We could be fat and solvent right now if we were different people."

"We're what we are," he said. "You were born rich and I was born hungry."

They walked quietly through the kitchen, through the entry hall and down the hall that led past the children's empty bedrooms. The children were at summer camp.

At their bedroom door, Steve said, "I'm going to sit up for a while. I want to go over the story again."

"Kiss me good night then."

He kissed her.

She said, "It's been a good day, hasn't it, all in all?"

"Pretty good."

"Then why am I frightened?"

"I don't know. Everybody is. *Everybody.* Go to sleep now. Forget about tomorrow."

In his study, he sat for a while without looking at the script, vaguely disturbed. It couldn't be only his temporary insolvency that nagged at him; despite his income through the good years they had always ridden the precarious edge of insolvency. It was a part of the local pattern.

Was there some threat beyond the financial, something in his now almost firm alliance with Harry Bergdahl? Harry was only a man trying to survive and he needed Steven Leander for that. Steve picked up the script and began to read.

He didn't get to bed until two o'clock. And there he had a long and involved dream of searching a mammoth parking lot for his Bentley and not being able to remember where he had parked it. Finally, in his dream, he found the battered, rusty Model T Ford that had been his father's pride for years.

chapter three

Hart Jameson's signing for the new picture was mentioned in Hedda Hopper's column next morning. Hedda didn't bite on the promotional gimmick of the insurance policy, but the paper's local cinema columnist gave it a paragraph. In this account Jameson was identified as "that exciting newcomer who caused such a sensation in *Sunburst Alley*."

Across the breakfast table from him, Marcia said, "You're happy again. You're never happy when you're not functioning, are you?"

"I'm happy," he agreed. "I'm going to take my coffee into the study. Send Dave in when he comes."

Dave Sidney arrived at ten o'clock and they spent the next two hours on the story changes and projected screenplay. Steve had no reason to complain about the young man's willingness to rewrite. What disturbed him was his doubt about Dave's ability to produce credible dialogue. With luck, that could be corrected off the cuff and on the set. With luck—and co-operation from Harry Bergdahl. Some producers could be hard-nosed about sticking to the final shooting script.

He said to Dave, "Lines that look good in print often don't come over when voiced. I hope Harry won't be difficult about any impromptu changes."

David Louis Sidney smiled knowingly. "My uncle isn't going to interfere with you, Steve. Don't give it another thought."

"What made you say that? How can you be sure?"

"I explained it all to Uncle Harry. About your four years of screenwriting and my hope I could learn the trade under you. I have his promise that he won't interfere with us."

"Well," Steve said. "Well, thank you! You've earned yourself a free lunch. We've done enough for one morning."

Everything was working out. There would be some friction, he knew, but the basic conflicts he had anticipated were not developing. The enthusiasm he needed came back.

He viewed some film on Hart Jameson that afternoon. The youth was photogenic and intense. His technique showed a gaucherie that careful direction could eliminate.

Steve came home to his dinner well pleased with his day. His agent had battled to an advantageous contract with Harry, and he knew his star was going to work out.

He came home to his dinner and a phone call from Laura Spain. She had been the star of his first picture, and the box-office magic of her name had been an important part of the picture's success. She had required masterful make-up to play in ingénue even then; she cherished the illusion that she still could.

She said brightly, "I'm looking for work, Steve, and I heard you were casting a Harry Bergdahl picture."

"All the good parts are cast, Laura," he lied.

A silence and then she said quietly, "I'm not looking for a *good* part. I'm looking for *work*, Steve. I mean any kind of work."

Embarrassment touched him. "Don't talk like that. Your name has value only as long as you think it has."

"I'm not thinking of my name these days," she said. "I'm really broke."

His embarrassment deepened but he kept his voice casual. "In that case, let's talk about it. Why don't you come over and have dinner with us? We'd love to see you again. We'll be eating in about an hour."

"I'll be there," she promised, "with last year's bells on. I'm serious about needing work, Steve."

"We'll talk about it," he said.

Marcia was out at the pool. Steve went out to tell her Laura was coming for dinner. "She phoned twice this afternoon," Marcia told him. "I hope you're not soft enough to give her a job in that picture."

He stared at his wife. "Why the sudden animosity? I thought you liked Laura."

"I do. But she is perhaps the world's third worst actress, as both of us know."

"She's a star," Steve explained, "not an actress. Often, that's more important. Anyone can learn to act. Stars are born."

"Loyal, loyal Steve," Marcia teased. "Mix me a martini."

Laura came before they had finished their drinks. She was still fashionably slim and her face still held the delicate bone structure that had been her fortune.

She kissed Marcia and held Steve's hand for a long time. Steve asked, "Drink?"

She shook her head sadly. "No, thank you. Not an ounce for eleven months. It was—becoming—a problem." Her smile was falsely bright. "That's just between us, of course."

Steve felt the same emphatic embarrassment he had felt while talking with her on the phone. Now, in sudden decision, he said, "I've been thinking of you since we talked, Laura. I wouldn't be surprised if you could handle the mother in this epic. Are you ready for mothers?"

"I'm ready for maids," she said. "I'm strapped, honey."

"Well, don't admit it to Harry Bergdahl," he advised her. "I'm going to phone him right now."

Harry wasn't home. Dotty told Steve that he was out on the town with his Texans, and heaven only knew when he would be home.

"Would you have him call me, honey, if he gets in before midnight? I've just had an inspirational idea for casting the mother in our masterpiece."

"I'll tell him, sweet," Dotty answered. A pause. "Give my love to Marcia—if she's listening."

Steve hung up and smiled at his wife. "Dotty sends her love. *If* you're listening."

Marcia sniffed. "And what was the 'honey' for? That's not Leander terminology."

"Dotty isn't standard," Steve explained. He looked at Laura. "Right, Miss Spain?"

"I'll say she isn't," Laura agreed. "That's how Harry is able to sign up these young actors so cheaply. They all come over to sniff around Dotty. That's how he hooked Hart Jameson. And Brad Amherst—for that last horror picture of his."

Steve finished his drink and said, "You're an incurable gossip, Laura. Let's get to the food."

It was an enjoyable dinner, spiced by the reminiscences of Laura's classic and multitudinous feuds, warmed by nostalgia for a better time.

At eleven-thirty Bergdahl returned his call. Steve said, "I think I can get Laura Spain for the mother. How does that sound to you, Harry?"

"Expensive," Bergdahl answered. "Look, I'm a little drunko right now. Let's talk about it tomorrow."

Steve hung up and faced the anxious gaze of Laura. He said, "Harry's too drunk to think tonight. He did say he thought you might be expensive."

"But he's interested?"

"I'm sure he is. Now don't fret about it. You get a good night's sleep, and Harry will probably phone your agent in the morning."

She leaned over to kiss him. "Bless you, Steve. You're one of the anointed."

In the dark and quiet house Steve lay awake, planning. He thought of the children, away at summer camp; he thought of his Sue, aged nine, away from home for the first year, sleeping so far from him.

He thought of Harry Bergdahl and John Abbot and Laura and Dotty. He fell asleep thinking about Dotty and was glad that Marcia couldn't read his mind.

In the morning he had another session with Dave Sidney that went well. Dave's ineptness was due to lack of experience, not lack of discernment, and Steve no longer worried about their ability to work together.

He phoned Harry right after lunch and Harry told him, "I was talking to Dotty about Laura Spain. Dotty thinks she's poison for a picture."

Steve kept his voice casual. "I see. And what do *you* think about her, Harry?"

A pause, "I don't know. Have her come in and talk to me, huh? Maybe, if she's cheap enough . . ."

"I'll call her agent," Steve said. "Everything else going all right, Harry?"

Another pause, "You heard something different?"

"Not a thing," Steve said lightly. "Should I have heard something different?"

"I'm having a little trouble with one of my pigeons. I worked on him four hours last night. Could you raise some quick money, Steve?"

Was this a test, a gauge of Steve's need? He said easily, "I couldn't even raise any slow money, Harry. Uncle Sam is living in my pocket."

"Ain't it the truth?" Harry said. "Well, don't worry. Half of it is solid, and the other boy is beginning to soften. You get together with Dave and get that script straightened around. Okay?"

"Right," Steve said.

Then he went into Hollywood to have lunch with his agent, and learned he was lucky to be working. All the live drama shows on TV were being dropped; the filmed shows already under the control of various studio hacks. Hollywood exhibitor production was down forty per cent from the corresponding period of last year, and last year hadn't been a world-beater.

This picture had to be made and it had to be successful. Viewing it as objectively as possible, Steve knew it could easily be the most important crisis in his career.

chapter four

They began shooting on a Monday, and the first straw in the wind was the nonappearance of Hart Jameson. Steve had talked with Jameson Friday and learned he had signed his contract. The lad had made no mention of not being able to make the Monday call.

At ten o'clock Bergdahl told Steve to go ahead with the scenes that didn't include Jameson. Steve had spent the day working with Laura and the other principals.

He was working with a cast of highly receptive professionals and a cameraman who knew his trade. Things went as well as anyone could expect for a first day's shooting.

Tuesday and Wednesday they were on location in Santa Barbara, and five more days of shooting had been planned for that city. Hart Jameson had not appeared.

Wednesday evening Laura came back from Santa Barbara in Steve's car. It had been a grueling day, hot and full of retakes, and Laura was unusually quiet.

As they came into Ventura, Steve said, "You're doing very well, trouper. Was I rough on you today?"

"No. Even when you are, you always make sense to me. I was thinking about Jameson, wondering about him. Aren't you?"

"Yes. But no gossip now. It's been a hot day."

"All right," she said wearily. *"All right!"*

They were past Ventura and approaching Oxnard when Steve said, "Okay, let's have it."

Laura took a breath. "Well, first, you know he had a criminal record, or course?"

"Not quite a *criminal* record. A juvenile delinquency record a few years back, yes."

"So a record, anyway. Tie that up with this insurance policy Harry took out on him. And some drunken bragging Jameson did at a party a few nights ago to a friend of mine. Hart said he might just possibly have a little accident in his Jaguar, something that might injure his back."

"Kid talk," Steve scoffed. "I hope he doesn't think a faked back injury would fool those insurance doctors."

"Maybe he does. And maybe Harry does, too." Laura paused. "You knew that one of Harry's angels backed out, didn't you?"

"No." Steve slowed his car. "Laura, you're not *looking* for trouble, are you?"

She shook her head slowly. "I've had enough trouble to last me the rest of my life. All I want is to keep working."

"We both have to keep working," Steve said quietly. "I think we had better forget we ever had this conversation."

"I've already forgotten it," she said. "And my friend told nobody but me. She *claims*. Don't you think you should have a talk with Harry Bergdahl, though?"

"I intend to, tonight," Steve said. "We can't continue to shoot around Jameson indefinitely."

The financial shenanigans of Harry Bergdahl were not his business, Steve tried to tell himself. His job was to direct a picture and make it the best picture that could be made with the people and money committed to it. Finance was the producer's realm and the producer's problem.

He dropped Laura off in Brentwood and reminded her, "Forget about Jameson's drunken bragging. Let's concentrate on the problems we have on the set."

She nodded. She patted his hand before stepping from the car.

It was the housekeeper's half-day, and Marcia was in the kitchen preparing dinner when Steve came home.

"Your drink's in the refrigerator," she said. "How did it go today?"

"Fine. That Laura's a real pro. I'm glad I cast her."

"There's something else on your mind. I can tell."

"Nothing," he said irritably. He went to the refrigerator. "It's been hot up there in Santa Barbara."

"It's been hot here, too. I see in the *Times* that your star got into a bar brawl last night."

He turned from the refrigerator. "Jameson?"

She nodded. "The paper's in the living room. It's on the front page. The picture was mentioned."

He didn't go to the living room. He sat at the kitchen table and sipped his drink.

Marcia asked casually, "How is David Louis Sidney doing?"

"Well. I enjoy working with Dave. We understand each other."

"And he's good for your ego," Marcia added. "You haven't kissed me yet, big man."

"I'm too tired to get up," he told her. "Come over here and I'll kiss you."

She came over to him. She stroked his hair and said, "There's a letter from the kids. I think they miss us. Could we go up there Sunday?"

He nodded.

She massaged the back of his neck. "Do you want to tell me what's bothering you, now?"

"Nothing serious. I'm in a complicated business and it has a million tedious problems and a million minor decisions every day. I'm bushed, that's all."

"Has Harry been giving you trouble?"

"He hasn't opened his mouth. He's giving me less trouble than I imagined in my rosiest dreams."

She leaned over to kiss him again. "All right, working man, I'll get off your back. Let's eat outside like the Corn Belt refugees."

He stayed in the shower a long time, letting the warm spray relax his neck and shoulder muscles, trying to dissolve his problems and his doubts in the soapy water that gurgled through the drain at his feet.

He had always tried to divorce himself from the gossip, the rumors, the angle shooting that was the sustenance of so many in the industry. Perhaps it was not wise to stay too aloof from the machinations of his contemporaries.

Marcia was setting the table on the sundeck when he came out from the dressing room. He went into the study and dialed Hart Jameson's number.

Jameson's voice was faintly blurred and annoyingly jovial. "I'll bet you're worried about me. Don't be. The bum didn't lay a hand on me."

"I'm worried about the picture," Steve said.

Over the wire came a muffled, feminine giggle and a less muffled, feminine "Stop that!"

Steve said stiffly, "I hope I'm not interrupting anything. Would it be possible for me to see you tonight?"

Jameson chuckled. "It all depends. This one may take some time to get to. She's the coy type. Does Harry want to talk to me, too?"

"I don't know," Steve answered. "I—heard a rumor and I want your version of it. But not over a phone."

Silence for a few moments, and then Jameson said, "Why not drop over here? It's not far. I can always send the—company out for another bottle or some cigarettes."

Steve carefully kept the indignation from his voice. "Would eight-thirty be all right?"

"Dandy," Jameson said. "Don't forget to knock."

Steve sat by the phone a few minutes before going out to the deck. He told Marcia, "I'm going over to see Jameson tonight. I'll only be gone for about an hour."

"*That's* what's been bothering you," she declared. "I knew there was something."

He didn't argue with her. He sat quietly in the shade of the overhang, looking down at his neighbors. Beyond the house immediately below, the canyon wound, dry and gray, lined with stunted chaparral. In the flood season the canyon would run high water; and the hills would be green.

Marcia must have been reading his thoughts. She said, "All this country really needs is summer rain."

"Summer rain," he agreed, "and a tenth as many people and some New England thrift."

She made a face. "I could start using oleomargarine."

"Bring me another drink," he said. "I'm beginning to feel almost human."

The apartment of Hart Jameson was on the second floor of a stucco building in a less desirable section of Brentwood. Mr. Jameson's success was recent, and his address obviously had not caught up with it.

Steve heard voices before he turned the mechanical chime in the door. Silence followed the chime and then Jameson called, "Just a minute."

It seemed longer than that before the door opened and the bright brown eyes of Hart Jameson considered Steve genially. "Eight-thirty on the dot. I'm not used to punctual people." He stood aside. "Come in."

Steve came into a small living room smelling of gin, perfume and cigarette smoke. A short hall to the right served the bedroom and bath. The bedroom door was closed.

Steve said meaningly, "I'd hoped to catch you alone."

"You did," Jameson said. "I'm all by my lonesome."

Steve hesitated and then headed for a studio couch at the far end of the room from the small hall. He sat down and looked around the room and up at Jameson.

"Speak freely," the youth assured him. "We're alone."

Steve kept his voice low. "I heard a very silly rumor at a party the other night. I heard you were planning a back injury."

Jameson's blunt-featured face twisted in a grin. "You hear the damnedest things at parties, don't you? I was figuring it even heavier than that. I figured to roll the Jag once over lightly to give it some realism. No risk. I used to roll my souped flivver all the time."

"Don't," Steve warned quietly. "You'd never get away with it. Those insurance investigators are extremely able men, Hart."

Jameson chuckled. "So we had another idea. I could run her off a cliff and then go down on foot, tear up my clothes a little and scuff around in the dirt. I don't worry about the Jag. She's insured to the hilt."

Steve almost whispered. "You said 'we.' Who else is involved in this absurd idea?"

Jameson smiled. "Now, who would be? Who's kept me out of the shooting all along?"

"Harry. Is this *his* idea?"

"I'm not going to say it," Jameson answered. "Look, what's all this to you? You're the great artist. The money isn't your department."

"It's not as simple as a question of raising money," Steve answered. "It's a question of morality."

Jameson shrugged. "Oh, come on . . . ! *Mortality,* where a billion-dollar insurance company is involved? That's cutting it real thin, man."

"Their morality isn't involved," Steve explained. "Yours is. And something that might be more important to you—your future. What you plan is already a rumor. If you go through with it, the rumor will be substantiated. Your career could be finished."

Jameson shook his head. "You know, I got a couple of real cornball opinions left over from my kid days. And one of them is that talent will *always* make out. I may not be any Brando, but I sure as hell got more on the ball than most of the slobs that are coining it today."

Steve nodded. "I'll buy that. And this picture could do a lot for your career."

Jameson laughed. "Come *on!* Man, I read that miserable script. This is going to be a dog to end all dogs. Level with me. It stinks, right?"

"No," Steve said firmly. "Originally, it was an unrealized story. It's been fixed now, and the rushes have been impressive."

Silence. Jameson stared at him in doubt. To Steve's nostrils came the odor of that unusual perfume again, stronger than the gin or cigarette smoke.

Jameson said, "You're leveling? I got a lot of regard for your opinion, man. I saw every picture you ever directed. That's why I couldn't figure you on this dog."

"It's not going to be a great picture," Steve said quietly, "but it's going to be a good one. And more important to you at this stage in your career, it's going to be financially successful."

Jameson sat down at the other end of the studio couch and lighted a cigarette. Belatedly he offered one to Steve.

Steve shook his head.

Jameson said softly, "I could have been conned, you know? It happens all the time in this town, right?"

Steve nodded.

After a moment Jameson said, "I promise nothing. And for the record, I admit nothing, either. But I'm going to do some thinking. I'll call you tomorrow night, right?"

Steve stood up. "Do that." He smiled. "And Mr. Self-Admitted Talent, I'll tell you something else. You have enough on the ball, but also a big fat need for good direction."

Jameson grinned. "From maybe three people in this phony town, I'd take that remark. You're one of 'em. Go home and rest easy now. And this little visit stays a secret between us, huh?" Steve nodded and then looked again at the closed bedroom door.

"Rest easy," Jameson repeated. "Leave the finagling to the guys that live by it."

It wasn't bad advice, Steve reflected, but it had come a little late. If Jameson had a change of heart now and appeared for the picture, perhaps there would be no picture. The involved financial shenanigans of Harry Bergdahl were too complicated for an amateur to tamper with.

But he felt better for having made the trip. Laura's rumor had proved to be factual, and it was possible he had saved a talented young man from committing a disastrous act. He smiled at his own pomposity. What he had probably done was to jam the financial machinery that would have kept him solvent.

At home Marcia said, "You look smug. What happened?"

"I did my good deed for the day. Why don't we go to a movie? Movies are better than ever, I heard."

"I thought you were bushed."

"Not any more. Let's go. I'm restless."

It was a long show and well after midnight before they left the theater. Then Marcia developed a gnawing urge for a hamburger, so they stopped at a drive-in.

Consequently, it was after one o'clock when they drove up the long and winding road that led to their hilltop home.

The lights of the Bentley illuminated a little MG as they swung around the last curve, and Marcia said, "Isn't that Dave Sidney's car? What would he be doing here this time of the night?"

"This town is full of MG's," Steve answered. "It must be someone visiting a neighbor."

"It's Dave," Marcia insisted. "See? He's getting out of the car."

She was right. Dave Sidney stood next to his car now, watching their headlights. Then, as Steve swung into the driveway, Dave came across the lawn toward them.

Steve killed the engine and got out. "What's the matter, Dave? Trouble?"

"Plenty," Dave answered. "Uncle Harry sent me over. He's been phoning you for an hour. Hart Jameson's had an accident."

Steve stood rigidly, staring through the darkness at Dave's face, barely visible in the reflection from the headlights. "My God! I talked with him earlier this evening." He paused. "Was he injured seriously?"

"His car went over the bluff above the Coast Highway in the Palisades," Dave said softly. "He was killed."

chapter five

For seconds Steve stood there quietly, unable to speak. Then he said, "Let's go into the house. Let's not stand out here."

Marcia put the car away as Steve and Dave walked toward the front door.

Dave asked, "Was Hart sober when you talked with him?"

"He'd been drinking, I'm sure," Steve said hesitantly. "Dave, I'm trying to decide whether or not I should tell you *why* I went to see Jameson tonight."

Dave stopped walking. "You went to see him? For some reason, I got the impression you talked with him over the phone."

Steve shook his head. "I went to his apartment. And I'm going to tell you why. Right here, without Marcia. I don't want her to know about it."

He told Dave about the rumor but not where he had heard it. He told him about the talk with Jameson and about hearing the voices before he went into the apartment and about the perfume.

When he'd finished, he said, "Except for the girl, I could be the last man to see him alive. I suppose I had better tell the police about it."

"And the rumor, too?" Dave asked.

"I don't know. I can't decide about that. It could make your uncle look bad, couldn't it?"

"It could easily cost him a quarter of a million dollars," Dave said. "Uncle Harry is no angel, Steve, but I can't see him as a murderer. Can you?"

Steve said no and knew he was lying.

"What must have happened," Dave went on, "is that Jameson got stinking drunk and had an actual accident. I don't see what else it could be. He certainly didn't commit suicide in order to accommodate Uncle Harry. But if this rumor gets out, the insurance company has a case."

"That's true," Steve agreed. "I don't know what good . . ."

From the doorway Marcia asked, "Can't you two talk in the house? Is there something I shouldn't know?"

"A number of things," Dave said lightly. "This is all dull man talk."

She looked between them anxiously. "Something's wrong. Is it about the insurance?"

Steve said calmly, "No, honey. We'll be in in a minute. Why don't you put some coffee on?"

Again she looked between them. Then, without speaking, she closed the door.

Steve said, "I should tell the police I talked with Jameson tonight, don't you think? That girl could tell them I was there, and they might wonder why I didn't phone them."

"If they ask you," Dave said, "you can't tell them. And I'm sure they'll ask you. I'm too young to be giving you advice, Steve, but if I were in your position, I'd sit tight until somebody else opened."

They stood in silence for a moment. The headlights of a car grew brighter as it came up the hill.

Dave said softly, "I could never understand the mechanics or morality of money, and I'm sure it's a confusion we share, Steve. This much you know, *you* haven't done anything wrong."

The car turned off at a driveway and they were in darkness again. Steve said, "Let's go in and have some coffee." Dave nodded. "And I'd better phone Uncle Harry."

Marcia had the electric percolator bubbling on the counter in the breakfast room. From the other room they could hear Dave dialing his uncle's number. Steve stared at the bright chrome of the percolator.

Marcia said quietly, "It can't possibly be anything I shouldn't know about."

He transferred his stare at her. "What can't?"

"Whatever you're being so secretive about. Whatever you and Dave were whispering about outside."

From the other room Dave called, "Uncle Harry wants to talk with you, Steve."

Bergdahl's voice was worried. "Dave tells me you talked to Jameson tonight."

"That's right, Harry."

"What about? Was he despondent or anything? I mean—do you think it could have been suicide?"

"I doubt it. I went over to his apartment to check a rumor I'd heard."

"Oh . . . ? What kind of rumor?"

"One I'd rather not voice"—he paused—"over a phone."

There was a silence which seemed to stretch. Then Bergdahl said quietly, "It looks bad—him not being in any of the shooting yet. It will look bad to the insurance people."

"It looks bad," Steve agreed. He took a breath. "Though we really didn't need him this early."

Harry sounded relieved. "That's right. You'll vouch for that. Well, I can handle 'em. I wonder what happened . . . ?"

"I'm wondering, too, Harry. We'll talk about it tomorrow. I think we both need a good night's sleep."

"You'd better stay up for a while," Bergdahl told him. "A Sergeant Morrow is on his way over to see you right now."

Apprehension moved through Steve. "A policeman?"

"That's right. A detective from Homicide, yet. Don't ask me why."

Steve hung up and sat quietly by the phone, and with some shame that he wasn't thinking about the dead Hart Jameson at the moment. He was thinking of the picture.

The picture must be saved. Hart Jameson was dead; nothing could help him now.

In the breakfast room Dave was telling Marcia, ". . . And one Texan stayed in but the other backed out. Uncle Harry has more than half the money he needs, though."

Marcia asked coolly, "Would the insurance on Hart Jameson make up the rest?"

Steve glared at his wife. Dave Sidney looked uncomfortable.

Marcia said, "I'm sorry, Dave." She met Steve's glare defiantly.

Steve said, "There's a detective coming over to see me. A Sergeant Morrow—from Homicide."

Nobody said anything for seconds. Then Dave said lamely, "I'd better go. I'll see you tomorrow, I suppose, Steve."

Marcia went to the door with him as Steve sat down and poured himself a cup of coffee. How much of his dialogue with Hart Jameson should he repeat to Sergeant Morrow? How much of it had that girl in the other room overheard?

Jameson had as much as admitted that the rumor was true. But when he had left Jameson this evening, Steve had felt sure he had convinced the youth the whole scheme was absurd and dangerous.

Tonight's accident might have been a catastrophic coincidence. But if he told Sergeant Morrow about their dialogue . . . ?

He heard the front door close and then Marcia came back to the breakfast room. "I think I'll go to bed. I think you've made it plain that you won't need me tonight."

He looked at her dully. "You're being ridiculous."

"Perhaps. I'm tired. I'm going to bed."

He didn't look at her. He sipped his coffee. For a moment, she stood in the doorway, staring at him. He wanted to look up, to ask her to stay. But he didn't.

She turned and left him.

In his mind Steve damned Harry Bergdahl and his financial shenanigans. In his mind, he framed words for Sergeant Morrow. And he realized he had already made his moral decision when he had told Bergdahl that they hadn't needed Jameson in the early shooting.

Mortgages and Magnin's and the new Bentley . . . The picture must be saved.

Sergeant Morrow was a bony man with gray hair and a weary horse's face. A shorter, stockier man was with him, a Detective Sommers.

Steve said, "I was just having some coffee. I can imagine both of you gentlemen could use a cup about now."

Morrow looked at Sommers and Sommers nodded. They all went into the breakfast room. The officers sat where they would be facing Steve.

As he poured Morrow's coffee, Steve said, "I talked with Hart Jameson earlier this evening. He had been drinking then."

"On the phone?" Morrow asked.

Steve shook his head. "I went to see him. I—read about that bar brawl he'd been in and I thought a little advice wouldn't be amiss."

Morrow asked, "Was he alone?"

Steve frowned. "I couldn't swear in court that he wasn't. But I heard him talking to a woman before I rang his bell and I'm sure she was in another room all the time I was there."

"What time was this?"

"I got there at eight-thirty. I stayed about fifteen minutes."

Morrow sipped his coffee. Sommers sipped his coffee. Steve said, "I get the impression Jameson's death isn't considered accidental. Is there a suspicion of murder?"

Morrow said dryly, "When a quarter of a million dollars is involved, there's always a suspicion of murder." He looked at Steve bleakly. "Wouldn't that make sense to you?"

Steve didn't answer. His mouth was dry. Even when he thought only of the picture.

Sommers said, "You can be damned sure there'll be an insurance dick camped in your hair for a while. If you've got anything that might help us, now would be a real bright time to speak up."

"There's nothing I can think of," Steve said quietly. "Absolutely nothing."

They talked for only a few minutes after that. Both detectives finished their coffee and stood up. Morrow said, "We've got a full night ahead of us. We'll be back tomorrow, Mr. Leander."

"I'll be on location in Santa Barbara all day," Steve said.

"Why?" Morrow asked. "You won't be going ahead with the picture until you get a new star, will you?"

"We'll be going ahead with the picture," Steve answered. "We can always get another actor."

Morrow paused for a moment before saying, "We'll keep in touch with you. Good night."

Steve went to the door with them. After he closed it, he waited until he had heard their car pulling away. Then he went into the bedroom. Marcia was asleep or feigning sleep. He didn't disturb her.

His lies didn't seem to affect his own sleep; he dropped off as soon as his head hit the pillow.

He was at the breakfast table when Bergdahl phoned in the morning. Harry said, "I've had agents on my neck since the morning paper came out. Goddamned, vultures . . . ! What do you think of Tom Leslie for Jameson's part?"

"I think we'd be lucky to get him. Do I go to Santa Barbara today?"

"Why not?"

Steve said nothing.

Harry asked, "How long did the law stay last night?"

"Only long enough for a cup of coffee. I have a feeling that the insurance investigators are going to give it more time than that."

"Why . . . ? Jesus, the punk had a record of drunken driving. And a criminal record, too."

Again Steve said nothing.

Bergdahl asked sharply, "Is there something on your mind, Steve? What's on your mind?"

"Hart Jameson, of course. He had a tendency to brag, Harry."

"I heard about that. So all punks brag. Cripes, man, you don't think I killed the kid, do you?"

"I'm wondering what the police will think."

"Think, think, think . . . ! Who cares what anybody thinks? *Proof*—that's what the judge listens to." Harry lowered his voice. "Listen, you worry about the picture. That's enough to worry about. I'll worry about the money. Okay, Steve?"

"Fair enough," Steve said. "Are we agreed on Tom Leslie for the part?"

"I'll let you know. I won't sign anybody until I let you know. Now, remember, all you think about is the picture. You forget about everything else, okay?"

"Okay, Harry. Good luck."

"Yeh. Oh, yeh. Good-by."

Steve came back to the breakfast table and the *Times* account of the Jameson tragedy, complete with pictures. There was a view of the cliff over which the Jaguar had tumbled and a picture of the battered car lying on its side on the Coast Highway.

It was early and Marcia was still in bed. He ate alone. He read that an autopsy was planned and that the police were searching for two people: the girl who was reported to have been with Jameson before the accident and an unidentified man who had been seen in the exclusive area on top of the bluff from which the car had fallen.

There was no reason given why an unidentified man should not be in the area. Steve assumed the police had more reason than his presence to be suspicious of him. The police weren't likely to reveal all of their information to the newspapers.

None of it was his business, he told himself firmly. He had a picture to make. He had Hart Jameson's part to cast and Laura Spain's jitters to look forward to. Laura had voiced that rumor only fourteen hours ago. And now Hart Jameson was dead. If they could get Tom Leslie for the part . . .

Before leaving to pick up Laura, he went into the bedroom to see if Marcia was awake. She wasn't. She was lying on her back, her eyes closed, both hands clenched at her sides.

He experienced a moment of unreasonable fright before he saw that she was breathing. He went out quietly.

Laura was waiting out at the curb when Steve drove up. Her face was drawn and she had the morning *Times* under her arm.

As she got into the car, she said, "I've had the acid test. I have never in my life wanted a drink more. But I didn't take it."

"Good girl," Steve said warmly. "Let's not think about it. It's really Harry Bergdahl's headache, isn't it? It's none of our business."

Her voice was tight. "It's not our business that a man is dead? After what I told you? We should have talked to Jameson."

"I did," Steve told her. "Last night. And I'm sure he had no intention of rolling his car over that cliff. I'm sure I convinced him he should show up for the picture."

Steve had to keep his eyes on the traffic but he could sense that Laura was staring at him. Finally she whispered, "Steve, could it have been murder?"

He nodded. "Two men from Homicide were over to my house last night. Incidentally, I didn't tell them about that rumor you told me. And you had better forget it."

"Why . . . ? If it isn't murder, why?"

"Because if it wasn't murder, the insurance company could still claim collusion. And then there might not be a picture."

Silence. He came to a break in the traffic and stole a glance at Laura. She was staring straight ahead, her face rigid.

"We're not the police," Steve reminded her gently. "And Hart Jameson is dead. *Nothing* can bring him back."

Laura was silent for blocks. And then she said hoarsely, "I wish I weren't so goddamned broke!"

chapter six

It was a bad day. Laura was jittery and the others were wooden. It was a day of almost completely wasted film. Steve fought his irritation and tried to think of nothing but the picture. He was not successful. He was a man with a conscience.

Laura had voiced a rumor and Jameson had verified it. And he had withheld that information from the police. No matter how he tried to rationalize it, that had been morally, if not legally, wrong.

Dave Sidney had argued in support of his silence, but Dave had admitted he took a light view of the morality of money.

Involved financial manipulations had always been an accepted part of the picture business. Since the advent of confiscatory income taxes, those manipulations had ventured farther and farther from the true intent of the Federal law. So far as he knew, however, they had never before ventured into the realm of murder.

He told himself that he couldn't be sure it was murder. The police would decide that. They had experts whose job it was to decide that definitely. And if they should discover it wasn't murder, there would be no moral problem for him to solve.

The script girl rode home with them. He and Laura carefully avoided any discussion of Hart Jameson's death.

He dropped Laura first, and told her, "It was a bad day. Tomorrow will be better."

She patted his hand. "I was abominable. It won't happen again, I promise you."

As they drove on, the script girl said, "I wonder who'll take Hart Jameson's part? He's going to be difficult to replace, isn't he?"

"Very," Steve agreed. "Mr. Bergdahl is working on that now."

And what else, he wondered, was Mr. Bergdahl working on now? On his alibi perhaps? He hadn't seen a paper since this morning's *Times*. By now the wet-eyed cinema columnists had undoubtedly taken over and the public would be deluged with another tidal wave of bathos. The "exciting newcomer" was dead, dead, dead.

A cerise Cadillac convertible was parked in his driveway, and he tried to remember which of his or Marcia's friends drove a car like that.

It was Harry's car. He was sitting out on the sundeck, a drink in his hand. Marcia sat near by in a terry-cloth robe over her swim suit.

Steve went over to kiss her and she turned her cheek.

Harry said, "Some kiss. If Dotty tried that, I'd throw her into the pool."

Steve took a deep breath and turned to face Bergdahl. "I suppose the columnists are pulling all the stops."

Bergdahl shrugged. "I only read the financial page. I can get Leslie for the lead. I can get him pretty cheap, too. Okay?"

"Fine," Steve said. "I wasted your money today, Harry."

Bergdahl shrugged again. "That figured. Did Laura show up sober?"

Steve nodded and went over to mix a drink. With his back to Harry, he asked, "Has Sergeant Morrow been around?"

"No. There's a real nasty slob nosing around for the insurance company, though. Polack bastard named Tomkevic. He's got a nasty mind, Steve. Keep your temper under control."

Steve turned to find Harry looking at him meaningfully. He said, "I haven't any temper left. I didn't even have the gumption to horsewhip that cast today."

"It's the first bad day," Harry said soothingly. "Don't fret, Steve." He looked at Marcia and away. He sipped his drink.

Marcia murmured, "Excuse *me!*" She rose and went down the steps to the pool.

Harry inclined his head. "What's with her?"

"I guess she's annoyed with me. She thinks I'm keeping some deep, dark secret from her."

"Are you?"

Steve shook his head.

Harry said quietly, "Dave told me about the talk you had with Jameson. Did you tell Marcia about that, too?"

Steve shook his head again.

"Smart boy," Harry said. "Women—they can't keep nothing to themselves."

Steve sipped his drink.

Harry finished his and expelled his breath. He stared at Steve steadily. "For Christ's sake, you don't think I killed him, do you?"

Steve said evenly, "Of course not. It was an accident, wasn't it? Have the police decided?"

"I think they're willing to write it off as an accident, but that Polack Tomkevic sure as hell ain't about to. You watch out for him, Steve."

"I'll be careful," Steve promised. "Will Leslie be ready tomorrow?"

"I'll have him there." Harry stood up. "And Dave will ride with you." He studied Steve thoughtfully. "Have you ever decided who your real friends are, Steve?"

Steve smiled. "Mmmm-hmmm. People who don't interfere."

He went to the door with Harry and then came to watch Marcia splashing in the pool. She was blithely ignoring him. He started down the steps to the pool when the housekeeper came out to tell him a Mr. Tomkevic was waiting to see him.

The pressure mounted in Steve's chest. He said, "I'll see him out here."

He was mixing a drink when the brown-eyed, soft-voiced man came out to the sundeck.

Steve indicated a chair and asked, "Drink, Mr. Tomkevic?"

"No, thanks. My first trip here doesn't seem quite as silly now as it did to you then, does it?"

Steve shrugged.

Tomkevic sat down and stared at Steve. Then, "I suppose you're about to have dinner. I'll try to be brief."

He went on then, to explain about the accident. Jameson's car had gone over the bluff from an empty lot, and it had to bump across an extremely rough stretch of ground in order to reach the edge from which it fell.

"He was probably drunk," Steve explained.

"It's been established that he'd been drinking. And drunken drivers have accidents. But not accidents like this. It would have required a rather high degree of rationality simply to keep the engine running across that field. You must remember there was no automatic transmission in that car, and that field could not be traversed in high gear."

Steve asked quietly, "Why are telling me this, Mr. Tomkevic? I'm not a detective."

Tomkevic said blandly, "Everything I've learned about you today indicates you're a man of exceptional integrity, Mr. Leander. I want you to re-examine your conversation with Hart Jameson and determine if there isn't something you overlooked."

"I'm not following you," Steve said.

Tomkevic frowned and leaned forward. "Frankly, I'm checking a rumor. The rumor is that Jameson never had any idea of appearing in this picture, for which he was insured."

Steve could feel the pulse beat in his wrist. He looked down at the pool. Marcia had taken off her swimming cap and was drying herself.

"Well . . . ?" Tomkevic prompted.

Steve said easily, "You hear a lot of damn-fool rumors in this business, Mr. Tomkevic. Jameson was signed to play and he would have been in legal hot water if he hadn't."

"Perhaps. Are you telling me now that you and Jameson didn't discuss his appearance in the picture?"

"I'm not obligated to tell you anything, am I?"

"That would depend on your conscience, Mr. Leander. A man is dead. Anything you can tell me that would help to uncover the reason for his death is important. Don't you agree with that?"

"I agree with that. But I don't believe any other conversation we may have had about the picture is anybody's business but mine."

Tomkevic's face tightened. "Well, you've told me enough to confirm my suspicion. I'm sure you'll realize later that honesty is your only sensible course."

Steve flushed. He asked, "Confirm *what* suspicion?"

"That Jameson's death was no accident."

"Isn't that a question for the police to decide?"

Tomkevic said wearily, "The police are overloaded. Even for a death as headline-worthy as this one, their time is limited. Mine isn't, and they'll ride with me."

"But will the courts?"

Tomkevic stood up. "Mr. Leander, I think I can safely say that by the time this mess gets into a court, it will be a *criminal* court. And the state will be the plaintiff."

Steve's flush deepened. "Is that an accusation?"

Tomkevic met his glare. "At the moment, I can only accuse you of a serious error in judgment. I am going to get to the truth of this accident. You would have done *both* of us a service if you had been completely co-operative with me today."

Steve said nothing.

Tomkevic said, "It still isn't too late."

"I'm sure you can find your way out," Steve told him.

Tomkevic smiled bitterly. He glanced past Steve to where Marcia was coming slowly up the steps. Then he turned abruptly and left.

Marcia went past to the portable bar and began to mix a drink.

"And why are you sulking?" Steve asked.

She kept her back to him. "I'm not. Who was that man?"

"An insurance investigator."

She turned around. "If this marriage means as much to you as it does to me, I think I've a right to know what you and Dave were talking about last night."

"We were talking about Hart Jameson. There's a suspicion afloat that he may have been murdered. Now, do you think either Dave or I could murder?"

"No. But I do think you know something about Jameson's death that you're not telling me. Or the police." She inhaled heavily. "And I think you've made a very bad moral decision."

"Only the nonparticipants," he said, "can afford this flawless morality."

Her voice was high. "Now what in hell did that mean? How am I a nonparticipant in anything that happens to you?"

"You're a nonparticipant in the frightened, scrambling, conniving world I work in. That's what I meant."

"I see. And you've decided to be a frightened, scrambling conniver. Is that it?"

He held his tongue for seconds and then said quietly, "You didn't mean that."

"They were your words," she answered. "Steve, this picture has become so important to you, you're letting Harry Bergdahl destroy you."

"That is absurd," he said. "Harry hasn't interfered once. I'm shooting this picture exactly the way I want to." He finished his drink. "And making the best picture I'm capable of is the only kind of morality I'm concerned about."

"Oh, God . . . !" she said. "Do you realize how pretentious you just sounded?"

"You tell me," he answered evenly. "You're good at it."

She glared, and tears came to her eyes. She set her untasted drink on a table and walked quickly into the house.

He sat there, trying to blank his mind. He couldn't get emotionally involved in a domestic crisis now. He needed every ounce of energy and serenity he could find to make this picture successful.

He was eating dinner alone when Marcia went out. He called after her and though he knew she had heard him, she didn't pause. The front door slammed with a force that shook the floor.

He finished his meal and took the percolator of coffee with him into the study. He was well into the script when the phone rang.

He picked it up and a doubtful masculine voice asked, "Mr. Leander?"

"Yes."

A pause, and then hesitantly, "This is a—a friend of a friend of Hart Jameson's. I wonder if I could see you tonight?"

"I'm very busy," Steve said. "Could I have your name, please?"

"Not unless I can see you," the man said. "This friend of Jameson's that I know, she was—over at his apartment last night."

Steve said steadily, "The police are looking for her. If she's a friend of yours, you'd be doing her a service by advising her to report to the nearest police station."

"She doesn't want to. She's innocent, see? But she doesn't want any part of the police."

"If she's innocent, why not?"

The man's voice was lower now and slightly shaky. "Well, it would just cause a lot of trouble. She heard something she wasn't supposed to hear, I guess, and she doesn't want to cause anybody any trouble."

The pressure was building up again in Steve's chest. He took a deep breath. "Why do you want to see me?"

"I'm an actor. I thought you might have a little something for me in this picture you're shooting."

"I see. How did you get my phone number?"

"Hart Jameson had it, and my friend got it from him."

"He had Mr. Bergdahl's number, too. He's the producer. Why didn't you phone him?"

"To tell you the truth, Mr. Leander, because I'm scared to death of Harry Bergdahl."

"But not of the police? Do you realize you're withholding information from them by not telling them the name of the girl?"

"I'm going to protect her. I wouldn't want her to get on the wrong side of Harry Bergdahl, not in this town."

"Oh . . . ? She's an actress, is she?"

"She likes to call herself one." A pause. "Am I wasting your time, Mr. Leander?"

"I'm not sure what you're doing," Steve said frankly. "And I'm also not sure why I'm listening. Why don't you want to give me your name?"

There was a silence that lasted for seconds. And then the man asked, "Did you see *Dim Thunder?*"

"Yes."

"Do you remember that bar scene, where the drunk went loco?"

"I most certainly do."

"I played that drunk. My name is Mitchell Morton. I wouldn't ask for a part any bigger than that."

Steve stared at his desk top and then at the script. Finally he said, "There's a part that small and that good in this picture. Why don't you come over here and we'll talk about it?"

After he had hung up, he went over to the bookcase and pulled

two books from a shelf. There was a .32 there which he kept because the house was so isolated.

After a few moments, he replaced the books without touching the
gun. What did he have to fear from an actor?

chapter seven

Had he been blackmailed? Not yet, of course. He had not promised
Morton a part. He had agreed to talk with him about it but he had
promised nothing. He went out onto the front lawn to wait.

The santana was blowing, and the evening was unusually warm
and dry. To his right the shoreline of Santa Monica Bay was clear
from Point Dume to Palos Verdes.

He hadn't come out to enjoy the view. He kept his eyes on the
glistening traffic of Sunset Boulevard, far below.

A car turned off from the artery, and he felt a flutter in his
stomach. It turned again at a driveway halfway up the hill. He
waited.

Now, another car turned off from the main road, and this one
was coming all the way up. He went out to the curb to wait. It was a
three-year-old, two-door Plymouth sedan.

He had seen Mitchell Morton only in that memorable bit in *Dim
Thunder,* but he recognized him as he stepped from the car.

He had a brush haircut and impressive shoulders. He was young
and his youth was apparent in the present situation. Steve sensed
that beneath the true actor's cultivated poise, young Morton was
uncertain and frightened.

He came over to stand squarely in front of Steve and he managed
to smile. "Call me a son-of-a-bitch and send me packing. I'm sure
that's what I deserve."

Some of Steve's apprehension disappeared, and his own poise
returned. He smiled. "Nobody's perfect. I'm not sure whether I'm
being blackmailed or not. I've been trying to decide."

"It's certainly not blackmail," Morton said quietly. "My friend
isn't about to go to the police, no matter what happens to the career

of Mitchell Morton." His chin lifted. "I used that line so you wouldn't hang up on me. Slimy, right?"

Steve shrugged. "You're in a rough profession."

They stood silently a moment. *He's scared,* Steve thought. *He's young and desperate and gutty, but he's scared.*

It was growing dark now, and the lights were beginning to dot the hills. Steve said, "You must be very hungry and you're only asking for a crumb. Come on into the house. I have an extra copy of the script I can give you."

Morton made no move. He said hoarsely, "Why don't you tell me to beat it?"

"Forget how you got here," Steve advised him gently. "You're something new, an actor with a conscience. Come on."

In Steve's study they talked for about ten minutes, and Steve learned that Mitchell Morton had studied with Jameson in New York. They hadn't been exactly friends, Morton was quick to explain, but when he had come out here, Jameson's had been the only familiar face.

"And through Jameson you met this girl?"

Morton said, "I'd rather not talk about the girl, Mr. Leander."

"I'd like to, a little. For instance, can you be sure she's not connected with Jameson's death in some way?"

"I'm positive," Morton answered.

"And you weren't, by any chance, the unidentified man who was seen in the area on top of the bluff there, were you?"

Morton shook his head. "I don't know anything about him and neither does my friend. I asked her about that when I read it in the paper."

Steve looked at the young man levelly. "Do you think Jameson's death was an accident?"

Morton nodded.

Steve smiled. "It's easier to lie with a nod than with words, isn't it? You don't really think his death was an accident."

"Maybe not. But I swear to you that I don't know it was anything else."

Steve stood up and handed Morton the script. "Okay. I'll tell Mr. Bergdahl you've been promised that bit. Phone me the early part of next week. We'll probably shoot that Thursday or Friday."

"Thank you," Morton said warmly. "Thank you for treating me better than I deserve."

It was, Steve reflected, the first time in his life he had been accused of that. He went out to the car with Morton and stood there long after Morton was out of sight, hoping that another car would turn up from the road. Where could Marcia have gone? To John Abbot?

She was being unreasonable, but that was a failing of her sex. He had worked with enough temperamental women to be able to cope with their absurdities. With Marcia, because of the emotional attachment, it was more difficult. But she'd come back to reason eventually, he assured himself.

He phoned Bergdahl and found him at home. He said, "I promised a lad named Mitchell Morton a piece in that lake cottage scene. Know him?"

"The name only . . . Wait, did I see it on a list? Was he listed in *Red Channels?*"

"I have no idea," Steve answered.

"Or did some broad mention his name? It sticks in my mind, for some reason."

"If you saw *Dim Thunder,* he played that pathological bit in the bar scene."

"I didn't see it," Harry said. "Well, I'll check; I've got all the lists. That Tomkevic was here right after dinner. The son-of-a-bitch is going to wind up with a bloody nose if he don't get out of my hair."

Steve said nothing.

"I talked to Sergeant Morrow," Harry went on, "and the law's about convinced it was an accident. So what's bothering the Polack? Jesus, it ain't *his* money!"

"He'll give up after a while," Steve said soothingly. "Remember your ulcer, Harry."

"Yeh, yeh. Mitchell Morton, Mitchell Morton—damn it, I'll bet he's a Commie."

"Check it," Steve said. "Is Dave coming over here in the morning or does he want me to pick him up?"

"He'll come here. Look, we're planning a cast party for Saturday night. You and Marcia going to be free?"

"I'm sure we are. I'll let you know. Marcia's not home right now."

Harry chuckled. "If she's out on the town, tell me where. That's some doll you got, mister."

"Thank you. I'll tell her you said that. I'll *warn* her. Now don't fret, Harry. Everything is going to work out well."

Bergdahl chuckled again. "That's a switch, *you* telling *me* not to fret. Be seein' you, kid."

Steve went back to the script, searching for soft spots he could discuss with Dave Sidney tomorrow.

At eleven he went out to the front again, and it was still warm for a California night. He stayed out until midnight, looking at the lights and waiting for Marcia. Finally he went in and to bed. He was asleep when she came home.

In the morning *Times* he read that an autopsy had discovered nothing beyond the exorbitant amount of alcohol in the body of Hart Jameson. The police, however, were still not ready to write off the death as accidental. No reason was given for this attitude, but Steve could guess that a man named Tomkevic might be mainly responsible for it.

The signing of Tom Leslie for Jameson's part was given a fat two paragraphs in Hedda's column, and the local columnist gave that and the Jameson tragedy his entire column. Harry would be happy about the free ink.

Steve was drinking his coffee when Dave Sidney came. Dave looked haggard.

"Sit down and have some coffee," Steve suggested. "Hung over?"

Dave shook his head as he sat down at the far end of the table from Steve. "I've been playing amateur detective. I was up until three this morning."

"Now, Dave what can you learn that a police department and a private detective can't?"

"Well, to begin with, I know a couple of Hart's girl friends. To my mind, that floozie who was with Hart Wednesday night could be the big key."

"I'll know her if I ever meet her," Steve said. "That is, unless she changes her brand of perfume. I'll never forget that odor."

"It could be a common perfume," Dave suggested.

Steve shook his head. "I've worked with women at all income levels, and I never smelled anything like this before." He poured Dave a cup of coffee. "Run into my study and get the script, will you? There are some shots I've marked for sharpening."

It was the start of a rewarding day. Tom Leslie, unlike Jameson, was a trained and disciplined talent. He would be another plus for the picture. And Laura moved through her scenes with competence and grace. There were moments when she seemed almost like an actress.

At the first break, Dave Sidney told Steve, "I don't know what's happening, but it's coming alive, isn't it?"

Steve nodded and smiled. "To tell you the truth, I'm not sure what's happening either, but I think this Leslie is a boy who pulls the best out of all the others."

There was a silence and Steve wondered if his shameful, fleeting thought had been shared by Dave. The death of Hart Jameson had not been a completely ill wind.

Dave said quietly, "I hope Uncle Harry gets the rest of his money."

Steve said confidently, "With stuff like this to show angels, he's got sound collateral." And he reflected that neither of them had used the word "insurance."

Laura got a ride home with Leslie that evening. Steve and Dave were the only occupants of Steve's car. Dave dozed as they drove along the Coast Highway, and Steve thought back on the day with satisfaction.

This picture had to be finished. Harry would have to get the money any damned way he could. This picture had to be done right. There were some expenses ahead. There were some sets they couldn't cheat on without damaging the picture.

Dave mumbled something and Steve glanced his way, but Dave's eyes were closed. This picture could do a lot for Dave's reputation, and Dave was Harry's nephew. This picture would be financed. Harry would see to that.

As he got out of the car in Steve's driveway, Dave asked, "Are you and Marcia going to the party tomorrow night?"

"Probably," Steve answered. "Though I can't vouch for Marcia. She's not talking to me."

"She's not still angry because of Wednesday night, is she? I mean —when you and I talked outside?"

Steve nodded. "I'll probably go, either way. I could use a real Bergdahl wingding about now."

"Don't forget the funeral is tomorrow," Dave reminded him. "Uncle Harry would like to see us all there."

"I'd forgotten," Steve said slowly. "Yes, we'd better all go."

It wasn't anything he was looking forward to, and he was sure Harry wanted them there only for the promotional effect. But it was no time to flaunt tradition.

And the party—he hoped Marcia would agree to go. A Bergdahl party would do them both a lot of good. If they drank enough.

Marcia wasn't home. She had left a note: "I decided to spend a long week end with the children. I'll be home Monday."

In the kitchen the housekeeper told him, "Mrs. Leander won't be home until Monday. Did you get her note?"

Steve nodded.

The woman hesitated. Then, "Is there something wrong, Mr. Leander? I know it's none of my business, but you two always got along so fine . . ." Her voice trailed off and she looked uncomfortable.

"There's nothing wrong, Mrs. Burke," Steve said placidly. "She simply went up to camp to see the children." He smiled. "I think I'll eat at the club tonight. That way you can make the early movie at the Bay."

He felt lethargic after his shower. He lay on the bed in his robe and tried to nap. Usually he could doze off in a few minutes, but not tonight.

Both John Abbot and Laura had warned him against Harry Bergdahl, and they were a pair of old pros. Of course, neither of them had been proved right so far. He had had no interference from Harry on the picture, and he would not have been involved in the death of Hart Jameson if he hadn't listened to Laura's gossip. And he wouldn't have been in a position to listen to Laura's gossip if she hadn't begged him for a part in the picture.

No, that wasn't fair. He had gone to see Jameson of his own volition, and he had lied to the police about the conversation they had had. He couldn't blame Laura for any of that. If Harry Bergdahl was not a murderer, what harm had been done by his lie? A lie is a lie is a lie . . .

He thought of Marcia, and desire swelled in him. He got up irritatedly and dressed.

In the grill of the Canyon Country Club, Dow Allen and Jack Delahunt waved to him from a table overlooking the eighteenth green. Steve went over.

Dow said, "You have the look of a man with a free evening. How about some poker?"

Steve sat down. "Maybe. My wife's out of town for the week end."

"Great," Dow said. "That was too bad about Jameson. Harry was ready, though, wasn't he?"

Jack laughed and Steve looked between them grimly. "I hope

that was a gag, though it was a bad one. Am I getting that kind of reputation?"

Dow smiled. "Not you, buddy. Harry's always had that kind of reputation."

"As a murderer? Not *quite.*"

Jack said seriously, "As anything he needs to be to stay in business. I wouldn't put murder past him, Steve."

"Nonsense," Steve said angrily. "Let's talk about something else."

"Let's talk about the picture," Allen said genially. "The word is you've got a winner. And now you come up smelling like roses with Tom Leslie."

"And Laura Spain," Delahunt added. "How did you ever convince her it was time to act her age?"

"Laura and I are old friends," Steve said.

"Is she off the soup?" Dow asked.

Steve nodded and picked up a menu. "Laura is doing very well. She's a real pro."

Dow laughed. "You sounded smug, kid."

"Why not?" Jack put in. "He's working, isn't he?"

They all had dinner in the grill, and then some others came and they went into the card room.

It was a table stakes game, and the cards were kind to Steve. He didn't concentrate properly and completely misplayed the best hand he was dealt all evening.

Despite this, when they broke up at three o'clock, he was an even four hundred dollars ahead for the session.

Dow Allen said, "You're the luckiest and lousiest poker player in the world. Kid, you stink."

"I'm not usually this bad," Steve answered. "I just couldn't get my mind on the cards."

"I'll vouch for that," Delahunt said. "Next to Harry Bergdahl, I think Steve is the best poker player I know." He smiled. "I would have loved to have been there when you two talked terms."

"My agent did that," Steve said. "I wouldn't dare to cross swords with Harry Bergdahl."

chapter eight

Sylvan Glade advertised quite honestly that it took the burden of decision from the bereaved relatives of the departed. It had its own interdenominational chapel, crypts, mausoleum, crematorium, casket salesroom, limousines, ushers, social secretary, publicity department and grave-digging machine with skilled operator. And photogenic professional mourners, if required.

It also had fountains, statuary, gigantic murals, wide winding drives and everything else that could contribute to the general bad taste of a town that specialized in bad taste. As one of the directors had boasted in an alcoholic moment, "We put on one hell of a show. But Jesus, a man only dies once!"

A package deal, Steve thought, in the terminology of his trade. He and Laura were driving in his car through the gaping teen-agers and sagging housewives who lined the green macadam drive that led to the chapel parking lot.

"Where's the ringmaster?" Laura asked. "God . . . !"

"Easy, girl. This is nothing, compared with Valentino's funeral."

"You don't remember that," Laura answered. "That was before your time. And mine, too."

Steve smiled. "It was before *mine,* at any rate. There were giants in those days."

Laura shook her head. "There was a sucker audience. . . . I'm a lousy actress, aren't I, Steve?"

"No," he said firmly. "Because you were a star, you never had to learn to act. But you were great yesterday. This picture could start a whole new career for you, Laura."

"An acting career," she said musingly. "Well, that would be a change."

They both laughed, and then Laura said, "Heavens, what will all these cretins think? We had better look sad."

Harry Bergdahl looked sad. He sat in the second row with a handkerchief in his hand, occasionally dabbing at his eyes.

"Smog?" Laura whispered to Steve. "I didn't notice it."

"Shut up," Steve whispered. "I suppose we'd better go up to view the body?"

"You go," Laura said. "I never could do that."

It was going to be a full house. As he returned to sit next to Laura, Steve saw Tomkevic in one of the back rows near the entrance. Mitchell Morton was in the front row. He was apparently one of the pallbearers. Dave Sidney sat next to his uncle, his face perfectly blank, almost bored. From the other side of Harry, Dotty smiled timidly at Steve. In one of the corners a flash bulb flared.

Were these causal onlookers representative of the mourners? Steve saw no genuine tears. Hadn't Jameson any family? He felt a cold sickness growing in him as he took his seat.

Laura sat rigidly, staring at the neck of the man ahead, while the cleric supplied by the management spoke unctuously of "this untimely departure of a young and brilliant talent."

There were a few wet eyes when he had finished. In the sixth row a chunky teen-ager sobbed noisily. Steve thought of the waiting kids lining the macadam drive outside and he asked Laura, "Should we go to the grave with the procession?"

"No," she said. "We put in an appearance. Harry can't have any complaints if we don't contribute further to this—circus."

Steve frowned, hesitating.

Laura said, *"Please,* Steve . . . ? I don't like funerals. I think they're vulgar."

"All right," he said soothingly. "Let the others get ahead of us and we'll go directly to the parking lot."

The parking lot was almost deserted when he and Laura walked over to his car some minutes later. There was a green Pontiac parked two stalls away.

Tomkevic stepped from the Pontiac as Steve opened the door for Laura.

He asked in his soft voice, "Could I have a minute, Mr. Leander?"

Steve closed the door and turned to face the investigator. "Yes . . . ?"

Tomkevic said, "I understand Mitchell Morton is going to have a part in your picture?"

"A small part," Steve agreed.

"Did you hire him, or Mr. Bergdahl?"

"I talked with Mr. Morton. No contract has been signed. Is there some reason why I shouldn't hire him?"

"None that I know of. I simply wanted to learn who had hired him. He hasn't worked in any of your other pictures, has he?"

"No."

"You knew him personally, did you, before casting him?"

Steve shook his head.

Tomkevic frowned. "Mr. Bergdahl did. I'm surprised he didn't go to Mr. Bergdahl."

Steve said nothing.

"Aren't you?" Tomkevic asked quietly.

"Not particularly. Anything else, Mr. Tomkevic?"

The investigator's eyes hardened. "Yes. Do you think you need to be as frightened and secretive as you are? You have a sound reputation in this town." He paused. "Or *had.*"

Steve said heatedly, "Don't be insolent. You're not heavy enough to carry it off."

The investigator smiled. "I'm not too big, I'll admit. But then, I'm not frightened, either. I'll see you again, Mr. Leander."

"I'm not looking forward to it," Steve said, and went around the car to the driver's side.

Laura said, "Well! And what was all that about?"

"I've no idea," Steve said angrily. "He's an investigator for the company that insured Jameson."

"I thought this morning's paper said the police had decided it was an accident?"

"There's absolutely no reason in the world," Steve said, "to consider it anything else. Let's not see any more goblins, Laura. We went through that phase."

She sighed and said nothing. She said nothing for the rest of the trip. As Steve dropped her he said, "I'll see you at the party tonight."

"I'm not sure I'm going," she answered. "I hate to sit around and watch everybody drink. Do you think Harry would mind very much if I didn't come?"

Steve shrugged.

"Is Marcia going?"

"She's out of town. She went up to the kids' camp."

A moment's silence, and then Laura said, "I suppose it would be good politics to go. Don't worry about me; I'll get there all right. I'll want to leave early."

Steve went home to his big and empty house. The parking-lot dialogue with Tomkevic had unsettled him again. And Tomkevic's claim that Harry had known Morton was a disturbing item. Harry had made too much of a point of his *not* knowing Mitchell Morton.

Damn it, Jameson was dead. Dead and now buried. And the police had decided it was an accident. They were the official arbiters.

He lay on the couch in his study and thought of Marcia, and desire grew in him again and his irritation deepened. She had never earned a dime in her life. She had no idea of the savage and incessant competition in the industry. Her duty was to sustain him, not to judge him.

It had been two weeks since their matinée session and he was no benedict and she was well aware of that. She was not exactly frigid herself.

He put on his trunks and went down to the pool. He dived, he swam, he lolled in the sun. He tried to forget Jameson and Morton and Tomkevic and Bergdahl. But the thought of Marcia stayed with him.

At five o'clock Harry phoned. "Dave tells me Marcia's out of town?"

"That's right, Harry. But I'll be there, bright and sober."

"Maybe I should invite something special for you? About eighteen or nineteen, something stacked?"

"I wouldn't know what to do with one like that. I'm sorry I didn't —go to the grave, Harry, but funerals give me the creeps."

"Oh . . . ? I thought maybe it was Laura that didn't want to go."

"No," Steve lied, "it was my idea. Tomkevic was waiting for me on the chapel parking lot. He won't give up, will he?"

"He don't scare me," Harry said. "Well, there'll be a lot of broads here, kid, so don't drink too much."

"I'll be careful. See you, Harry."

"Wait . . ." Bergdahl said. "That Mitchell Morton—he's okay, he's clean. I checked him."

"Glad to hear it," Steve said. "He'll be another small plus for the picture."

How did Dave know that Marcia was out of town? He had left him at the front door yesterday and not talked to him since. And when they had parted, even Steve hadn't known Marcia wasn't home.

Perhaps Dave had learned it from Laura. Or perhaps his amateur detective work had extended into the private life of the Leanders.

The rear patio was lighted by gay Japanese lanterns, and the concrete badminton court had been waxed for dancing. The bar was built-in near the huge, used-brick fireplace. Small wrought-iron and glass tables were set back around the wide deck of the pool.

Next to Steve at the bar, Mitchell Morton said, "Simple suburban living. I wonder if I'll ever make it."

Steve laughed. "Not unless you can get into a position to use a capital-gains gimmick. Not on salary alone, not any more."

From the other side of Morton, the girl he had brought said, "Okay, Mitch, don't I meet the important people, too?"

She was a thin girl with her black hair in a Hollywood version of a Dutch cut. Her voice was low and pleasant.

Morton performed the introduction and then Dotty Bergdahl came over to tell him coyly that there were "oodles of people just gasping to meet Steven Leander."

He met four of the oodles, three women and one man, and then Dotty led him to the badminton court, where Tom Leslie was dancing with a spectacular blonde.

"I want to talk to you," she explained, "and I don't want Harry to think I'm pumping you. Let's dance."

Steve frowned. "Pumping me . . . ? About what?"

"About a rumor I heard, that Jameson was *planning* to have an accident in his car."

"Dotty, in this business we hear ridiculous rumors every day." He moved her along the edge of the court, aware of her fine body, of her firm breasts tight against his chest.

"I know that," she admitted. "But what is Harry so nervous about? Why is that insurance detective bothering him all the time?"

"I have no idea."

"He's been going out practically every night. Why?"

Steve smiled sadly. "Honey, how in hell would I know?"

"Men . . . !" she said. "And you and Marcia had a fight, too, didn't you? And there's some big, mysterious secret about that."

"She went up to see the kids. Marcia and I have fought before, Dotty. We're not newlyweds."

She looked up at him beseechingly. "I know there's something horrible going on, Steve. Why don't you tell me what it is?"

He said gravely, "If there's anything horrible going on, I swear to you, Dotty, that I don't know what it is. Horrible things are going on in this town every minute."

"Not things Harry's involved in." She took a deep breath. "I know what you think of me—a peroxide nitwit. But I've been good for Harry. I brought these young people around, and he's put out some pictures with vitality and youth in them. If he's in trouble, don't be too sure I can't help him."

"Dotty, I never thought of you as a peroxide nitwit. I can't seem to think of you as anything but about the most seductive female in the county. And if Harry's in trouble, he hasn't told me about it."

She moved closer and desire quickened in Steve. She asked softly, "Is it about Hart Jameson?" Her voice was even quieter. "Or is it a girl? Tell me, please, Steve."

"I don't know. So help me, honey, I don't know. You're closer to him than I am. He'd tell you things he wouldn't tell me."

"Not if it's about a girl," she insisted. "And I think it is."

Steve didn't have time to answer. A genial voice at his elbow said loudly, "Get one of your own, Leander. This one's mine."

Steve smiled and relinquished Dotty Bergdahl to her leering husband.

He went back to the bar. Morton's black-haired girl friend was talking with Dave Sidney there. Morton was at one of the tables, talking with Laura Spain and the dialogue director.

Dave said, "Jean thinks you dance very well for an older man."

The girl grimaced. "I didn't say anything about an *older* man. Dave's trying to blight my career."

"Don't butter him," Dave said. "He's the last local bastion of integrity." He looked around the yard. "I wonder where my giddy companion has disappeared to?"

Jean yawned. "You could check the bedrooms and the bushes. That one belongs on a leash."

Steve asked the bartender for a Scotch and water and turned to watch Harry dancing with Dotty. Harry was talking to her very earnestly, and Dotty's face looked grim and stubborn.

The conversational murmur was higher now and more people were coming in. Dave said, "I love Uncle Harry's idea of a *cast* party. He means the casts of all his pictures and all the people they ever met."

Above the swaying lanterns the stars were clear and the moon full. Steve drank slowly and thought of Marcia.

Dave said, "Ah, here comes my lovely now."

Jean said, "She's looking petulant. Somebody must have said no to her."

Steve saw a girl in a white sheath dress coming toward them, walking carefully, as though on the edge of drunken oblivion. Her full breasts were almost emerging from the top of the tight dress, and its tautness emphasized the functional, rounded beauty of her behind. She had large brown eyes and a sulky, full-lipped mouth and a tangle of dark brown hair. Dave had brought a tigress.

Then Laura beckoned to him and he went over to her table. As he sat down she said, "I'm here to keep you out of the clutches of females like that one you were ogling. It's the least I can do for your absent and mistreated wife."

Steve smiled. "All woman, isn't she? I had no idea Dave was that virile."

Morton smiled. Laura said, "I had no idea *you* were. Heavens, the way you were *leering* at her . . ."

"My party look," Steve explained. "She probably considers me a licentious old man."

Laura raised his eyebrows. "Old . . . ?"

Morton said, "Not her, not Pat Cullum. The adolescents can't afford her."

"An actress?" Steve asked.

"She likes to think she is," Morton answered.

It was almost the same phrase he had used about his friend, the night he had phoned Steve. Steve looked at him searchingly now.

Morton met his gaze and said, "I use that expression too much. I suppose it's because of envy. I really only know the girl by hearsay."

Laura stared at her admiringly and murmured, "I often wonder how far I could have gone with a larger cup size."

Steve laughed and rose. "Why don't we dance, Laura, and dream of better days?"

She sighed. "What a romantic approach! Let's go, gallant."

They had danced together before and discovered they were well suited, and they enjoyed it now. The music was continuous, fed to the yard through speakers from a record player in the house.

They had danced without speaking for perhaps three minutes when Laura said, "I think the young actors coming up are more serious than they used to be."

"Morton, do you mean?"

"For one. And Tom Leslie for another. They're more thoughtful, more analytical about their profession."

"And less colorful," Steve added. "Though they're certainly easier to work with, except for the sweat-shirt gang."

"If we ever come into the age of reason in this business," Laura asked, "what's going to happen to men like Harry Bergdahl?"

"In any age, men like Harry are going to survive, Laura. They're adaptable. Harry's not stupid."

"No. That's right." She sighed. "I keep thinking of him as a murderer. But he wouldn't be that stupid, would he?"

Steve didn't answer. Dave Sidney went by, dancing with Pat Cullum, and the girl didn't look drunk now, flawlessly following the intricate pattern of Dave's steps.

"I wish I were twenty-four," Steve said.

Laura chuckled. "I'd settle for thirty-four. But you're that now, aren't you?"

"Thirty-seven," Steve answered, "but tonight I mean to howl."

"Not I," Laura said. "A funeral and an orgy in the same day are too much for me. I've made my token appearance at both shows and I'm ready for my hot Ovaltine." She grimaced. "I need all my strength for my new career."

She left soon after that and Steve went to the bar again. Harry was there, talking with the black-haired Jean. Though the night was cool, Harry's forehead and neck were wet with perspiration and his tongue was thick.

He put a heavy hand on Steve's shoulder. "Met Jean yet, kid?"

Steve nodded. "Dave introduced us. She's too young for us, Harry."

Bergdahl said heavily, "She's two years younger than my wife. Speak for yourself, sissy." He laughed, and said to the girl, "I leave you in safe hands." He swaggered away.

Jean exhaled audibly. "What do I say? Not what I'm thinking; or I go back to typing for a living."

"Smile and look tolerant," Steve advised her. "Self-discipline, that's the virtue. Control, control, control . . ."

"Isn't there," she asked, "some *vertical* way to get ahead in this business?"

"There are a number of ways," Steve said. "Some of them vertical. I think the best way is to be stubborn and disciplined." He asked the bartender for a Scotch and water.

"Wouldn't talent help?" Jean asked, as he turned back to her.

"Always. But there's damned little of it around. You stick with that Morton boy. He's going up."

"I don't want to ride anybody," she said firmly, "and I want to decide who rides me. If you'll pardon the vulgarism, which I'm sure you will. In New York, talent was very important. I should have stayed there."

"And why didn't you?"

"Because everything is moving out here."

"Including Mitchell Morton?"

She shook her head. "Mitch is about the best friend I have. But we don't ring any bells in each other. I wish we did. He's a damned saint."

Then Dave was coming over with his tigress, and Steve was introduced. And as the girl moved closer, to face the bar, Steve smelled the fragrance he couldn't forget, the perfume he had first smelled in Hart Jameson's apartment.

He said a little shakily, "I watched you dance with Dave. You're very good."

"Thank you." She smiled at him and pushed her hair back. "I was watching you, too. You're very good yourself."

Jean said coolly, "Dance with me, Dave. Your friend is occupied."

Dave grinned and took the black-haired girl away.

"She hates me," Pat Cullum said wonderingly. "I hardly know her and she hates me."

Steve said lightly, "I imagine a lot of women do. And I don't suppose it bothers you much, does it?"

She laughed. "Not at all. What are you drinking?"

"Scotch and water. Why?"

"I always drink what the man I'm with drinks. It's a whim of mine."

"You're only with me momentarily," Steve pointed out. "You can get mighty sick mixing drinks, you know."

"I know," she said amiably. "But how do you know I'm only with you momentarily? You're not here with anyone else. I noticed."

He grinned at her. "Now, we don't want to annoy Dave. Not while he and I are working together."

She reached for her drink. "Don't you worry about Dave. He's dancing with his sad and secret love this second, and he's had enough whiskey to tell her about it."

Steve danced with her and they danced well, and the challenge of her body almost made him forget the significance of her perfume.

The crowd noise grew and the alcohol poured and someone fell into the pool. A fight started but was quickly broken up. A little after one o'clock Dotty asked Steve if he would help to encourage the guests to eat.

"Harry's disappeared somewhere," she explained. "We've just got to get some food and coffee into these drunks."

By two o'clock they had managed to inveigle some coffee into the drunker of the drunken and food into all the others. Steve's own fine edge had worn off by this time. He sat quietly with the script girl near the pool, nursing a big mug of coffee and scanning the crowd for Pat Cullum.

She was not in sight. Nor was Dave Sidney. Harry and a number of other men had come from the garage crap game. Practically all the people Steve knew were visible except for Dave and Pat. Perhaps it was just as well. Adultery had never been one of his comfortable vices.

He said good night to the Bergdahls and Dotty thanked him for helping to subdue the revelers, explaining loudly enough for most of the guests to hear that "Harry is *never* any good at parties."

He went around to the parking area, and it looked as though there was someone in his car.

There was. Pat Cullum looked up, rubbed her eyes, yawned and said, "It's about time!"

"Where's Dave?" Steve asked.

"He passed out. He's sleeping here tonight."

Steve got behind the wheel. "And with a yardful of handsome young men to choose from, you picked me. Why?"

"Call it a simple case of lust," she said. "Let's go."

chapter nine

She was active and demanding. She was artful and violent; her teeth brought blood from the lobe of his ear. Finally she was quiescent.

Her apartment was on the second floor of a fairly new building on a slope north of Hollywood. She had quite a view from her southern windows. It was not a cheap apartment.

On the broad, low bed, Steve stretched, spent and faintly uncomfortable. She was a girl who might soon demand more, and he was sure he could not supply the demand.

He said, "That's an unusual perfume you use."

"It ought to be, at fifty dollars a dram."

"Fifty dollars a dram . . . ! That's four hundred dollars an ounce."

"I guess. A man named Dostel makes it. He claims that each fragrance is tailored for only one person. But I'll bet he sells the same odor to women in other towns. This particular number is Dostel Number 263 if you're thinking of buying me some."

"At four hundred dollars an ounce? I'd have to give up smoking. Tell me, do you buy it for yourself?"

Her laugh was low and mocking. She asked, "Do you like peanut butter sandwiches?"

"I don't think so. Why?"

"I want one," she answered. "And a big glass of milk. Shall I bring you a drink?"

"No. But maybe the milk . . . Wait, I'll go with you."

They went to the kitchen, naked as sparrows, and she turned on the bright overhead light and pointed to a chair in the breakfast area. "You sit, I'll serve."

In her full, bronzed body there was no hint of sag. In her friendly, natural behavior there was no hint of shame.

She was reaching to open one of the cupboard doors when Steve said, "You were with Hart Jameson Wednesday night, weren't you? Why didn't you go to the police?"

She paused, her body tense, and turned to stare at him. "Are you crazy? I had a date Wednesday night. Why did you say that?"

"I smelled your perfume in his apartment when I went to see him. I know it was yours."

She continued to stare. "Is that why you came here, why you came up, to question me about Hart Jameson?"

Steve shook his head.

"You lie," she said hoarsely. "You've—spoiled *everything.*"

He raised a hand. "Be sensible, listen to . . ."

"Listen, hell! Get out! Do you think I brought you here because you were a director or because you had money or because I was drunk? I wanted *you,* just as you are, just for tonight. Now, *get out!*"

Steve said quietly, "Please, will you listen to . . ."

She reached up and got a pitcher and she lifted it high. "I swear I'll kill you if you're not out of here in two minutes."

Her voice was loud enough to arouse the neighbors. It was that threat as much as the pitcher that sent Steve to the bedroom without further argument.

He dressed hurriedly. He was out in the cold night three minutes later.

There were only two cars in sight. One was his Bentley, in front of the apartment. The other, a green Pontiac half a block away on the other side of the street, was either Tomkevic's car or a duplicate.

Steve got into his car and started the engine. He drove almost to the Pontiac before switching on his headlights. And then he put them on the high beam.

Behind the windshield of the Pontiac the blank face of Tomkevic blinked in the sudden glare.

Had he followed Steve here or the girl? The car hadn't been there when they'd arrived. The detective had another item for his dossier. And a lever? A bit of blackmail he could use to pry some honest answers out of Steve?

No. He hadn't been up there very long. If he had stayed all night, Tomkevic would have had his lever.

It seemed to Steve the smell of perfume still lingered in the car. He drove slowly, watching to see if the green Pontiac would follow. There was a pressure in his chest again and a bad taste in his mouth.

Casual, he told himself, *think of it as that. A half-drunken romp in the hay with a girl who was begging for it. Casual . . .* Would he consider it casual if Marcia had been the guilty one?

The car swerved and the driver of the car flanking him sounded his horn angrily. Perspiration broke out on Steve's neck and forehead, and nausea expanded in his stomach.

That miserable, ubiquitous, tenacious Tomkevic. He might not be building a case solid enough to stand up in court, but he was probably building a case that would delay the payment of the insurance money to Harry.

Steve sucked deeply of the cold night air. He thought of Pat Cullum, naked in her bright kitchen, angrily eating a peanut butter sandwich, and he laughed to himself. But the nausea remained.

An incident, a casual nothing, a meaningless moment; how could any evil be read into that? He had been a tame domestic animal for a number of years. Tonight he had been a willing victim of circumstance. It had been a frustrating six months just past, and he had desperately needed the cathartic effect of this ridiculous night.

Adjusted now? he asked himself. A small lie, a trivial succumbing to blackmail, a momentary infidelity. Nothing to fret about, really. Nothing but the nausea.

He was in Beverly Hills, where the lots were wide and the houses set well back. He pulled to the curb and left the car and found some bushes and was sick.

He drove home carefully after that, alert for prowl cars and the green Pontiac. The clock on his instrument board showed exactly four o'clock when he left the car on the drive in front of the garage.

He slept without dreams and woke to a hot Sunday afternoon and a hangover. When he came into the living room, Mrs. Burke told him that Dave Sidney had phoned and left a number.

The number was Harry's and Steve dialed it.

Dave answered the phone. "I've been thinking of that bit with the torch singer, Steve. Don't you think Jean D'Arcy could handle that well?"

Steve smiled to himself. "Do you? Is this a form of non-family nepotism? Sweet on her, aren't you?"

"So, maybe. But you know I wouldn't risk spoiling the picture for anybody or anything. She's very good and she'll work at minimum."

"She can read for it," Steve said. "I've been thinking of that girl in the diving-board scene at the lake. And who would I be thinking of for that?"

"Pat Cullum. She's got the figure."

Steve asked, "But can she swim?"

"Swim?" Dave chuckled. "Like a mink." A pause. "I hope she got home all right last night."

"I'm sure she did. How are you and your drunken uncle feeling today?"

"Fit and happy. Look, why don't you come over for dinner, as long as Marcia is out of town?"

"I'd be bad company. At the moment I'm only looking for a hole to crawl into." He sighed. "We're taking care of our friends, aren't we?"

"The mark of a Harry Bergdahl picture," Dave said lightly. "Would it be all right if I came over later in the day? I'd like to talk with you."

"I guess. I should be human in a few hours. I'll be here."

He drank some tomato juice and ate some heavily buttered toast. He took the percolator of coffee and the Sunday papers out to the sundeck.

The death of Hart Jameson as news had retreated to one of the inner pages in the local news section. But as a feature story in the drama-arts section of the *Times,* it received the full lachrymose treatment.

There was a picture of Hart at the age of seven, riding a rented pony and staring belligerently into the camera. There were some stills from *Sunburst Alley* and a bleak shot of an Oklahoma orphanage where he had spent a few of the formative years.

Finally, on one of the inner pages where the text had carried over, there was one more picture of Hart. He was standing with his arm around the jet-haired Jean D'Arcy. The caption asked: *Romance?*

The text informed the reader that the lovely television star, Jean D'Arcy, had been a frequent companion of Hart's in the East. It was rumored that she had followed him out here after a quarrel had sent him west.

Steve poured himself another cup of coffee. Maybe they wouldn't get Miss D'Arcy at minimum after today's publicity. Or maybe the inclusion of her name in the piece was the work of Harry's cunning hand?

No. Finding a spot for Jean had been Dave's idea, not Harry's. And it hadn't even been suggested until today.

The sun soaked him, baking out the alcohol. He ate two cold-beef sandwiches and drank some milk and spent an hour in the pool. He felt almost human when Dave Sidney arrived.

Dave didn't come alone. Jean D'Arcy was with him, and they had brought their swimming clothes.

"So it shouldn't be a total loss," Dave explained. "Jean wanted to read for that two-bit side, but I thought you might not be in a mood for that."

"I'm not," Steve answered. "Has Harry okayed it?"

Dave smiled. "He told me to tell you he has complete faith in your casting judgment."

"That was generous of him," Steve said dryly. He looked at Dave steadily. "Yesterday, you told him Marcia was out of town. How did you know that?"

Dave frowned. "Laura told me when I phoned her to see if she had a ride to the party. Why did you ask that, Steve?"

Steve shrugged.

Dave colored. "I guess we—caught you in a bad mood, didn't we?"

Steve sighed. "You did, and I apologize." He put a hand on Dave's shoulder. "Come on, let's get into that pool."

Jean D'Arcy's swim suit was an unrelieved white, trim and scanty. And though she lacked the extraordinary mammary and posterior development of Pat Cullum, Jean wore the suit to advantage.

Steve sat with a cigarette on the sunny side of the pool and watched Dave and the girl dive and swim. They were a well-matched couple, intelligent, personable and young. And innocent? The girl had been a companion of Hart Jameson's, and Dave was a much more complicated person than Steve had first assumed.

Jean came out of the water near where Steve sat and asked, "Would you light me a cigarette? My hands are wet."

Steve lighted her one and handed her a towel before giving her the cigarette. He said casually, "I see you had some publicity in today's *Times.*"

She nodded. "Though it was all hogwash about my romance with Hart Jameson." She puffed deeply and looked candidly at Steve. "What happened to your ear?"

He reached a hand up in sudden remembrance. "I must have scraped it, diving. Is it bleeding?"

"The lobe is discolored. It looks as though somebody bit it."

Steve stared at her unblinkingly, and she met his gaze. Finally, he said with a smile, "I guess you heard Dave tell me Harry had complete faith in my casting judgment?"

She smiled in return. "I heard. Believe me, I had no idea my remark had any significance."

"It didn't," he said. "Was that story about you and Jameson in the paper a *complete* lie?"

"Almost. I didn't follow him out here; that's absurd. I did go to a few places with him in New York, but that was because we were both studying at the Studio. We rarely went anywhere alone and we always went Dutch."

"Did you meet Mitchell Morton through him?"

"No. Mitch was at the Studio, too. I met him there." She smiled doubtfully. "Am I being interviewed or investigated?"

"Only making conversation," Steve answered. "One more question while Dave's out of earshot—do you like him?"

She made a face. "I like him, Uncle Steve. Do you like him?"

Steve nodded, and said with the false gravity, "I was thinking of Pat Cullum for that bit you want to read for."

"It's your picture," she said, "yours to ruin with bad minor casting." She put her cigarette out in an ash tray, turned abruptly and dived into the pool.

The young ones, he thought, *the good young ones.* They were coming out here in swarms from New York, and what was there for them to do? Eastern television, which had started with such invigorating promise for the early hour-long dramas, was retrogressing to the 1912 cinema level. There was always a place for the bad actors, but what could the good ones do?

Dave came out of the water and padded over to pick up a towel. As he wiped the back of his neck, he asked, "Isn't she nice? Jean, I mean?"

"Very nice. What do you know about Mitchell Morton, Dave?"

Dave shrugged. "He's a good actor. He's hungry. But he's young enough so that doesn't matter."

"He's ambitious, too, isn't he? He'd go to some extremes, I would bet, to get his face in front of the public."

Dave frowned. "I guess. Steve, how far would you go to protect a picture you thought a lot of?"

Steve smiled and didn't answer.

Dave asked, "How about that—bit?"

"She can have it."

Dave sat down. "Thanks. What happened to your ear?"

"The housekeeper bit it last night," Steve explained carefully, "repelling my advances."

For seconds, they said nothing as they watched Jean swim the length of the pool and back. *The young ones,* Steve thought again, *the good young ones, the firm young ones, the ear-biters and the black-mailers.* At thirty-seven, he decided, the firm young ones looked so damned interesting. . . .

At seven it turned too cool to swim, and they went into the house to raid the refrigerator. After that they sat in the playroom, watching the image on the monster, this particular image being an hour-long comedy from New York.

The pair made caustic comments from time to time, but Steve

rested, too well aware of the medium's limits to expect the perfection only the young demanded.

At ten-thirty Dave and Jean left, and the house seemed lonely. Steve went out to the front yard. It was a clear, cold night, and he could see the lights flashing along Sunset Boulevard.

It was then he remembered he had promised Marcia they would go up together today. She had gone to the camp alone, but he wondered if she had expected him to drive up to join her.

A car turned up from the highway below, and from a driveway a quarter of the way up the hill another car turned down, its headlights illuminating the car coming up.

It was the Buick, it was Marcia. He went over to the driveway to wait for her.

She had no greeting for him. Her face was grim, she avoided his eyes. He followed her from the garage to the kitchen, and she refused to look at him or answer his questions.

She was opening the refrigerator door when he went into his study. He sat there, smoking and staring at nothing, his thoughts black, his temper boiling. Who in hell did she think she was?

He heard her walking around in the kitchen and later he heard water running in the bathroom. But it was the guest bathroom. He heard a door close and there was silence.

In a few minutes he rose and went to their bedroom. She was not there. A nightgown and robe and pair of slippers were missing from her closet.

He went to the guest room. The door was closed. He opened it and turned on the bright overhead light. She was lying with her back to the doorway.

He said, "Marcia, I've a right to know why you're acting like this."

"You promised to come up," she said. "And I told the kids you had promised. And they waited for you. They waited and waited and waited."

"I'm very sorry about that. I went to a party at Bergdahl's last night and I didn't get home until late. I didn't wake up until this afternoon."

"Explain that to the children. Write them a letter and explain that, if you think you can."

He took a deep breath. "And how long do you intend to sleep in here?"

"Forever, probably."

With fine, unconscious hypocrisy, he said, "It's been over two weeks, you might remember. And I'm not made of stone."

She said quietly and coldly, "It's been over two weeks for me. I'm not sure it has for you."

His stomach churned and his hands trembled. He looked at her back doubtfully. "God damn it," he said, "turn around!"

She turned over to glare at him.

He asked, "Just exactly what did you mean by that last crack?"

Her voice was even and calm and cold. "You've been going downhill morally so fast lately it wouldn't surprise me to learn you had tried *anything.* And one of Harry Bergdahl's parties would be a logical place to start off on an adultery kick."

"You don't mean that."

"I mean that."

He said hoarsely, "I'm thinking of the kids. That's all that's keeping me home tonight."

She turned over again. She said wearily, "Turn out the light and get out of here. Don't threaten me—not until you're ready to do it in court."

The fever of unrighteous indignation burned in him, and he said harshly, "I'll be glad to go into court any time you're ready."

"I'm ready now," she said. "Good night."

He stared at her familiar back, and the sickness welled in him again and his knees trembled. A life without Marcia would be worse than death. A life without Marcia and the kids would be . . .

He couldn't imagine it. He said softly, "I hope you'll be more reasonable tomorrow." He turned out the light and closed the door gently.

chapter ten

He sat for an hour in his unlighted study, thinking back on it all from Laura's first bit of gossip. That had been Wednesday, as they drove home from Santa Barbara.

And after he had gone to see Jameson that same evening, a few new facts had been revealed to him. He could see no pattern in them but if he gave them to Tomkevic, perhaps the detective could.

What then was preventing him from phoning Tomkevic? The unadmitted fear that Bergdahl was the murderer? If Harry wasn't, the insurance money was safe. If Harry was, did he want him revealed?

Harry's own nephew wanted to *know;* he wasn't afraid of the truths. But Harry's own nephew wasn't thirty-seven years old and he wasn't carrying the financial load Steve was. He could afford his militant morality.

He thought back on John Abbot's phrase: "the sanctity of solvency." John could afford morality, too. He had been active in a seller's market before the days of confiscatory taxation.

Your job is making pictures, Steven Leander, not moral judgments. That would be the pragmatic view. If he had sinned, they had been sins of omission. Overlooking, of course, one small sin of commission on Pat Cullum's wide, low bed.

Tomkevic was not concerned with sin; he was concerned with crime. Though the crime that concerned him now was also a sin, the sin of murder.

I am innocent of murder. So far as I know there has been no murder.

That was the thought that he took to bed with him—so far as he knew, there had been no murder. It helped to bolster the righteousness of his anger over the deportment of his unreasonable wife.

It didn't help him to sleep. But there were pills for that, and he took them after the first restless hour, falling asleep to dream of his personal Javert, the brush-haired, brown-eyed, soft-voiced Tomkevic.

Marcia didn't join him at breakfast. Mrs. Burke served him with a minimum of dialogue, and Steve wondered if she had overheard last night's quarrel. He had finished eating by the time Dave came, and they left immediately to pick up Laura.

Steve had always managed to divorce his personal troubles from his professional problems. Today he didn't achieve this. He was short-tempered and sarcastic. He had a hopelessly disrupted cast halfway through the morning's shooting.

He knew he was dealing with temperamental people and he knew he was handling them badly. But some perversity in him persisted. His temper grew shorter and his tongue sharper.

They stopped for a break at ten-thirty, and Laura came over to tell him quietly, "You'll have a mutiny on your hands any minute. What's wrong, Steve?"

"Everything," he said curtly. "You know you're not delivering, don't you?"

She flushed. "No, I didn't. But I'll take your word for it." Her voice was bitter. "Possibly the role is too big for me."

He almost said *possibly* but stopped in time. He said, "It seems to be too much for you this morning. It wasn't Friday."

She started to say something, paused, and turned away. He watched her walk over to the table where Dave sat and take a seat next to him. Dave glanced guiltily at Steve before he and Laura started to talk.

Tom Leslie came over to ask genially, "Am I really that lousy, Steve, or are you having a bad morning?"

Steve said evenly, "You weren't lousy. You were just barely—adequate, to use the critics' cliché. I expect something better than that."

Leslie continued to smile. "I think we're all trying to give you something better than that." He paused. "We—could stand a little patience."

Steve stared at him for seconds. "Mr. Leslie, you haven't been in it long enough to learn the director is *never* argued with."

Leslie's smile turned cold. "I've learned that, Mr. Leander. I'll remember it from now on."

Steve watched him walk over to join Laura and Dave at the table. And he knew this would be a lost day. And he knew it was his fault. Or Marcia's? Or Bergdahl's? Or Tomkevic's?

Laura rode home with Tom Leslie. Dave came back with Steve. Dave was unusually quiet.

After about twenty minutes of silent driving, Steve said, "Okay, speak up. Who's leading the mutiny?"

Dave smiled weakly. "Boy, you are edgy today. Were they that bad?"

"Probably not. But they were so great Friday, and I suppose my own—state of mind magnified the letdown."

"Are you still thinking about Hart Jameson?"

Steve nodded without taking his eyes from the road. "Aren't you?"

"Mmmm-hmmm. But it looks more like an accident every day."

"Did you learn anything, Dave, that the police don't know?"

Dave paused before saying too casually, "Nothing important."

"Anything I should know?"

"Nothing," Dave said definitely. "Can't we talk about something else?"

"All right. Let's talk about the picture. Are we going to be able to finish it?"

"I don't know. I don't see why not. Uncle Harry is very good at raising money and he has over half of it."

There was a long and uncomfortable silence. Finally Dave said, "Ever since Jameson's death you've been—different. It's none of my business, but is it because of the quarrel with Marcia?"

"Partly, I suppose," Steve admitted. "Though I was never an easy man to get along with while working. I—expect too much from people."

"And too much from yourself, maybe? And at the moment, you might be hating yourself?"

Steve said slowly, "That could be. Since I lied to the police about why I went to see Jameson, I've been—unhappy."

"That's easily corrected, Steve. Go to them and tell them you lied. Tell them the real reason you went to see Jameson."

"That would involve your uncle. Do you want me to do that?"

"No."

"So . . . ?"

Dave said earnestly, "*I* wouldn't want my uncle involved, but do you always do what others want you to do? I'd rather see Uncle Harry involved than see you do a bad job on the picture."

Steve said gently, "Don't worry, I'll come to terms with myself. We had a good day Friday, and there'll be more of them."

There had been, he reflected, a funeral and a party since Friday, and both had added to his general despondency. There might be more revelations in store, though he hadn't actively sought any.

Would it help, he wondered, if he could prove to himself that Harry wasn't a murderer? And how could he prove it to himself? Perhaps by co-operating with Tomkevic or the police, by telling them all he knew that they didn't.

Though they had a gardener three times a week, Marcia was out in front feeding the roses when Steve drove up. Marcia liked to work when she was emotionally disturbed.

She smiled at Dave and ignored Steve. She didn't speak to either of them.

Dave said quietly, "I'll see you tomorrow." He went directly to his car.

Steve started to walk over toward Marcia and then decided against it. He went into the house through the garage.

In his study he looked up Dostel in the western phone book. There were four in his end of town, and one of them was Dostel Laboratories, Inc. This had the same address as a Paul Dostel. He dialed the residence number.

A pleasant voice answered, "Dostel Laboratories, Paul Dostel speaking," and Steve asked, "Are you the Dostel who makes those individualized perfumes?"

"Yes."

"My name is Leander. Would it be possible for me to see you this evening?"

"Steven Leander, the director?"

"That's right."

"I'll be here all evening, Mr. Leander."

Steve thanked him and hung up. If he should learn that Jameson had bought the perfume Pat Cullum used, it would seem to indicate she had been the girl in Hart's apartment.

And if she was? What did he do with the knowledge? Take it to the police? Or Tomkevic?

He could decide that when he learned more. He didn't mix a drink this evening. He went directly in for his shower.

Dinner was quiet. Marcia spoke when spoken to, maintaining a rigid formality. He stopped speaking to her after the first few minutes.

He was on his coffee when Bergdahl phoned.

"A little birdie told me something," Harry said coyly. "He told me you had trouble today on the set."

"A little birdie named Dave?" Steve asked.

"Not him. I'm his dumb uncle, remember? To be frank, Tom Leslie phoned me."

"I had to put him in his place, that's true," Steve said.

"His place . . . ?" A pause. "What's his place?"

"Subordinate to the director. I'm sure we all agree on that. At least he did."

A sigh. "Well, when I see the rushes, I'll know if the day was wasted." Another pause. "Is something bothering you, Steve?"

"A number of things, all personal. Don't worry about me, Harry. I'm coming out of it."

"Good. You got any problems you need help on, old Harry's here every minute, right?"

"Right. Thanks for calling."

He hung up, annoyed. Leslie had gone over his head. He had figured the man for more of a trouper than that.

When he went back to the table to finish his coffee, Marcia looked at him inquiringly but said nothing.

"Bergdahl," Steve said. "I was owly today and Tom Leslie complained to him about it."

Marcia nodded, saying nothing.

Steve sat down and looked at her. "We're not children. This is unnatural behavior for us. Shall I tell you why I went to see Hart Jameson that night?"

"It's not important any more," she answered.

"Not important . . . ? Why not? If you love me, it's important."

"I used to love you and admire you," she said. "I think I need to do both—or neither."

He kept his temper from his voice. "That's—soap opera. You're too intelligent to talk that way."

"It's the way I feel, Steve."

"All right. I'm sorry about Sunday. If you had stayed home Friday, we both would have gone up to camp Sunday. That was the way we planned it."

She said nothing.

"I haven't the best disposition in the world," he went on, "but you've known that for a long time. Why is this last flare-up any more important than the others?"

"I've learned to live with your disposition," she said, "and your childish insecurity. Because you were honest and dedicated, I could take a lot of nonsense. I can't live with dishonesty."

"That's what I'm trying to correct now, a temporary dishonesty. And you told me it wasn't important any more."

"Let's talk about it later," she said wearily.

"I'd like to talk about it now. You're failing me, Marcia. I need your moral support *now.*"

Her smile was cynical. *"I'm* failing *you?* Even if it were true, it would be the first time, wouldn't it?"

Anger grew in him but he maintained a calm voice. "No. You have the impossible code of a person who *never* had to worry about money. I think it's fair to say you have never tried to understand the problems of people who weren't that lucky."

"I understand your problems," she argued. "It's your behavior that I can't understand. I don't want to talk about it, Steve."

Harsh words came to his tongue but he held them back. "All right, Judge," he said smilingly. "Yes, Your Honor." He stood up. "I have to see a man this evening. I won't be late."

She nodded and said nothing.

Damn her, damn her, damn her . . . And all her smug and gilt-edged friends. There wasn't a damned one of them who had the faintest idea of what was going on in the working world.

As he drove over to the address of Paul Dostel, Steve wondered why he had suddenly decided to inquire into the death of Hart Jameson. And the guilty thought came that perhaps it was because of today's wasted film. The death of Hart Jameson had finally begun to interfere with the successful creation of a motion picture. *His* picture.

Well, there were a number of reasons for morality, not all of them admirable.

Paul Dostel looked like a skinny Yul Brynner, a tall, thin, bright-eyed man with a head as hairless as a cue ball.

His apartment was above and behind the one-story brick laboratory that fronted on the street. It was an elegant apartment, and Mr. Dostel wore a rather ornate lounging robe and alligator slippers.

After Steve was seated in the living room, Dostel said, "I imagine you're here to see about a fragrance, and I can hope it's for your wife." He sighed. "So few of my clients order for their wives."

"Most of your clients are men?"

"About two-thirds. You're married to Marcia Bishop, aren't you, Mr. Leander?"

Steve nodded. "Did you look that up after I phoned?"

Dostel shook his head. "I keep myself informed as well as possible about the histories of our more socially prominent women. Sometimes, you see, an odor that brings back a pleasant memory is all my client is seeking. This is a complicated business, dealing in intangibles, and the more I know about my clients' backgrounds, the more success I'm likely to have."

Steve smiled politely. "It sounds like a fascinating business. However, I'm not here to buy. I'm here for information."

"Oh . . . ?"

The single exclamation had been meant to show surprise. Paul Dostel had voiced it badly, and there had been no surprise on his face.

"Yes," Steve said. "I'd like to know who your customer, or client, is for Number 176."

Now there was surprise on the face of Paul Dostel. He asked doubtfully, "One seventy-six . . . ?" before he recovered his composure.

Steve smiled. "Did I say 176? I meant 263."

A silence while Dostel stared at him. Finally he said, "I never reveal the names of my clients. I think you can understand why. I explained it a few moments ago."

"I'm not looking for scandal," Steve said. "I'm looking for information that might uncover a murderer."

Dostel frowned. "A murderer . . . ? Who has been murdered, Mr. Leander?"

"It's possible Hart Jameson was murdered."

"And one of my perfumes is involved, somehow?"

Steve nodded.

Dostel continued to frown. "Then why haven't the police contacted me? You're not working for the police, are you?"

"Not officially," Steve said. He stood up. "Well, I suppose you're right. This is their business, not mine. I'll tell them about the perfume." He half turned toward the door.

"One moment, Mr. Leander," Dostel said thoughtfully.

Steve waited.

Dostel said slowly, "I can't afford to court any unpleasant publicity. Would you mind telling me where you learned about my fragrance 263?"

"I'd mind," Steve answered shortly. "I'm not looking for scandal and I certainly don't intend to spread it."

Dostel took a deep breath. "You realize, I hope, that you are forcing me to violate an important professional principle for the first time?"

"I'll take your word for it."

Dostel rose. "The information is downstairs in the office. I'll be right back."

Steve was almost sure the other man would come back with a fraudulent name. But if he did, that, too, would be a straw.

He came back with a small file card in his hand. He read aloud: "Edward Ambrose Brown, 730 South Plumer Street, Tucson, Arizona." He looked at Steve blandly. "Is that any help, Mr. Leander?"

Steve shook his head. "It has no meaning for me. But perhaps it will have for the police. Isn't there some other local customer that fragrance could have been sold to?"

Dostel shook his head. "One client to a fragrance, that's my guarantee. Of course, I have no way of knowing who Mr. Brown bought the perfume for."

"I thought you said you like to know the backgrounds of the people who use your perfume?"

"I did say that. And I do like to. But it's not always possible."

"I see. What is the price of that Number 263?"

"Fifty dollars a dram, four hundred dollars an ounce."

Steve thanked him and left. He was only about two blocks from the Hotel Beauchamp. He walked over.

And there, in a Tucson telephone book, he looked up Edward Ambrose Brown and found a man by the name of Edward A. Brown at 730 South Plumer. If Dostel was lying, it had been a careful lie.

He went back to his car and drove north. On a slope north of Hollywood, he parked in front of a fairly new apartment building and stared at the light in a secondfloor window.

He had left there hurriedly Sunday morning, and he wondered if Miss Pat Cullum was inclined to nurse a grudge. It seemed reasonable to guess she wouldn't relish his coming back with questions.

Well, he had gone this far . . . He got out of the car and went up to the second floor to ring her bell.

She was wearing a white knit dress tonight and her hair was up. She stared at him and said, "Migawd, you're not gutless, are you?"

He smiled. "I came with an apology, an offer and a question. Should I leave?"

She studied him. "Come in."

"If you'll promise not to throw any crockery."

"I promise. You can forget the apology. What kind of offer did you have in mind?" She held the door wide.

Steve came in. "A nothing, really. A very small bit in this picture we're making. It involves wearing a swimming suit and posing on a diving board. A few lines might be written in."

"I'll take it," she said. "Now, what was the question?"

"Do you know a man named Edward Ambrose Brown?"

She looked at him blankly. "So help me, I've never even heard the name. Am I supposed to know him?"

"Mr. Dostel told me half an hour ago that Edward Ambrose Brown is the only purchaser of Number 263."

"You can tell Mr. Dostel from me that he's a goddamned liar. And if you want to know where I was Wednesday night from nine o'clock until way past midnight, I can give you the names of three people who were with me."

"You don't need to do that," Steve said. "I'm not a detective."

"Even if you were," she said, "you wouldn't learn from me who gave me the perfume. But I can guarantee you it didn't come from Jameson."

"I didn't assume it did," Steve told her. "Well, perhaps the person who gave you the perfume is a friend of this Brown. That can be checked, I suppose."

She shrugged.

Steve said, "I don't want to crowd you, but do you think you're acting in your own best interest? There's a possibility Mr. Jameson was murdered. I'm sure you're not equipped to protect yourself against a murderer, Pat."

"Possibly not," she agreed. "But if I wanted protection, wouldn't the Police Department be the logical place to go for it?"

He nodded.

She smiled. "You wouldn't want me to go there, would you?"

"Why not?"

"I don't know why not. But knowing what you do about the perfume, why didn't you go to the police?"

He looked at her candidly. "Because I think you're innocent of murder or involvement in murder. And, thinking that, I certainly wouldn't want to involve you in an embarrassing investigation."

"I've been told that any kind of publicity is good publicity."

"Not today. However, I'm not your father, am I? And you're of age."

Her smile was mocking. "I'm of age. And I hope you're not my father. You know, Steve, I think you might be a nice guy if you could ever forget how important you are."

"Thank you," he said coolly. "I'll have somebody get in touch with you about that bit. Good night, Miss Cullum."

"Good night, Steve," she said lightly. "Drop in any time."

chapter eleven

A faint resentment flickered in him as he went down the steps to the street and over to his car. He climbed in behind the wheel and looked at the lighted street ahead. *Where next, Dick Tracy?*

A green Pontiac came up from behind and parked in front of his car. Steve waited.

Tomkevic got out on the street side and walked behind his car, heading for the apartment building.

Steve leaned over and called, "Mr. Tomkevic!"

The investigator turned, frowned and then walked toward the Bentley as Steve opened the door.

He stood there without getting in. "I'm not here to see you."

"I didn't think you were. Would you sit in the car for a few minutes?"

Tomkevic looked up at the lighted window and then stepped into the car. "Decided to turn honest, Leander?"

"A little. What interest do you have in Miss Cullum?"

"Frankly, only a suspicion because of your interest in her. You're still my key to this puzzle."

"This much I'll tell you about her," Steve said. "She wears the same perfume as the girl who was in Jameson's apartment the night he died. And the man who makes the perfume told me an hour ago each individual fragrance is sold to only one customer."

"Oh . . . ? What's the man's name?"

Steve told him and gave him a full account of his conversation with Dostel. And he told him about the Brown he'd found at the right address in the Tucson phone book.

Tomkevic took out a card and handed it to Steve. Then he wrote Brown's name and address in a notebook. "I can check that easily enough. He could be a friend of this Dostel, you know."

"I suppose it's more than possible. You're not going to tell Miss Cullum I gave you this information, are you?"

"No. I'll tell her I'm checking her because she was a friend of Hart Jameson's."

"Was she?"

"Yes. And young Sidney brought her to the party, didn't he? And he's a nephew of Harry Bergdahl's. Now, what excuse could I have for giving up on this case?"

Steve didn't answer.

Tomkevic asked, "Is that why you came home with the Cullum girl Saturday night, because you were trying to learn something?"

"Partly."

Tomkevic looked out at the street. Finally, "I was going to be a real son-of-a-bitch, Leander. I was going to tell your wife you brought that bomb up there home Saturday night."

"Why . . . ?"

"To stir up some action. Quite often truth comes out of turbulence."

"What made you think I hadn't told my wife I brought this—bomb home Saturday night?"

Tomkevic said dryly, "I'm a married man. I know I wouldn't have told *my* wife, not if she'd ever seen the girl."

"My wife has never seen Miss Cullum."

There was a silence, which Steve broke. "I've given you some help. Now give me this—if Jameson was murdered, who is your favorite suspect?"

"Until five minutes ago," Tomkevic said candidly, "you were."

"*I* was . . . ? I was at a movie with my wife. You knew that."

"How could I be sure? I have a long list of wives who lied to protect their husbands. And that's why I was going to—create this domestic turbulence."

There was another silence, and this time Tomkevic broke it. "Why are you getting interested in Jameson's death?"

"I'm trying to resolve a moral dilemma I found myself in."

"I figured you would, eventually. And there's a possibility you could learn things I couldn't. You already have. Do you want to work with me? I mean unofficially, informally, of course."

"And possibly cost poor Harry Bergdahl a quarter of a million dollars? And put myself out of work? Do you realize what you're asking?"

"I do. And you were well aware of all those potentials when you decided to investigate for yourself."

Steve pointed out, "I was looking for innocence. You're asking me to help establish guilt."

"I don't think you were looking for innocence. I think you were merely looking for information. To forestall a decision on your moral dilemma. But the decision would have to be made eventually if you learned what you didn't want to learn. Am I right?"

"I don't know. It all sounds very logical, but I can't seem to establish my motives as clearly as that."

Tomkevic smiled. "I'm heartened to find a man wrestling with a moral problem. It isn't a situation I've come upon recently."

Steve said lightly, "I'll give you a moral problem of your very own to ponder—you could be stopping production on a worth-while motion picture. And when was the last time you saw one of *those?*"

Tomkevic chuckled. "That's not a moral problem. That's an esthetic problem. And what would a dumb Polack like me know about esthetics? Carry on, Leander, keep in touch. I've got to run up and see that bomb before her date gets here."

"Who's her date? Someone I know?"

"A man named Mitchell Morton," Tomkevic answered. "Small damned world, isn't it?"

Small, damned, tight world. Revolving around a man named Harry Bergdahl. Steve started the engine and turned back toward Sunset. He drove over to Laura's.

In her flush days Laura had owned one of the most impressive estates in Beverly Hills. The apartment she lived in now was not cheap, but it was a number of plateaus below her former eminence.

She opened her door and said with surprise, "This is an unexpected pleasure."

Clichés for all occasions, Steve thought, and smiled. "I was going by, so I thought I'd stop in to apologize."

"Going by alone or is Marcia in the car?"

"Alone," Steve answered. "I was a beast today, wasn't I?"

"Come in," she said.

He came into a small living room crowded with massive furniture, undoubtedly remnants from her former home.

"Drink?" she asked.

He sat down on a carved walnut davenport upholstered in mohair. "No, thanks. Tom Leslie complained to Harry about my treatment of him."

Laura sighed and looked at the floor. "Tom's—young and temperamental."

Steve nodded. "And not completely trustworthy, I'm beginning to suspect. Are you going to Santa Barbara with him tomorrow, or shall I pick you up as usual?"

She stared at him blankly. "Tomorrow . . . ? I was notified that we weren't working tomorrow."

"When?"

"About an hour ago. Are we working?"

"Not if you were notified. Harry must have had a brainstorm. He's probably been trying to get me. May I use your phone?"

She inclined her head toward the dinette. "It's in there."

Harry answered the phone and Steve asked, "What's this I hear about not working tomorrow?"

"That's right. I've been trying to call you. I've had a chance to look over the film, and we don't need any more from up there. We can fake the rest."

"No, Harry."

"What's *that?*"

"We can't fake the rest. We can't fake anything. I've got this picture firmly in mind now, and we have to go up there for at least two more days."

"Oh . . . ? You got the picture in mind? You got the money, too?"

"No. Haven't you?"

A silence. Then, "Look, Steve, don't go off half-cocked. Don't say anything you'll be sorry for later."

"I'm trying not to. May I come over and see you now?"

"Not tonight, Steve. I've got an important engagement in twenty minutes and I'm leaving right now. We can talk it over tomorrow."

"When tomorrow? Could we make the date now?"

"Stevie, Stevie boy, what kind of talk is this—make the date? Do we have to be formal? Tomorrow. I'll call you or you call me, who-ever gets up first."

"All right, Harry. I'll see you tomorrow."

"Sure. And cool off, huh? Today's been a bad one for you."

Steve hung up and went back to the living room. "Cut-rate Harry is back in form," he said bitterly. "We are about to create a turkey."

Laura said soothingly, "Easy now, Steve. Harry's the man who understands money. That's the first concern in any business, you know, to show a profit."

"I'll match the profits on my five best pictures against the total of any *fifteen* of his. The intelligent way to make money is to make a good picture."

"Always, Steve?"

"It's the safest. It's the surest. Unless you're making Grade-Z quickies. Christ, why did I ever get tied up with that man?"

Laura said nothing, staring at the floor.

Steve said wearily, "Well, I'm going home. Relax tomorrow. If I have to, I'll settle for one more day in Santa Barbara. But if that happens, it will be a long day and you'll need all the energy you can store up."

She rose. "All right, Steve. And watch your temper."

He came over to kiss her forehead. "I'll try. Lady, you were sensational Friday. And you will be again."

He drove home. He sat for some minutes in the car after killing the engine. He thought of the three people he had visited tonight and of Tomkevic. But mostly he thought of Laura, who had come from the estate in Beverly Hills to that apartment.

Tomorrow he would be going up against Harry Bergdahl for the first time since they were allied. He would be fighting for what he considered a major decision and Harry undoubtedly considered minor. His position would seem unreasonable to Harry, the capricious arrogance of a pretentious man.

He went into the house and found Marcia reading in the living room. She looked up to say, "John Abbot phoned. He wants you to call him." She went back to her reading.

"Thank you," Steve said formally. He went into the study to phone.

Abbot said, "I hear there's a possibility of money trouble on your picture."

"It's possible, John. Harry doesn't confide in me too much about the financial end, but you're probably right. Where did you hear the rumor?"

Abbot chuckled. "From one of my stoolies."

"Marcia, maybe?"

"No. What made you ask that, Steve?"

"I don't know. We're having money troubles, John."

"Well, that's why I phoned. I've a few contacts left, you know, and I've been scouting around. I'm positive I can get you some money if the picture looks promising."

"Thanks, John. Of course, the money is really Harry's department."

"But if you had a source, it would be a weapon, wouldn't it?" A pause. "You could afford to stay honest."

"You *have* been talking to Marcia."

"This wasn't her idea."

"I see. Well, thank you very much. Even if we don't need it, the knowledge that it's available is a—weapon. How are you feeling, John?"

"Like an old man. But that's in character. Steve, I've heard some surprising rumors about you around town."

"Did you believe them?"

"Not completely. Are you all right?"

"Is anybody ever? I'm struggling. I'm not in the ministry, John."

Abbot chuckled again. "No, you certainly are not. You call me, now, if it's necessary, Steve."

"I'll call you even if it isn't," Steve answered. "As soon as this picture is finished, we'll go fishing again, like we used to."

"Sure."

"And thank you again," Steve said. "Thank you very much."

He went back to the living room. Marcia continued to read. He said, "Harry's starting to give me trouble."

She didn't lift her eyes from the book. "Is that supposed to be news?"

"I thought it might be of interest to you," he said stiffly. He went into the study and turned on the television set.

Garbage, garbage, garbage . . . This was the machine that had crippled his industry. And only because his own industry had built up a public hunger for garbage.

That was what Harry Bergdahl understood, garbage. God damn it, Harry didn't need him for that. But he had thought he needed him or he never would have hired him. Had something changed his mind?

He went to bed early but couldn't fall asleep. He thought about tomorrow and wondered about tonight, wondered if he would hear Marcia's step in the hall, hear her come into the room.

He lay quietly and anxiously, waiting for a reconciliation. He didn't fall asleep until long after he heard her go into the guest room.

chapter twelve

Dotty said, "Come in Steve. Harry's taking a shower. He'll be out in a few minutes."

Steve came into the low-beamed, provincial living room and sat on a davenport near the high-hearth fireplace.

"Drink?" Dotty asked.

"Never in the morning," he answered. He smiled at her. "Recovered from the party, have you?"

Her answering smile was vacant and superficial. She looked at him anxiously. "Are you and Harry fighting about something?"

"Not yet," Steve said mildly.

"Money," she said. "It's money, I'll bet. It's all he fights about. He's been a horrible bear, lately." She looked at Steve closely. "It is only money, isn't it? He's been so nasty and secretive."

"Is the honeymoon over, Dotty?"

"Honeymoon . . . ? In a motel, that's where we spent our honeymoon. He never wanted to get out of bed except to go to the bathroom. Why don't you answer my questions, Steve? Why are you covering up?"

Steve said firmly, "I'm not covering up anything. Harry thinks we've shot enough film in Santa Barbara, and I don't. So we're going to discuss it this morning."

"That isn't all. You had trouble with Tom Leslie, too. I heard about that. Tom's a troublemaker, Steve."

"All the young talents give us occasional trouble, Dotty. I'm not worried about Tom."

She leaned over to take a cigarette from a box on the coffee table. Under the loose V of her blouse, Steve could see her firm breasts. She was wearing no bra. He looked away as he fumbled for a match.

Again she leaned forward to get the light he held for her. He said softly, "Easy, sister, that's a loose blouse. And I'm not as old as you think."

"Old . . . ?" She blew smoke into his face. "You're a kid, compared to Harry. Does Pat Cullum think you're old?"

Steve looked at her blankly. "Who's Pat Cullum?"

"Huh!" she said. "Don't give me that innocent look. I've got ears."

"All right," he said, "then *you* tell *me* what's eating Harry."

She sat on the davenport near him. "I wish I knew. I wish to hell I knew." She stared at the fireplace. "Do you think it could be connected with Hart Jameson's death? And that insurance policy?"

"I suppose it could. But how?"

"That's what I don't want to think about," she said quietly. "And then that damned detective pestering him . . ."

Steve said gently, "Look, Dotty, we know Harry's no murderer. It's probably money that's bothering him."

"We don't know anything," she said. "We don't *really* know anything about anybody."

Steve glanced over quickly, startled by the despair in her voice. She looked lonely and frightened, staring at the high-hearth fireplace.

Then Harry was there in a toweling robe and straw slippers, his hair wet, his face unshaven. "Cuddling on the couch, you two, huh? A guy can't even take a shower any more."

Dotty stood up without smiling. Steve's smile was purely facial. Dotty said, "Steve thinks he's too old for me."

Harry looked at her without expression. "Business, honey. Run along."

She went out without another word. Harry came over to take the seat she'd vacated. "Well, Steve, speak your piece."

"It's simple enough. I need two more days up there."

"I want to show you the film, how we can cut it and fake the rest. You'll wait until I show you that, won't you?"

Steve said nothing, thinking.

Harry said, "Jesus, Laura was lousy yesterday."

"They were all bad, Harry."

"Not Leslie. Wait until you see the film. Leslie was all right."

"It's his scene," Steve pointed out. "He has to be better than all right in it. Are we running short of money, Harry?"

"We could, if that damned Polack keeps stalling things. Anyway, what's wrong with saving money on a picture? That's a sin?"

"At times. I might be able to get some money if we can show the investors the potential of a first-class picture." He paused, to drop the name with emphasis. "John Abbot phoned me last night."

Harry was silent, respectfully silent. "Abbot, huh? He's a friend of yours, isn't he?"

"Yes."

Harry frowned. "Jesus, I don't know. He'd want a bigger hunk of it than he's entitled to. He's all business, that Abbot."

"I don't think it would be his money."

Harry stared. "So then what does he want? A big commission for introducing us to the money?"

"Of course not," Steve said patiently. "He simply wants to help me. He's a friend."

Harry's laugh was short. "I got dozens of friends. Some of 'em have money. That don't mean they want to give me some of it. Stevie boy, there's got to be an angle. John Abbot's no dummy."

Steve was silent, realizing the impossibility of explaining to Harry about friends.

Harry said, "Maybe he wants to be like a silent partner? Maybe it would be that you got a bigger hunk of the picture, and you two would be silent partners?"

Steve laughed. "Harry, for heaven's sake, you're calling me a crook!"

Harry shook his head. "Nothing like that. No, Steve, I don't want to tangle with John Abbot."

Steve's hands trembled. He sat quietly, not looking at Harry. Finally he said, "Ask any of them what they think about yesterday's film. Ask Dave."

"That snot-nose? Since when is a writer consulted? Why should I ask anybody? Am I a greenhorn, am I new to the business?"

Steve said slowly, "Maybe to this kind of picture you're new, Harry."

In the silence, Steve thought he could hear his heart pound.

After a few seconds, Bergdahl asked quietly, "Make that clearer. What kind of crack was that?"

Steve forced himself to look at Harry fully. "Don't you agree that this picture is more—serious than most of those you've produced? You were known for your series pictures, Harry."

Were known? I'm still known. Would you like to take a look at their grosses?"

"Let's not quibble, Harry. I'm sure both of us can quote some impressive figures. One question though—why did you want me? I didn't come to you, remember."

"You're a director. I needed a director. You're a good director and you weren't working."

"And as a good director, I'm asking for two more days in Santa Barbara. I'm not asking for the moon, you know."

"As a director," Harry said implacably, "you're entitled to ask. As the producer, I got a right to decide whether I let you. That's right, isn't it?"

"Technically, yes. But we discussed the possibility of friction before I signed. And you promised me a free hand with this picture."

Harry started to answer but was interrupted by a voice behind him. The voice was Dave Sidney's and it was indignant. "That's right, Uncle Harry. And you promised me, too, that Steve would have a free hand."

Startled, Harry turned to face his nephew. "Where'd you come from? Who invited you into this?"

Dave said stubbornly, "You promised before I signed. It's my script you want to ruin. I'll take it to the Guild."

Harry looked at Steve and shook his head. "He'll take it to the Guild. He's threatening me." He looked again at Dave. "What will you take?"

"Your promise. I sold you the script with the agreement that Steve was not to be interfered with."

Harry smiled contemptuously. "I promised? In writing?"

"No," Dave said evenly, "not in writing. But before a witness." He looked over at Dotty, standing in the doorway to the dining room.

Harry glanced coldly between his nephew and his wife. "What is this? What's going on here?"

Dotty said, "That's right, Harry, you promised Dave. I was there when you promised."

Bergdahl's face was grim and ugly. "Get out of here, both of you. I'm discussing business. Go!"

"Come on, Dave," Dotty said softly.

But Dave stood rigidly, glaring at his uncle. "I warn you, Uncle Harry, I've got a case."

"One more word out of you," Bergdahl said harshly, "and you'll wind up driving a bakery truck. Go, right now!"

Dave turned and walked out toward the dining room. Harry

turned around again, breathing heavily. "Crazy," he said. "They're both crazy. He must have been in the kitchen all the time."

Steve rose. "I guess we've nothing to discuss, Harry. I don't know what's happened to you."

"Sit down, God damn it!" Bergdahl said hoarsely. "You, too?"

Steve asked quietly, "Has something happened, Harry? Is there something I don't know about that's frightening you?"

Bergdahl glared at him. "Frightening *me?* What scares me? Nothing scares me." Saliva flecked his lips.

"You're a lucky man, then. A number of things scare me. At the moment, you're one of them."

"I scare you? That's good. I'm glad to hear it. Maybe you'll listen to some sense if you get scared enough."

"I think I'd better go," Steve said. "We can talk about this later."

Harry looked up coldly. "Maybe you got a better job, huh? Maybe that's why John Abbot called you?"

Steve shook his head. "I've no new job nor prospects, Harry. But maybe I'd better look for one."

Harry said balefully, "Sit down. We're not through talking. You came here to talk. Sit down."

Steve stood for a moment looking down at Harry doubtfully. Then he smiled and said, "Okay, boss." He sat down.

"You bastard," Harry said. "You knew the right words, don't you? You're good with words."

"I made a living from words for four years, Harry. And while we're on the subject, I think you were unnecessarily rude to Dave. You might need him someday. Someday he's going to be very good with words."

"He'll learn respect for his superiors first, or he won't get the chance to be good."

Steve took a deep breath. He had come here to reason, hoping that logic would prevail. It hadn't. He said, "I think we both need a drink, don't you, Harry?"

Harry nodded. He sighed. His body was slumped in an attitude of resignation, but there was no surrender in his broad face. He mixed a pair of drinks, and Steve lifted his.

"To better understanding," Steve said.

"That I'll drink to." Bergdahl downed half of his at a gulp.

Steve said quietly, "One long day could do it up there, Harry. How about settling for one long day?"

"All right, all right! You think I'm chintzy? You think I'm cheap? God damn it, all I wanted to do was save the picture."

"We're allies then," Steve said. "Because that's all I want to do, too." He finished his drink. "Thanks a lot, Harry. I knew you'd be reasonable."

"Don't soap me," Bergdahl said. "Fight me but don't soap me. I'll see you later."

Outside, Jean D'Arcy was sitting in Dave's MG, which was parked on the circular drive near the kitchen. Steve went over. "Aren't you permitted in the house?" he asked jestingly.

"Not today. What's going on in there? I could hear the shouting way out here."

"Story conference," Steve said. "When did Dave come?"

"About fifteen minutes ago. Just before the shouting. He told me he'd be right out. Now, why didn't he invite me in?"

"I've no idea. Your friend Morton is a good friend of Pat Cullum's, I understand."

She studied him. "Why did you say that? Mitch *despises* Pat Cullum. I'll bet that's what you were waiting to hear. You were being tricky, weren't you?"

"No, I was being serious. I thought he dated her."

She shook her head vehemently. "Not Mitch. Tom Leslie now— Pat is exactly the kind of dish Tom is always looking for."

"Tom and every other red-blooded male. Why do you dislike Pat so much?"

"I'm not sure," she said honestly. "Probably because she'll get further with her bust than the rest of us will with our small talents."

Then Dave was there. He looked at Steve and asked, "Well . . . ?"

"We go up tomorrow. I wanted two days but settled for one. Dave, don't fight him. He's a very tough pro, and you're still an amateur."

"I'll fight for my script," Dave said. "He doesn't scare me. I'll fight anybody for my script."

Jean D'Arcy smiled at Steve. "Does he scare you, Mr. Leander?"

Steve said lightly, "I have a wife and two children and a number of oppressive financial obligations. Practically everything and everybody scares me these days."

He left them, faintly annoyed, as usual. Dave would fight for his script, being single and related to a producer. Dave didn't have a script worth fighting for, he thought, until I practically rewrote it.

Easy now, Leander. Don't let a bruised ego embitter you. The young one can be innocently unkind.

He drove away remembering the fine, firm breasts of Dotty Bergdahl. He had no urge to go home and face the cool reserve of his wife. He searched his wallet for the card Tomkevic had given him. From a drugstore he phoned the investigator.

He was informed that Mr. Tomkevic was out but would be back in an hour. Steve left his number and drove home.

Marcia wasn't there, and Mrs. Burke didn't know where she had gone. Steve went into the study, restless at his enforced inactivity. Once he started a picture, delays nettled him. Harry could have arranged to do some shooting at the studio today, and Steve wondered why he hadn't.

It had been a quick and unexpected decision Harry had made last night. Steve thought of Dotty's concern. It was possible that something beyond money was bothering Bergdahl. What would be more important than money to Harry?

Jail?

In the papers, there had been no more mention of the unidentified man who had been seen at the top of the bluff. Perhaps it had only been the meaningless remark of a neighbor, and the newspapers had blown it up for its mystery value.

One thing seemed certain. It was time to convince Mitchell Morton he should reveal the name of Jameson's companion on the fatal night. If the girl was innocent, there was no reason for her to stay unidentified. Unless, of course, she had seen or heard something that put her in danger of reprisal. That kind of fear would be strong motivation to stay silent. Who would she fear?

Mitchell Morton feared Harry Bergdahl. He had admitted that. Did his unnamed friend, too? In all the theories, the paths of suspicion seemed to lead back to Harry.

Harry had said he didn't know Morton. Yet Tomkevic had claimed he did and wondered why Morton hadn't gone to him for the job. Jameson had strongly implied that keeping him out of the picture and faking an accident had been Harry's idea. And Dotty had told him that something serious was bothering her husband.

They didn't need the insurance money now. They could get money enough to finish the picture through John Abbot. Steve asked himself, *Is that why I've turned moral?* He had gone investigating *before* John's call last night, he reminded himself, and felt properly noble.

The phone rang and it was Tomkevic. Steve asked, "Are you sure Mitchell Morton had a date with the Cullum girl last night?"

"I'm sure. Jealous, Leander?"

"Not very. But I heard today that Morton despised the girl."

"So? She could still have her uses, I imagine."

"They went out? He didn't only stay a short while?"

"They went out and got drunk. What's bothering you about it?"

"Something I didn't tell you about Morton."

"I'm waiting to hear it."

"Could you come here? Or could I come over to your office?"

"What's wrong with telling me over the phone?"

"I need some time to think, Mr. Tomkevic. I could give it to the police, but I don't want any innocent people smeared. I'll expect some promises from you."

A silence of a few seconds and then Tomkevic said, "I have to be in that neighborhood anyway, this afternoon. I'll be at your house in half an hour."

Steve was eating lunch when Tomkevic came. He said, "Sit down and have some coffee. Or eat, if you haven't."

"I'll have some coffee," Tomkevic said. "I've eaten." He sat down.

Steve said, "You'd look very big to your boss, I suppose, if you saved the company a quarter of a million dollars."

"I look big to my boss right now. I'm not out to prove anything that isn't true, Mr. Leander."

Steve smiled at him. "But you told me truth comes out of turbulence. You're out to stir up turbulence, aren't you?"

Tomkevic returned Steve's smile and didn't answer.

"There are some young people involved in this," Steve went on. "Scandal could stop their careers before they were properly started. I'm expecting a high degree of discretion from you."

"I'm sorry. I can't promise that."

"All right, Mr. Tomkevic, enjoy your coffee. Because that's all you'll be getting from me."

"Perhaps the police could get more."

"Perhaps. And perhaps not. I'd be sure to tell them how you tried to blackmail me."

Tomkevic stared. "I—what . . . ? Are you crazy?"

"I'd tell them simply what you told me, that you had planned to tell my wife I had taken Miss Cullum home from a party. I'd tell them it was perfectly innocent but might not look that way to my wife, who was out of town at the time. I'd tell all my friends in the industry about it, too. Your firm gets a lot of studio business, I understand."

Tomkevic continued to stare, his face rigid.

Steve asked, "Isn't Donald Allison on your board of directors?"

Tomkevic nodded.

"I know Don very well," Steve said.

Tomkevic's voice was softer than usual. "Are you trying to frighten me? Or impress me? You're not making it."

"I'll quit, then," Steve said. "More coffee?"

Silence. Tomkevic seemed to be breathing more heavily than usual.

Steve said, "Personally, I would benefit if the insurance money was never paid. Because Mr. Bergdahl might then be in financial trouble, and I'm in a position to take advantage of that."

Tomkevic smiled. "Really? My information doesn't show your financial position to be that sound."

"I'll be getting the money through a man named John Abbot," Steve explained. "He's one of my closest friends. You could check that statement and check Mr. Abbot's credit at the same time."

Tomkevic shook his head slowly. "You fooled me, mister. You're a real tough, son-of-a-bitch, aren't you?"

"Basically," Steve said lightly, "I'm an artist. But in my trade there are times when it's necessary to be a real tough son-of-a-bitch. I don't suppose you ever have a need to be anything else."

Silence again and Tomkevic finally said, "Maybe. Maybe now would be a good time for me to turn into a diplomat."

"Try one of those rolls," Steve said. "They're very good."

chapter thirteen

He went back to the beginning, to Wednesday, and told Tomkevic everything but the reason for his trip to Jameson's apartment. Silence on the rumor was a half-lie he still owed to Harry Bergdahl, and he had no compunction about not repeating it.

When he had finished, Tomkevic said, "It's simple enough. I go up against Morton. If he refuses to tell me who the girl is, he'll have to answer to the police."

"He's a stubborn man."

Tomkevic said nothing.

Steve asked, "Did you check that Brown, from Tucson?"

"Our Phoenix office is going to check on it today." He stood up. "Well, I'll talk to Morton. I'll take it easy."

"Good luck," Steve said. "You'll—keep me informed, won't you?"

Tomkevic smiled wryly. "Of course, Mr. Leander. I wouldn't want you to report me to your friend, Don Allison."

A good man, Steve thought. An active, perceptive, courageous, efficient man. Earning how much on a job like his? He put in long, tedious hours and probably earned less than a studio electrician.

He went into his study for a nap. His haven, that study, lined with unread books, overlooking the pool and housing the television set. His base of operations, his refuge. *Actually,* he thought, *it's all I need, this one room. The rest is for Marcia and the kids, whether they appreciate it or not.*

Honest, self-sacrificing Steven Leander, one of this area's three great directors, lay on his air-cushioned, soft leather couch, contemplating his essential nobility. It was a fine couch, well worth the fourteen hundred dollars it had cost him. He dozed.

At three o'clock, the phone rang and he picked it up in time to hear the housekeeper tell Tomkevic he was sleeping.

Steve said, "I'm awake. I'll take it, Mrs. Burke."

Tomkevic waited for the extension to click before he said, "That Morton's not home. He's out at Zuma Beach. I'll get him tonight. We got word from Phoenix, though."

"And . . . ?"

"This Edward Ambrose Brown in Tucson is a chemist. He came to work in Tucson a year ago. His job application sheet shows his last place of employment as the Dostel Laboratories in Los Angeles."

"And I suppose you went over immediately to see Dostel?"

"Naturally. But he's not there. The man who runs the delicatessen store across the street told me that Dostel told him he was taking a week or two off, roughing it up in Yosemite."

"Isn't anyone in the laboratory? Hasn't he any help?"

"One helper, the delicatessen man told me. But he doesn't know his name and I'm stymied." Tomkevic paused. "Unless we involve the police now and break in to get Dostel's records."

"We don't need the police yet, do we? We can try to get the real customer's name from Miss Cullum, can't we?"

"She isn't home either."

"Let's wait," Steve suggested. "Both she and Morton should be home for dinner. It's only a couple of hours."

A second's silence. Then Tomkevic said, "All right. I'll want you along tonight. In the meantime, I'll try to get the name of Dostel's current employee from the unemployment people."

Steve hung up and went back to sit on the couch. There was nothing unusual about Pat Cullum and Morton not being home, but Dostel's sudden vacation was suspicious. It seemed logical he would have left someone in charge of the business.

He had lied last night. That would indicate he had been forewarned. But who had known that Steve had recognized the perfume? He had told Dave he would remember it and he had accused Pat of wearing it. Pat was the only person who knew Steve had learned the name of the perfume's maker.

Had she warned Dostel? That seemed unlikely. She had called Dostel a liar when Steve had told her about the fictitious customer. Dostel could be trying blackmail. It had been a mistake to mention murder last night. He had gone at Dostel badly. He had blundered in his approach to the man.

He was sunning himself next to the pool when Marcia came home at five o'clock. She stood on the sundeck above, looking down at him, and he sensed that she had something on her mind.

Then she called down, "Shall I mix you a drink?"

He looked up, startled at the change. "Please," he said.

Five minutes later she came down the steps with a pitcher of martinis and two glasses. She poured a pair on the rocks and sat near him in an aluminum and plastic chair.

"I had lunch with Ellen," she said.

Here we go, he thought, *here we go . . .* He said mildly, "That's nice. How is she?"

"The same. She—asked me to ask you if you knew a Pat Cullum."

Steve smiled. "And how! You'll have to meet her. She's quite a girl."

Marcia stared at him perplexedly. "Ellen doesn't make remarks like that to be sociable. What did she mean?"

"I have no idea," he answered. "I could never understand Ellen. Pat Cullum is a girl who wears the same kind of perfume as the girl I smelled but didn't see in Hart Jameson's apartment the night he was murdered. It's a perfume called Dostel Number 263. Have you ever heard of the Dostel perfumes?"

She nodded. "Individualized, aren't they?"

"Exclusively, according to Mr. Dostel. I went to see him about it last night, and Tomkevic and I have reason to believe he lied to me about who bought that number from him."

"Tomkevic and you . . . ?"

"That's right, the insurance investigator. You remember him, don't you?"

"Yes, but what is your connection with him?"

"He and I," Steve said evenly, "have been working very hard on the strange death of Hart Jameson. Together. There are people who will talk to me who won't talk to Mr. Tomkevic. So he asked me to help him. What did you think I've been doing the last few nights?"

"Steve," she asked, "is that the absolute truth?"

He sipped his drink and looked resigned. "In my wallet, up in my lonely bedroom, is Mr. Tomkevic's card. I would be happy if you would phone him and check my story. And then ask Mrs. Burke who I talked with on the phone two hours ago."

"I believe you," she said. "And where did you happen to meet this Pat Cullum?"

"At Harry's party. She was with Dave Sidney. That doesn't automatically make Dave a suspect, because Dave is investigating this strange death, too."

"For heaven's sake, why?"

"Because he wants to know if Harry was in any way responsible. And so do I."

"And you thought it was necessary to keep that information from me. That's what you and Dave have been so secretive about?"

He nodded. "It wasn't a part of my life where I wanted you and the children involved."

She looked at him searchingly. "I know you're a con man when you need to be. You won't be too hurt, I hope, if I don't fall immediately into your arms?"

"I can wait," he said. "It's only been three weeks."

"Two and a half," she corrected him. "And that's another thing that made me suspicious, this apparent sex-discipline of yours."

"Apparent . . . ?" He frowned at her. "Suspicious? Of what?"

"Don't be naïve, Steven Leander. Where did you go this morning?"

"To Bergdahl's. Harry had an idea we didn't need any more film from Santa Barbara. He wanted to fake some shots. We fought that out to a compromise. I get one day up there. I wanted two and he didn't want me to go at all. I'll make it a long day, so don't expect me home early tomorrow night."

Marcia stared at him. He smiled at her.

"You and your light touch," she said finally. "The guiltier you've been, the lighter your touch."

"Yes, Your Honor," he said. "I'm sorry, Judge." He held out his glass. "Will you pour me a little more?"

"If I didn't have a case," she went on doggedly, "you'd be furious now, you'd be lividly indignant."

"Never mind another olive," he said amiably. "I saved this one. I'm starting to economize."

She poured him another drink. "I'll find out. Ellen will know."

"If you don't mind a vulgarism," he said, "your friend Ellen doesn't know her ass from third base. Did I ask you where you stormed to Thursday night? Did I check to see if you *really* spent the week end with the kids? Am I going to ask my friend Harry if he knows something evil about you?"

"Your friend Harry, that's a good one."

He smiled tolerantly. "You're pressing. Have another drink."

She shook her head. "I had two at lunch with Ellen."

He leaned back and stretched. "Still on the booze, old Ellen, eh? Harry told me it runs in her family."

She stood up and looked down at him musingly. "You know, when you try to be, you can be the most insufferable creature alive. You haven't heard the last word on this."

He nodded sadly. "That's always the trouble. The last word can always be yours and it can so easily be no. That's your sword."

"Perhaps," she suggested acidly, "this Pat Cullum would be more —available."

"Perhaps," he agreed. "I'll probably be seeing her tonight. Of course, Tomkevic will be along, but maybe he'll go out for a sandwich or something."

"One thing is certain," Marcia said thoughtfully, "the girl must have money if she buys her own perfume."

"She doesn't. Tomkevic and I are trying to learn who buys it for her. Dostel lied about it, as I told you."

From the deck above, Mrs. Burke called down, "It's Mr. Tomkevic again, Mr. Leander. He wants to know if he can pick you up here after dinner."

"Tell him I'll be waiting," Steve said.

Mrs. Burke went back into the house and Marcia looked doubtfully at Steve. Then she said quietly, "Be careful tonight, won't you? Promise?"

"I promise," he said solemnly.

As he steered the green Pontiac along Sunset, Tomkevic said, "I figured you could run in and hit that Morton first. You've got a wedge with him; he's in your picture."

"So is Miss Cullum," Steve told him, "since last night. Do you know that they're both home?"

"No."

Steve asked, "Did you find out the name of Dostel's helper?"

"I did. And he's out of town, too. Real strange, isn't it?"

"Everybody's running," Steve said. "I knew the minute I got on this case the action would start."

Tomkevic chuckled and shook his head. "Man, you certainly have changed attitudes since last week. Come into some money or something?"

"I made a moral decision," Steve said smugly.

"To stay out of that Cullum girl's bed?"

"There's no need to be vulgar, Mr. Tomkevic."

The Pontiac turned right, heading into Hollywood, toward the same section of Brentwood, where Hart Jameson had lived. In front of a two-story, weathered-stucco apartment building, Tomkevic parked behind Morton's Plymouth.

"Jameson lived only a block from here," Steve said.

"That's right. Coincidence?"

Steve didn't answer.

Tomkevic said, "Explain to him that if this thing can't be handled quietly, the police will be called in. Well, I guess you'll know what to say."

Steve shrugged and stepped from the car. In the open lobby the mailboxes informed him that Mitchell Morton occupied apartment 6B. That was on the second floor, and Steve walked up the outside staircase.

There was the same kind of mechanical door chime there had been on Jameson's door, and he turned it.

Mitchell Morton came to the door in swimming trunks and terry-cloth jacket. He stared at Steve in surprise.

Steve asked, "May I come in?"

"Of course. I'm sorry . . ." He stepped aside. "Something about the picture?"

Steve came into a small, cluttered living room. "No. About the girl you're protecting. Is it Pat Cullum?"

Morton shook his head slowly. "What made you think that? She's no friend of mine."

"You had a date with her last night. You went out and got drunk together."

Morton opened his mouth—and closed it. He stared at Steve doubtfully.

Steve said, "She wears the same perfume as the girl you're protecting. It's a special perfume and we—and I'm running down the buyer now."

Morton took a deep breath. "You started to say 'we.' "

"I made a mistake. Who was the girl, Morton?"

Morton looked at Steve steadily. "I don't know. I just used that gimmick to blackmail you. I lied to you."

Steve shook his head. "You couldn't. How would you know Hart Jameson and I talked about something which you claimed the girl overheard, something I wouldn't want repeated?"

"Hart told me long before you went to see him that he was planning an accident. Hell, it was no secret."

"You still wouldn't *know* that was why I went to see him."

"I could guess," Mitchell said, "and I did. And I was lucky." He swallowed. "I suppose I'm out of the picture now."

"This has nothing to do with the picture. But I'll have to tell the police what you told me that night at your house."

"Tell them that I blackmailed you?" Disbelief was apparent on Morton's face. "How could that do either of us any good? I swear to you that I'll tell the police exactly what I told you tonight."

"Was it Jean D'Arcy?" Steve asked.

"I don't know who it was. That's my story, Mr. Leander. From now until I die."

"You're being very foolish," Steve said harshly. "You can't afford this kind of foolishness."

Morton met Steve's gaze. "Yes, I can. I don't owe anybody in the world a dime."

"Do you want to tell me why you took Pat Cullum out last night?"

Morton shook his head. "No more than you want to tell me why you took her home from Mr. Bergdahl's party."

"I took her home because I recognized her perfume. And also because she asked me to take her home."

"You don't owe me an explanation," Morton said.

"How did you know I took her home from the party?"

"She told me last night."

"Did she tell you anything else you want to tell me?"

"She told me she had a small bit in the picture, and she told me what you said about her perfume."

"Did she tell you who bought it for her?"

"No."

"I don't imagine, at four hundred dollars an ounce, she bought it for herself."

Morton shrugged. "I know very little about her."

"All right," Steve said. "Good night, Mr. Morton." He turned irritatedly and went out.

In the car Tomkevic listened to the story and said, "Maybe somebody got to him. That's the way it sounds to me. But who?"

"Have you checked him? Do you know where he was the night that Jameson died?"

Tomkevic nodded. "He was out with that D'Arcy girl. They went up to Pasadena to see a play."

Steve asked, "Do we have to go to the police now? I threatened Morton with that."

Tomkevic said dryly, "The Department isn't anxious to get into it, not yet. Not until I can almost wrap it up for them." He tapped the steering wheel and stared out at the street. "Have you noticed where all the fingers point in this mess?"

"You tell me."

"I don't have to. Toward Harry Bergdahl." He turned to face Steve. "Right?"

Steve said, "Harry has a reputation for being tricky. But I'm sure he's no murderer. For that matter, there's been no evidence of murder established."

"Not yet," Tomkevic admitted. "But I think you'll agree there has been considerable evidence of trickery established." He started the engine. "Well, we'll see what luck you have with the Cullum girl."

They had no luck there. Her apartment was dark and there was no answer to Steve's ring.

Tomkevic said wearily, "I've had enough for today. I've been going since eight o'clock this morning. We'll come here again. Tomorrow morning I'll see if there's some way I can get into that laboratory without involving the police."

"Some crooked way?" Steve asked.

"Some way. If I hadn't promised you I'd be discreet, it would be easy."

Steve lighted a cigarette. "Actually, with all your running around, you're no closer to proving murder than when you started, are you?"

"Murder? Probably not. But the possibility of collusion grows stronger, doesn't it? Is murder the only crime that would motivate your helping me?"

"Probably." Steve admitted quietly. "I'm not a policeman."

"You're a citizen, aren't you?" Tomkevic turned back toward Sunset.

Steve didn't answer. He was thinking of tomorrow, planning the day, hoping his cast would be at their Friday level so this morning's compromise from Harry would not be wasted.

As Tomkevic pulled up in front of Steve's house, he told him, "I'll wait until tomorrow night to see Miss Cullum. Will you be able to go alone?"

"I'll try. Tomorrow is going to be a full day."

"And that D'Arcy girl, too," Tomkevic added. "I'd like to have you talk to her."

Steve stared at the detective. "You don't think she's involved in any of this, do you?"

"She's a good friend of Morton's. And of Bergdahl's nephew, too. And she was a friend of Jameson's. What makes her special?"

Steve smiled. "I don't know. I suppose you're right. I like to think she's special. I'll see you tomorrow probably."

"I hope so. You've been a big help."

Steve watched the Pontiac go down the hill and stood on the front lawn for a few minutes after it disappeared, looking out at the light-dotted hills and the illuminated curve of the bay.

It was quiet and peaceful here, but all around him was the city. A big, noisy, complex, struggling, hating, frightened city. He had forgotten, up on his hill, that all of them at all the levels were secretly afraid of tomorrow.

That was their terrifying unknown—tomorrow. And Harry Bergdahl's. And his.

He went into the house. Marcia was in the kitchen, making cinna-
mon toast. "I got this sudden and ridiculous urge for some," she
explained. "Do you think I might be pregnant?"

He smiled. "Maybe. Miss Cullum wasn't home. I think I'll go to
bed. Big day tomorrow."

She smiled and said, "Good night."

He didn't fall asleep immediately. He lay in the dark room, remembering her smile.

And he wasn't at all surprised, half an hour later, to hear her
open the door quietly and ask, "Too tired . . . ?"

"Never," he assured her. "Not for you. You're one of my favorites."

chapter fourteen

In the morning she had breakfast with him. And when Dave came,
she insisted he join them for a cup of coffee.

Dave said teasingly, "I'm glad we're all friends again. What did
you buy her, a mink?"

"Marcia isn't interested in material things," Steve answered.
"She's never had to be."

She glanced between them and said nothing.

Dave said, "I talked with Tom Leslie yesterday. He's ashamed of
himself. For complaining to Uncle Harry, I mean. He asked me to
tell you that."

"Is he afraid to tell me directly?"

Dave shrugged. "I wouldn't blame him. You've been a hard man
to get along with this past week."

It was Wednesday. Last Wednesday Hart Jameson had died. And
because he had died, this was going to be a better picture. Tom
Leslie would make it one.

There was a new suspect for the suspicious Tomkevic. From the
vantage point of now, Tom Leslie had more reason than any of

them to kill Jameson. More reason than any of them, he corrected himself, except Harry Bergdahl.

It was a good day. Steve started it with a short speech, apologizing for any excessive rudeness of his on Monday, and he told them that today was important and their performances would decide its length.

They came back to their Friday level, and it didn't turn out to be a long day after all. Again it was Leslie who pulled them up, drawing from them performances to match his own, which was flawless.

In the car, as they waited for Dave, Laura asked, "How were we, Steve?"

"Perfect. I wasn't joking, Laura, when I said this would start a new career for you."

She sighed and smiled and relaxed in the seat.

Then Dave was coming toward the car and he looked troubled. He glanced at Laura before telling Steve, "Uncle Harry wants you to stop at his house on the way home."

"Okay. You look worried."

"I am," Dave said anxiously. "He sounded drunk, Steve. And indignant."

What now, what now, *what now . . . ?*

Dave got into the car. "It's probably about expenses. I can't see him getting mad about anything else."

Laura said nothing but she was no longer smiling and no longer relaxed. She sat silently staring out through the windshield almost all the way home.

When they dropped her, she said, "Watch your temper, won't you, Steve?"

He winked at her. "Yes, mama. I'll see you tomorrow."

As he cut back into the traffic, Steve said, "There's no point in taking you to your car first. You may as well come along."

"He wants me there," Dave said. "I guess he's mad at me, too."

"You don't think it's a relapse from our argument with him yesterday?"

"It could be. He might have got drunk and begun to look back on it with a drunk's belligerence. He never used to drink like he has lately. What could be happening to him, Steve?"

"The same thing that's happening to all of us. We're insecure. We're scared. It's a bad time for the industry."

"Hell, there's always TV."

"For you and young Leslie and Morton and your girl, maybe. Not for Harry and me. Our own trade is ridiculous enough; this new one needs younger nerves. Harry and I aren't the type who can kowtow to sponsors and hucksters."

"You and Harry . . . ? You're the same type?"

"In the most important relationship, we're blood brothers."

Dave asked lightly, "And what's the important relationship, Uncle Steve?"

"Belief," Steve answered quietly. "We believe in our medium."

Dotty opened the front door for them. She said softly, "He's in the living room. He's drunk." She walked ahead of them into the provincial living room.

Harry sat in a big chair near the fireplace, sweating, scowling and obviously drunk. He stared at Steve, transferred the stare to Dave and then brought it back to Steve.

He said, "Leave, Dotty. This is business."

"I want to stay. If Dave can stay, I can."

He turned his head slowly to look at her. "Dave is not here as my nephew. Go, now."

For seconds she met his gaze, then turned and left the room.

Harry looked back at them. "You're a pair. Detectives, huh? Nosing around, trying to pin something on Harry. That will be the day."

Steve said gently, "Neither Dave nor I are trying to pin anything on you, Harry. If you were sober, you wouldn't talk like this."

"Stirring up the cast," Harry accused him. "Slowing up the picture." He glared at Steve. "Why? You think you can get money from Abbot and buy me out?"

Steve shook his head. "That's absurd and you know it, Harry. You're not making sense to me, and I'm sure you aren't to Dave, either."

"You're thinking for him now? He's your nephew now?" He stared at Dave. "That Cullum girl—she's a friend of yours?"

Dave shook his head.

Harry asked, "But the D'Arcy girl, maybe?"

Dave nodded. "A good friend. I'm hoping she'll be more than that. What's wrong with her, Uncle Harry?"

"You tell me. She's in the picture all of a sudden. Morton's in the picture. Now the Cullum girl. Jameson's friends. Maybe they all told you something and you paid them off that way, huh?"

Steve looked at Dave and then went over to sit on the davenport. "Harry," he said evenly, "I don't know exactly what you're getting at, but if you're talking about Jameson's brag, that's the worst-kept secret in town. It's why I went over to see him last Wednesday night. And it's why Tomkevic hasn't given up on this case. But neither Dave nor I had anything to do with starting or spreading that rumor."

"Who started it then?"

"Jameson, with his bragging at a party. And when I went to see him, he practically told me this accident he had planned was your idea."

"And you told Tomkevic that?"

"No."

Harry squinted suspiciously. "You've been riding around with him. You're been working with him."

"Yes. But I didn't tell him what Jameson told me and I never will."

Silence. Dave said, "Jameson was a bad man to confide in, Uncle Harry. He was all mouth."

Harry sat without speaking, breathing heavily, glaring at both of them.

Steve asked, "Who told you I'd been working with Tomkevic?"

"What difference does it make? Don't worry, I got friends with eyes and ears. You know you damned near scared off my angel? But you didn't make it. You were trying to scare off my money, weren't you?"

"Of course not," Steve said sharply. "I thought that money was firm."

Harry sneered. "Firm . . . ? That's some word. What does it mean? When you've spent it and they ain't got grounds to sue you, then it's firm. You talk like a real-estate peddler. Firm—*Jesus!*"

There was a silence, broken only by the sound of Harry's heavy breathing. Then Dave said, "I'll get my car later, Steve. I'll stay here for dinner."

Harry glared at his nephew. "I don't need you here for dinner. Who asked you?"

"I'd like to stay, Uncle Harry. I'd really like to try to explain a lot of things to you."

For a moment, Harry's glare seemed to dim. Finally, he said grudgingly, "Maybe it's about time." He looked at Steve. "We'll talk some more later. We'll talk straight."

Steve nodded. He left without another word.

A new alliance, Dave and Harry against him? Or an old alliance re-established? He stilled the thought; he was beginning to think like Harry. To Harry, all who weren't one-hundred per cent with him were enemies.

At home Marcia said, "You're earlier than I expected. Where's Dave?"

"At Harry's." Steve told her about the scene in Harry's living room.

She shook her head and said nothing.

"He was drunk," Steve explained. "Drunk and belligerent. He'll be more reasonable when he sobers up."

She nodded absently. She stared at Steve. "You know I'm not in his fan club. But can you see him as a murderer?"

"No. Though I couldn't say why."

"I can't either," she said. "Oh—Mr. Tomkevic phoned and said he'd pick you up about eight-thirty." She made a face. "He wants you along when he visits Miss Cullum."

"I suppose I'd better go." He rubbed the back of his neck. "I could use a drink."

She patted his cheek gently. "I'll bring you one. Sit down and relax."

As he sat there, waiting for his drink, he thought of Harry's scorn for the word "firm." It was a new scorn; Harry had used exactly that word when he had first talked with Steve. Perhaps the Texan had definitely backed out. Perhaps Harry had lied about that. It was strange that the Texan hadn't been at the cast party.

At eight o'clock Dave came for his car. Dotty had driven him over and she told Steve that Harry was asleep.

Marcia said sweetly, "Then why don't you and Dave stay here and visit with me for a while? Steve has to go out this evening."

Dotty looked pleased and surprised. Dave smiled at Steve. Steve kissed his wife and murmured in her ear, "Don't get too nice. It's out of character." He went out front to wait for Tomkevic. Perhaps, if he caught him in front, Dave wouldn't see him.

He didn't tell the investigator about this afternoon's session with Harry. He asked him if he had been able to locate Dostel or his assistant.

"No, but I did send a list of names on the Phoenix office, and our man there will go to Tucson to see if that Brown recognizes any of them as Dostel customers. Of course, he's been gone from here for a year."

"And he probably wouldn't remember the numbers if he should remember the names."

"Maybe not. But it will be another wedge." He turned toward the Palisades. "I want you to see the D'Arcy girl first tonight. See if you can shake her alibi for Morton."

"You mean, you think they didn't go to Pasadena that night?"

"It's highly doubtful. I checked for that night, and the house was sold out for a P.T.A. benefit. The lady I talked to up there this morning swears that every seat was sold to Pasadena residents two days before the presentation. Morton and the girl probably saw the play together some other night and decided it would make a good alibi."

"I can't see Jean D'Arcy as a liar."

"How about Morton? All his friends claim he's a real square joe. But he tried to blackmail you, didn't he?"

Steve said quickly, "I never told you that."

"You damned near told me that. You will, eventually."

Steve smiled. "You still don't trust me, do you?"

"Should I, completely? Think before you answer."

Steve thought—and didn't answer. The Pontiac went drumming along toward the Palisades.

Tomkevic said, "Remember now, unless Morton and the girl were somebody's guests, they didn't see the show that night. And if they were somebody's guests, I want the name of their host. That woman is sending me the entire reservation list."

"Tiger, tiger," Steve murmured.

"What's that?"

"Nothing," Steve said. "You certainly are a hard worker, aren't you?"

"And I deal with such miserable people," Tomkevic added. "Present company excepted, of course."

The apartment building was on Sunset, west of the Palisades shopping district. Tomkevic pulled around the corner and told Steve, "Remember, now, it's Morton's alibi you're checking. If you make her realize she's not under suspicion, you'll be likely to get more honest answers."

The apartment was on the first floor, on the corner, and there was the sound of music coming from an open window as Steve went past it to the door.

The sound of music stopped before she opened the door. She looked at Steve in perplexity. "Well . . . ! Didn't you bring a bottle? Isn't that the standard opening gambit?"

"You overestimate your charms," he told her. "I came for information."

She flushed faintly, staring at him. Then she said quietly, "Come in."

He came into a small, uncarpeted and sparsely furnished living room. The record player was on a card table in one corner. Another card table was set for dinner.

Steve stood right inside the still open doorway and said, "I came to check on Mitchell Morton. He claims to have been with you last Wednesday night."

"He was. We went to the Pasadena Playhouse."

"Not Wednesday night. All the seats were reserved, and there is no record of your reservations."

She frowned. "The seats are reserved every night. But tickets can be bought at the box office, and there would be no record of who bought them."

"You mean he didn't reserve the seats in advance?"

"That's right. He bought two reserved seats when we got there."

Steve shook his head. She stared at him.

Steve said, "Last Wednesday night all the seats were sold before the box office opened. It was a P.T.A. benefit, and we have the listing of every purchaser."

"We . . . ?" She licked her lips. "Who did you mean by 'we'? Why are you checking me? What right have you to investigate me?"

"No right," Steve answered. "But to save all of you from being investigated by the police, I'm working with the insurance-company investigator on the death of Hart Jameson."

"To save all of *us?* Who do you mean by that?"

"At the moment, I mean you and Mitchell Morton."

"Nonsense," she said hoarsely. "What are we to you? Why should you want to save us from anything?"

"It's complicated," he told her gently. "But believe me, I do."

"I've nothing to fear from the police," she said. "You have my permission to stop protecting me from them. Good night, Mr. Leander."

"You're being foolish."

She smiled thinly. "Good night. I don't need that part. Don't slam the door."

"This has nothing to do with the part," he told her. "And you're not under suspicion. It's Morton's alibi I'm concerned with."

"And Mitch is my best friend. Will you go?"

He nodded. "I'll go. Ask your best friend how he happened to get *his* part in the picture. Ask him to tell you the truth, if it's in him."

"Go, *please!*" she whispered. Her chin quivered.

He went out and down to the car. Tomkevic looked at him questioningly.

"I feel like a twenty-two-carat bastard," Steve said.

"But you didn't learn anything."

"Nothing. She's being loyal to Morton. Is that a crime?"

Tomkevic shrugged. "I don't know. If Jameson was murdered, it's a crime."

Steve said grimly, "There's not the slightest goddamned shred of evidence that Jameson was murdered. Actually, there's just your two hundred and fifty thousand-dollar motivation for wanting the accident to look like a murder."

Tomkevic smiled. "You're beginning to hate me again. Either me or your conscience. Does this mean you don't want to go over and see the Cullum girl with me?"

"That's right. I'd tackle Morton with you. But no more women, no more lambs."

"Morton isn't home. Look, Leander, let's run over to see the Cullum girl, and then I'll take you home. Then, if you want to drop out of further participation, I'll take what I have, and what I intend to get, to the police. And your lousy lambs can go up against some real wolves. Okay?"

"Okay," Steve said wearily. "Now you're hot. Why?"

"Your bleeding heart. Your great compassion for liars and blackmailers and whores. If you want to bleed for worth-while people, Leander, the town is loaded with them. And not a single one of them has a Guild card."

"Don't lecture me," Steve said. "You're not qualified. Drive on, Hawkshaw."

They had no further words for each other on the long trip to the apartment building that housed Pat Cullum. There Steve said curtly, "I'll wait in the car."

Tomkevic turned to stare at him for seconds before getting out and going up the walk. There was, Steve saw, no light visible in the windows of the girl's apartment.

Tomkevic disappeared around the turn of the stairs, and Steve lighted a cigarette. In about a minute Tomkevic came down the steps again, but he didn't come to the car. He went to an apartment on the first floor and rang the bell.

A few seconds of conversation and then Tomkevic and the man who had answered the door went up the steps together. Steve watched the windows of Pat Cullum's apartment and saw the light go on.

Apprehension moved through him, and he watched the steps anxiously. A few minutes later Tomkevic and the man came down. The man went into his apartment, and Tomkevic came down to the car.

He didn't get in. He stood on the curb and said woodenly, "We'll wait here for the police. One of your lambs is dead, and this time I know it wasn't an accident. She was murdered, stabbed to death."

chapter fifteen

In a small and dreary room in the Hollywood station, Steve and Tomkevic waited for Sergeant Morrow. He worked out of Headquarters, but he had been called after Tomkevic had explained the connection between Hart Jameson's death and Pat Cullum's.

Steve had phoned Marcia. Dave and Dotty had still been there. Dave was on his way down to the station.

Tomkevic smoked a cigar and stared at the floor. He didn't look at Steve. There has been very few words between them since their angry words in front of Jean D'Arcy's apartment.

A detective came in to tell Tomkevic, "She's been dead about ten hours, as close as we're able to figure so far. Does that ring any bells with you?"

Tomkevic shook his head. "That would make it around one o'clock. I don't know what any of them were doing at that time. How about her neighbors?"

"They're being checked now." He glanced at Steve and then moved closer to Tomkevic. He began to speak quietly, too quietly for Steve to hear.

Steve lighted a cigarette. He was not a heavy smoker, but he had been smoking constantly since the discovery of Pat Cullum's death. His mouth was dry, his throat irritated.

The door opened and a uniformed man came in. Jean D'Arcy
was with him. She looked exceptionally young and frightened,
standing next to the big policeman, staring bewilderedly at Steve.

Steve rose and went over to ask her, "Would you like a lawyer,
Jean? I'll phone mine, if you want."

The uniformed man said, "Let the little lady do her own thinking,
mister. We'll inform her of her rights."

Jean said, "I don't need a lawyer. I don't need anything from you,
Mr. Leander."

The detective came over then. "Miss D'Arcy?"

She nodded.

"I want to talk to you and Mr. Tomkevic in another room." He
looked at Steve. "You wait here." He turned to the uniformed man.
"How about that Morton?"

"Ebey is looking for him now, Sergeant. He wasn't home, hasn't
been home all day."

Steve went back to sit on the hard chair near the window. Dave
would be surprised to find his true love here when he arrived. Or
perhaps he wouldn't. Maybe Dave knew more about everything that
had happened than anyone in this room.

They were all going out when Sergeant Morrow came in.
Tomkevic talked with him for a moment at the door and then
Tomkevic left with the others and Morrow came over to the small
desk in one corner of the room.

He said, "Bring your chair over here, Mr. Leander." He sat down
behind the desk.

Steve brought the chair over and sat where he would be facing
the officer.

Morrow glanced through some papers on his desk and then
looked up at Steve. "You weren't honest with me last time we
talked, were you?"

"Yes. What makes you think I wasn't, Sergeant?"

"We'll get to that. Consider it from my angle. So far as we know,
you were the last man to see Hart Jameson alive. Tonight you discover the body of this Cullum girl. What would you think, sitting
where I am?"

"I don't know, Sergeant. I didn't discover the body of Miss Cullum. Mr. Tomkevic did."

"You were along."

Steve nodded.

"Why?"

Steve frowned. "Why not?"

"You're a director, aren't you? You're not an investigator. At least you're not licensed as an investigator."

"Mr. Tomkevic thought I might be helpful to him. The death of Hart Jameson bothered me and I wanted to help."

"Why should it bother you? We had about written it off as an accident."

"Not *about*. You *had* written it off as an accident. Tomkevic wasn't satisfied with that decision and he asked me to help him. I'm sure he'll tell you I was a help."

Sergeant Morrow asked, "And did you withhold from him, as you did from us, the real reason you went to see Hart Jameson on the night he died?"

"Withhold what?" Steve asked. "What do you think my real reason was for visiting him?"

"To try to talk him into faking an accident."

Steve said heatedly, "That's not true. Nothing could be further from the truth than that."

Morrow's smile was cynical. "You'd swear to that under oath?"

"I certainly would. Now, or in court."

"You'll probably get the chance. Well, an officer should be in here any minute to take your statement. You can go, after that."

Steve nodded.

Morrow said, "I'm going easy on you, at the moment, because Mr. Tomkevic told me you'd been very helpful. But you're not out of the woods by a long shot. Give it a lot of thought, Mr. Leander, and I'm sure you'll realize complete frankness is your best course now."

Steve nodded again.

Dave arrived before the stenographer came in. He seemed nervous and his voice was high. "Where's Jean?"

"I don't know. She went to another room with Tomkevic and a detective. How did you know she was down here?"

"The desk sergeant told me."

There was a silence, and then Dave asked, "Why did you go to see her tonight?"

"To find out why she lied about Morton. Your girl's in trouble, Dave, and not because of me. She would have saved herself a lot of trouble, though, if she hadn't lied to me."

Dave's chin came up. "I don't believe she lied. I'm getting her a lawyer. They won't push her around."

"How did you know I went to see her tonight?"

Dave took a deep breath. "I phoned her from your house, right after you'd been there. You're not a policeman, Steve, or an investigator."

"I stayed with it longer than you did," Steve said quietly. "What made you quit so suddenly, Dave?"

Dave started to say something and then stopped. He asked plaintively, "Why are we fighting? This is—embarrassing to me."

"And to me," Steve admitted. "But, Dave, tell your girl she's making a mistake in trying to protect Morton. He's not at all what she thinks he is. He tried to blackmail me last Thursday night."

Dave stared, his mouth open. "Mitchell Morton . . . ?"

"That's right. He phoned to tell me he knew the girl who had been in Jameson's apartment and she overheard what Jameson and I were talking about. And now he can't be found. You tell Jean that."

Dave shook his head wonderingly. "Why should she want to protect him? What did she lie about?"

"She claimed she went to Pasadena with Morton last Wednesday night. Tomkevic can almost prove she didn't."

"Wednesday night? That's the night Jameson was killed."

"Right."

Dave said slowly, "I know she wasn't with Morton. She had a date with me that night."

"So. And a few minutes ago you said you wouldn't believe she'd lie. Do you now?"

Dave didn't answer.

"And only to protect a man who's not worth it." Steve added. "You'd better find her and give her the word."

An officer came in with a stenographer's notebook as Dave went out. The detective who had been with Tomkevic came in a few minutes later.

Steve asked him, "Have you located Mitchell Morton?"

The detective shook his head. "Why?"

"He seems to be the key, doesn't he? He even went out with Miss Cullum the other night, though I know they weren't friends. Why would he date her?"

"Do you know they weren't friends or is that just something you were told?"

"I was told that by Miss D'Arcy and by Morton himself."

The detective smiled. "I'm sure you don't believe everything that pair tell you. Let's get on with the statement, Mr. Leander."

Steve started with his visit to Jameson's apartment and related all that seemed pertinent, omitting the information that he had first heard the rumor from Laura. The police already had the rumor, through Tomkevic; there was no point in involving Laura.

When he had finished, the detective told him, "Tomkevic will be around here for quite a while yet, but Mr. Sidney told me he'd take you home. He's waiting in the hall."

Jean was in the hall with Dave, Steve said, "We can't all ride in that little bug of yours, can we?"

"I brought Dotty's car," Dave answered. "She took mine home from your house." He smiled at Jean. "Aren't you going to say it?"

She glanced at Dave and then looked steadily at Steve. "Dave thinks I owe you an apology. And I guess I do."

"You don't," he said. "Loyalty is a rare but still admirable virtue."

She continued to look at him steadily. "Even when it's misplaced?"

"Especially then. It's easy to ride with a winner. Let's go home. I'm worn out."

Dave chewed his lip and stared at Steve. "I guess you and I will have a loyalty test soon, too."

Steve looked at him quizzically.

Dave nodded toward a closed door. "The way Tomkevic is shaping things up in there, all the fingers are pointing at Uncle Harry."

"They always did," Steve said dully. "Let's go."

As they rode along in Dotty's convertible, Steve thought of Tomkevic. He had compared him mentally with Javert, but the man was changing into a different image. Tomkevic, despite his unctuous speeches, was less concerned with the law and justice than he was with saving his firm's money.

Steve asked, "Did your uncle know Morton before I gave him that part?"

"I don't think so. Why?"

"Tomkevic claimed he did."

"Tomkevic has made a lot of claims. And he's got reason to."

"That's what I've been thinking. Are you going to stay at your uncle's tonight?"

"I doubt it. Did you want to talk with him?"

"I think both of us should talk with him. But he's probably still sleeping. Well, I'll phone him early in the morning. Or, if he's awake when you go to pick up your car, have him phone me tonight. I'll stay up for a while."

Dave said, "If he's awake, he's probably still drunk. Tomorrow should be soon enough, don't you think?"

"I suppose. Dave, tell him we don't need the damned insurance money. Tell him we can get the money through John Abbot, and Harry will still be boss."

Dave smiled wearily. "Okay, I'll tell him. But you know damned well what he'll tell me."

Steve smiled and didn't answer. Dave was right. Harry Bergdahl had grown up in a world where survival was a tricky business, where proffered friendships needed critical and cynical examination. *Don't do me any favors.* That was the motto on Harry's shield.

At home, Marcia said, "I've made some cocoa. You used to like cocoa after a bad day."

He kissed her. "It's been a good day and a bad evening. Did anyone call? Are we going to work tomorrow?"

"Harry called," she said. "You're not working. He said you shouldn't call him back until tomorrow morning."

"Why not?"

She shrugged. "He didn't say. Steve, have the police learned anything?"

"I don't know. They don't confide in me."

"Harry sounded drunk—drunk and frightened."

"He's probably both. Let's get to the cocoa."

She nodded. "And then you soak in a hot bath. And sleep late tomorrow."

The hot bath helped. He lay in it, trying to blank his mind, trying to forget the picture Tomkevic's words had triggered, the mental picture of Pat Cullum in her dark apartment, stabbed to death. He reached one wet hand up to touch his bitten ear. It was almost healed.

chapter sixteen

The morning *Times* had a new development in the murder since Steve had left the Hollywood station. Mitchell Morton had appeared of his own volition at Central Headquarters. He had brought two things with him: a new story and Leon Spangler.

Leon Spangler was the most expensive criminal lawyer in this town of expensive criminal lawyers, and he had never been known to work for charity. That fact was strange enough.

Morton's new story was even stranger. In this new fantasy, he claimed that he had been on his way to see Jameson when he had seen Jameson drive off with a girl. It had been dark and he couldn't be sure of the girl's identity, but he had been *almost* sure that she was Pat Cullum. Jameson was obviously drunk and Morton had followed in his car, remembering the rumor he had heard about Jameson planning an accident.

Jameson, he related, had lost him momentarily on one of the curving streets in the area near the bluff. Then, as he swung around a turn, his headlights had picked up the picture of the Jaguar sliding over the edge of the cliff. And a girl was running along the sidewalk toward another car parked at the curb.

He had not been able to see the driver of the car, he had been aware that there were "big-money interests" involved in the planned accident of Jameson, and at this stage in his acting career he could not afford to alienate them. Further than that, on advice of his expensive counsel, deponent said naught.

It was a ludicrously vulnerable story in many ways. It was a very weak story, but Spangler had permitted him to bring it in to the police. It was logical to guess that it was the strongest story Morton could devise out of those elements already known to the police.

Tomkevic had said that truth quite often came out of turbulence. The turbulence had swirled around Mitchell Morton, and there could be some truth, some necessary truth, in his statement.

He could easily have been the unidentified man the police had not been able to uncover. He could have seen Jameson's car go over the cliff. Identifying the waiting car as an MG could be the truth or it could be a red herring. His uncertain identification of Miss Cullum was understandable. If the friends Miss Cullum had been with that night didn't come forward to dispute this story, it would stand. If they did come forward, Morton had not made positive identification.

The statement could explain why he had gone out with Pat Cullum the other night. He could say he had hoped to get her drunk enough to admit she had been the occupant of Jameson's car. With a man of Spangler's cunning staging it for a jury, this could even be believable.

There would be no urgent reason to take Morton to court. His previous lies had not been told to police officers, and he had not told them under oath. Withholding information from the police was his only known crime. He was much more valuable to the police as a witness.

"He's a goddamned liar," Steve said.

Across the table from him, Marcia looked up, startled. "Who is?"

He handed her the paper. When she had finished reading the account, she said hesitantly, "That—part about the MG—didn't Dave bring this Cullum girl to Harry's party?"

"That's right. And Morton was at the party; he knew Dave had brought her. That's what makes that bit look like a red herring to me."

"But why should this Morton want to involve Dave?"

"Because Dave's already involved to some degree. And that makes Morton's lie more plausible." He paused. "If it is a lie."

"How is Dave involved?" he continued. "He brought Pat Cullum to the party. Pat Cullum wore the same perfume as the girl in Jameson's apartment. Dave is Harry's nephew, and Harry took out the insurance policy. It's a real involved deal Mr. Morton has hinted at."

"And you don't believe it?"

"Should I? Who told him I'd visited Jameson? How did he know the girl in the other room overheard us? Who are the big-money interests he's so scared of?"

"Harry Bergdahl?" asked Marcia.

Steve smiled dryly. "Harry would be very pleased right now to be known as a big-money interest. Only he isn't."

Marcia said slowly, "This town is full of MG's. There's nothing unusual about them out here."

"That's right. And Dave has his alibi for that night: Jean D'Arcy. And she has Dave. That forced Morton to change his story and could be another reason why he identified the waiting car as an MG."

Marcia poured herself another cup of coffee. She looked at the cup as she said, "Well, anyway, you're not involved. Harry might be, but you're not."

"Look at me," Steve commanded her.

She looked at him.

"I'm involved," he said evenly. "Harry's involved, so I'm involved. Because he took me from the ranks of the unemployed, and let us not forget that for even one second."

"Nonsense," she said. "He needed you. He never would have called if he hadn't needed you."

"And I needed him even more," Steve answered. "And maybe he needs me now. I'm going over to find out."

Morton had lied. So had Dostel and Jean D'Arcy. Who else had lied? Rather than lie, Pat Cullum had refused to answer. Harry Bergdahl had admitted nothing tangible, but there had been no proof he had lied. Morton, Dostel, D'Arcy—they were amateurs, and lying badly was the mark of amateurs. Leon Spangler was no amateur. Who was paying his fee?

Dave was just getting out of his little black car when Steve drove up in front of Bergdahl's. He waited on the driveway.

Steve said, "I'm surprised you're free after your friend Morton identified the getaway car."

"I've just come from the station," Dave explained. "He's no friend of mine. Or Jean's either, any more."

"Are they holding him?"

Dave shook his head. "Not with Spangler representing him. And will you tell me where the bum got the money to hire expensive help like Leon Spangler?"

"That's a question I should think the police would ask. Do you know if Harry's awake and sober?"

Dave shrugged. "We'll soon know." They walked to the front door and Dave opened it.

Somewhere in the house a radio was tuned to a news report, and the commentator was talking about the death of Pat Cullum. Dave led the way to the kitchen.

It was a huge, beamed, farm kitchen, and the breakfast table had been set near the used-brick fireplace. Harry and Dotty were at the table, reading the morning paper.

Dotty smiled in greeting, and her glance rested appraisingly on Steve. Harry said sourly, "The detectives, the investigators."

Dave laughed. Steve said, "We're here to comfort you, Harry. We're here to hold your hand."

Dotty said smilingly, "There's a whole pot of coffee. Get some cups, Dave."

Steve sat down as Dave went to the cupboard. Harry said growlingly, "So what's on your mind?"

"I wondered if you had phoned your lawyer. Tomkevic seems determined to railroad you, Harry."

"That would bother you?"

Steve nodded solemnly.

Harry looked away. "I don't need a lawyer. They rob you blind. What do I need with a lawyer? I'm clean."

Steve said nothing. Dave brought a pair of cups and saucers. Dotty smiled at Steve and winked at Dave.

Harry asked, "Why are you worried? Since when does Steven Leander worry about cornball Harry Bergdahl?"

"Since you gave me a job when I needed it. Do you want me to go, Harry? It's your house."

Dotty said softly, "Harry doesn't know who his real friends are. He doesn't trust anybody." She poured Steve a cup of coffee.

"Friends . . . ?" Harry said bitterly. "Some friends, a pair of suspicious associates, nosing into my business. I can live without friends like that."

Steve said jestingly, "Why worry? You're clean."

Harry glared. "A hundred per cent clean nobody is. Are you?"

Steve shook his head.

"Nobody working and me paying rent at the studio," Harry went on. "And why . . . ? Tell me, *why?*"

"I don't know, Harry. It was your idea."

"To start all the trouble it was my idea? Oh, no. You and my loving nephew here, it was your idea."

Dave asked, "And whose idea was it to insure Hart Jameson?"

Harry transferred his glare to his nephew. "Mine." He gestured impatiently. "The old days are dead. Now a guy's gotta make pictures with class. That means stepping up publicity about stars, their insurance gimmicks, tough location breaks—all that flapdoodle.

You know how the columns like to kick it around." Then more softly, "But the accident idea—that was *his*. He thought we had a dog of a script. He thought it would hurt his nothing reputation."

Steve said, "I wouldn't admit all that to Tomkevic, Harry."

"Was I born yesterday? I'll get to him. His time will come."

Dave asked, "Could I fry myself a couple of eggs, Dotty? I'm starving."

"Ask me," Harry said. "I pay for the eggs around here."

Dotty said sweetly, "I'll fry them for you, Dave. He can take them out of my allowance."

Dave smiled. Steve managed to keep a straight face.

Harry tapped the newspaper. "Did you read this Morton's bull? Who's the big-money interests?"

Dave said mildly, "I wouldn't be surprised if he meant you, Uncle Harry."

Bergdahl nodded. "I never liked that man. I still think he's on a list somewhere. He's a liar. I'll bet he made a deal with that Polack insurance man."

Steve said soothingly, "Harry, let's not think about anything but the picture. If the insurance money isn't paid, we'll get money somewhere else and you'll still be kingpin. But let's worry about nothing but the picture."

"*Now* you talk like that. After you and Dave mess around for a week with your big noses."

"So we're not messing around any more. I think we should get right back to work tomorrow, and I think Mitchell Morton should still have that part."

Harry stared. "Are you crazy? Is he a buddy of yours or something?"

"I despise him. But he's the man for the part, and we'll get him at minimum. Harry, I said we should think *only* of the picture."

Bergdahl studied him thoughtfully. Finally he said, "You're right. Yeh, you're right. I hope we can get him before he goes to jail. Because that's where he's going to wind up."

Dotty brought the eggs over and Dave began to eat.

Bergdahl was still studying Steve. His chin went up. "You know, I always had the feeling you figured me for a bastard. Maybe I was wrong about that, huh?"

Steve shook his head and smiled. "It's only that I'm beginning to realize you're my kind of bastard, Harry."

Bergdahl's dour face was impassive for a moment and then he

also smiled. "We're going to have a picture, ain't we? Nobody's going to stop that."

"We're going to have a picture," Steve promised.

The phone rang and Dotty picked it up. She said, "Yes, he's here." She looked at Steve. "It's for you."

It was Sergeant Morrow. He said, "We got that statement typed up that you dictated last night. You can drop in at the Hollywood station any time today to sign it."

"I'll do that, Sergeant. How is it you didn't hold Mitchell Morton? It's obvious from my statement that his story was fabricated, isn't it?"

"It's obvious either his story was fabricated or your statement is fabricated, Mr. Leander. Or maybe both."

"Thanks, Sergeant. Next time I'll know better than to answer a summons for help."

"The summons didn't come from us, Leander."

"You're right, it didn't, Morrow. Good-by." He replaced the phone on its cradle roughly.

"Temper, temper . . ." Dotty said.

Dave said, "That Morrow can be nasty. If I was twenty pounds heavier, I'd have slugged him this morning."

Harry was doing the smiling now. He said nothing.

Steve said, "I'll go over and sign the statement. And then I think I'll go to the studio and see if I can find anyone there to run yesterday's rushes for me. They should be terrific."

"They'd better be," Harry said. "Because you'll remember we agreed yesterday was your last day up there."

"I remember, skinflint. Now, you call me if Tomkevic sends any law over here. I've got the best attorney in town."

Dave said, "Not for this kind of trouble. Morton's got *him.*"

At the Hollywood station, the desk sergeant told him, "Sergeant Morrow has the statement. He's in that first room on the right off the hall."

It was the same room Steve had waited in last night. Sergeant Morrow sat behind the small desk in the corner. He looked up without smiling as Steve walked in.

He nodded at a chair on the other side of the desk. "Sit down, Mr. Leander."

Steve sat down and took out a cigarette.

Morrow asked, "Cool off? I've heard about your temper."

Steve didn't answer.

"You've got some reason to hate Mitchell Morton, have you?"

"He's a liar. He's a blackmailer."

"Blackmailed you, did he?"

"Not quite. He was the man for the part and he got it. He's still got it, as far as Mr. Bergdahl and I are concerned. That is, if he's not in jail by the time we get around to shooting it."

"Jail . . . ? What has he done?"

"Withheld information from the police, at the very least."

"So did you, and you're not in jail."

"All right," Steve said vexedly. "You win, Sergeant. It's your baby, not mine. Where's the statement?"

Sergeant Morrow's smile was slight. "You're turning in your badge, are you? Getting out of the investigation business?"

"That's right. And I here and now apologize for letting Tomkevic talk me into it in the first place."

"No need for an apology," Morrow said. "You helped. And now maybe things are getting too hot?"

Steve stared at him. "Is that an accusation? If it is, I'd like to phone my attorney."

Morrow lifted a hand. "Now, take it easy. Nobody's accusing you of anything. It's your boss I was thinking of."

Steve said patiently, "Only because Tomkevic steered your thinking that way. And I'm sure you know why Tomkevic would want Mr. Bergdahl involved."

Morrow nodded. "I considered all that. And I figured Morton for what you called him, a liar and a blackmailer. But a smart liar knows just how much truth to put into his story, and I figure Morton for a smart liar. The parts of his story that check with other stories point directly at Mr. Bergdahl. Right now, we're running down a pretty solid rumor that this Pat Cullum was Bergdahl's girl friend."

"That could be," Steve agreed. "His and any other available male's. At least that was the girl's reputation."

Morrow frowned. "She's dead. Is that a nice way to talk about the dead?"

Steve looked at the unlighted cigarette in his hand and put it absently into his pocket. He looked at Morrow and said nothing.

Morrow said quietly, "I meant Mr. Bergdahl's *special* girl friend, special enough for him to pay her rent. That's the rumor we're running down. Now, what have you got to say?"

"I came here to sign a statement. Where is it?"

"You're being insolent, Mr. Leander."

"I'm trying not to be. Consider this—you and your Department friends wrote off the death of Hart Jameson as an accident. Tomkevic, for financial reasons, and I, for moral reasons, weren't satisfied with that decision. We nosed around. And probably, because of that, Pat Cullum was killed. If we had let it go as an accident, Pat Cullum would probably still be alive and I wouldn't have to sit here and listen to you tell me I'm not out of the woods. I was *way* out of the woods before I turned moral."

"Turned moral?"

"Turned actively instead of passively moral. There's a distinction there I'm not sure you're mentally equipped to understand."

"There goes that insolence again."

Steve nodded. "The trouble with you boys is you think a man has to wear a badge to be insolent."

Morrow leaned back in his chair and shook his head. "Jesus, I'd hate to work for you. You must be a real tiger."

Steve said nothing. He put his trembling hands in his lap. Morrow shuffled through some papers and picked out a stapled sheaf of three. He pushed it across to Steve. "There's your statement. Better read it carefully before you sign it."

Steve read it and signed it. Morrow gave him two more copies. "These are carbons."

Steve signed those. He finished and asked, "Assuming you prove that Pat Cullum was Mr. Bergdahl's *special* girl friend. How does that connect him with Jameson's death?"

"She was with Jameson, wasn't she? Maybe working for Bergdahl?"

"She wasn't with Jameson when he died. She told me she went on a double date that night and there would be three witnesses to testify she had been with them."

"Why haven't they come forward? If they can read, they should be here, shouldn't they? And you're overlooking one thing, Leander."

"What's that?"

"Your boss could be innocent of what happened to Jameson and still be guilty of Miss Cullum's death. We haven't been able to prove where he was at the time she died."

"Have you asked him?"

Morrow nodded.

"I just saw him half an hour ago. He didn't tell me that."

Morrow smiled. "You know, there could be a lot of things he hasn't told you. Or us. Thanks for coming in, Mr. Leander."

chapter seventeen

Steve went out into an overcast day and drove to the studio. It was time to concentrate on the important thing, on the picture. He was not a detective and certainly not a lawyer. He had been a writer, was now a director and would one day be a producer. God and TV willing.

He found a projectionist he knew and they ran yesterday's film. It was what he had been sure it would be; it was perfect. Laura was getting better and better, and Tom Leslie was superb. The others milked their bits to the ultimate, and the cameraman hadn't missed a nuance.

The cameraman had been Harry's choice, and Steve suddenly remembered Harry had come to prominence through the technical end of the business. Looking back on the pictures of Harry's he had seen, he remembered now how technically sound they had been.

But even the best cutter in the business could not have contrived the dramatic impact they had captured in yesterday's fought-for trip. Harry would be forced to admit that when he saw this film.

An empty day leered at him. He drove over to John Abbot's. He pulled up behind a green Pontiac and got out of his car as Tomkevic came down the walk from the house.

Steve stared at him. "Here, too? Are you crazy? Now what in hell are you doing here?"

Tomkevic's smile was cool. "It was your idea. You asked me to check the man and check his offer of money."

"Oh? And I'm under suspicion again? Or have I always been?"

"You're practically a partner of Bergdahl's, aren't you? You admitted seeing Jameson earlier that night. How do I know you went to a movie later? How do I know you weren't the man in the MG?"

"I don't have an MG."

"Your buddy, young Sidney, has. His car could be one place while he's establishing an alibi somewhere else, couldn't it?"

Steve said coldly, "You're really reaching now, aren't you? You're determined to twist this accident to suit your own purposes, no matter how absurd your theory actually is. Is that why Morton's free? Did you buy him a phony witness and then con the police into releasing him?"

"Watch your language, Leander. I can get rough, you know."

"Please do. Now and here." A redness moved through Steve's mind. "Fool me. Show me the guts I'm sure you lack. Get rough."

"Take it easy, Leander. Don't do anything foolish."

Steve took a step toward the investigator.

And from the lawn the gentle voice of John Abbot said, "That's right, Steve—don't do anything foolish."

Steve turned to stare at John. Abbot said to Tomkevic, "You'd better go. I think it would be wise if you went quietly and quickly."

"He doesn't scare me," Tomkevic said.

Abbot smiled. "Everyone is entitled to an occasional error in judgment. Let me assure you that he's my best friend, but he scares me at the moment."

Tomkevic went away and the redness went with him and Steve stood on the walk trembling.

John came over to put a hand on his arm. "A drink will help. Lord, you looked—murderous. Aren't you ever going to learn to discipline that temper, Steve?"

"I have been disciplining it, John. Believe me, you'd be proud of me if you'd seen it. Ye gods, I've been getting along with Harry Bergdahl!"

Abbot chuckled. "You win. And I'll have to admit that Mr. Tomkevic even annoyed me for the few minutes he was here. What's happening that I don't know about?"

"Mix me a drink and I'll tell you," Steve answered. "Gosh, it's time for lunch, isn't it? I'd better phone Marcia."

"I'll phone her," Abbot said. "You sit down and relax. You're still trembling."

Steve had already mixed a drink when Abbot came back from phoning Marcia. Abbot went over to mix one for himself.

Steve asked, "Who's your wealthy friend who is willing to put money into a motion picture these days?"

"A man with money *and* faith," Abbot replied. "Johnson Waters."

"Money I knew he had," Steve said, "but not that much faith."

"He's always had faith in you, Steve. He's been in your fan club since your first picture."

Steve looked at his drink. "John, are we going to survive?"

"The industry, you mean? The present setup? Through exhibitors?"

"I mean without making pictures for TV."

"Of course we'll survive," Abbot said. "Forty years ago a supposedly learned man assured me the movies meant the death of the publishing business. And a little later all the bright ones were positive that radio would ruin the record business. I hope you don't think a commercial-studded wrestling match will ever replace Laurence Olivier."

"That's hardly a fair comparison," Steve said.

"I'm not trying to be fair," Abbot told him smilingly. "It's my industry I'm defending."

"You know who else believes in it?"

"Harry Bergdahl. Is that who you meant?"

Steve nodded.

Abbot said, "There are angles to this business Harry knows very well. And he knows another very important thing—he knows enough not to interfere with a competent subordinate."

"That isn't his reputation. He has a reputation as a meddler."

"He's had to be. He rarely had competent subordinates. He never paid enough to get them. When cheap pictures sold, Harry made cheap pictures. He has never before had any reason to make a good one."

Steve smiled. "What a switch . . . You were the man who warned me against him."

"Because I knew you and I knew his reputation, and I felt that in a showdown, he'd win. I overlooked one of your less obvious attributes."

"What's that, John?"

"You're a con man. You're glib and occasionally tricky."

"Thanks," Steve said wryly.

"Well, aren't you?"

"Maybe. Yup, I guess. At times. When I have to be." He held up his empty glass.

"Mix your own," Abbot said mildly. "You don't scare me."

They had lunch together, and the reminiscences of John Abbot were not boring today. They were the background of a continuing industry, the colorful, impressive, illuminating history of a giant now sick but far from dead.

Steve left at two-thirty and drove toward home. But as he drove along Wilshire, an impulse moved him and he turned toward Brentwood. Mitchell Morton's Plymouth was parked in front of his apartment building. Steve sat in his own car for seconds before going up to turn the mechanical chime.

Morton came to the door in T-shirt and polished cotton Ivy League trousers. He stared at Steve without speaking.

"We'll shoot your bit tomorrow," Steve told him. "We want to get it into the can before you go to jail."

"I don't think I'm going to jail," Morton said calmly. "I had to tell some kind of story, didn't I?"

"Who's paying for Leon Spangler? Not you, working at minimum."

Morton didn't answer.

Steve said, "Patience, that's all you needed. The talent you have. You had to work a short cut. You're young. What was your hurry?"

"I don't understand you, Mr. Leander."

"You understand me. That lie about the MG, was that malice?"

Morton colored.

Steve asked, "How much did Tomkevic pay you to stooge for him?"

"That's enough, Mr. Leander. I don't need you."

"Don't you? I'll bet you'll show up for that part tomorrow, though. Show me some integrity; spit in my face."

Morton asked quietly, "Why? I don't have to prove anything. I know you're as scared as I am. I've known that for a week."

The redness came to Steve again, and his hands clenched. The vision of Mitchell Morton wavered—and the door closed. He held onto the guard rail as he went down the steps.

At home Marcia was in the kitchen with Mrs. Burke. She told him, "Dave called. He wants you to phone him back."

"Is he home or at Bergdahl's?"

"I imagine he's home or he would have mentioned he wasn't. His phone number's in that little black book attached to the telephone book."

Dave, too, had an unlisted number. For a moment that casual thought stirred something in Steve's unconscious mind but brought forth nothing tangible. He dialed the number.

Dave said, "I have a visitor, a young actor. He's a friend of mine.

He was on a double date with Pat Cullum last Wednesday night. He came to me for advice."

"Why? He knows his duty, doesn't he?"

A pause. "He doesn't want to make any enemies."

"Then he's in the wrong business. In this business, a man's reputation is established by making the right enemies. You're not *personally* afraid of what he might tell the police, are you, Dave?"

"Of course not. All right, I'll tell him to go directly to Sergeant Morrow. That's the man to see, isn't it?"

"Right. And tell him not to talk to Tomkevic at all."

"That's for sure." Dave lowered his voice. "Steve, when did you develop this new faith in Uncle Harry?"

Steve laughed. "When I learned we were brothers."

"Okay, Uncle Steve. I'll see you tomorrow."

"Early," Steve reminded him. "That scene of Morton's needs some polishing." He hung up before Dave could protest.

Outside, the sun was breaking through the overcast. In the kitchen Marcia asked, "More shenanigans?"

Steve glanced openly and meaningly at the kitchen extension.

"No, no," Marcia protested. "I could hear you from the living room. I heard you mention the police."

He told her about his conversation with Dave.

She sighed. "Harry Bergdahl and Steven Leander, that's a pair you can draw to, as Tom Duggan would say."

"It's a winning pair," Steve said. "With Dave, it makes a very potent three-of-a-kind."

"That I'll buy," she agreed. "Three egocentric monsters."

Mrs. Burke said, "You shouldn't talk like that, Mrs. Leander. I don't know this Mr. Bergdahl, but Mr. Sidney and your husband are as fine a pair of men as it has ever been my privilege to meet."

Steve smiled smugly. "Mrs. Burke, you have just earned yourself a free trip to the early show at the Bay. Mrs. Leander and I are going out for dinner this evening."

Marcia said sadly, "And then to a movie, I suppose? Couldn't we think of some better entertainment for a change?"

"There is no better entertainment," Steve said, "anywhere in the world."

And Mrs. Burke nodded in complete agreement.

chapter eighteen

Mitchell Morton was an actor. With the turmoil of his recent publicity and aware that the man directing him hated him, it would have been logical to expect some garbled lines and wooden gestures from him Friday morning. Nothing of the sort happened. He moved through the scene with a touch reminiscent of Tom Leslie and, like Tom, he brought the others in the scene up to his dramatic level. He finished faultlessly in one take.

Dave said quietly to Steve, "Hard man to hate, isn't he?"

Steve nodded. "A damned fool, a talented damned fool."

"Maybe he's not so foolish," Dave pointed out. "Somebody with money is certainly paying for his lawyer."

Morton came over to ask, "All right, Mr. Leander?"

"Excellent, Mr. Morton." Steve nodded a dismissal and turned away.

Morton stood there stubbornly. "You don't give a man any breaks, do you?"

Steve looked at him coldly. "Don't I? You worked this morning, didn't you? I overlooked your first disreputable approach to me, didn't I? Exactly how many breaks do you think you're entitled to, Morton?"

They stood there silently a moment, staring at each other. Then Dave said, "Let's go to lunch, Steve. It's time for lunch."

Something stirred in Steve's unconscious mind again, and this time it came to the surface. He watched Morton walk away and he said to Dave, "Something just occurred to me."

"What?"

"When Morton phoned me, he said he got my telephone number from Hart Jameson. He couldn't have. Jameson didn't have it."

Dave said, "There are people who make a business of selling unlisted phone numbers. He probably bought it."

Steve nodded absently and began to enumerate in his mind those people who had his phone number. Dave, Harry, Laura. If Morton had bought his number, there would be no reason for him not to admit it. A man attempting blackmail wouldn't be reluctant to admit he bought an unlisted telephone number.

Harry joined them in the commissary for lunch. "How did the bastard do?" he asked.

Steve smiled. "I've got bad news for you, Harry. He was great."

Harry sighed. He looked at the tablecloth. "I—that film you shot Wednesday, Steve—it was—well . . ." He shook his head.

Dave supplied, "Spectacular? Sensational? Superb? A producer shouldn't run out of superlatives, Uncle Harry."

Harry frowned. "So I've been wrong before. You know somebody who hasn't? You young snots . . ."

Steve asked, "Did you ever give Hart Jameson my telephone number, Harry?"

Bergdahl stared. "I don't remember. No, I'm sure I didn't. Are we on that kick again? The picture, the picture, the picture—let's think about the *picture*. Okay?"

Steve winked. "Okay, boss."

Across the table from them, Dave said, "And I didn't give it to him. So that leaves who, Steve?"

"Only Laura," Steve answered.

"The picture," Harry said ominously.

"The picture *and* Laura," Steve said. "She's doing well, isn't she, Harry?"

Bergdahl nodded. "And we know why, don't we? You almost got her an Academy Award the first time you directed her."

"How sweet of you to remember," Steve said. "I'll remind you of it next time we tangle." He buttered a roll carefully. "Harry, I've been thinking of that money John Abbot was talking about."

Harry looked up suspiciously. "So . . . ?"

"Johnson Water's the man with the money," Steve went on. "I was thinking if we didn't need it for this picture, it would be a shame to let it go to waste, wouldn't it?"

Harry looked less suspicious. "So . . . ?"

"We ought to get it for our next picture."

Surprise wiped out the remnants of suspicion on Harry's face. *"We . . . ? Our* next picture? Why am I in?"

"Because I'm not a producer, yet. I've a few hard facts to learn about economy and audience acceptance before I take that jump. You're a good producer."

Bergdahl said nothing. A variety of emotions seemed to play over his broad face.

Dave said lightly, "I know an available screenwriter."

Bergdahl smiled. "A *cheap* available screenwriter?"

The afternoon moved less smoothly than the morning had, but it was far from wasted. It had been another good day.

Steve drove home with an unreasonable sense of premonition. Things were going too well; he had an adolescent uneasiness about smooth sailing.

It was a hot day and Marcia was in the pool. He put on his trunks and went down to join her. He dived deeply and stayed under, swimming toward her legs.

They had a few drinks on the sundeck after their swim and it was eight o'clock before they sat down to dinner. At eight-twenty Dave phoned.

He said, "You'd better get that lawyer you were bragging about. Sergeant Morrow has just come out here and picked up Uncle Harry."

"Why? What happened now?"

"They located that perfume man. Uncle Harry is the real customer for that Number 263."

"What does that prove? They must have something else."

"Probably. Morrow looked confident. Could you run over here after you phone the lawyer? Dotty's—unnerved. I'm going down to Headquarters."

In the background Dotty said, "Stop that, Dave. I don't need anyone to hold my hand."

The words triggered an incident in Steve's memory. He said, "I'll get right over there. I'll be there in twenty minutes."

"I'll leave now then," Dave said.

Steve hung up and stood by the phone, thinking back.

From the dining room Marcia called, "What's the matter, Steve? What's happened?"

He came back to the dining room. "I've been stupid. I overlooked the obvious. The police have just picked up Harry Bergdahl."

"That isn't what you meant by overlooking the obvious. What did you mean by that?"

"I meant I've been as blind as Tomkevic. I want you to phone my lawyer, Craig Medoff, and tell him Harry's been picked up. I'm going over to Bergdahl's."

She stood up. "All right. But what did you overlook?"

"The girl in Hart's apartment. You stay here; Harry may phone. And call Medoff right now." He went out to the car.

Dotty opened the door to Steve's ring. She seemed to be swaying and her voice was thick. "I appreciate your coming."

He grinned at her. "That isn't what you told Dave."

"I didn't think it was necessary," she enunciated very carefully. "There was no point in disrupting your evening. Harry's not in serious trouble anyway, is he?"

Steve followed her into the living room. "Of course not. Morrow was probably egged on by Tomkevic to make a grandstand play. There'll be some red faces in the morning, I guarantee you."

Dotty nodded. "I thought so. Would you like a drink?"

"I could use one. Bourbon and water."

She mixed a pair. She was ludicrously careful as she poured the whisky, added water, and slowly walked to the davenport with both of them. She handed him one and sat a few feet from him.

Steve chuckled. "I can see Harry now, giving them all hell. There'll be a false arrest suit filed, I'll bet."

Dotty said nothing. Her smile was labored.

Steve said, "I had a weird idea this afternoon. Are you superstitious?"

She shook her head. She sipped her drink and stared at him.

Steve said, "Pat Cullum had a small part in this picture we're making. Why don't you take it?"

"I'm not an actress," she said heavily. "I gave up my career."

"Because you don't need the money now, married to Harry. But just for fun? As a gag?"

She shook her head stubbornly.

"It's only a line," Steve explained. "You're supposed to be a little tipsy, see? And this fellow is talking on the phone, but he's well—fondling you at the same time. And you giggle and say, 'Stop that!' You'd have fun doing it and . . ."

"Shut up," Dotty said. She glared at him.

Steve shrugged and sipped his drink. Dotty finished hers and went over to pour another.

Steve said, "Somebody told me that Harry met Jameson through you. Is that right?"

She nodded and sat down on the davenport again with a full glass.

"You knew Morton, too? Through Jameson?"

She said nothing.

Steve sipped his drink. "Tomkevic was sure Harry knew Morton, but it was you who knew him. Did you give him my phone number?"

"I don't know what you're talking about," she said warily.

"Morton told me yesterday that he didn't need me. Was that because he thought he could get to Harry through you? Are you paying for his attorney?"

She stared at the fireplace.

He asked gently, "Don't you want to talk, Dotty?"

She shook her head.

"Do you mind if I do?"

"Suit yourself."

Steve leaned back. "What Morrow overlooked is that when a man buys perfume, he buys the kind *he* likes, quite often. He likes to smell it on his women, on all of his women. Do you wear Dostel Number 263, Dotty?"

She shook her head.

"Harry bought you some. Didn't you ever wear it?"

She stared at the fireplace.

"What I overlooked," Steve went on, "was the obvious fact that Jameson was no gentleman. There would be no point in his hiding a woman just because I came to visit him. Not unless I knew the woman, and she wanted to hide."

Dotty turned her head. "What are you trying to prove, Steve? What can you prove?"

"I'm just expounding a theory. Does it bore you?"

She shook her head slowly.

"And another thing," he continued, "Jameson didn't worry about the girl overhearing the accident gimmick. That could indicate the girl already knew it. Through her husband?"

Dotty turned to face him again.

"What beats me," Steve said thoughtfully, "is why the girl would want to kill him."

Dotty said carefully, "Maybe she didn't. Maybe they were both crazy drunk and Jameson bragged about how easy it would be to ride on the edge of the bluff and the girl got scared and jumped out of the car and ran away."

"And was picked up by Mitchell Morton," Steve went on, "and taken home. And Mitchell tried to blackmail her. He didn't want much, just a part in the picture. And the girl said it would look suspicious coming through her. She suggested he phone Steve Leander and tell him that he knew something the police should. And the girl gave Morton my number."

"And what difference does it make?" Dotty asked hoarsely. "It's still an accident, isn't it?"

"Yes," Steve agreed, "it certainly is. Can I mix you another drink?"

"I've had too many already," she said. "Why don't you leave?"

"All right." He finished his drink and stood up. "What you forget is that Morton is an actor and an ambitious one. His allegiance is going to go to the person who can do him the most good. Unfortunately, you're not a producer."

She stared at him. "No, but with Pat Cullum dead, Harry has only his little Dotty, hasn't he? With Pat Cullum dead, Dotty is again queen; and if I tell Harry I want Mitchell Morton out of the business, what do you think will happen?"

Steve said softly, "Is that why you killed her? Don't you think there will be other Pat Cullums? Don't you think this town is loaded with them?"

"There'll never be another Pat Cullum," Dotty said. "I can guarantee you that. Harry and I have talked it over very carefully, and there will never be another Pat Cullum. She was the first infidelity in our marriage and now she's dead. I don't know who killed her, but I'm glad she's dead. Harry's mine now, *all mine.*"

"You know who killed her, Dotty. You did. And it was senseless. Because you can't control Harry forever. He's just not that kind of man. He has to dominate."

Dotty smiled blearily and shook her head.

Steve asked, "Was Morton working for you when he took out Pat Cullum? Did you send him over to find out how she'd learned the mystery girl was wearing your perfume?"

"I know how she found that out," Dotty said thickly. "You told her. She was going to tell the police about that, too, about the perfume. She threatened me with that."

"And then you killed her?"

"I didn't kill her. I didn't, I didn't, I didn't . . ." Her voice rose hysterically and her head shook savagely. "You can't prove I killed her. *Nobody* can prove that!"

"I can prove you had reason to. Do you want to tell me about it?"

Dotty's impressive bosom rose and fell. "Hart Jameson's death was an accident. That's God's gospel truth. When you told Pat Cullum about the perfume, she knew I must have been the girl with Hart that night, the mysterious missing woman."

"Did she threaten you with that?"

Dotty took a deep breath and looked at Steve anxiously. "She did. She said if it ever came out, it would ruin me. It could send me to prison. She told me that if I interfered with her—her *romance* she called it—her affair with *my* husband, she would tell the police I was with Hart Jameson the night he died."

Steve stared. "She—threatened you? My God, did she think Harry was going to marry her?"

Dotty nodded mutely, her eyes beseechingly on Steve. "The silly little tramp thought Harry would divorce me. Steve, I swear to you Hart Jameson's death was an accident. He was showing off. He was always showing off."

Steve looked at the carpeting and up at Dotty. "You haven't told the whole truth, Dotty. You've admitted Pat threatened you. Well, Morton has already told me that you killed her."

"You're a liar," she said hoarsely. "You're trying to trick me. I can have you destroyed, too, Steve. I know about you and Pat Cullum. I can ruin your marriage."

Steve shook his head. "Why don't you come with me to the police? Harry must suspect, too. You claimed to be worried about him, but in reality he was worried about you. He knows, doesn't he?"

"I don't have to listen to any more of this," she whispered. "Get out of my house."

"I'm going. I'm sure the police will listen more politely than you did. Good night, Dotty."

He was halfway to the door when she whimpered, "Steve, wait—Steve, please . . ."

By the time he got back to the davenport, she had passed out. He went to the phone and called Headquarters. He asked for Sergeant Morrow.

"Sergeant Morrow is busy at the moment, sir. May I be of help?"

"No," Steve answered. "This concerns the murder of the Cullum girl, and I will talk only to Sergeant Morrow. Tell him Steven Leander is on the phone."

"One moment, sir."

It was a little longer than that before Morrow came on. Steve said, "I want you to try something. I want you to pull in Mitchell

Morton and tell him Mrs. Bergdahl has confessed to everything. Tell him there's no point in his sticking to that ridiculous story of his."

"We don't have to pull him in; he's down here. What kind of a game are you trying to run now, Leander?"

"Sergeant, have you considered that all those fingers that pointed at Harry Bergdahl were really only pointing at his house? Get Morton alone and tell him what I've told you to, and I guarantee you'll come up with something solid."

"Where's Mrs. Bergdahl now?"

"Ten feet from me. Dead drunk and fast asleep. As soon as one of your men gets here to her house, I'll come down. Don't let Bergdahl know what you're questioning Morton about."

A silence.

Steve said, "How much help do you need, Sergeant? Haven't I given you enough even before tonight?"

"All right. *All right!*"

From the direction of the davenport Dotty Bergdahl moaned in her sleep.

The room was as dreary as the little room in the Hollywood station, but this one was bigger. Harry and Steve sat on chairs against the wall. Dave sat behind the desk.

Detective Sommers came in to tell them, "I guess you can all go home. That Morton is singing like a parakeet."

Harry said gruffly, "Who can believe him? You flatfeet ain't had enough experience with that bastard? That don't mean my wife had anything to do with Miss Cullum's death."

Sommers looked at him compassionately. "We don't need Morton for that, Mr. Bergdahl. We had some prints from the girl's apartment we've been trying to match up." His voice was lower. "Your wife fills the bill."

Harry took a deep breath and stared at the floor. Sommers went out.

Dave said, "We'd better get home, Uncle Harry. It's late."

Harry nodded, still staring at the floor. "The little bitch. The dirty little bitch."

Steve came over to put a hand on his shoulder. "You can always get another wife, Harry. We've got more important things to worry about. We've got a picture to finish."

Ed Gorman has worked in virtually every genre but seems to be at his best when combining history and fiction, as here. If you read accounts of Nickelodeons and their social impact, you'll soon learn that movies in all forms became addictive to a certain portion of the population—addictive to the point that movies often became more real than reality. Here is Gorman's take on this phenomenon.

Gunslinger

Ed Gorman

He reaches Los Angeles three days early, a scrawny forty-eight-year-old man in a three-piece black Cheviot suit made of wool and far too hot for the desertlike climate here. He chews without pause on stick after stick of White's Yucatan gum. He carries, tucked in his trousers beneath his vest, a Navy Colt that belonged to his father, a farmer from Morgan County, Missouri.

As he steps down from the train, a Negro porter accidentally bumping into him and tipping his red cap in apology, he takes one more look at the newspaper he has been reading for the last one hundred miles of his journey, the prime headline of which details President Teddy Roosevelt's hunting trip to the Badlands, the secondary headline being concerned with the annexation by Los Angeles of San Pedro and Wilmington, thereby giving the city a harbor. But it is the third headline that holds his interest: DIRECTOR THOMAS INCE, NOW RECOVERED FROM HEART TROUBLE, STARTS NEW PICTURE THURSDAY WITH HIS FAMOUS WESTERN STAR REX SWANSON.

Today was Monday.

He finds a rooming house two blocks from a bar called The Waterhole, which is where most of the cowboys hang out. Because real ranches in the west have fallen on hard times, the cowboys had little choice but to drift to Los Angeles to become extras and stunt riders and trick shooters in the silent movie industry. Now there is a whole colony, a whole subculture of them out here, and they are much given to drink and even more given to violence. So he must be careful around them, very careful.

In the street below his room runs a trolley car, its tingling bell the friendliest sound in this arid city of 'dobe buildings for the poor and unimaginable mansions for the rich. It is said, at least back in Missouri, that at least once a day a Los Angeles police officer draws down on a man and kills him. He has no reason to doubt this as he falls asleep on the cot in the hot shabby room with its flowered vase lamp, the kerosene flame flickering into the dusk as his exhausted snoring begins.

In the morning he goes down the hall, waits till a Mexican woman comes out of the bathroom smelling sweetly of perfume, and then goes in and bathes and puts on the things he bought just before leaving Morgan County. A bank teller, he is not particularly familiar with real Western attire, but he knew it would be a mistake to buy his things new. That would mark him as a dude for certain. He had found a livery up in the northern edge of the county that had some old clothes in the back, which he bought for $1.50 total.

Now, looking at himself in the mirror, trying to be as objective as he can, he sees that he does not look so bad. Not so bad at all. The graying hair helps. Not shaving helps. And he's always been capable of a certain blue evil eye (as are most of the men in his family). Then there are the clothes. The dusty brown Stetson creased cowhand-style. The faded denim shirt. The Levi's with patches in knee and butt. The black Texas boots.

For the first time he loses some of his fear.

For the first time there is within him excitement.

In his room, before leaving, he writes a quick letter.

Dear Mother,

By the time you read this, you will know what I have done. I apologize for the pain and humiliation my action will cause you but I'm sure you will understand why I had to do this.

If it were not for the man I will kill Thursday,

you would have had a husband all these years, and I a
father.

I will write you one more letter before Thursday.

Your loving son,
Todd

The next two days . . .

In the Los Angeles of the movie cowboy extra, there are certain
key places to go for work. On Sunset Boulevard there is a horse
barn where you wait like farmhands to be picked for a day's work;
then there are a few studio backlots where you can stand in the
baking sun all day waiting for somebody already hired to keel over
and need to be replaced; and then there is Universal's slave-galley
arrangement where extras are literally herded into a big cage to
wait to be called. Five dollars a day is the pay, which for some men
is five times what they were getting back in the blizzard country of
Montana and Wyoming and Utah.

It is into this world he slips now, making the rounds, trying to get
himself hired as an extra. If he does not get on Ince's set Thursday,
if he does not get that close, then he will be unable to do what he
has waited most of his life to do.

He is accepted. Or at least none of the other cowboys question
him. They talk in their rough boozy way of doing stunt work—
something called the "Running W" or the even more frightening
"Dead Man's Fall" are particularly popular topics—and they gossip
about the movie stars themselves. Which sweet young virginal types
can actually be had by just about anybody who has taken a bath in
the past month. Which so-called he-men are actually prancing
nancies afraid to even get close to a horse.

All this fascinates and frightens him. He wants to be back home
in Morgan County, Missouri.

All that keeps him going is his memory of his father. The pennies
on Father's eyes during the wake. The waxen look of the coffin. The
smell of funeral flowers. His mother weeping, weeping.

The Navy Colt burns in his waistband. Burns . . .

Late on Wednesday, near the corral on the Miller Brothers 101
Ranch where Ince makes his two-reelers, a fat bald casting director
in jodhpurs comes over and says, "You five men there. Can you be
here at sunup?"

He has traveled fifteen hundred miles and forty-one years for this moment.

Dear Mother,

I never told you about where I saw him first, in the nickelodeon six years ago. He used a different name, of course, but I've seen so many photographs of him that even with his dyed hair and new mustache I knew it was him. I see now that his whole so-called "murder" was nothing more than a ruse to let him escape justice. He is not dead; he's alive out here . . .

He is very popular, of course, especially with the ladies, just as he was back there. He is also celebrated as a movie hero. But we know differently, don't we? If Father hadn't been riding back from the state capital that day on the train . . .

In the morning I go out to the Miller ranch where the picture is to be shot.

It will not be the only thing being shot . . .

Say hello to Aunt Eunice for me and think of me when you're making mince meat pie next Thanksgiving.

I think of your smile, Mother. I think of it all the time.

Your loving son,
Todd

All he can liken it to was his six-month stint in the army (six months only because of what the post doctor called his "nervous condition")—hundreds of extras milling around for a big scene in which a railroad car is to be held up and then robbers and good citizens alike are attacked by an entire tribe of savage Indians. It is in this way that the robber will become a hero—he will be forced to save the lives of the very passengers whom he was robbing.

The trolley car ran late. He did not sleep well. He urinates a lot. He paces a lot. He mooches two pre-rolls from a Texas cowhand who keeps talking about what a nancy the casting director in the jodhpurs is. The smoke, as always, makes him cough. But it helps calm him. The "nervous condition" being something he's always suffered from.

For two hours, waiting for the casting director to call him, he wanders the ranch, looks at the rope corral, the ranch house, the two hundred yards of train track meant to simulate miles of train track. There's even a replica of the engine from the Great Northern standing there. Everything is hot, dusty. He urinates a lot.

Around ten he sees Rex Swanson.

Rex is taller than he expected and more handsome. Dressed in a white Stetson, white western shirt with blue pearl buttons, white sheepskin vest and matching chaps, and enough rouge and lipstick to make him look womanly. Rex has just arrived, being dispatched from the back of a limousine long enough to house thirty people. He is instantly surrounded and in the tone of everybody about him there is a note of supplication.

Please Rex this.

Please Rex that.

Please Rex.

Rex *please.*

Just before lunch he sees his chance.

He has drifted over to a small stage where a printed backdrop depicts the interior of a railroad car.

It is here that Rex, in character, holds up the rich passengers, a kerchief over his face, twin silver Peacemakers shining in his hands. He demands their money, gold, jewelry.

A camera rolls; an always-angry director shouts obscenities through a megaphone. Everybody, particularly the casting director, looks nervous.

His father knocking a baseball to him. His father bouncing him on his knee. His father driving the three of them—how good it felt to be the-three-of-them, mother son father—in the buggy to Sunday church. Then his father happening to be on the train that day/so waxen in the coffin/pennies on his eyes

He moves now.

Past the director who is already shouting at him.

Past the actors who play the passengers.

Right up to Rex himself.

"You killed my father," he hears himself say, jerking the Navy Colt from his waistband. "Thirty-seven years ago in Morgan County, Missouri!"

Rex, frantic, shouts to somebody. "Lenny! My God, it's that lunatic who's been writing me letters all these years!"

"But I know who you really are. You're really Jesse!" he says, fear gone once again, pure excitement now.

Rex—now it's his turn to be the supplicant—says, "I'm an actor from New Jersey. I only play Jesse James in these pictures! I only *play* him!"

But he has come a long ways, fifteen hundred miles and forty-one years, for this moment.

He starts firing.

It takes him three bullets, but he gets it done, he does what Robert Ford only supposedly did. He kills Jesse James.

Then he turns to answer the fire of the cowboys who are now shooting at him.

He smiles. The way that special breed of men in the nickelodeons always do.

The gunslingers.

Henry Kuttner was one of the great pulp writers. While he was frequently criticised for writing too much and too quickly, not even his detractors could deny the fact that he wrote several real masterpieces, including one of the most perfectly conceived horror tales ever written, "Call Him Demon." Here is another story of Kuttner's at top form, a most curious tale that will stay with you a long time.

The Shadow on the Screen

Henry Kuttner

Torture Master was being given a sneak preview at a Beverly Hills theatre. Somehow, when my credit line, "Directed by Peter Haviland," was flashed on the screen, a little chill of apprehension shook me, despite the applause that came from a receptive audience. When you've been in the picture game for a long time you get these hunches; I've often spotted a dud movie before a hundred feet have been reeled off. Yet *Torture Master* was no worse than a dozen similar films I'd handled in the past few years.

But it was formula, box-office formula. I could see that. The star was all right; the make-up department had done a good job; the dialogue was unusually smooth. Yet the film was obviously box-office, and not the sort of film I'd have liked to direct.

After watching a reel unwind amid an encouraging scattering of applause, I got up and went to the lobby. Some of the gang from Summit Pictures were lounging there, smoking and commenting on the picture. Ann Howard, who played the heroin in *Torture Master,* noticed my scowl and pulled me into a corner. She was that rare type, a girl who will screen well without all of that greasepaint that makes you look like an animated corpse. She was small, and her hair and eyes and skin were brown—I'd like to have seen her play *Peter Pan.* That type, you know.

I had occasionally proposed to her, but she never took me seriously. As a matter of fact, I myself didn't know how serious I was about it. Now she led me into the bar and ordered drinks.

"Don't look so miserable, Pete," she said over the rim of her glass. "The picture's going over. It'll gross enough to suit the boss, and it won't hurt my reputation."

Well, that was right. Ann had a fat part, and she'd made the most of it. And the picture would be good box-office; Universal's *Night Key,* with Karloff, had been released a few months ago, and the audiences were ripe for another horror picture.

"I know," I told her, signaling the bartender to refill my glass. "But I get tired of these damn hokumy pics. Lord, how I'd like to do another *Cabinet of Doctor Caligari!*"

"Or another *Ape of God,*" Ann suggested.

I shrugged. "Even that, maybe. There's so much chance for development of the weird on the screen, Ann—and no producer will stand for a genuinely good picture of that type. They call it arty, and say it'll flop. If I branched out on my own—well, Hecht and MacArthur tried it, and they're back on the Hollywood payroll now."

Someone Ann knew came up and engaged her in conversation. I saw a man beckoning, and with a hasty apology left Ann to join him. It was Andy Worth, Hollywood's dirtiest columnist. I knew him for a double-crosser and a skunk, but I also knew that he could get more inside information than a brace of Winchells. He was a short, fat chap with a meticulously cultivated moustache and sleekly pomaded black hair. Worth fancied himself as a ladies' man, and spent a great deal of his time trying to blackmail actresses into having affairs with him.

That didn't make him a villain, of course. I like anybody who can carry on an intelligent conversation for ten minutes, and Worth could do that. He fingered his mustache and said, "I heard you talking about *Ape of God.* A coincidence, Pete."

"Yeah?" I was cautious. I had to be, with this walking scandal-sheet. "How's that?"

He took a deep breath. "Well, you understand that I haven't got the real lowdown, and it's all hearsay—but I've found a picture that'll make the weirdest movie ever canned look sick."

I suspected a gag. "Okay, what is it? *Torture Master?*"

"Eh? No—though Blake's yarn deserved better adaptation than your boys gave it. No, Pete, the one I'm talking about isn't for general release—isn't completed, in fact. I saw a few rushes of it. A one-man affair; title's *The Nameless.* Arnold Keene's doing it."

* * *

Worth sat back and watched how I took that. And I must have shown my amazement. For it was Arnold Keene who had directed the notorious *Ape of God,* which had wrecked his promising career in films. The public doesn't know that picture. It never was released. Summit junked it. And they had good cause, although it was one of the most amazingly effective weird films I've ever seen. Keene had shot most of it down in Mexico, and he'd been able to assume virtual dictatorship of the location troupe. Several Mexicans had died at the time, and there had been some ugly rumors, but it had all been hushed up. I'd talked with several people who had been down near Taxco with Keene, and they spoke of the man with peculiar horror. He had been willing to sacrifice almost anything to make *Ape of God* a masterpiece of its type.

It was an unusual picture—there was no question about that. There's only one master print of the film, and it's kept in a locked vault at Summit. Very few have seen it. For what Machen had done in weird literature, Keene had done on the screen—and it was literally amazing.

I said to Worth, "Arnold Keene, eh? I've always had a sneaking sympathy for the man. But I thought he'd died long ago."

"Oh, no. He bought a place near Tujunga and went into hiding. He didn't have much dough after the blow-up, you know, and it took him about five years to get together enough *dinero* to start his *Nameless.* He always said *Ape of God* was a failure, and that he intended to do a film that would be a masterpiece of weirdness. Well, he's done it. He's canned a film that's—unearthly. I tell you it made my flesh creep."

"Who's the star?" I asked.

"Unknowns. Russian trick, you know. The real star is a—a shadow."

I stared at him.

"That's right, Pete. The shadow of something that's never shown on the screen. Doesn't sound like much, eh? But you ought to see it!"

"I'd like to," I told him. "In fact, I'll do just that. Maybe he'll release it through Summit."

Worth chuckled. "No chance. No studio would release that movie. I'm not even going to play it up in my column. This is the real McCoy, Pete."

"What's Keene's address?" I asked.

Worth gave it to me. "But don't go out till Wednesday night," he said. "The rought prints will be ready then, or most of them. And keep it under your hat, of course."

A group of autograph hunters came up just then, and Worth and I were separated. It didn't matter. I'd got all the information I needed. My mind was seething with fantastic surmises. Keene was one of the great geniuses of the screen, and his talent lay in the direction of the macabre. Unlike book publishers, the studios catered to no small, discriminating audiences. A film must suit everybody.

Finally I broke away and took Ann to a dance at Bel-Air. But I hadn't forgotten Keene, and the next night I was too impatient to wait. I telephoned Worth, but he was out. Oddly enough, I was unable to get in touch with him during the next few days; even his paper couldn't helpe me. A furious editor told me the Associated Press had been sending him hourly telegrams asking for Worth's copy; but the man had vanished completely. I had a hunch.

It was Tuesday night when I drove out of the studio and took a short cut through Griffith Park, past the Planetarium, to Glendale. From there I went on to Tujunga, to the address Worth had given me. Once or twice I had an uneasy suspicion that a black coupé was trailing me, but I couldn't be sure.

Arnold Keene's house was in a little canyon hidden back in the Tujunga mountains. I had to follow a winding dirt road for several miles, and ford a stream or two, before I reached it. The place was built against the side of the canyon, and a man stood on the porch and watched me as I braked my car to a stop.

It was Arnold Keene. I recognized him immediately. He was a slender man under middle height, with a closely cropped bristle of grey hair; his face was coldly austere. There had been a rumor that Keene had at one time been an officer in Prussia before he came to Hollywood and Americanized his name, and, scrutinizing him, I could well believe it. His eyes were like pale blue marbles, curiously shallow.

He said, "Peter Haviland? I did not expect you until tomorrow night."

I shook hands. "Sorry if I intrude," I apologized. "The fact is, I got impatient after what Worth told me about your film. He isn't here, by any chance?"

The shallow eyes were unreadable. "No. But come in. Luckily, the developing took less time that I had anticipated. I need only a few more shots to complete my task."

He ushered me into the house, which was thoroughly modern and comfortably furnished. Under the influence of good cognac my suspicions began to dissolve. I told Keene I had always admired his *Ape of God.*

He made a wry grimace. "Amateurish, Haviland. I depended too much on hokum in that film. Merely devil-worship, a reincarnated Gilles de Rais, and sadism. That isn't true weirdness."

I was interested. "That's correct. But the film had genuine power—"

"Man has nothing of the weird in him intrinsically. It is only the hints of the utterly abnormal and unhuman that give one the true feeling of weirdness. That, and human reactions to such supernatural phenomena. Look at any great weird work—*The Horla,* which tells of a man's reaction to a creature utterly alien, Blackwood's *Willows,* Machen's *Black Seal,* Lovecraft's *Color Out of Space*—all these deal with the absolutely alien influencing normal lives. Sadism and death may contribute, but alone they cannot produce the true, intangible atmosphere of weirdness."

I had read all these tales. "But you can't film the indescribable. How could you show the invisible beings of *The Willows?*"

Keene hesitated. "I think I'll let my film answer that. I have a projection room downstairs—"

The bell rang sharply. I could not help noticing the quick glance Keene darted at me. With an apologetic gesture he went out and presently returned with Ann Howard at his side. She was smiling rather shakily.

"Did you forget our date, Pete?" she asked me.

I blinked, and suddenly remembered. Two weeks ago I had promised to take Ann to an affair in Laguna Beach this evening, but in my preoccupation with Keene's picture the date had slipped my mind. I stammered apologies.

"Oh, that's all right," she broke in. "I'd much rather stay here— that is, if Mr. Keene doesn't mind. His picture—"

"You know about it?"

"I told her," Keene said. "When she explained why she had come, I took the liberty of inviting her to stay to watch the film. I did not want her to drag you away, you see," he finished, smiling. "Some cognac for Miss—eh?"

I introduced them.

"For Miss Howard, and then *The Nameless.*"

At his words a tiny warning note seemed to throb in my brain. I had been fingering a heavy metal paperweight, and now, as Keene's attention was momentarily diverted to the sideboard, I slipped it, on a sudden impulse, into my pocket. It would be no defense, though, against a gun.

What was wrong with me, I wondered? An atmosphere of distrust and suspicion seemed to have sprung out of nothing. As Keene ushered us down into his projection room, the skin of my back seemed to crawl with the expectation of attack. It was inexplicable, but definitely unpleasant.

Keene was busy for a time in the projection booth, and then he joined us.

"Modern machinery is a blessing," he said with heavy jocularity. "I can be as lazy as I wish. I needed no help with the shooting, once the automatic cameras were installed. The projector, too, is automatic."

I felt Ann move closer to me in the gloom. I put my arm around her and said, "It helps, yes. What about releasing the picture, Mr. Keene?"

There was a harsh note in his voice. "It will not be released. The world is uneducated, not ready for it. In a hundred years, perhaps, it will achieve the fame it deserves. I am doing it for posterity, and for the sake of creating a weird masterpiece on the screen."

With a muffled click the projector began to operate, and a title flashed on the screen: *The Nameless.*

Keene's voice came out of the darkness. "It's a silent film, except for one sequence at the start. Sound adds nothing to weirdness, and it helps to destroy the illusion of reality. Later, suitable music will be dubbed in."

I did not answer. For a book had flashed on the gray oblong before us—that amazing tour de force, *The Circus of Doctor Lao.* A hand opened it, and a long finger followed the lines as a toneless voice read:

"These are the sports, the offthrows of the universe instead of the species; these are the weird children of the lust of the spheres. Mysticism explains them where science cannot. Listen: when that great mysterious fecundity that peopled the worlds at the command of the gods had done with its birth-giving, when the celestial midwives all had left, when life had begun in the universe, the primal womb-thing found itself still unexhausted, its loins still potent. So that awful fertility tossed on its couch in a final fierce outbreak of life-giving and gave birth to these nightmare beings, these abortions of the world."

The voice ceased. The book faded, and there swam into view a mass of tumbled ruins. The ages had pitted the man-carved rocks with cracks and scars; the bas-relief figures were scarcely recognizable. I was reminded of certain ruins I had seen in Yucatan.

The camera swung down. The ruins seemed to grow larger. A yawning hole gaped in the earth.

Beside me Keene said, "The site of a ruined temple. Watch, now."

The effect was that of moving forward into the depths of a subterranean pit. For a moment the screen was in darkness; then a stray beam of sunlight rested on an idol that stood in what was apparently an underground cavern. A narrow crack of light showed in the roof. The idol was starkly hideous.

I got only a flashing glimpse, but the impression on my mind was that of a bulky, ovoid shape like a pineapple or a pine-cone. The thing had certain doubtful features which lent it a definitely unpleasant appearance; but it was gone in a flash, dissolving into a brightly lighted drawing-room, thronged with gay couples.

The story proper began at that point. None of the actors or actresses was known to me; Keene must have hired them and worked secretly in his house. Most of the interiors and a few of the exteriors seemed to have been taken in this very canyon. The director had used the "parallel" trick which saves so much money for studios yearly. I'd often done it myself. It simply means that the story is tied in with real life as closely as possible; that is, when I had a troupe working up at Lake Arrowhead last winter, and an unexpected snowfall changed the scene, I had the continuity rewritten so that the necessary scenes could take place in snow. Similarly, Keene had paralleled his own experiences—sometimes almost too closely.

The Nameless told of a man, ostracized by his fellows because of his fanatical passion for the morbid and bizarre, who determined to create a work of art—a living masterpiece of sheer weirdness. He had experimented before by directing films that were sufficiently unusual to stir up comment. But this did not satisfy him. It was acting—and he wanted something more than that. No one can convincingly fake reaction to horror, not even the most talented actor, he contended. The genuine emotion must be felt in order to be transferred to the screen.

It was here that *The Nameless* ceased to parallel Keene's own experiences, and branched out into sheer fantasy. The protagonist in the film was Keene himself, but this was not unusual, as directors often act in their own productions. And, by deft montage shots, the audience learned that Keene in his search for authenticity had gone down into Mexico, and had, with the aid of an ancient scroll, found the site of a ruined Aztec temple. And here, as I say, reality was left behind as the film entered a morbid and extraordinary phase.

There was a god hidden beneath this ruined temple—a long-forgotten god, which had been worshipped even before the Aztecs had sprung from the womb of the centuries. At least, the natives had considered it a god, and had erected a temple in its honor, but Keene hinted that the thing was actually a survival, one of the "off-throws of the universe," unique and baroque, which had come down through the eons in an existence totally alien to mankind. The creature was never actually seen on the screen, save for a few brief glimpses in the shadowed, underground temple. It was roughly barrel-shaped, and perhaps ten feet high, studded with odd spiky projections. The chief feature was a gem set in the thing's rounded apex—a smoothly polished jewel as large as a child's head. It was in this gem that the being's life was supposed to have its focus.

It was not dead, but neither was it alive, in the accepted sense of that term. When the Aztecs had filled the temple with the hot stench of blood the thing had lived, and the jewel had glamed with unearthly radiance. But with the passage of time the sacrifices had ceased, and the being had sunk into a state of coma akin to hibernation. In the picture Keene brought it to life.

He transported it secretly to his home, and there, in an underground room hollowed beneath the house, he placed the monster-god. The room was built with an eye for the purpose for which Keene intended it; automatic cameras and clever lighting features were installed, so that pictures could be shot from several different angles at once, and pieced together later as Keene cut the film. And now there entered something of the touch of genius which had made Keene famous.

He was clever, I had always realized that. Yet in the scenes that were next unfolded I admired not so much the technical tricks— which were familiar enough to me—as the marvelously clever way in which Keene had managed to inject realism into the acting. His characters did not act—they *lived*.

Or, rather, they died. For in the picture they were thrust into the underground room to die horribly as sacrifices to the monster-god from the Aztec temple. Sacrifice was supposed to bring the thing to life, to cause the jewel in which its existence was bound to flare with fantastic splendor. The first sacrifice was, I think, the most effective.

The underground room in which the god was hidden was large, but quite vacant, save for a curtained alcove which held the idol. A barred doorway led to the upper room, and here Keene appeared on the screen, revolver in hand, herding before him a man—over-all-clad, with a stubble of black beard on his stolid face. Keene swing open the door, motioned his captive into the great room. He closed the barred door, and through the grating could be seen busy at a switchboard.

Light flared. The man stood near the bars, and then, at Keene's gesture with his weapon, moved forward slowly to the far wall. He stood there, staring around vaguely, dull apprehension in his face. Light threw his shadow in bold relief on the wall.

Then another shadow leaped into existence beside him.

It was barrel-shaped, gigantic, studded with blunt spikes, and capped by a round dark blob—the life-jewel. The shadow of the monster-god! The man saw it. He turned.

Stark horror sprang into his face, and at sight of that utterly ghastly and realistic expression a chill struck through me. This was almost too convincing. The man could not be merely acting.

But, if he was, his acting was superb, and so was Keene's direction. The shadow on the wall stirred, and a thrill of movement shook it. It rocked and seemed to rise, supported by a dozen tentacular appendages that uncoiled from beneath its base. The spikes— changed. They lengthened. They coiled and writhed, hideously worm-like.

It wasn't the metamorphosis of the shadow that held me motionless in my chair. Rather, it was the appalling expression of sheer horror on the man's face. He stood gaping as the shadow toppled and swayed on the wall, growing larger and larger. Then he fled, his mouth an open square of terror. The shadow paused, with an odd air of indecision, and slipped slowly along the wall out of range of the camera.

But there were other cameras, and Keene had used his cutting-shears deftly. The movements of the man were mirrored on the screen; the glaring lights swung and flared; and ever the grim shadow crawled hideously across the wall. The thing that cast it was never shown—just the shadow, and it was a dramatically effective trick. Too many directors, I knew, could not have resisted the temptation to show the monster, thus destroying the illusion—for papier-mâché and rubber, no matter how cleverly constructed, cannot convincingly ape reality.

At last the shadows merged—the gigantic swaying thing with its coiling tentacles, and the black shadow of the man that was caught and lifted, struggling and kicking frantically. The shadows merged —and the man did not reappear. Only the dark blob capping the great shadow faded and flickered, as though strange light were streaming from it; the light that was fed by sacrifice, the jewel that was—life.

Beside me there came a rustle. I felt Ann stir and move closer in the gloom. Keene's voice came from some distance away.

"There were several more sacrifice scenes, Haviland, but I haven't patched them in yet, except for the one you'll see in a moment now. As I said, the film isn't finished."

I did not answer. My eyes were on the screen as the fantastic tale unfolded. The pictured Keene was bringing another victim to his cavern, a short, fat man with sleekly pomaded black hair. I did not see his face until he had been imprisoned in the cave, and then, abruptly there came a close-up shot, probably done with a telescopic lens. His plump face, with its tiny mustache, leaped into gigantic visibility, and I recognized Andy Worth.

It was the missing columnist, but for the first time I saw his veneer of sophistication lacking. Naked fear crawled in his eyes, and I leaned forward in my seat as the ghastly barrel-shaped shadow sprang out on the wall. Worth saw it, and the expression on his face was shocking. I pushed back my chair and got up as the lights came on. The screen went blank.

Arnold Keene was standing by the door, erect and military as ever. He had a gun in his hand, and its muzzle was aimed at my stomach.

"You had better sit down, Haviland," he said quietly. "You too, Miss Howard. I've something to tell you—and I don't wish to be melodramatic about it. This gun"—he glanced at it wryly—"is necessary. There are a few things you must know, Haviland, for a reason you'll understand later."

I said, "There'll be some visitors here for you soon, Keene. You don't think I'd neglect normal precautions!"

He shrugged. "You're lying, of course. Also you're unarmed, or you'd have had your gun out by now. I didn't expect you until tomorrow night, but I'm prepared. In a word, what I have to tell you is this: the film you just saw is a record of actual events."

Ann's teeth sank into her lip, but I didn't say anything. I waited, and Keene resumed.

"Whether you believe me or not doesn't matter, for you'll have to believe in a few minutes. I told you something of my motive, my desire to create a genuine masterpiece of weirdness. That's what I've done, or will have done before tomorrow. Quite a number of vagrants and laborers have disappeared, and the columnist, Worth, as well; but I took care to leave no clues. You'll be the last to vanish —you and this girl."

"You'll never be able to show the film," I told him.

"What of it? You're a hack, Haviland, and you can't understand what it means to create a masterpiece. Is a work of art any less beautiful because it's hidden? I'll see the picture—and after I'm dead the world will see it, and realize my genius even though they may fear and hate its expression. The reactions of my unwilling actors—that's the trick. As a director, you should know that there's no substitute for realism. The reactions were not faked—that was obvious enough. The first sacrifice was that of a clod—an unintelligent moron, whose fears were largely superstitious. The next sacrifice was of a higher type—a vagrant who came begging to my door some months ago. You will complete the group, for you'll know just what you're facing, and your attempt to rationalize your fear will lend an interesting touch. Both of you will stand up, with your hands in the air, and precede me into this passage."

All this came out tonelessly and swiftly, quite as though it were a rehearsed speech. His hand slid over the wall beside him, and a black oblong widened in the oak paneling. I stood up.

"Do as he says, Ann," I said. "Maybe I can—"

"No, you can't," Keene interrupted, gesturing impatiently with his weapon. "You won't have the chance. Hurry up."

We went through the opening in the wall and Keene followed, touching a stud that flooded the passage with light. It was a narrow tunnel that slanted down through solid rock for perhaps ten feet to a steep stairway. He herded us down this, after sliding the panel shut.

"It's well hidden," he said, indicating metal sheathing—indeed, the entire corridor was lined with metal plates. "This lever opens it from within, but no one but me can find the spring which opens it from without. The police could wreck the house without discovering this passage."

That seemed worth remembering, but of little practical value at the moment. Ann and I went down the stairway until it ended in another short passage. Our way was blocked by a door of steel bars, which Keene unlocked with a key he took from his pocket. The passage where we stood was dimly lighted; there were several chairs here; and the space beyond the barred door was not lighted at all.

Keene opened the door and gestured me through it. He locked it behind me and turned to Ann. Her face, I saw, was paper-white in the pale glow.

What happened after that brought an angry curse to my lips. Without warning Keene swung the automatic in a short, vicious arc, smashing it against Ann's head.

She saw it coming too late, and her upflung hand failed to ward off the blow. She dropped without a sound, a little trickle of blood oozing from her temple. Keene stepped over her body to a switchboard set in the rock wall.

Light lanced with intolerable brilliance into my eyes. I shut them tightly, opening them after a moment to stare around apprehensively. I recognized my surroundings. I was in the cave of sacrifice, the underground den I had seen on the screen. Cameras high up on the walls began to operate as I discovered them. From various points blinding arc-lights streamed down upon me.

A grey curtain shielded a space on the far wall, but this was drawn upward to reveal a deep alcove. There was an object within that niche—a barrel-shaped thing ten feet high, studded with spikes, and crowned with a jewel that pulsed and glittered with cold flame. It was grey and varnished-looking, and it was the original of Keene's Aztec god.

Somehow I felt oddly reassured as I examined the thing. It was a model, of course, inanimate and dead; for certainly no life of any kind could exist in such an abnormality. Keene might have installed machinery of some sort within it, however.

"You see, Haviland," Keene said from beyond the bars, "the thing actually exists. I got on the trail of it in an old parchment I found in the Huntington Library. It had been considered merely an interesting bit of folk-lore, but I saw something else in it. When I was making *Ape of God* in Mexico I discovered the ruined temple, and what lay forgotten behind the altar."

He touched a switch, and light streamed out from the alcove behind the thing. Swiftly I turned. On the wall behind me was my own shadow, grotesquely elongated, and beside it was the squat, amorphous patch of blackness I had seen on the screen upstairs.

My back was toward Keene, and my fingers crept into my pocket, touching the metal paperweight I had dropped there earlier that evening. Briefly I considered the possibility of hurling the thing at Keene, and then decided against it. The bars were too close together, and the man would shoot me at any sign of dangerous hostility.

My eyes were drawn to the shadow on the wall. It was moving.

It rocked slightly, and lifted. The spikes lengthened. The thing was no longer inanimate and dead, and as I swung about, stark amazement gripping me, I saw the incredible metamorphosis that had taken place in the thing that cast the shadow.

It was no longer barrel-shaped. A dozen smooth, glistening appendages, ending in flat pads, supported the snake-thin body. And all over that greyish upright pole tentacles sprouted and lengthened, writhing into ghastly life as the horror awakened. Keene had not lied, and the monstrous survival he had brought from the Aztec temple was lumbering from the alcove, its myriad tentacles alive with frightful hunger!

Keene saved me. He saw me standing motionless with abysmal fear in the path of that gigantic, nightmare being, and realizing that he was being cheated of his picture, the man shouted at me to run. His hoarse voice broke the spell that held me unmoving, and I whirled and fled across the cave to the barred door. Skin ripped from my hands as I tore at the bars.

"Run!" Keene yelled at me, his shallow eyes blazing. "It can't move fast! Look out—"

A writhing, snake-like thing lashed out, and a sickening musky stench filled my nostrils. I leaped away, racing across the cave again. The arc-lights died and others flared into being as Keene manipulated the switchboard. He was adjusting the lights, so that our shadows would not be lost—so that in the climax of *The Nameless* the shadow of that ghastly horror would be thrown on the cave wall beside me.

* * *

It was an infernal game of tag we played there, in those shifting lights that glared down while the camera lenses watched dispassionately. I fled and dodged with my pulses thundering and blood pounding in my temples, and ever the grim shadow moved slowly across the walls, while my legs began to ache with the strain. For hours, perhaps, or eons, I fled.

There would come brief periods of respite when I would cling to the bars, cursing Keene, but he would not answer. His hands flickered over the switchboard as he adjusted the arc-lights, and his eyes never paused in their roving examination of the cave. In the end it was this that saved me.

For Keene did not see Ann stir and open her eyes. He did not see the girl, after a swift glance around, get quietly to her feet. Luckily she was behind Keene, and he did not turn.

I tried to keep my eyes away from Ann, but I do not think I succeeded. At the last moment I saw Keene's face change, and he started back; but the chair in Ann's hands crashed down and splintered on the man's head. He fell to his knees, clawing at the air, and then collapsed inertly.

I was on the far side of the cave, and my attention was momentarily diverted from the monster. I had been watching it from the corner of my eye, expecting to be able to dodge and leap away before it came too close; but it lumbered forward with a sudden burst of speed. Although I tried to spring clear I failed; a tentacle whipped about my legs and sent me sprawling. As I tried to roll away another smooth grey coil got my left arm.

Intolerable agony dug into my shoulder as I was lifted. I heard Ann scream, and a gun barked angrily. Bullets plopped into the smooth flesh of the monster, but it paid no attention. I was lifted through a welter of coiling, ropy tentacles, until just above me was the flaming jewel in which the creature's life was centered.

Remembrance of Keene's words spurred me to action; this might be the monster's vulnerable point. The paperweight was still in my pocket, and I clawed it out desperately. I hurled it with all my strength at the shining gem. And the jewel shattered!

There came a shrill vibration, like the tinkling of countless tiny crystalline bells. Piercingly sweet, it shrilled in my ears, and died away quickly. And suddenly nothing existed but light.

It was as though the shattering of the gem had released a sea of incandescent flame imprisoned within it. The glare of the arc-lights faded beside this flood of silvery radiance that bathed me. The cold glory of Arcturus, the blaze of tropical moonlight, were in the light.

Swiftly it faded and fled away. I felt myself dropping, and pain lanced into my wrenched shoulder as I struck the ground. I heard Ann's voice.

Dazedly I got up, expecting to see the monster towering above me. But it was gone. In its place, a few feet away, was the barrel-shaped thing I had first seen in the alcove. There was a gaping cavity in the rounded apex where the jewel had been. And, somehow, I sensed that the creature was no longer deadly, no longer a horror.

I saw Ann. She was still holding Keene's gun, and in her other hand was the key with which she had unlocked the door. She came running toward me, and I went swiftly to meet her.

I took the gun and made sure it was loaded. "Come on," I said, curtly. "We're getting out of here."

Ann's fingers were gripping my arm tightly as we went through the door, past the prone figure of Keene, and up the stairway. The lever behind the panel was not difficult to operate, and I followed Ann through the opening into the theater. Then I paused, listening.

Ann turned, watching me, a question in her eyes. "What is it, Pete?"

"Listen," I said. "Get the cans of film from the projection booth. We'll take them with us and burn them."

"But—you're not—"

"I'll be with you in a minute," I told her, and swung the panel shut.

I went down the stairs swiftly and very quietly, my gun ready and my ears alert for the low muttering I had heard from below.

Keene was no longer unconscious. He was standing beside the switchboard with his back to me, and over his shoulder I could see the shadow of the monster-god sprawling on the wall, inert and lifeless. Keene was chanting something, in a language I did not know, and his hands were moving in strange gestures.

God knows what unearthly powers Keene had acquired in his search for horror! For as I stood there, watching the patch of blackness on the cave wall, I saw a little shudder rock that barrel-shaped shadow of horror, while a single spike abruptly lengthened into a tentacle that groped out furtively and drew back and vanished.

Then I killed Arnold Keene.

Ron Goulart is the pro's pro. Name it, he's written it. But his work is oftentimes not as easy and breezy as it might first appear. An otherwise lightweight book such as *Brinkman* looks a lot more serious when you go back through it a second time. As do many of his novels. Here is Goulart at peak form.

How Come My Dog Don't Bark?

Ron Goulart

They couldn't use those final pictures of him. The photos were too much even for *Worldwide Intruder,* which is why the last picture of Kerry Dent to run in that particular tabloid showed him looking tan, fit, and relatively unwrinkled.

It was the other photos in the *Intruder* which caused Dent to do what he did. If it hadn't been for those earlier pictures, and the unflattering little stories and captions accompanying them, he wouldn't have ended up out in San Fernando Valley in such terrible shape.

Well, his wife had something to do with it, of course. And that impossible dog, too.

Dent told me his suspicions concerning his wife when I visited him on the set of his television show late in the spring of last year. I'm sure you know he was married to Sue Bee Brannigan who does all the commercials for Galz beer. A striking girl, if not overly supportive. He was a shade over 29 years older than Sue Bee.

His suspicions and complaints about the dog I was already pretty familiar with. His feelings concerning Demon were why I was on the Wheelan Studios lot that bright, relatively clear morning. My advertising agency had bought his new show, "Demon & Co.," for our client, the Barx Smoke Alarm. That's the one that barks and howls like a dog to warn you that your house is on fire. Dent's show seemed perfect for Barx and within three weeks of its first airing,

"Demon & Co." had shot up to the number three spot in the ratings. Not bad for a television show starring a German Shepherd and a 59-year-old daredevil actor.

The trouble was, Dent had developed the notion the dog was jealous of him. He took to calling me at the ad agency, and eventually at my home in the best part of Santa Monica, to tell me how insanely jealous Demon was of him. Dent was convinced Demon was deliberately flubbing scenes, wasn't growling on cue, was mugging and letting his purplish tongue loll out during Dent's best dramatic moments and, on three occasions at least, nudging him off high places where only the actor's agility and long experience in action films saved him from serious injury. I'm not overly fond of animals, but I still found it difficult to accept most of what Dent told me.

As I approached the indoor set where Dent was supposed to be rescuing, aided by Demon, a country-and-western singer who was marooned in a flood I heard a great deal of snarling, barking, and shouting.

"Out, I want that gink out of here! Let me go, let me smack him in the beezer!"

That was Dent. You couldn't mistake his voice, which had never quite shaken his Bronx childhood.

"Easy, Kerry. Your pudgy face is getting all flushed. It's going to be coronary time if you don't watch it."

I reached the set in time to see Dent break free of the assistant director and key grip who'd been restraining him from charging at Ben Walden.

Walden was a tall, lean, and moderately handsome young man in his late twenties. He set his camera safely on a vacant canvas chair, pivoted, and stepped out of Dent's way.

"Gigolo!" accused Dent, spinning around. "I told you what I'd do with your camera if I ever caught you around me again!"

"Relax, Kerry," suggested Walden. "Your flabby body can't stand such stress."

"Flabby! I'll shove that—"

Dent, his narrowed eyes on the reporter, didn't notice the approach of Demon. He tripped over the dog and landed with a smack on the sound-stage floor.

Walden, snatching up his camera, clicked off six shots of the actor. "Beautiful, beautiful. All your chins are showing nicely." Then cradling the camera in his arms like a football, Walden jogged away.

He was out of the place by the time they got Dent on his feet again. "Didn't I give strict orders that nobody from the *Intruder* ever be allowed near me?"

The director patted Dent on the shoulder. "The guy slips in, Kerry, he's elusive."

"And you!" Dent kicked out at the dog, missed, and nearly lost his balance.

"Why don't we take five," the director urged. "Pull Dolly out of the tank, Skipper. We'll try the scene again in a few minutes."

"I can do it now," said Dent.

"Few minutes. Go sit down and have a drink."

"I don't drink. I haven't had a drink in three years, no matter what you read in the damn *Intruder*. 'Aging Hasbeen, Looking the Worse for Booze, Totters out of Gollywood Bistro on Arm of Long-Suffering Wife.' You better keep Walden off my set, off the lot. Otherwise there's going to be real trouble." He noticed me then and came hurrying over.

"You're looking well, Kerry," I made the mistake of saying.

"Why shouldn't I look well? I'm in damn fine shape. I do all my own stunts in this halfwit show," he told me, face still flushed. "Which is more than I can say for Demon, my illustrious co-star. He needs a double for all the difficult stuff. Come into my dressing room so we can talk."

I followed him through a doorway and down a corridor. "The client is a little worried about—"

"Did you see what he did just now? Tripped me so I couldn't wind Walden's clock for him."

"An accident, dogs aren't as bright as—"

"And look at this dressing room." He jerked the door open. "Cozy."

"Cozy my fanny! It's tiny. You know who had this dressing room before me? That clunk who starred in *Cybernetic Midget*. Yeah, this is a dwarf's old dressing room." He stalked to a small refrigerator, took out a bottle of Perrier water. "Demon has a kennel the size of Pickfair, while I—"

"The client was worried by the last story in the *Int*—"

"Listen, I'm a part of your life, right?" He gestured at one wall with his glass of sparkling water.

There were framed stills from some of his old movies mounted on the wall. A shot from *The Dancing Pirate*, two from *Captain*

Juggernaut, one from *Fort Gordo,* and a whole series from *The Avenging Cavalier,* which was Dent's most popular movie.

"I saw most of your pictures," I admitted, "when I was a kid."

"Ha, ha. Very funny. You're as old as I am."

"I'm forty-four, you're fifty-nine."

"Forty-four isn't that far from fifty-nine. However, I don't have the problems you civilians do." He sipped at the water. "I take care of myself, good care." He patted his chin. "That's *one* chin you see, no matter what snide lies Walden writes in the *Intruder.*"

"It's not so much the lies as the photographs. The client feels—"

"That bum hounds me! He sneaks around and snaps pictures of me when I'm at my worst. He waits for some unfortunate pose, then snaps and runs."

"The picture in this week's tab is particularly unfortunate. When you're hitting that blind beggar woman over the head with her own accordion."

"It only *looks* that way. Because of that wily jerk Walden," explained the actor. "I was helping the old bat adjust the damn thing and *snap* there's Walden and his camera."

"You were caught standing in front of the Naked Nikelodeon," I reminded. "With that poster behind you promising explicit romantic action inside."

"You don't understand what it is to be a celebrity," Dent said. "I can't take a walk or meet a friend without some nitwit reporter or photographer popping up and trying to make me look bad. The worst offender is that—"

"Maybe you should quit strolling in places like the Los Angeles tenderloin."

Finishing his Perrier, Dent turned to face me. "You recall the picture of me three weeks ago in the *Intruder?*"

"The one where you're doing a bellyflop in your pool. Flabby Kerry Does Flop. The client thought—"

"He climbed over the wall of my estate to snap that." The actor turned his back on me. "At least, I thought that was his only reason for being there. Now I—well, it's one of those little everyday troubles you have to live with."

I said, "I don't think the Barx Brothers can live with many more of your little everyday troubles, Kerry. What is it?"

He gestured at another wall of photos. "I've had four wives, everybody knows that. I swear the only one I ever cared for is Sue Bee."

"She's a striking woman."

"Of course she is. I only marry striking women. Sue Bee is also intelligent. How many people do you know who've read all the way through Proust's *Remembrance of Things Past?*"

"I read it in college, and my wife read it while she was in the hospital with—"

"Never mind," he cut in. "The trouble is, despite her intelligence —well, Sue Bee is being unfaithful."

I nodded. "These days, Kerry, with society in a state of—"

"Unfaithful to *me!* And do you know who the guy is?"

"No, who?"

"Him! The jerk with the camera!"

"Ben Walden?"

"That bum with the camera, yes. Walden is cuckholding me."

"You're absolutely sure?"

"Figures, doesn't it? Explains why he's trying to destroy me in the pages of that filthy rag. Over-the-hill Swashbuckler makes Feeble Attempt at Comeback. Feeble? He knows we knocked off the two top shows. The network ought to have a few more feeble swash-bucklers like me."

"Wait now," I said. "Do you know for certain your wife's having an affair with Walden, or do you just suppose she is?"

"I know *here!*" He thumped his handsome chest. "Look, if you're an artist you *sense* things. I know. Old Man Dent Takes Snooze After Too Much Booze. He's trying to make me look ridiculous in the eyes of Sue Bee."

"But a woman of her intelligence wouldn't—"

"Just because she's read Proust doesn't mean she wouldn't have an affair with Walden."

I was silent for several seconds. "Going to be tough using any of this with the Barx Brothers," I finally told him. "If true, this is a logical explanation for why the *Intruder* seems to be picking on you. But the idea of your wife fooling around will upset them even more than—"

"You can tell the Barx boys to stick some of their smoke alarms—"

"Kerry, let me think about this. I'll see if I can—"

"Always the ad man. You can't react to anything with your *guts.* You have to write memos, take a couple dips in the think tank."

I cleared my throat. "This probably isn't the best time to ask you about the publicity stills."

"What stills?"

"Ones of you and Demon standing under a Barx alarm."

"Tell you what." Dent put a hand on my back. "We can use Demon's stand-in. That dog is an angel, a gem of a hound. Sweet, considerate, the absolute antithesis of Demon. I keep telling them to take Demon out and retire him or something and use the damn stand-in. They won't hear of it, especially Tessica Janes, the bimbo who claims to be Demon's trainer. She's got them all hoodwinked into thinking Demon is unique. He's unique all right, but—"

"Ready to shoot again, Mr. Dent," someone called outside the door.

Dent straightened, smiling. "Don't brood too much about anything that's happened today," he said to me. "I have an uncanny ability for bouncing back. And you're going to see one hell of a bounce any day now."

The agency sent me to Mentor, Ohio, a few days after that encounter with Kerry Dent and I didn't see him again for nearly a month. We'd been test-marketing a new bread in Mentor, a loaf which was 20 percent sawdust and called Lumberjack Bread, and some problems had arisen. Nearly everyone who ate so much as a slice of the experimental bread had come down with a disease closely resembling the flu. There was a definite danger of the media getting hold of the story. We couldn't afford to have the whole country hearing about a new blight known as the Lumberjack Bread Disease.

I was able, with a mixture of diplomacy and bribery, to keep the whole mess hushed up. Working very covertly we got all the test loaves out of the supermarkets and dumped into a handy river. That dumping gave us another problem, since it turned out that Lumberjack Bread was capable of killing fish even with its wrapper on.

As I say, I didn't get back to Los Angeles until a month or more after my meeting with Kerry Dent on the "Demon and Co." set. Not that I hadn't been in communication with him, or rather he with me. Dent, possibly because he knew I'd been a fan of his swashbucklers in my youth, decided I was the one person he could confide in.

The phone in my slightly mildewed Mentor motel room rang at all hours. Dent's complaints were all variations on ones I'd heard before. Sue Bee continued to be unfaithful with Ben Walden of *Worldwide Intruder,* Demon loathed him and was making enormous efforts to sabotage his comeback, Walden was so audacious that when he sneaked into Dent's mansion to woo his wife he managed to snap unflattering photos of the dozing actor. Despite his claims of renewed vigor, Dent seemed to nap a good deal, as the frequent pictures showing up in the *Intruder* attested.

One particularly bleak morning in Ohio, just after my lovely secretary had rushed in to tell me 5000 dead fish had been sighted floating down the river with several loaves of Lumber-Jack Bread leading the pack, Dent phoned me collect. He claimed he had absolute proof that Demon not only hated him but was actually trying to kill him. In a scene for the eleventh episode of their show the dog was supposed to remove a smoking stick of dynamite from the vicinity of the bound-and-gagged Dent. He swore, and claimed to have witnesses, that Demon switched a real stick of dynamite for the prop one. If Dent hadn't sensed something was wrong and gone rolling over a low precipice he would have been blown up.

I pointed out that real dynamite could just as likely have blown up the dog when he snatched it up in his powerful jaws. Dent told me the dog had deliberately dawdled instead of rushing in to pick up the dynamite stick. Pacifying him as best I could, I went out to do something about all those dead fish.

My last, although I didn't know it at the time, encounter with Kerry Dent took place by accident. I was out in San Fernando Valley to call on a well-known sci-fi writer in Woodland Hills to see if we could persuade him to endorse a new pizza line the agency was involved with. The author, an extremely surly man, was not at all impressed by the Unidentified Flying Pizza and came close to punching me. Feeling very much like someone in an *Intruder* gossip item, I slunk away from his home and dropped into a valley restaurant for a cup of coffee to calm my nerves.

It was a noisy place, because of the prerecorded whip cracking and pistol shooting, and at first I wasn't aware of the hissing.

"Hsst, over here."

It was Dent, wearing a nylon jumpsuit and dark glasses and without his hairpiece. "Are you incognito?" I inquired, joining him in his booth.

"Used to know Whip in his heyday and I stop by here now and then."

Whip Wigransky's Burger Rancho was one of six such spots in the valley. It didn't seem to me that a nostalgia for the old

B-Western actor was what had brought Dent here. "You have," I mentioned, "paw prints all over your front."

He glanced down, frowning, and brushed off some of the muddy spots. "Ho, ho," he said.

"You sound happy. I take it those prints aren't the leftovers from another attack by your co-star."

"That dumbunny isn't a co-star. I'm a star and he's only a bit player." Dent appeared considerably more relaxed than he'd been lately.

"I'm glad you're in a jovial mood. I thought maybe the picture in this week's *Intruder* would have—"

"Ho, ho, ho. That sort of guff rolls off my back. Fat Old Actor, Looking Terrible, Escorts Stunning Much Younger Wife to Premiere. Walden'll have to do a lot better than that to dampen Kerry Dent's spirits."

"I'll pass that news on to the Barx Brothers."

"Give them my love."

I watched his partially masked face. "What are you up to?"

"Having a Bar-B-Q Burger, Owlhoot Style," he said, smiling. "That's all."

"You're out here, disguised, looking smug. It's not like you."

"You didn't know me in my heyday," he replied. "I often went around looking smug. Recently I've found a way to return to the happier moods of yesteryear."

"Are you drinking again?"

"You can't drink and do your own stunts and keep a crazed hellhound from destroying you." He chuckled, relaxing even more. "I was stupid for a spell, now I'm getting all my old smarts back. There was a rock-and-roll tune I used to be fond of years ago. About a guy who suspected his wife was two-timing him. He asks the suspected lover, 'How come my dog don't bark when you come round to my door? Maybe it's because you been here before.' I was like that, stupid. Now I see things as they really are. I've devised a plan to bring me complete and total happiness."

"You haven't gone and joined some lunatic cult?"

"Cults join me." He locked his hands behind his head. "You and the Barx brood need have no fears. In a short time I shall have everything worked out to the satisfaction of one and all."

"Tessica Janes lives out here in the valley somewhere," I said, recalling the fact all at once. "You haven't been visiting her and making threats?"

"That bimbo and I have little to do with each other," Dent assured me. "She trains Demon, I am forced to act with him. That's our only link."

"She's a pretty large young woman. Doesn't look as though she could be intimidated."

"I don't blame Tess for what Demon does. He hates me and plots against me entirely on his own," he said. "Say, look who's coming in. It's old Whip Wigransky himself. Excuse me while I go wrestle with him. It's a long-standing custom."

"Sure, certainly." I sat there, not even turning to watch the good-natured horseplay which was amusing all the other customers. Deep inside I felt very uneasy. I had a premonition something was going to happen, something which would affect the show and annoy the Barx Brothers.

Immediately after this I had to leave town again. There'd been a disastrous fire in the Barx Brothers main factory in Trenton, New Jersey. The place had burned to the ground and not one of the 10,000 smoke alarms sitting in there had so much as yelped. The wire services had picked up the story and both *Newsmag* and *Tide* were sending people in. The Barx Brothers, with the exception of Carlos who refused to come back from Bermuda, met with me for two days while we worked out a rush campaign to counteract the effects of what had happened.

By the time I came up with a copy approach which satisfied us all, except for Jocko who went off to join Carlos in Bermuda, and wrote some commercials three weeks had passed. I was on the plane back to L.A. when the news came through. I learned about it because my stewardess was sobbing and I asked why.

"The poor darling old man," she managed to say between sobs. "He's been a part of my life since earliest girlhood. I simply adored his swashbuckuling films and his TV shows and—"

"Wait a minute. You can't be talking about—"

"Yes, isn't it awful? Kerry Dent is dead."

"Kerry Dent is dead?"

"I heard it on the news just before takeoff."

"How did it happen?"

"Oh, it's too terrible."

She was referring of course only to the official version of Dent's passing. Nobody ever released the true story, which was fortunate I suppose. It's possible that Ben Walden knows most of the truth, but he won't be writing it up in the *Intruder*. Not unless he can figure a way to make his own part of the events seem admirable. Which isn't likely.

As you probably know, I don't like to get too involved in affairs of this sort. Since I was curious, though, and since I felt I owed it to the agency to find out why the star of our top-rated show had been torn to pieces, I did some digging.

What follows is, I believe, a relatively accurate account of how Dent met his end. Some of it I've had to guess.

Dent had come up with a plan to remove the two prime sources of grief in his life—Ben Walden and Demon. He was certain Sue Bee would return to him completely when there was no more Ben Walden around. He also believed Demon could be very easily replaced on the show by the stand-in, a much more admirable dog. He figured it would be to the benefit of all concerned not even to let on there'd been a switch. One German Shepherd looked pretty much like another.

He arranged things so he could put his plan into action the night Tessica Janes, Demon's trainer, was not at home. The girl was scheduled to attend a screening of the punk rock remake of *Boys Town* on the night in question. Dent, with the help of Whip Wigransky, had already planted in Ben Walden's mind the idea that Dent was having an affair with Tessica. That fateful night Whip phoned Walden with a tip that the girl was going to skip the screening and spend the night with the aging actor. Dent assumed Walden wouldn't pass up a chance to get pictures of him in such a compromising position.

Dent had been, very secretly, working out in San Fernando Valley at a seedy dog-training school. That was where he'd been the day I ran into him. The paw prints I'd noticed had come from the vicious German Shepherd that Dent was training. This dog was designed to be a watchdog, eager to kill anyone his master ordered him to kill. Dent was his master.

Actually it wasn't a bad plan. Lure Walden to Tessica's place and set this killer dog on him. The police would find the body of a snooping reporter who'd obviously been torn to pieces by a mad German Shepherd. There would be Demon in his cage looking sheepish.

Even if Tessica claimed the dog had been locked up all night, the evidence of a dead *Intruder* reporter would contradict her.

Dent arrived a half hour before the ten-o'clock assignation time that he'd had Whip pass on to Walden. It was an exceptionally clear night with more stars out than you usually see in Southern California.

Parking his rented van in a wooded area behind Tessica's spread, Dent led his killer dog out of the vehicle and down to the ranch. By diligent spying earlier he knew there was only one old servant to worry about. The man was in his late sixties and slept in a cottage near the main entrance of the ranch. There was a cyclone fence around the three acres, but it wasn't electrified. Dent had no trouble clipping a section out of it.

The police would naturally assume that Walden, hot after a hot story, had done the snipping.

Up to here Dent's plan went well. He crossed onto the ranch grounds with his dog.

There was an arbor to the left of the ranch house. He took the German Shepherd there and crouched in the shadows to await Walden.

He debated whether or not he ought to let Demon loose after the killing. He decided it would be safer not to. As he'd already figured out, no matter what Tessica and the old servant might claim, they'd never convince the police that it wasn't Demon who'd done the killing. There were only two collies and a spaniel in the kennels here. None of them could be blamed. The frame would fit only Demon.

Unfortunately there were three things Dent couldn't have anticipated. For one thing, he couldn't have known that Walden, who was spending some time with Sue Bee, would be late by about 20 minutes. Nor did Dent know that on the evenings when Tessica was away the old servant let Demon loose for a romp around the ranch.

The third thing he couldn't have expected was that his killer dog, while aggressive with people, was fearful of other German Shepherds.

So when the roaming Demon, sensing the presence of Dent and the dog in the arbor, came galloping in there, the killer dog yelped and ran away through the hole in the fence.

Demon then leaped straight at Dent.

I'd always thought Dent was exaggerating about the animosity Demon felt toward him. It turned out, though, Dent was absolutely right.

That dog really hated him.

Ray Russell began writing in the early fifties, went on to have a close association with *Playboy*, and to write some of the most notable horror fiction of the ensuing decades. Recently, the Horror writers of America gave him a Life Achievement Award. The following story will demonstrate why.

Ding-Dong, the Lizard's Dead

Ray Russell

The era of the old Hollywood studio system has passed forever, and along with it the legendary breed of studio moguls who built the fledgling industry from scratch. MBAs and market research have replaced the crude but effective showmanship of the Golden Age. But were the days of the Selznicks, the Zanucks, and the Warners really the good old days? When Lieutenant Garcia of the LAPD is called in to investigate the death of the last of the great Hollywood patriarchs, in Ray Russell's "Ding-Dong, the Lizard's Dead," he finds that the good old days concealed some unpleasant secrets.

Garcia found himself humming the old tune as he turned off Doheny onto Pico and drove deeper into West Los Angeles. Old tune, but revised words. Not "the witch is dead," but "the lizard's dead." That's the way it was being sung the past few days by all the registered smartballs in town. Garcia was tired of it, but he couldn't keep it from running through his head.

On his left, he noted the kosher eatery owned and operated by Steven Spielberg's mother; on his right, where shops used to be, was the discreetly walled enclosure of an oil company's slant-drilling operation, always smelling faintly of unrefined petroleum. (Progress!)

Just the day before, one of his younger colleagues, Jameson, had been trying to tell him that the world was getting better. He had snorted at the presumptuous pup and said, "Better? Are you nuts? Have you seen the latest numbers on narcotic addiction? Have you waded through your phone bills since they busted up Ma Bell? Do you know how many people are dying of AIDS—a disease that hadn't even been *invented* when I was your age? Don't give me 'better.' The world is the *pits*. And it's getting worse every day."

"Come on, Garcia," Jameson had persisted. "When you were my age, a black dude like me wouldn't even be on the same payroll with you." Garcia had refrained from responding that there hadn't been many Garcias or Gomezes or Rodriguezes on the strength back then, either, and there still weren't enough to suit him. The black man had continued, "When you were a kid, I bet they didn't even have TV. Now, guess what I bought yesterday? I went out and got myself a VCR."

"Great," Garcia had groaned. "Now you can rent *Casablanca* for more than I paid to see it first run on the *big* screen."

"*Casablanca!* That old thing? I can rent X-rated stuff, and me and my little honey can watch it together."

"Exactly! The pits, like I said. You and your little honey will probably end up with herpes."

"From a *cassette?*"

It was well before noon, but the Southern California sun was already threatening to turn the car into a potter's kiln, even with the windows open. He closed them and turned on the air conditioner as he passed the green, woody fragrance of Rancho Park golf course on his left. Garcia put pressure on the gas pedal and picked up speed. He didn't want to be late for the show.

Because that's what it would be. A show. A display. He didn't expect to accomplish anything this morning, do any business, conduct any interviews. Wrong time, if not wrong place. All he could do would be to study the . . . cast of characters. He touched his chest and felt the crinkle of paper in the inside pocket of his jacket.

He passed Twentieth Century-Fox—now shrunken to a wraith of its sprawling former self by a real estate sell-off to developers. Garcia, a native Angeleno, was saddened by such changes. A big blue bus of the Santa Monica line roared past him, leaving behind a black cloud of diesel flatulence. He was glad he had closed his windows.

He passed the warm Spanish architecture of St. Timothy's: a reminder that he hadn't been to confession for . . . he couldn't remember how long. He let his wife take care of all the religious stuff.

Well, what the hell, what did *he* have to confess? *He* didn't shoot dope or watch X-rated filth with a little honey. But he made a mental note to visit the confessional box anyway. Tomorrow. Or over the weekend, at the very latest. It couldn't hurt.

His destination was almost on top of him, and he quickly moved into the next lane without signaling, luckily avoiding any traffic mishaps.

As he drove under the giant arch bearing the letters O-Z, a uniformed guard stopped him with an authoritative gesture. Garcia lowered the driver window, and before the guard had a chance to speak, he flashed his ID and said, "I'm looking for Stage Twelve."

"Straight ahead, then turn right. Just follow the rest of the parade."

Parade. Nice word for it. Garcia drove on, slowly trailing the stately procession of long, costly sedans and limousines. His eyes narrowed in the sunlight as he watched the huge sound stages go by his car window.

It had been a long time since he'd been on the "Oz" lot, as it was often called by people who liked to be considered in the swim. But the real insiders called it either O-Z or just Oracle, short for Oracle-Zodiac Pictures. The company had been formed, decades earlier, by a merger of two studios, Oracle and Zodiac.

The string of cars came to an end at Stage Twelve, its colossal doors open wide. Garcia parked as best he could, climbed out, and watched the collection of notables do the same. Stretch limos, stretch jeans. The people were of both sexes and all ages, and many of the faces were familiar to him. Some he had seen all his life on the screen. He tried to blend in with them as he sauntered into the cavernous interior of the soundstage.

There, pinned like a rare butterfly by the dramatic beam of an overhead spotlight, was an ornate open coffin banked by floral wreaths. Organ music—recorded, Garcia assumed—softly cushioned the assembled mourners. Inside the coffin lay the mortal remains of the studio's late production head, Baruch Isaac Gross. Mister B.I.G. The Lizard of Oz.

"He ruled his kingdom, Oracle-Zodiac, with despotic genius," the newspaper eulogy had said. "A man of clashing contradictions, he could one minute be crassly commercial, and the next minute he might approve an experimental project by a bright young student fresh out of cinema school. A brilliant if untutored armchair psychologist, he knew what made his employees tick, and that knowledge was power. Crude, forceful, admired by few, hated by many, he countered accusations of 'grossness' by responding: 'You know what Gross means? It don't just mean the grosses. Gross means Great! Look it up.' And, in his way, B. I. Gross was indeed great, the last of the old-style tyrannosaurs that once were wont to do battle with each other in the primeval jungles of Hollywood. . . .''

Dead, he didn't look much like a lizard, Garcia thought. You needed to see the teeth when he smiled that mirthless smile; you had to shrivel before those glittering eyes moving under the canopy-like lids.

"Yep," a man standing next to Garcia whispered, "Gross was absolutely right. Look at this turnout, will you? Like he always said, 'Give the marks what they want and they'll line up like sailors at a whorehouse.' " The cynic was a burly middle-aged man with sandy hair going gray and thin.

"You mean," asked Garcia, "all these people are glad he's dead?"

"Well, you don't see any tears, do you? Except from one or two crocodiles, maybe. They all hated him, every one of them, the whole ball of wackos."

"You could be right. Pardon me, you're . . . ?"

"Hammond."

"Buck Hammond, the cameraman?"

"Cinematographer," Hammond corrected with an ironical grin.

"Right. I'll be talking to you later. You live up in Bel-Air, don't you?"

"Talk to me about what?" asked Hammond, with a scowl of suspicion.

"The death of Mr. Gross."

"Who the hell are you?"

"Name of Garcia. Lieutenant, LAPD." Garcia smiled. "Homicide Division. Nice to meet you, Mr. Hammond."

Earlier that week, a lawyer named Creeley had phoned and asked Garcia to drop by his office. The office was located in one of Century City's twin triangular forty-four-story high-rises, a cold structure like an upended ice cube tray, in a synthetic "city" without houses, without litter, without children, without dogs or cats; a place avoided by most birds, where even the severe platoons of trees, though real, seemed to be clever plastic fakes; where all the parking was hidden underground, and nothing was permitted to exist that did not turn a large profit.

In years gone by, the 180-acre complex had been the backlot of the Twentieth Century-Fox film studio. It could be argued that the long-gone fabulous backlot had been no less relentlessly commercial in its goals than its rigid, frigid successor. Certainly it had been far more tawdry. But to be tawdry, Garcia reflected, is to be human. He hated Century City.

When he had complied with the request and visited Creeley's office, the attorney had handed him a sealed gray envelope addressed in longhand to Sergeant P. Garcia, LAPD.

"From my client—well, my former client, the late B. I. Gross," Creeley had said. His eyes were about the size of poppy seeds. "It was among his effects, to be delivered to you upon his death. If you *are* the correct Garcia, that is. This says 'Sergeant,' but my secretary announced you as Lieutenant. . . ."

"I was still a sergeant when Mr. Gross and I met some years ago. A little scrape his son got into. Nothing serious. I wasn't in Homicide then."

Garcia had thanked Creeley and had declined to open the letter there in the office, despite (or possibly because of) the attorney's obvious curiosity.

At a taco and hot dog stand well away from Century City, Garcia had avoided the tacos as being a desecration to the memory of those his mother had made with such care and authenticity and settled for a hot dog with sauerkraut. Chewing his lunch and washing it down with diet root beer, he had opened the letter and read it. Written in Gross's hand on heavy, rat-gray personal stationery, it said, in effect, that if the writer were to die from causes other than natural, certain people were to be investigated because they all wanted him dead. A list of nine names followed.

Garcia, fighting back the threatened eruption of a volcanic root-beer belch, had put down his hot dog half-eaten. Causes other than natural? Gross had died of barbiturate poisoning. Accidental? Suicide? Murder? Suddenly this letter had made murder the odds-on favorite. A much closer look into the matter was in order. A more thorough search of the dead man's house. And a microscopic examination of the nine suspects.

That was when Garcia had assigned a team to the house and had made it his personal business to attend the funeral service that was held, with typical B. I. Gross showmanship, on one of his own soundstages. Among those in attendance, the lieutenant noted with interest, were all nine of the people on the Lizard's list.

He had researched all of them, and in the week following the burial of Gross, he sought out and interviewed them, one by one.

First, he interviewed the one he already knew: the dead man's son, Martin. The sullen, delicately pretty young man of twenty-seven lived in a tastefully appointed little house in that part of the Hollywood Hills sometimes known as the Swish Alps. He opened the door himself.

"Hello, Martin," said Garcia.

"Do I know you?" Martin blinked and seemed the worse for drink, an assumption enhanced by the alcoholic odor that radiated from him like a halo.

"You were only eighteen when we last met. Lieutenant Garcia, LAPD."

"Oh, sure, the *cop!* Come on in, friend."

Declining the offer of a drink, Garcia got right to the point. "Your father left me a letter," he said, "naming several people I should investigate if he died."

"And I'm one of them?"

"I'm afraid so."

Martin Gross laughed. "Love it! I *love* it! What's my motive supposed to be?"

"You tell me," Garcia suggested.

"Oh, no. That's what *you're* paid for."

"Well," Garcia said casually, "I know you're gay, and your father knew it, too . . ."

"And hated the idea, yes indeed, but that's a motive for *him* to kill *me,* not me him."

"What I started to say was, I know you're gay because of that little scrape when you were still a high school senior, when you tried to pick up that fellow in the bar, and he got all uptight about it and swore out a complaint against you . . ."

"I'm eternally grateful to you, Lieutenant, for smoothing that over and convincing my father it had something to do with pot. Bad enough in his eyes, the devil's weed and all that, but if he had found out the *truth* . . ."

"He did find out later, though, didn't he?" said Garcia. "It's only gossip, of course, but the way I heard it, he caught you and another man—"

"In flagrante delicto, or do I mean *delicious?"* Martin laughed. "Yes, he certainly did, Lieutenant."

"And he couldn't take that. So, for appearances, he forced you to marry some starlet under contract to his studio . . ."

"As you say, for appearances. But also 'to make a man of me.' Can you imagine the naiveté of the old fool? To think that marrying me off to some tart would 'cure' me? The marriage didn't last, of course. Oh, I never blamed *her,* the poor little bubble-brain. She'd been servicing the old man for years, and most of his friends as well, like that spic Montoya . . . oh, sorry about that! . . . but anyway, I was just another assignment to her."

"The story goes that the whole experience turned you into a lush. Sorry about *that,* Martin."

"Oh, I *am* a lush. I've been a lush for simply *years.* But it wasn't the marriage to little Charlaine that did it. Good grief, that was only a bore. And an inconvenience. What made me a lush was being the son of that unspeakable pig!"

"Then you hated him?"

"Of *course* I hated him! Who didn't?" Martin began to sing: *"Ding-dong, the lizard's dead . . ."* He broke off, and said, "My stepmother hated him, too. Why don't you talk to her?"

"I will," said Garcia. For she was on the list.

It was not Martin's stepmother Garcia visited next, however. The next name on his list was Fawn Blake, and in order to interview her, he had to drive into the San Fernando Valley. He wisely resolved to schedule his further interviews more efficiently, to cut down on driving time.

He eased his car across Sunset Boulevard and kept driving north on Highland until that avenue obligingly became the Hollywood Freeway, conveying him smoothly into the Valley. Fawn Blake. . . . Garcia smiled as he recalled her pictures with affection. . . .

Signaling right, he drifted deftly across the lanes and made it to the off ramp just in time, curving gracefully down onto Lankershim Boulevard and leaving only one angry horn honking in his wake. "Same to you, buddy," he muttered to his steering wheel.

He found Fawn Blake at Universal, on the set of a top-rated television series, where she was doing a guest appearance.

"As an aging actress," she said sweetly. "But it's a job. Come, Lieutenant, let's take a break in my dressing room. They won't be needing me for a while."

The dressing room was only a trailer, but it contained the necessities of television life, as well as the thick, cloying odor of makeup. "Sit down somewhere," said Fawn Blake, easing off her shoes, "and tell me what this is all about."

She had always been, if not a great beauty in the classic sense, the epitome of girl-next-door innocence and sincerity. Much of this essence still clung to her.

Garcia perched himself precariously on a small folding chair and told her about the list. She smiled. "That's just dear Biggie making trouble for everybody," she said. "Doesn't mean a thing."

"Biggie?"

"B.I.G. A lot of us called him Biggie. Of course, *some* called him the Lizard of Oz or even worse. The killer will probably turn out to be somebody not even *on* the list."

"Maybe," Garcia admitted. "But you did have a motive, Miss Blake."

"Do tell." She smirked, not unattractively.

"Well," said the lieutenant, "the characters you played in your films . . ."

"Movies," she said primly. "I made movies. We all made movies in those days. It was when they started making *films* that they began to lose the public."

He nodded. "Anyway, you always played—how should I put it?— wholesome ladies . . ."

"Pure as the well-known driven snow," she added.

"Right, both on and *off* the screen. Not a breath of scandal. Never in the gossip columns. Your private life was spotless. You were held up as some kind of ideal, by church groups and so on."

"You have a good memory, Lieutenant."

"You were my mother's favorite actress," said Garcia, and when he saw her face begin to harden, he quickly added, "Mine, too."

"On your dear mama's lap? Very well, I was the original Mrs. Clean. Where is all this leading?"

"The inside story is that although you were a big star, very popular—especially after you made that picture about St. Therese—you worked for low pay under contract to Mr. Gross—"

"Peanuts," she snapped. "I wasn't a very good businesswoman."

"You worked for low pay," Garcia continued, "because Mr. Gross possessed the only existing print of a one-reel movie you made when you were fifteen. The kind of movie they used to call a stag film and that was shown only at men's smokers. Today, movies

like that are shown in theaters, rated X, big screen, color, stereo-
phonic sound. But not then."

"Rumors, Lieutenant," said Fawn Blake, "just rumors."

"The film was in Mr. Gross's wall safe," said Garcia. "As part of
this investigation, I screened it. It pretty much supports the rumors,
Miss Blake. They say you moved heaven and earth to have all the
prints destroyed, but Gross had the last remaining copy, and he
held it over your head."

"And I killed him because of that? After all these years? Don't
be silly." The warm crinkle of her eyes took the sting out of the
admonition.

"It's a valid motive," Garcia insisted.

Fawn Blake shook her head. "You're barking up the wrong lady,
Lieutenant. Oh, I admit that I used to be terribly afraid of that little
strip of celluloid. But that was back in the old days, when people
took things like that very big. Now?" she shrugged. "Frankly, my
dear, I don't give a damn—as Clark said in the movie." She giggled.
"What a stir that caused! When he said 'damn.' And today they say
anything they please. Well, *autres temps, autres moeurs.*"

"I'm sorry?"

"Never mind—just a French proverb I picked up from Charles
Boyer. As for that little old one-reeler of mine, you can book it into
all the trendiest theaters in Westwood, for all I care. I only wish my
last two pictures were as good as that one!"

"It certainly doesn't have any dull moments," Garcia conceded.

"You saw it, you say?" Garcia nodded. Fawn Blake sighed wist-
fully. With a faraway gaze in her still-innocent wide eyes, she said,
"I had great tits in those days, didn't I?"

The next name on the list took Garcia back to the O-Z lot and the
office of Sidney Warren, executive vice-president of the studio. He
was a crisply tailored, gray-haired man, well into his sixties, thin and
angular as a praying mantis. A hint of lime-scented aftershave lotion clung to him.

"Is this sort of thing really necessary?" he asked. "Wasting people's time . . . bothering them in their hour of grief? I thought
these days the police solved crimes in the forensics laboratories."

"We do, some of them," said Garcia. "And our police labs here
in L.A. are among the best in the country. But I guess I'm old-
fashioned. Also, it so happens that the Justice Department, not too

long ago, completed a three-year study of local, state, and federal crime labs. Know what they came up with, Mr. Warren?"

"I haven't the faintest idea," said Warren, bored.

"Fully *half* of the labs couldn't identify dog hair. Thirty-four percent couldn't tell three kinds of paint apart. Twenty-two percent couldn't differentiate among three different metals. Thirteen percent couldn't analyze which guns bullets came from. So, yes, this sort of thing really *is* necessary."

Glancing at his watch, Warren said, "I have a full agenda today, Lieutenant. I can allow you five minutes."

Garcia told him about the list, adding, "You were Mr. Gross's second-in-command here, isn't that right?" Warren nodded. "That means you're first in line for the top-dog position, now that he's dead."

"It seems likely," said Warren.

"The talk around town, though, is that you never had his showmanship or daring, and he didn't have much respect for your opinions."

"I'm surprised you listen to 'the talk around town,' Lieutenant," Warren responded. "Actually, Baruch and I got along very well."

"He called you the Accountant, I understand."

"I *was* an accountant when we first met."

"He made fun of your cautious attitudes."

"And I criticized his lack of caution. It was a nice check and balance."

"They say," Garcia went on, "that a long time ago, when you were a young employee at a credit-reporting agency, he came to you with a proposal. If you would fiddle with the files and give his financially shaky company, Zodiac, a phony triple-A credit rating so he'd be in a better position to merge with Oracle, he'd reward you with a large slice of stock and a position in the new company."

Warren said, "I've heard that story. But whether or not it's true, it doesn't give me a reason to kill him."

"No, it doesn't," Garcia agreed. "But the other things do. The resentment, the desire to be main man . . ."

Warren looked at his watch again. "Your five minutes are up. If you'll excuse me?"

As long as he was on the O-Z lot, Garcia figured he might as well visit Barry Birmingham, who was acting in a picture being shot on Stage Four. He was one of the people on the list. The handsome leading man was not to be found on the soundstage at the moment, however, and Garcia was directed to his bungalow.

There, resting between acting chores, Birmingham was dressed in a burgundy velour robe and, presumably, nothing else. His tanned bare feet and ankles seemed aggressively casual, particularly in light of the fact that he was not alone. With him in the bungalow was a handsome, if glassily brittle, woman in elegant early middle age—forty?—dressed exactly the same as Birmingham. His and Hers matching robes? wondered Garcia. Her toenails were tinted tea-rose pink. Her face seemed faintly familiar to Garcia, but he couldn't place her.

"What can I do for you, Lieutenant?" the actor asked amiably after Garcia had identified himself.

"Actually, Mr. Birmingham, I'd like a few words in private."

"You can speak in front of Mrs. Gross," Birmingham assured him. Now Garcia recognized the former Regina Thayer, who had been a minor contract player at O-Z until Gross had married her some fifteen years before. Garcia had noted the widow's veiled presence at the funeral service, as she had been helped from her limo by a black chauffeur. "We have no secrets from each other," said Birmingham. "Right, Regina?"

The woman drawled, "If that's the way you want to play it, Barry."

Birmingham smiled. "What does the Bard say? 'Man and wife are one flesh . . .' "

"We're not married yet, darling," Regina Gross reminded him. "There has to be a decent interval between the death of one husband and marriage to the next."

"True," said Birmingham. " 'The funeral baked meats' mustn't 'coldly furnish forth the marriage table.' "

Regina smiled wryly at Garcia. "Don't mind all that Bard stuff, Lieutenant. Barry has been boning up on Shakespeare, now that my late lamented has croaked."

Birmingham winced. "Please, dear," he said. "Not 'croaked.' 'Shuffled off this mortal coil.' "

"Whatever." She sauntered over to the refreshments table. "Something to drink, Lieutenant?"

"I'm on duty," said Garcia, "but maybe some of that Perrier water? It's a hot day."

As she handed him the icy drink, Garcia apologetically said, "I guess I'm a little slow, but I don't get the connection between Shakespeare and the death of Mr. Gross."

Barry Birmingham replied, "Biggie always kept me trapped in pretty-boy roles. But I'm meant for better things. Dramatic parts. The classics."

"I see. Then I guess that's one reason you're on the list, Mr. Birmingham."

"List?"

Garcia explained, adding, "That gives you a pretty good double motive for murdering him. Better parts, and Mrs. Gross's inherited fortune, if you marry her."

Birmingham frowned hammily, in a jocose mockery of malevolence. "Aha, so I'm cast as a villain . . . a 'bloody, bawdy villain . . .'"

"Barry, for Christ's sake, knock it off with the *Hamlet,* will you?" Regina pleaded. "Lieutenant, believe me, he's a pussycat. Wouldn't hurt a fly."

Garcia asked, "What about you, Mrs. Gross? You're on your husband's list, too."

"Not exactly an exclusive club, is it? What's my motive?"

"The money," said Garcia. "A say in studio business. The freedom to marry Mr. Birmingham. Plus you hated Mr. Gross. Your stepson says so. And you certainly had plenty of opportunity."

"So did the butler, the gardener, the chauffeur, the maids. Why don't you grill *them?*"

"I'm going to," said Garcia. "One of them is on the list, in fact." Turning back to Barry, Garcia asked the actor, "Are you sure I can talk about anything at all in front of Mrs. Gross?"

"As I said," Barry replied, "no secrets."

"Okay," said Garcia, "then you had another motive, too. A reason for fearing B. I. Gross—and for him hating you."

"You mean because I was banging his wife?"

"That, too. But mainly because you were banging his son. He caught you and Martin together. He couldn't stand the thought of a son of his being that way, and he forced the boy to marry a starlet. He punished you by locking you into insipid parts. You might have wanted Gross dead not only because of the money and the classic roles, but also because he knew you were gay and he could spill the beans about it."

Birmingham laughed. "Spill *what* beans? Everyone knows I'm AC/DC. I swing both ways, Lieutenant, and give equal satisfaction

to both genders. Ask Regina. Ask Martin. They've never complained." He rolled his eyes skyward. "To be or not to be a pederast
—who *cares* anymore?"

Maybe *I* care, Mr. Pretty Boy Birmingham, Garcia muttered to
himself that evening. Maybe I care that *cabrones* like you are committing adultery, sodomy, screwing other people's wives and sons
and *dogs,* for all I know!

"What are you mumbling about, Pablo?" asked his wife as she
put an aromatic platter of *carne asada* on the table. She was a
bright-eyed, energetic woman in her fifties, with a remarkably Aztec
profile. She had kept her svelte figure and peppery personality
through a quarter century of marriage and two children, both now
grown, married, and in the process of producing the lieutenant's
first grandchildren.

To his wife's question, Garcia replied, "Nothing. Just talking back
to Barry Birmingham—in my own mind."

Serving him the meat, she said, "I don't care very much for him.
Seems too stuck on himself, at least on the screen."

"You wouldn't like him any better in person."

"Who are you going to interview tomorrow?" she asked as she
sat down.

"I think I'll talk to Kleinbaum first."

"Who's he?"

"A composer. Writes movie music."

"Songs?"

"I don't think so. The music that goes on behind the action."

"Never heard of him."

"He was supposed to be fairly big back in the old country."

"Why did Gross put him on the list?"

Garcia shook his head. "Maybe he figured Kleinbaum hated
him."

"Why?"

Garcia chewed his meat thoughtfully. "The story is, Kleinbaum
barely made it out of Vienna during the Nazi days, but not before
having some pretty nasty experiences with the Gestapo, and losing
some family members, like both parents and a sister, in concentra-
tion camps. When he got over here, he got a job at Oracle-Zodiac,
in the music department. . . ."

"Then he was luckier than most. So?"

"So B. I. Gross used to think it was a lot of fun to sneak up behind him and yell *'Heil Hitler!'* in a loud German accent—making Kleinbaum jump about three feet in the air and come down shaking like Jell-O for half an hour."

"What a terrible thing to do!" she said, appalled.

Her husband shrugged. "That's the kind of guy he was."

She shuddered. "I'm surprised he stayed alive as long as he did."

"Pass the tortillas, please."

Kurt Hermann Kleinbaum's study was a small, restful, cluttered room in his Pacific Palisades home. He lived there alone—"with my memories," he said, perfectly straight, as if unaware that it was a hackneyed phrase.

A bust of Bach occupied a focal place on a bookshelf. A musical score stood open on the gleaming mahogany piano. Photos of dead friends glowered from the walls. Kleinbaum introduced Garcia to them: "Erich Korngold . . . Arnold Schönberg . . . Anton Webern . . . Alban Berg . . . I knew them all, Lieutenant, in Europe. And some of them over here, as well. Korngold wrote music at Warner Brothers, for Errol Flynn pictures. Schönberg taught at UCLA. They named a building after him."

"Oh, *that* Schönberg," said Garcia.

"And I . . ." He laughed sourly. "I worked for the great Gross. Do you know, I was the one who told him that the German word *gross* means 'big' or 'great'? As in Beethoven's Great Fugue, the *Grosse Fuge.* He repeated that again and again, to everybody— 'Gross means Great!' He loved it. But he kept me writing monster music."

"Monster music?"

The old composer nodded. "I wanted to write the music for important films, beautiful films. After all, in Vienna I was considered a serious artist. I wrote symphonies, operas, concertos. But Gross assigned me to such stuff as *The Shrieking Dead . . . The Snake Woman . . . Return of the Snake Woman . . .*"

"Must have been quite a comedown," said Garcia.

Kleinbaum's eyes narrowed. "I see these young ones today, with their rock scores, their electronic sounds, their computerized music . . . I see them winning Oscars, making millions of dollars . . ."

"Hard to take," Garcia suggested.

"Hard? No, Lieutenant. Easy. Because next year their trash will be totally forgotten, replaced by other trash. There will be rust on their Oscars. But my work, my *real* work—my *Rhapsodic Symphony,*

my Double Concerto for Viola and Harp, my opera *Abraham*—
these will *live*. They will live forever!"

"Sure," Garcia said. "But even so, you must have resented Mr.
Gross."

"I deplored his taste, his manners, his ghastly sense of humor. I
was also very sorry for him."

"Sorry? Why?" wondered Garcia.

"He was a man who had nothing. No friends, no loved ones. His
own wife and son hated him. He was desperately unhappy. But I
had friends, and the respect of my colleagues, and the talent God
gave me. That is why he envied me. That is why he played his
pathetic, sick little jokes on me, and kept me writing music for
monsters and maniacs. That is also why he put me on his list. . . ."

To himself, Garcia said: I'll be the judge of that.

Doretta Mulvane also lived in the Palisades, so when Garcia left
Kleinbaum's house, he sought out the home of that madcap star of
yesteryear.

"Yes, Lieutenant, I've heard about your list," said the stately
grande dame who bore scant resemblance to the light comedienne
of so many screen romps. A veritable mist of lavender aroma surrounded her, as if she had bathed in cologne.

"News travels fast in this town, Miss Mulvane," said Garcia.

"It's like Gilbert and Sullivan, isn't it?"

"Pardon?"

She chirped a tune: " 'I've got a little list . . . they never will be
missed . . .' And am *I* on the little list?"

"I'm afraid so, Miss Mulvane."

"One wonders why. I had no motive for murdering the old boy."

"Mr. Gross seemed to think you did. Something about your
whirlwind romance with Arturo Montoya, maybe, and your marriage to him."

"But that was *ages* ago, Lieutenant!"

Garcia nodded. "I think Mr. Gross figured you hated him because he busted up the marriage."

"I did hate him for that," she declared. "I was very much in love
with Arturo. Gross was always messing about with people's lives.
Forced that boy of his to marry that silly little bit of candyfloss.
Forced me to divorce Arturo. Not that Arturo minded, the scamp!
He only married me because he'd got me preggers. People *did* that

in those days, you know. Got married *before* having babies. Now it's the other way round, more often than not."

"The baby was stillborn, I read," said Garcia.

"Yes," she said softly. "A little girl, they told me. I never saw her."

"Why did Gross disapprove of the marriage?" Garcia asked.

"He *said* it was because the public wouldn't accept a popular romantic idol like Arturo being married. Bad for box office. But the *real* reason was because *he* wanted me."

"Gross?"

"None other. He had a very high fever for me. Kept after me all the time. But I never let him take liberties. That made him furious! And that's why he hated me and broke up the marriage."

"Why are you on the list but not Montoya?"

Doretta Mulvane shrugged. "Search me. Ask Arturo."

On his way to Arturo Montoya's Malibu beach house, Garcia thought about something Fawn Blake had said: "The killer will probably turn out to be somebody not even *on* the list. . . ."

Like Montoya?

It was cooler near the ocean, and almost completely smogless. Garcia parked near Montoya's house, but he didn't walk up to the door immediately. He watched the Pacific waves breaking for a minute or so, inhaled the salt tang of the air, and appreciatively eyed a coven of high-school-age girls in bikinis that seemed to be constructed of dental floss. If they had dressed that way when *he* was a teenager . . . He shook his head, not so much in disapproval as in wonderment—wonder at changing times and at the beauty of the sea, the sun, the lithe young bodies of these unashamed kids. He had to get out to the beach more often, he told himself.

Despite the ocean breeze, the sun was beginning to draw glistening droplets of moisture from his forehead. Or was it those near-naked girls who were doing it? he pondered. Dabbing his face with a handkerchief, Garcia turned away from the pleasant scene and walked up to the beach house's door.

His knock was answered by a stunning black woman whose smooth chocolate flesh was in bold contrast to the French-cut maillot that clung to her like a coat of lemon-yellow paint. The one-piece swimsuit was, in its way, even more enticing than the all-but-nude models displayed by the girls outside, for the hip-high leg holes, waist-deep neckline, and porthole sides revealed easily ninety percent of a vibrantly healthy, trim, yet ample female body. A short beach robe of the same yellow shade hung, open, from her shoulders.

"Yes?" she inquired. After Garcia had identified himself and his mission, she invited him inside, saying, "I'm Mr. Montoya's secretary, Trisha Jones. I'll tell him you're here. Oh . . . and this is Mr. McCoy," she offhandedly added.

A casually dressed, tow-headed young man with glasses crouched over a coffee table, script and pen in hand. He looked up and nodded as the provocative Trisha left the room. "How's the investigation going?" he asked.

Garcia made a noncommittal gesture. "Slow but unsure," he said, studying the young fellow. "McCoy . . ." he muttered. "Are you Jack McCoy?"

"That's right."

"The director?"

McCoy nodded. "Heard of me, have you? That's a switch."

"Sure. You're up and coming."

"Was," said McCoy.

"Why was?"

"Ding-dong, the lizard's dead," McCoy recited, rather than sang.

"I know Mr. Gross signed you up right out of film school," said Garcia. "Let you direct some small stuff, then just recently gave you the green light on a major project. . . ."

"*The House of Atreus.* Greek tragedy, updated to the contemporary world. But Sid Warren will cancel it for sure. Too risky. Too big a budget, too small a director. Iffy subject matter."

"So now you're working on something with Montoya?"

"Just a favor. Helping him with a guest spot on a TV show. A little dialogue coaching on his lines."

"Sort of ghost-directing him?"

"In a way. I think they tried to get Cesar Romero for the part, but he was unavailable, so they settled for Montoya. Trish asked me to do it." McCoy smiled. "I'd do anything for her."

"She's a beautiful woman."

"I know. I'm crazy about her. So is Montoya." His face clouded. "No contest. He's a 'star,' and I'm the youngest has-been in town."

"Isn't he a little old for her?"

"He sure is. But she's blinded by his so-called Latin charm."

"Careful what you say about Latin charm, Mr. McCoy. My name is Garcia, remember."

Trisha Jones reappeared with her employer. He was clad in an immaculate blue-and-white running suit. The actor, his dark virility not entirely ravaged by the onslaught of time, flashed Garcia a brilliant smile and offered his hand.

"Lieutenant, a pleasure," said Arturo Montoya. "How can I help you get to the bottom of this terrible thing?" The Hispanic accent had remained intact over the years, Garcia noted, although the dazzling teeth were probably capped at the very least, and the curly hair was surely dyed that raven hue.

"Miss Mulvane suggested I talk to you," said Garcia.

"Doretta? Such a lovely lady, no?"

"Mr. Gross left a list of people he thought would be glad to see him dead. Miss Mulvane is on the list, but you're not. I wondered why."

Montoya looked dubious. "I do not believe that Doretta wished the *jefe* to be dead. She did not like him, true, because he broke up our marriage . . . but to desire him to be dead? That is a bad thing, a sin, no? Not Doretta . . . a sweet girl . . . no, no . . ." He shook his head.

"And you, Mr. Montoya, did you like him?"

Another flash of teeth. "I got along marvelously with him. We played cards, we got drunk, sometimes we swapped girls. We understood each other. He called me Wetback!" Montoya's brown eyes twinkled.

The term didn't sound like an endearment to Garcia. "What part of Mexico are you from, Mr. Montoya?"

"I am not Mexican, Lieutenant. I am from Bolivia."

"Oh," said Garcia. "I guess that explains the accent. It doesn't sound Mexican. My parents came from Mexico. Oaxaca."

"Well, we are both Latinos, eh, *amigo?*"

"Yes, sir. Didn't you hate Mr. Gross when he broke up your marriage?"

Montoya shook his head. "I understood Jefecito's reasons. Sound business reasons, from his point of view. He was not a sentimentalist. And . . . well, to tell you the truth, I was a restless young *muchacho* and did not really want to be tied down." He turned and looked lovingly at Trisha. "Not *then,* that is."

Trisha returned the loving look. "So you see, Lieutenant," she said, "Arturo has no motive. That's why he's not on the list."

"None of you are," Garcia told her. "Not you, or Mr. Montoya, or Mr. McCoy. But I had to ask, because of the old connection with Miss Mulvane."

"We understand," said Montoya, with a sympathetic smile.

"How many more on the list?" asked Jack McCoy.

"Two," said Garcia. "A cameraman and a chauffeur. I'll see them tomorrow."

"Chauffeur?" asked Trisha. "Mr. Gross's chauffeur?"

"That's right. Duncan Jones." Reflectively, Garcia repeated the surname: "Jones . . . it's a common name. . . . I don't suppose you're related to . . . ?"

"Yes," said Trisha, her voice hushed with concern. "He's my father."

"What are you doing here?"

"I have to talk to you before that cop does."

"Cop?"

"Garcia. If he starts to grill you, everything might come out."

"Why should it? No percentage in that for me."

"You might get careless . . . rattled . . . the pressure . . . he might scare you."

"Hmm . . . true enough. I *might* let the cat out of the bag, at that."

"You can't!"

"It sure will be hard keeping my mouth shut under all that *pressure,* like you say . . . unless I have a good reason to keep quiet."

"I'm already giving you plenty of good reasons—with pictures of presidents on every one of them. Have been for years!"

"But I want more."

"How much more?"

"As much as it's worth. Or else I'll tell."

"No!"

"And I'll tell the *other* thing, too. . . ."

"Other thing?"

"That's right. The thing even *you* don't know. Believe me, you're not going to like it when you hear it. You're not going to like it one little bit. . . ."

Garcia had scheduled the last two interviews for the same morning, to save himself unnecessary driving. Both men lived in the gracious northerly reaches of Bel-Air, Buck Hammond in a rambling ranch-style house, Duncan Jones in quarters over the ample multiple-car garage of the B. I. Gross estate. The lieutenant visited Hammond first.

The bulky cinematographer was on his knees, tending the roses in his garden. They exuded an oppressively sweet perfume that reminded Garcia of a funeral parlor.

"My wife loved roses, but they don't do so well in this dry climate," he said. "They like it wetter than this. Oregon. England. That's where they thrive."

"But these look great," said Garcia with admiration.

As Hammond led him inside to his den, he said, "I do the best I can with what I've got to work with."

"Just like your movies."

"That's right," Hammond agreed, pushing his thinning hair out of his eyes. "Even if the script is a load of manure and the actors are about as animated as those guys on Mount Rushmore, I try to make everything *look* good."

"You've certainly got the Oscars to prove it," Garcia said, indicating several burnished Academy Award statuettes on the mantelpiece.

"Well, I learned from the best. Jimmy Howe, Gregg Toland . . . Can we get down to business?"

"Sure, Mr. Hammond. You didn't like B. I. Gross very much, did you?"

"I didn't have to. He paid me to do a job and I did it. Liking him wasn't part of the contract."

"I mean, I remember some of the things you said when you and I were standing at his coffin."

Hammond grinned. "Well, I didn't know you were a cop or I would have kept my mouth shut."

"What exactly did you have against him?" Garcia asked. "He assigned you to some big pictures. You might say he made it possible for you to win those Oscars."

"Yeah, you might say that." Hammond sighed and lit a cigarette. "I'm a widower," he said, after exhaling a double lungful of acrid smoke. "About a year ago, my wife and I planned to take a long trip, just the two of us. Call it a second honeymoon. We both knew it would be the last trip we'd ever take together, because she was terminally ill. So we made all our plans, got all the reservations, and then Gross said he needed me on an important picture. 'But she's dying!' I told him. Know what he said? 'We're all dying. You'll be better off working and getting your mind off your troubles. It'll be better for her, too.' So Sally and I never took that trip."

"And you hated Gross for that?"

"Yep," Hammond admitted. "But, you know, the old bastard was probably right. Better to keep working, carry on a normal life. I couldn't see it that way at the time, though. . . ."

Hammond's phone rang, and he grabbed it, barking, "Yeah?" Then he handed it to Garcia. "For you."

"I gave the station this number." He took the phone. "Garcia speaking."

The voice of Sergeant Jameson crackled in his ear: "Hey, my man, you better get on up to the Gross place. There's been a shooting. We just got the call. You're near there, aren't you?"

"I'm on my way."

"And we've got some other late-breaking news, too, but that can wait," Jameson added.

"News about what?"

"The Lizard's choice of reading matter, for one thing," said Jameson.

When Garcia arrived at the Gross estate, Duncan Jones was being lifted into an ambulance on a stretcher, and a body bag was being stowed into another vehicle.

"Who's in the bag?" he asked the nearest officer.

"Some actor."

"Actor? *What* actor?"

An older policeman, closer to Garcia's age, supplied the name: "Arturo Montoya."

"What?"

"Yes, sir. He shot the chauffeur and then killed himself. A .455 Webley in the mouth. Took the top of his head right off."

"Christ!" Turning to a paramedic, Garcia asked, "How bad off is the chauffeur?"

"Pretty bad," said the paramedic. "He may not make it to the hospital."

"I've got to ride with him. There are some things I need to know." Garcia followed the paramedic into the back of the ambulance, where Duncan Jones lay, connected by plastic tubing to an IV bottle. The paramedic closed the doors and the ambulance rolled, siren blasting.

Garcia peered into the pain-dimmed eyes of the chauffeur. "Why did Montoya shoot you?" he gently asked.

"Name . . . not Montoya," whispered Jones, staring straight up.

"Then what *is* his name?"

"Arthur . . . Montrose. Light mulatto from Louisiana. Been passing for white all these years . . . fake accent . . . nobody knew . . . but Mr. Gross found out . . . and I knew . . . and Montoya *knew* that I knew . . ."

"How did he know, Mr. Jones?"

Duncan Jones seemed reluctant to answer.

"How did he know?" Garcia repeated, adding casually, "You were blackmailing him, is that right?"

Jones nodded. "When you said . . . you were going to talk to me today . . . he got scared . . . thought it would all come out . . . about him being black . . . so he offered me more money . . . but I wanted even more than he offered . . . or I'd tell the *other* thing. . . ."

"What other thing?"

The chauffeur's eyes glazed and he licked his lips. The siren relentlessly split Garcia's eardrums as the ambulance sliced through traffic. *"What* other thing, Mr. Jones?"

"Something Montoya didn't even know . . . until just this morning when I told him. . . ."

"Go on," Garcia urged.

"The way Mr. Gross found out Montoya was a black man . . ."

"Yes?"

"Because Miss Doretta's baby . . . Montoya's baby . . . was black . . . real dark . . . took after Montoya's grandpappy or something. . . ."

"Happens that way sometimes," said Garcia.

"Mr. Gross paid off the doctor, the nurses . . . to say the baby was born dead. . . . Miss Doretta didn't never know no different. . . . Montoya never knew different, neither. . . ."

"The baby wasn't stillborn?"

"No, sir. . . ."

"What happened to the child?"

"Mr. Gross gave the little girl to me and my wife to raise . . . we didn't have no children of our own. . . ."

"Then you mean *Trisha* is—"

"Montoya's daughter. And lately she's been . . . been . . ."

"Sleeping with him?" Garcia suggested.

"Yes, sir. When Montoya found out who she really was . . . he went crazy . . . said *she* mustn't ever find out she's his daughter, she'd die of shame. . . . That's when he pulled out the gun and . . . and . . ."

A long, hissing sigh emptied the lungs of the stricken chauffeur.

"I guess we don't need the siren anymore," said the paramedic.

"Jonesy sure must have done a whole lot of talking before he cashed in," said Sergeant Jameson. "And with those slugs in him! He must have been one big tough brother."

Jameson and Garcia were having a couple of beers at a bar near the station. "He was in pretty good shape for his age, all right," said Garcia. "But Lester Gillis weighed in at only a hundred and twenty-five pounds, soaking wet, and he took seventeen hits from an FBI agent with a submachine gun, then got up to live six more hours, kill that agent and two others, plus a couple of cops."

"Awesome," Jameson agreed. "Who was Lester Gillis?"

"Better known as Baby Face Nelson," said Garcia.

"Him I heard of. But getting back to modern times, I guess there wasn't any murder after all, huh?"

"Sure there was. What are you talking about? Montoya murdered Jones before he killed himself."

"I meant Gross," said Jameson.

"No, Gross wasn't murdered. You saw that report from the team we put on his house. Those books they found locked in the secret compartment of his desk . . . what were the titles again?"

Jameson pulled the report from his pocket and unfolded it. *"Justifiable Euthanasia: A Guide for Physicians,* by Dr. P. V. Admiraal . . . *Let Me Die Before I Wake,* by Derek Humphry . . . *Commonsense Suicide: The Final Right,* by Doris Portwood . . . *How to Die with Dignity,* by—"

"That's enough," said Garcia. "And his doctor started prescribing sleeping pills for him a whole year ago, but he probably never took them, just saved them, maybe till he worked up the nerve to overdose himself. 'We're all dying,' he told Buck Hammond a year ago. That must have been when he first learned he was terminal."

Jameson frowned. "Yeah, but then why did he make that list?"

"To stir up trouble, probably. 'That's just dear Biggie making trouble for everybody. Doesn't mean a thing.' That's exactly what Fawn Blake said. And, you know, I think maybe Gross had a pretty good idea that things might turn out the way they did, or close to it." Garcia sipped his beer. "Well, one good thing has come out of all this," he said. "Trisha's stopped bedding her own father."

"Yeah, that's an improvement," said Jameson, "specially for Mc-Coy, but you really think old man Gross could have foreseen that?"

"Maybe not. But he was a shrewd son of a bitch, and like that newspaper article said, he was a good amateur psychologist, he knew what made his people tick, how they'd react in certain situations."

"But what beef did he have with his chauffeur?"

"The kid Martin filled me in about that. Seems Duncan Jones was blackmailing Gross, too, not only Montoya."

"Blackmailing Gross? About what?"

"His son being gay. Gross didn't want that spread around."

Jameson shook his head. "Not a very nice dude, Jonesy."

"A lot of not very nice people in this mess," said Garcia.

"Beginning to think you're right about the world getting worse and worse," Jameson said glumly.

"No, I was wrong about that," Garcia admitted. "The world is getting better."

"Say what?"

"Well, look at all the fuss these old-timers had to put up with about being black or white or passing. Or being gay. Or having a porno skeleton in the closet. Or romantic stars not getting married because they thought it was bad for box office. All that crap, causing all that unhappiness and blackmail and loused-up lives. Today, it couldn't happen. Black, white, gay, married, unmarried, so what? No, the world is slowly getting better, believe it or not. Not much, but little by little. It's like an old movie I saw on TV a while back. William Powell is at a party and some drunk is bending his ear about how great it was back in the good old days. Powell tells him, 'Don't kid yourself. *These* are the good old days.'"

"Hey," said Jameson with a chuckle, "next thing you'll be getting yourself a VCR, just like me!"

"Why not?" said Garcia. "My wife has been after me to get one. And the first movie I'll rent will be *Gone with the Wind.*"

"That old thing?"

"Yeah," Garcia said, smiling. "I still get a kick out of the way Gable says, 'Frankly, my dear, I don't give a damn.'"

Pulp writers were much taken with Hollywood. Many pulps carried at least one Tinsletown story per issue. A few magazines published nothing but such stories. John K. Butler was a modestly successful pulp writer who worked in various fields but who never quite got the recognition he'd hoped for. He wrote one unabashed little masterpiece, this breakneck gem about Hollywood between the world wars.

The Saint in Silver

John K. Butler

One
A Fare for Valhalla

It was the drunk again. He had passed Siberia twenty minutes earlier in a low-slung cream-colored roadster doing at least fifty in the rain, on the wrong side of the street. Now he was coming back again, and still on the wrong side.

That night I'd done a pretty good business on account of the rain. About a dozen short local hauls and a couple of long ones. Altogether the meter had ticked off close to eighteen dollars. Tips had averaged well over a dime a ride. So I felt fine as I sat there in the hack counting over the night's winnings, and I continued to feel fine until this guy in the cream-colored roadster entered my otherwise happy existence.

I suppose it was just after 2 A.M., because the Carinthian Club had closed. The orchestra boys had come out into the rain carrying neat black instrument cases. The last car had coughed, with chill motor, out of the auto park and I had called good-night to Pete Sondergaard as he looked up. That left nothing on the main drag but the rain falling steadily and gurgling in the gutters, dim night lights burning behind the misty windows of the corner drugstore, an orange traffic globe blinking regularly at the intersection. No pedestrians, no passing cars, no patrolman—nothing. My cab stand after 2 A.M. might just as well have been in Siberia. And Siberia is what I always called it, after two.

I was just slipping the count back into my pocket when the roadster came roaring up behind me, doing fifty. It passed like a breath of wind, plump tires hissing on wet pavement. There was a guy at the wheel, laughing. There was a girl beside him, trying to wrestle the wheel from him. I just caught a glimpse as they went by. Then the car went out on the Amusement Pier.

I couldn't think of any good reason why they'd drive out there. In the first place it was against a traffic ordinance. In the second place the amusement concessions, from roller coasters to hot dog stands, had closed early. And in the third place there was nothing out there but darkness and rain and the Pacific Ocean.

I began to wonder if maybe they weren't a couple of lovers in a suicide pact. Drive the car right off the end of the pier. And while I was wondering that, not doing anything about it, the roadster came back again.

It was going slower now. It came down off the ramp at about twenty, couldn't decide which way to turn on Ocean Avenue, skidded a little, first right, then left, as if on casters instead of wheels. Then it came on across the intersection and straight toward me on the main drag, on the wrong side of the street.

I sat up in my hack and blasted the horn button. The sound of the horn was like a siren in the night. The drunk heard it, and saw my headlamps snap on, and decided not to have a head-on collision with a parked cab. He swerved the roadster to the other side of the street, his own side, and the girl grabbed the wheel and pulled the emergency brake. The roadster came to a jolting stop against the opposite curb, and the man's voice scolded drunkenly: "Hey! Wassa big idea?"

"Don't be such a fool," she said, and switched off the ignition and took the keys. There was a little struggle over that, but she pushed him, and his face came down limply against the wheel. He didn't struggle any more. He looked like he'd passed out.

She opened the door of the car and came across the street toward my cab, a small determined blonde in a yellow transparent rain coat with a yellow rubberoid hood drawn up over waved honey hair. She walked rapidly and aggressively on high spiked heels, the movement of her legs flapping the rubberoid skirt. She glanced once at the lettering on the side of the hack, the lettering which said: *Red Owl Cab Company*. Then she looked up into my face.

"You for hire?"

"Certainly."

"My boyfriend's too tight to drive," she said. "We need a cab. But you'll have to help me with him."

I got out of the cab. It occurred to me that maybe she was tight, too. Or anyway she had a peculiar combination of nervousness and rage.

"Come on," she said, leading the way back to the roadster. "I don't know how to drive, or I'd take the wheel from him. I hope he don't clip you."

But her boyfriend made no move to clip me. He was too drunk for that. With his head cradled in his arms, his arms folded on the steering wheel, he slept heavily.

I opened the door beside him and eased him out. He tried to get his feet on the ground, but his shoes skidded, and his body became dead weight in my arms.

"Wassa big idea?" he grumbled thickly.

I carried him over to the cab and propped him up in the back seat. He was nicely dressed in a tuxedo, trim-fitting, but now it was rumpled from his night's orgy. His black bow tie hung crooked on the white starched collar. He was a hefty man and hard to handle when his muscles turned to sand. His head rolled loosely and a lock of dark pomaded hair had come down over his eyes. He had lost his hat somewhere.

"Hey," he muttered. "Wassa . . ."

And then he was sound asleep again, in the corner of the cab.

The blonde got in with him and slammed the door.

"All right," she said. "Get rolling."

"You want to leave the car here?"

"The hell with his car," she said. "Anyway it's locked. I've got the keys. I guess it'll be all right here."

"There's a no-parking ordinance after twelve," I said.

"That's *his* worry," she said.

So I climbed into the front seat, switched on the meter and the headlamps, tramped a foot on the starter. The cab's motor growled and roared, and I called over a shoulder: "Where does he live?"

"It don't matter where he lives. We're not going there." She took a slip of paper from her purse and held it under the dome-light in the rear of the cab. "We want to go to Valhalla."

That was silly. I'd never heard of any apartment house, or hotel, or suburb, called Valhalla. The only Valhalla I knew was a cemetery on the other side of Los Angeles. And it wasn't an active cemetery. Nobody had been put to rest there in the last ten years. It was a neglected weed-grown burial park down near the Southern Pacific freight yards.

I said to the blonde: 'What's the address of the Valhalla Apartments?"

"It's not an apartment," she said. "It's a cemetery."

"You want to go *there? Tonight?"

"Yes," she said.

"The fare will run around nine dollars."

Her red lips sneered with impatience. "Did I say I was worried about the fare?"

So I got us rolling and didn't ask any questions. After all, you meet such screwy people when you drive a cab for a living.

It took us nearly an hour to get there, and Valhalla at 3 A.M., with dismal winter rain, was hardly what you'd label a romantic spot.

The front of it faced a macadam road, its surface battered and pitted by the passage of trucks during the day. There was a crumbling brick wall around it and behind the wall you could see the dark shapes of wind-lashed eucalyptus trees. There was a tall rusty gate, locked with chains, and back of that a small keeper's cottage that hadn't been occupied in ten years. I pulled up and came to a stop in front of the gate.

"Wait a minute," the blonde said, and passed a slip of paper forward to me. "See if you can make any sense out of this."

It was a note in a woman's handwriting, in green ink, and it read—

> The name is Valhalla. A place of the dead. Go around to the back. Dirt road above the railroad tracks. Find three trees by a break in the wall. Enter through the break, follow the trail to a marble crypt.
>
> Inside the crypt, where a forgotten body lies at rest, something awaits you.
>
> Have no fear.
>
> Seek and ye shall find.

There was no signature. That was all.

I returned the note. She took it in her left hand, her right being a support for the sleeping man. His shoulder leaned heavily against her. He looked like he might sleep that way forever.

"Well?" she asked. "Do you make any sense out of it?"

"A little," I said. "It tells you where to go."

"Let's go there," she said.

So I put the hack in gear and continued along the pitted macadam until there was a muddy road leading off to the side. I followed this in low gear. No cars had traveled on it in a long time. The wheels of the cab whirled and skidded in the mud, but I kept going and followed the road all the way around the cemetery wall to the rear of the park.

Below us now, down a long weedy slope, I could see the railroad tracks, half a dozen sets of them, gleaming like ribbons under the big headlamp of a switch engine as it puffed with a line of freight cars. All that was about half a mile down the slope.

To our right was the crumbling wall of the cemetery, and three tall dark eucalyptus trees beside a break in the wall.

"This is the place," I said.

"We've got to hurry," the blonde replied. "Hey, Lew! *Lew!*" She pushed him away from her into the corner of the cab. She smacked him open-handed. His head lolled with sleep. She took him by the shoulders and shook him. That didn't do any good either.

Then she turned angry eyes on me. "It's no use. He's out like a light. You'll have to go in with me. Do you mind?"

"Well—" I began.

Her red lips got that sneer again, and her eyes had a blue impatient sparkle in them under the interior dome-lamp. "What's the matter? Afraid of ghosts?"

"Do I look like a guy who might be afraid of ghosts?"

She studied my face appraisingly, studied my shoulders and hands. "No. You don't. Let's go."

I slipped out from under the wheel, killing the motor and the lights. I got a small pocket flash from under the seat and opened the rear door for the blonde and helped her step out into the mud.

"I'm not exactly superstitious," I told her. "Ordinarily, I'm not even curious. But this isn't any ordinary taxi trip. You can't blame me for wanting to know what that note means."

She laughed then, a sudden low-pitched throaty laugh. She reached out and patted my cheek with cool fingers, like a mother showing sympathy to a child. "Don't let it get you down, fella. This is only a treasure hunt. You know what a treasure hunt is?"

I thought I knew what it was. A party. People gather at some-body's house, and the host, or hostess, gives out notes to start them off. Then off they go, in couples, following the directions in the first note to find a second note. Then a third, a fourth—and so through the night, each couple trailing their own series of notes. The couple who returns first with the final note wins the hunt and the prizes.

"Is that what it is?" I asked.

"That's right. And I need a mink coat."

"You get a fur coat if you win?"

Her hooded head nodded vigorously in the dark. "Not just fur—mink. And the man gets a gold watch. I don't care about Lew, of course. We'll just let him sleep it off in the cab. But a mink coat can come in awfully handy during the cold winter nights. Come on, cabby, let's take a look in the graveyard."

The rain came down hard now, beating at us in the open places and dripping on us from the branches of trees. My flash cut a beam through the darkness, and we followed a narrow muddy footpath from the break in the wall and back into the solemn silence of the cemetery. There were a few empty tin cans along the path, probably left there by railroad bums who hiked up from the freight yards to find temporary haven. The path itself, no doubt, had been worn by the weary feet of men who ride the rails and who have to hide from yard dicks whenever they reach a city.

On each side of the path orderly rows of granite stones marked forgotten graves. Some of the stones had settled in the mud, canted rakishly, most of them were almost hidden by the wild growth of weeds.

Through this neglected burial park we trod steadily, with no sound about us but our own shoes slopping in the mud, the hush of falling rain, the distant chug of the switch engine down in the yards.

"This must be it," the blonde said.

My flash had picked out the front of a tomb that looked like a tiny saddened cathedral. Part of it was below ground, with a narrow flight of stone steps leading downward to a heavy iron door. And part of it, the dome, protruded eerily into the night, covered with ancient vines.

I went down the broken steps and tried the door. It had no lock on it, but something prevented it from moving inward at my push. I pressed my whole weight against it. But I couldn't budge it.

The blonde said in a whisper: "There must be some way to open it. Or else how did they get the note inside?"

"Maybe they got in by some other way."

I came back up the steps and shot the beam of the flash over the dome-like roof. There was a glass skylight up there, most of it shattered by kids who played here during the day and practiced their stone-throwing. It was probably a way to get in.

"I'll try it," I offered.

I grabbed a fistful of strong old vines and climbed up these to the skylight and lifted it on its rusty hinge. Broken panes of glass fell down inside the tomb and tinkled against stone. I pointed the flash downward.

"Can you get in?" the blonde called.

"It's a cinch," I told her. "But the fare is double. Ordinarily, the Red Owl Company doesn't figure on these extra services."

"I'll pay," she said. "What's ten or twenty dollars against a mink coat?"

By my flash, I saw I could climb through the skylight and step on an inside ledge, and then step to the top of an altar, and from there to the floor.

So I stowed the flash back into my hip pocket, and with both hands free, eased my body, feet first, through the opening. I groped downward until my shoes found the ledge. From there I slid my feet farther to the top of the altar, keeping hands gripped on a trail of vines that had grown inside through the broken skylight.

I was in absolute darkness now, hanging by my hands, groping with my feet. Rain lanced down from above and was cool against my face. That was good. I was sweating from the climb, and the interior of the crypt had a clammy warmness.

I got to my knees on top of the dark altar, then eased myself to the floor. I was just reaching for my flash again, when a pair of strong arms wrapped themselves about me and wrestled me back against the wall. My head struck stone with a blow that knocked my cap off.

It couldn't be a ghost, of course. This ghost was tough, and had a breath like garlic, and a fist that smashed me in the teeth like a straight left from Joe Louis.

I sat flat on the floor, with my back to the wall, and grabbed for something, anything, and got hold of an ankle. He jerked his leg away, kicked.

"You son-of-a———!" he said.

A ghost wouldn't say that.

We fought there in the dark of the tomb, and I kept trying to get up and fight him. Somehow I got the feeling he meant this fight to be my last one. He was in it for the finish, and his eyes had grown accustomed to the dark—mine hadn't. He kept slugging me time after time, slamming me hard, viciously. And then I knew it wasn't his fists he was using. He was slamming my body with something like a baseball bat or a pick handle. He got me twice on the shoulder and paralyzed my right arm. He swung against my kneecap, and I went down like a poled buffalo.

"You son-of-a———!" he said.

I could hear him grunt with each swing. He missed me a couple of times, and the heavy wooden weapon cracked against the stone wall, but I put my face into the next one. I got it right across the bridge of the nose.

Then the inside of the tomb became bright red, like water on fire, and I sank down through that fiery water, with a tremendous weight pressing against my nose and flashes blinding my eyes. I sank deeper and deeper through it, and nothing hurt me. It didn't matter when he kicked me in the ribs. It didn't matter when he snicked on a flashlight and put the beam into my face.

"What the hell?" he said.

Something smashed me on the side of the jaw, and brought new blinding flashes. It could have been a pick-handle, or a baseball bat, or a cane, or a stick, or even a toothpick. It just didn't matter.

Two
The Missing Mr. Walgreen

When I came around again, it was still night and I was still in the crypt. Something outside made a gentle scratching sound against stone. I fixed my eyes on the broken skylight and saw the branch of a tree moving sluggishly back and forth in the wind. The branch scratched and rustled.

I got to my feet with effort, and every part of my body had pain. I felt like a man hit by a truck and still lacking the knowledge of how seriously he's been hurt. A little rain pattered down through the skylight, touching my swollen face with cool drops. Nobody came out of the darkness to beat me down again.

In the upper pocket of my shirt, under my coat, I found the booklet of paper matches I always kept there. Striking a match, cupping its glow in my palms, I located my flash. I got it, snicked the catch, and it worked. It was good to have light again.

I groped for my watch to see what time it was; I didn't have any watch. I felt for my wallet and that was gone too. My pockets had been turned inside out. All I had left was a handkerchief, matches, cigarets, and a handful of small change.

I shot the beam of the flash around the inside of the crypt and found the weapon that had slugged me but not the man who had wielded it. I was entirely alone in the tomb, with just my own laborious breathing for company.

The weapon was the handle of a pick. No wonder I still felt groggy.

I saw other things scattered about on the stone floor. An empty gin bottle. A tattered blanket which had once been somebody's bed. Empty tins with canned heat labels, a whole batch of empty bottles that had once contained rubbing-alcohol.

The beam of my flash moved upward on the far wall. Here was a marble slab with engraved words on it.

JONATHAN CARNES HOLBROOK
1862–1927
FLORENCE SHAW HOLBROOK
1864–1928
His Ever Loving Wife
Here They Shall Rest

I wondered how much resting they had done while railroad bums used their tomb for a camp, and for a place to get drunk, on rubbing-alcohol and canned heat. I wondered if the Holbrooks, behind that marble slab, had enjoyed much rest while kids threw rocks at the skylight, and drunken adults used the place for treasure hunts, and while some guy tried to beat me to death with a pick handle.

While I was wondering that, my flash picked out a slip of folded white paper forced into a crack of the marble. I got the paper out and read, in a woman's handwriting in green ink—

*Find the small building at the end of the car tracks in
Playa del Rey. Between a drugstore and a liquor store.*

The Doctor is out, or the Doctor is in.

*And behind a little cardboard sign are further
instructions.*

Have no fear.

Seek and Ye shall find.

There was no signature; that was all. It was the next note of the
treasure hunt—next in the series leading my blonde fare to the goal
of a mink coat.

I put my turned-out pockets back in order again, stowed the note
in one of the pockets, and further explored the crypt with the beam
of the flash. There was only one more thing to see. The heavy iron
door of the tomb now stood open a little. There was a marble statue
broken on the floor beside it. The statue, even broken, was heavy to
lift. It had made a good barrier to keep the door shut. But somebody had moved it aside to get out of here in a hurry. It would take
strength to move it—the strength of a man who could wield a pick
handle.

I got my cap, and followed the beam of the flash through the
doorway and up the broken stone steps into the graveyard again.

It was cold outside, with the rain coming down hard through the
trees. I called: "Hello! Hello!"—meaning that for the blonde.

There was no answer.

I followed the path down through the weeds and the orderly rows
of forgotten tombstones, and climbed through the tumbled brick
wall and stopped under the three eucalyptus trees.

My cab stood there as I had left it, dark and silent. I crossed over
to it and shot the flash inside. The blonde wasn't there. Neither was
her drunken boy-friend. My fares had skipped out on me. I glanced
around the desolate, rainy landscape, and wondered where the hell
they had skipped to. Their skipping would cost me their fares and
tips. Furthermore, I had been robbed. And none of that was pleasant thinking.

I sat in the cab and tooted the horn. I kept that up for several
minutes, hoping my fares would return to the cab. But nobody returned. There was just darkness and the silence of the graveyard
and the lonely patter of rain. Far down on the railroad tracks a train
came along with a fast flicker of lights. Then it passed on, leaving

behind it only the memory of wheel-trucks hammering on rail-joints and the mournful toll of the big bell.

The hell with it, the hell with screwy people on treasure hunts, and husky thieves with pick handles who hide in forgotten tombs.

I started the motor of the cab.

Well, there was one satisfaction, anyhow. The blonde who ran out on me wouldn't win her mink coat.

It was sometime after 4 A.M.—maybe going on five—when I got back to my stand in Pacific Park. Still rain, and more rain, and dark as coal. My call-box clings to the wall outside the Carinthian Club, and the phone in it was ringing harshly when I pulled up at the curb.

I got out and answered the phone and the voice of Pat Regan, Red Owl's Chief Dispatcher, didn't have the rasp of rage I expected. Instead it dripped with sugary sarcasm.

"Well, well, if it isn't Steve Middleton Knight! It's sweet of you to answer the phone, Steven. Just lovely of you to get out of your cab in all this wet—" Then came the expected rasp of rage. It came in one prolonged ear-splitting bellow. "Where the hell you been for the last couple of hours? Or is it tactless of me to inquire? Listen, you shiftless son-of-a-flat-tire, I've had four calls in your district! Had to send Olie Greenberg over to cover 'em for you. Maybe I better have Olie cover your district *all* the time. Maybe—"

"Listen, Pat," I said, "I had a fare."

"Oh, yeah? Well, maybe you never heard it, but it's the custom of hackers to ring the office before they go out on pick-up runs. Maybe you didn't know that. Or maybe you just wanted to be sweet and not disturb me!"

"The fare was in a hurry, Pat."

"Yeah? Probably some blonde. Well, get this, Steven: you can't play Romeo on the Red Owl's time! Now take the red rose out of your smiling teeth and get over to the Surf Hotel and pick up an old lady who wants to go to the bus depot! Will you do that for me, Stevie? Or is it too much to ask?"

"Well, as a matter of fact—"

I was stalling. How could I go pick up a fare when my uniform was a mess, my nose swollen and bloody, and there was a six-inch cut on my forehead?

Pat Regan liked his drivers to put up a smart appearance. He'd canned me once for the mere fact of a black eye. I was afraid he'd do a lot more if he got a complaint from the old lady that a Red Owl driver looked like he'd just come out of Dunkirk.

"You'd better send Olie," I suggested politely. "I've got another fare, Pat. In the cab right now."

"Yeah? Another cutie, huh? It's wonderful the business you do with the cuties!"

He rang off sharply and left me alone with the dead phone in my hand. And left me alone with a problem.

Pat went off duty at 6 A.M., didn't come on again till eight in the evening. That gave me exactly fourteen hours in which to patch up my face, clean up my uniform, and somehow find enough money to pay in the meter receipts I'd been robbed of.

There was no use trying to explain to him I'd been robbed—that's why I had no intention of notifying the police. Pat Regan wasn't the kind of man to believe robbery stories. He fully trusted me for a distance of about six inches. He was deeply fond of me—the way Hitler is fond of Winston Churchill.

So I climbed back into the cab, and listened to the rain patter, and brooded over the problem of raising about thirty dollars in fourteen hours. If I failed to raise it, I'd have to raise another job.

Well, there was still a chance. The long cream-colored roadster still stood across the street from me, one front tire jammed against the curb. Somebody would have to return for it. And whoever came would find a very aggressive taxi driver who wanted double payment on a nine dollar run to Valhalla Cemetery. That would give me eighteen bucks, anyhow. And left me still a few bobs to raise before Pat Regan came snorting around for my meter receipts.

I was just considering a hike across the street to read the roadster's registration when a police prowl-car cruised slowly up from the Ocean Avenue intersection. It was a small black sedan that glistened like gun-metal in the rain. In it were Officers Purcell and Lasker.

They stopped just opposite my cab, motor idling. A big spotlamp cut a bright beam through the rain, examining the parked roadster. After the spot made a thorough examination, it snicked off. Lasker stuck his head out the window into the rain. His hands were resting on the driver's wheel. He wore white gloves.

He called: "That you, Steve Midnight?"

"In person," I called back.

"How long's this beautiful crate been parked here?"

"Since about two," I said.

"Then it gets a ticket."

"Swell," I said. "Give it a hundred tickets. The more the merrier. It's all okay with me."

Ed Purcell stepped out of the sedan and went over to the roadster. He got out a flashlight and a small book and a pencil. His big body leaned in over the door, his flat cap ducking under the rain-soaked fabric of the top. I saw the flash go on, as he examined the registration. Then the flash went out, and he didn't write a ticket.

"Walgreen," he said. "Lew Walgreen. You hear that, Jim?"

"I heard it," said Lasker, and got out of the police car and both of them crossed over to my cab. Rain-water dripped from the visors of their caps. They were suddenly stern, as if sore about something.

Purcell said: "Did you see the guy that left this crate here?"

"Sure. I took him for a ride. Stinko drunk. Had a blonde with him."

Purcell snicked on his flash and shot the beam at me—from close range. It made me blink.

"What's the matter with your face, Steve?"

"A little trouble," I said. "Beaten up. Robbed. Cab drivers get it all the time. Just part of the work."

"You report it?"

"No," I confessed.

"Why not?"

"Because the Red Owl Company has a certain night dispatcher named Pat Regan. He doesn't believe his employees ever get robbed. Know what I mean?"

"I get it," said Lasker. "But there's a jam here, Steve. Where'd you take the drunk and the blonde?"

"Valhalla. The cemetery. It was a treasure hunt."

Lasker shot a solemn glance at Purcell, and Purcell returned it. Then both of them looked back at me, with the light still shining bright in my eyes.

Lasker said: "You'd better come over to headquarters with us, Steve."

"Headquarters? Why?"

"Because a fellow named Walgreen got knocked off tonight. Down in the Southern Pacific freight yards. Near Valhalla."

Three
You Can't Get Prints Off Gravel

The room was small and hot, and I sat alone in it for three long dreary hours. A steam radiator in the corner gave off hissing heat. I didn't know how to turn it off. I tried to lift a window, but it was stuck tighter than a window in an old-fashioned Pullman. I couldn't budge it.

I finally relaxed in a straight oak chair and smoked cigarets until I ran out of them, and watched the rain patter against misty windows.

It was Captain Hollister's office, and nobody bothered me there until later in the morning when Hollister himself came in.

He was a tall, heavy-set man who smoked a ragged cigar and wore the same overcoat and battered hat which had done him service through many years. He had bushy gray brows, and eyes that could either smile on little children or make a condemned man squirm. The eyes were always changing—first pleasant, then shrewd.

He came briskly into the Homicide office and threw his hat at a brass hook on the wall. The hat missed, bounced off the wall and landed on the floor near a cuspidor. Captain Hollister ignored it. He went around the bare oak desk, plumped into a swivel chair, and put his feet on the desk. His shoes, his socks, the cuffs of his trousers, were coated with mud. He beamed on me pleasantly.

"Hello, Steve."

"Hello," I said.

"Poor old Steve Midnight. Whenever there's any trouble he lands right smack in the middle of it. Tough life, driving a cab—huh, Steve?" He laughed heartily, unlocked his desk and took out a box of cigars.

"Why am I under arrest?" I asked.

"Arrest?" His laugh boomed. "Nothing like that, Steve. Just a little talk. Seems you had a fare last night and the fare got knocked off."

"It's all news to me," I said. "The guy was drunk. Had a blonde with him. They were on a treasure hunt."

He waved a hand impatiently. "I heard all that from Purcell and Lasker. You got socked and robbed in a tomb down at Valhalla. Didn't report it." His eyes got shrewd. "Know who the blonde was, Steve?"

I shook my head.

"Neither do I," he said, "but I've got an idea. And the identity of your other fare is established. I traced him through some cards in his pocket and some laundry-marks on his clothes. Lew Walgreen. Bugsy Walgreen. That mean anything to you, Steve?"

"Not a thing," I said.

"Bugsy used to peddle hooch back in Prohibition. After that, a little dope. The feds gave him seven years on a narcotic rap. They paroled him last spring. He seemed to be getting along all right. Nobody caught him at any crooked stuff. Had a night club up on Sunset Boulevard, in the Strip. Somebody financed him, we don't know who. I grilled all the boys up there, and they don't know either. Bugsy seemed to be living a clean life, driving a nice car, running a legitimate night club. No trouble till last night."

"You identified the blonde?"

He chewed the tattered stub of cigar. "Think so. Bugsy had a blonde singer working for him named Maybelle Knapp. Had a date with her last night. The boys at the club didn't know what kind of a date, but they knew where she lived. I went to her apartment. She'd moved out early this morning. No trace of her."

I said: "A small blonde with lots of red lips and hard blue eyes, and knows her way around?"

"That fits," he nodded. "Only we can't find her. I'd like to."

"So would I," I told him. "She owes me eighteen bucks and my job."

"We'll get her, Steve." He said: "Who started this treasure hunt?"

"I don't know," I said.

"She didn't mention anything about it?"

"Just a mink coat for a prize. That's all."

"Did Walgreen say anything?"

"He was too drunk. Just slept in the back of the cab. Both of them disappeared when I got robbed in the cemetery. I didn't know he got killed. I still don't know *how*."

"I can tell you about that," Hollister said.

It seemed the police had had a call at 4 A.M. The call came from a track watchman in the S. P. Freight Yards. Walking up the tracks, just below Valhalla Cemetery, he had found a mangled body. It had been ground and pounded under the wheels of a fast freight.

"Suicide, robbery, or accident," Hollister said. "That's what it was supposed to look like. Too damned obvious. It missed by a mile."

I said: "Maybe some railroad bum robbed him and killed him. Maybe he wandered down there from my cab, and the bum got him. Maybe the same bum that slugged me and robbed me at the tomb."

"What makes you think a bum did it, Steve?"

"Well, bums use the cemetery for a hangout."

"Yeah," he nodded. "But most of the bums on the road don't fall into the killer class. Lazy, maybe. Drink a little rubbing-alcohol and canned heat, maybe. But not killers. No, Steve, there's something funny back of this."

"Was he robbed?"

"Sure. No money, or wallet in his pockets. But it doesn't have to make robbery the motive. It was just supposed to look like it."

"Couldn't be an accident or suicide?"

"Absolutely not," Hollister said firmly. I've got evidence on *that*. There's a water tower where Walgreen went under the wheels of the freight. Wooden tool-shed built under the tower. Somebody held Walgreen against the far wall of the tool-shed so the engine's big searchlight wouldn't pick them out. Then, after the engine passed, he shoved Walgreen under the wheels."

"Evidence of that?"

"Plenty. That's the crack freight from the Valley. Carries perishable fruit and travels like the very devil. A train passing that fast makes a big blast of wind—a fact this guy overlooked. He shoved Walgreen under the wheels all right, but the blast of wind knocked the killer back against the tool-shed. Walgreen's blood flew out from under those wheels like it had been thrown up from a bucket. The blood got on the killer, and some of it rubbed off his clothes when he fell against the tool-shed wall. There's a nice clear imprint of a bloody hand. It doesn't do us much good though. Not for fingerprints. The killer wore gloves. Cotton gloves. One of the gloves got torn on a nail. Doctor Dana, down in the Bureau of Criminology, tells me you can buy cotton gloves like that in any dime store in the country."

I thought that over as I lit one of Hollister's cigars. I said: "With all that rain, there was plenty of mud around. How about footprints?"

He wagged his head solemnly. "Too much rain. The water ran down that cemetery path like a spring creek. And the track-bed is all gravel. And gravel around the water tower. You can't get footprints off gravel."

"So that leaves you out on the limb, huh, Captain?"

"Way out," he said. "But I've climbed in off longer limbs than this. I'm gonna fingerprint everything in that tomb, Steve. I got a hunch the guy who slugged you in there was trying for Walgreen and didn't get him till later."

"Then you won't find prints," I offered. "He was probably wearing the same cotton gloves."

The captain waved a hand impatiently. "Sure. Sure. But cops play all the angles. It doesn't pay to skip anything. I'll take your prints downstairs, Steve, just to clear them from any other prints we get at the crypt."

"Then can I leave?"

"Sure." His bushy brows drew together over a thin hawk-like nose, and his eyes gave me a stern third-degree. "You wouldn't hold out anything, would you, Steve?"

"Why would I?"

"Just asking, Steve. And you didn't get any identification on this guy that worked you over with the pick-handle?"

"He called me a son-of-a-bat. That's all."

"And you don't have any idea who started this treasure hunt party?"

I shook my head. "Can I go now, Captain?"

"Why the hurry, Steve?"

"Because," I said, "I've got less than twelve hours to scratch up thirty dollars for Pat Regan. Otherwise, I can scratch up a new job."

The captain chuckled. "This Regan sounds like a nice guy. If he heard about the robbery he'd think you faked it to chisel the cab company's meter receipts. That it?"

"Exactly."

"But you can't hide the robbery, Steve. It'll be in all the papers."

"That won't matter as long as I dig up thirty bucks."

The captain laughed. "This Regan is wonderful."

"He's a louse," I replied sullenly.

Four
Seek and Ye Shall Find

It was about ten in the morning when I got away from Headquarters. I went back to Siberia for my hack and drove it over to the Red Owl Garage. Pat Regan had been off duty for some hours, so he wouldn't be climbing into my hair over the meter receipts until eight o'clock in the evening. But eight o'clock didn't seem such a long way off.

I hiked back across town to my hotel, had to listen briefly to the clerk's wisecracks regarding my battered appearance, and then I went to my room to clean up.

That was quite a job. My nose didn't feel broken but it was swollen so much that fat bluish bags surrounded my eyes. The gash on my forehead was a superficial break of the skin, and under it was a swelling. There was a bloated bruise on the right side of my jaw, sore to touch, and my bruised knee gave me a limp.

I sat in a hot tub for a while, then showered off cold and drank a frosty highball. I began to feel hungry and like myself again. But in the mirror I didn't look like myself. Not at all. The swellings had gotten worse. I looked like a one-round stumble-bum who'd tried to take Joe Louis.

I dressed into clean clothes, from underwear to tan tweed suit, and then groped absent-mindedly through the pockets of my taxi uniform to find my wallet. That reminded me I'd been robbed. I didn't find the wallet, of course, but in one of the pockets I found a slip of paper, folded. On it was a woman's handwriting, in green ink.

I'd forgotten about that. It was the treasure hunt note I'd found in the crypt. The next note the blonde was after on the trail of a mink coat.

I reached for the telephone and called police headquarters. Captain Hollister wasn't there; probably out at the cemetery with the fingerprint men.

"No message," I told the desk sergeant.

I went downstairs to the hotel's coffee shop, swallowed a fast breakfast, then boarded a big red interurban trolley for Playa del Rey.

The rain had stopped when I got to the end of the car line, but the sky hung low with dark angry clouds. The motorman climbed down from the trolley and strolled across the empty street to a little cafe. It was a deserted place—this end of the car line. Bare brown hills with scattered houses on them facing the sea; the Venice marshes, with tall skeletons of oil derricks. And right nearby, a grocery store, an abandoned real estate office, and a row of gloomy one-story stucco buildings near a gas station.

I limped over to these buildings, found a drugstore and a liquor store, and between them a narrow modernistic building with long glass windows and drawn venetian blinds. The brass placard read simply—

Dr. Otto C. Jelks
Physician & Surgeon
Hours 9:00 to 5:00

There was a blue Chrysler coupe parked at the curb. Its glass had been cranked up and was misted from last night's rain. So it had been there a long time.

I entered a small foyer and rang the bell. I could hear it tinkle musically inside, but there was no response to it, even after repeated ringings. A cardboard sign hung on a hook above the bell. It said that the Doctor was out and that he would return at 9 A.M.

I lifted the sign a little, and a folded slip of paper fluttered to the damp brick stoop. I picked it up and read another note in a woman's handwriting in green ink.

You have found it! Return to the starting point! And if you are the first to return, then the reward is yours!

As usual no signature. And unfortunately, no information on the starting point of the treasure hunt.

I tucked the note into my breast pocket, rang the bell again, still got no answer, and tried turning the door-knob. It wouldn't turn. It was locked.

I limped across the sidewalk and went around the blue Chrysler coupe to the driver's side and unlatched the door. The interior of the coupe was cold from last night and had a musty smell. The State Registration on the steering post said the car belonged to Dr. Otto C. Jelks of 1444 Hobart Street, Los Angeles. A neat leather keycase hung from the ignition switch.

I removed the keys and went around the car again and up the brick steps into the foyer of the building. There were six keys in the leather case and the third one worked.

I stepped into a rectangular reception room, furnished with low modernistic chairs and chromium magazine-racks.

"Hello?" I said. "Doctor?"

My own voice came back to me in muffled little echoes. I closed the door, locked it again, and used another key to enter the office.

This was sanitary and efficient, and full of gray daylight from frosted glass panels set slantwise up a slope of ceiling. Everything was white in the room except the floor—that was smooth green linoleum—white walls, a white roll-top desk, three white steel chairs, white filing cabinets, and a white enamel examination-table. Inside glass cases were rows of surgical instruments, laid out carefully on starched towels. The whole place was so sanitary and efficient, with a faint odor of disinfectant, that I felt glad the doctor was out and that I wasn't here to pay him a professional visit.

I found two other doors in the office. The first opened into a lavatory walled in white tile. The second opened into a dressing-closet—and that's where I found the doctor.

He was hanging by his neck from an exposed waterpipe that crossed just under the ceiling. The noose was cinched with cutting tightness about his throat, forcing his tongue to stick out blue and bloated from between his teeth. The knot about the waterpipe had slipped a little, the rope had evidently stretched, and his feet, in black patent-leather shoes, dangled only a few inches from the floor.

I reached out and touched one of his hands. It was stiff and cold and lifeless, and just touching it caused his body to swing gently on the rope.

He wore a tailored tuxedo, the trousers pressed into blade-like creases, and there was a wilting gardenia in the lapel of his coat. He was fastidiously dressed, except for the fact that his collar and tie were missing.

There was a small stepladder against the back wall, and it looked like he'd used this for his own gallows trap, standing on the top rung of it to fix the noose, to knot the other end of the rope at the waterpipe, before he jumped. And before he jumped, he had removed collar and tie and placed them side by side on the dressing-table. The tie had been folded. A very cool and calculated way to take your own life—if he had taken his own life.

I searched his pockets for a suicide note, didn't find any. Just a wallet with money and cards, a handkerchief, some loose change, and a small black case containing a hypodermic needle.

I looked up at his eyes. They were bugged from strangulation, but not the eyes of an habitual narcotic. So the hypodermic needle must've been intended for some patient.

I stepped out into the office and over to the desk. The top had been rolled up and there was a batch of papers but no suicide note. Most of the papers were bills he'd intended to mail, and ads from a physicians' supply house, and letters from patients explaining why they were unable to settle their accounts until next month.

But there was also a stack of dusty prescriptions—already filled—his personal copies. Those of them dated before July first of this year were on his own office pads, specially printed with his name and address. Those after July first didn't have his name printed, just serial numbers and his handwriting, and the paper was of fine quality—almost like the grade of paper the Government uses for currency.

I read his handwriting on all the prescriptions, and each was for Cocaine HCL, or Hyocine Hydro-Bromide, or for twenty-tablet bottles of morphine, one-half gram. The names of the patients were all different. The names of pharmacies where they'd been filled were all different too; some of the pharmacies were located outside the city of Los Angeles, and some even outside its suburbs.

I had just finished pawing the prescriptions when a bell tinkled musically behind me. I didn't quite jump out of my suit. It tinkled three times, the front doorbell, and I hoped it was some patient who would finally give up and go away.

I waited motionless for several minutes. The bell didn't ring again, and after a while I figured the patient had left. But he hadn't.

A key clicked in the outside door and somebody entered the reception room.

I tip-toed into the lavatory and drew myself flat against the tiled wall.

Another key clicked in a lock and the door opened into the doctor's office and a young woman entered swiftly. She didn't even bother to close the door behind her. She went straight to the dressing-closet where the doctor hung by his neck, and a little choked sigh escaped her lips, but not a sigh of surprise.

She carried a black leather overnight case, and this she placed on the floor near his dangling feet. She yanked out drawers in a wooden chest and removed the contents and stuffed everything hastily into the case. It all took less than a minute, this packing. She then snicked the latch, shoved the drawers back, shuddered as she took one last frightened glimpse of the doctor, and came out into the room carrying the case.

"Hello," I called gently. "What's the hurry?"

Her eyes swiveled toward the doorway where I stood, but her eyes never quite reached me. Another shudder passed down her body from shoulders to ankles, and the start of a scream never materialized into sound. Her knees gave, and she crumpled to the floor in a dead faint.

Five
Lady With a Knife

I picked her up and placed her on the white enamel table. That took effort; she was not small and light, and not the type for fainting. I must've given her quite a scare.

I loosened the ascot scarf from about her throat, and found a bottle of ammonia in one of the cabinets. Uncorking that, I held it under her nose. It did the trick. It revived her.

The lashes of her eyes flicked. Then she stared at me, and stared at the room as if seeing it for the first time.

"Everything's all right," I assured her. "You're in Doctor Jelk's office."

That didn't remove any of the fright from her pale cheeks. She put firm hands on the table, lifting herself, swinging legs to the floor. They were strong legs, and muscular under tan silk stockings. With her feet on the floor, hips and hands on the table-edge, she regarded me thoughtfully and the fright began to dim.

"Who are you?"—that from a throaty competent voice.

"I was about to ask you the same question," I replied.

She shrugged a little. "I suppose you're one of the G-men."

"Suppose I am?"

"Nothing. You've found the doctor, of course. And you probably think I'm involved in it." That was a flat statement of fact and was followed with another shrug of her shoulders. "Well, so what."

"So you'll have to do some explaining," I suggested.

Dark eyes looked deep into mine, but no thoughts were given away by them. She was not pretty, but not unattractive either—if you like them strong and capable. She wore a plain gray suit, tailored like a man's, and her shoes were low-heeled, efficient. She reminded me of the girls' athletic coach in the local high school.

"All right," she said, "I'll explain. I'll have a drink first. Do you mind?"

I shook my head at that, and she stepped past me and opened a glass case. I didn't see anything to drink in it, just surgical instruments laid out on starched white towels. I saw her hand swoop down and I yelled at her and reached for her arm, but I was too late.

She avoided me as she turned, her back against the open door of the case. A gleaming knife was in her hand, a surgeon's scalpel, and she lashed it across my chest in one lightning movement.

"Don't be a fool!" she snapped. "Look at your coat."

My fingers went up instinctively and discovered a ten inch cut in the tweed material of my best suit.

"I can do the same thing to your face," she said. "But I hope I won't have to."

"Lady," I said, "so do *I*."

"I want to leave here. *Now*." The scalpel was steady in her strong hand and pointed at me like a gun. "I don't expect to be followed. You can remain with the doctor for a while."

The blade of the scalpel backed me away in slow steps, and advanced with me as I backed. My legs hit a chair and upset it. The blade still advanced, and behind it came this determined, grim-jawed woman who reminded me of an athletic coach. She backed me through the doorway into the dressing closet, and I reached behind me and gave a sly push to the doctor's hanging body.

"Good God!" I shouted. "He's still alive!"

Her nerves were so tense that another violent shudder shook her body. My sudden shout, and her brief glimpse of Dr. Jelks swiveling slowly by the neck, caused the scalpel to drop a little and her eyes to stare for an instant at the body behind me.

I took advantage of that instant. I knocked her arm aside and smacked her flush on the jaw. It was even harder than I intended, and I felt a little ashamed about it afterwards. Somehow you don't like to hit a woman that hard—even a husky capable woman with a surgeon's scalpel.

I picked her up and placed her on the table again. But I didn't get the ammonia bottle, not right away.

Her purse was a flat bag of gray cloth, matching her tailored suit, and it was well stocked with money. About four hundred dollars in currency, a fistful of silver. There was a card in it that said she was Dorothy Tyler, a registered nurse. There was a personal check from Dr. Jelks for twenty dollars—probably her last week's salary. There was a railroad ticket for Omaha, Nebraska. Union Pacific, Train No. 49, leaving L. A. Station at 3:45 P.M. The ticket was dated today.

I put everything in the bag, closed it, put it where she'd dropped it when she first fainted. I opened the black leather overnight case and found it full of white starched dresses, the kind nurses wear in a doctor's office. There were laundry marks on them.

I closed that case too, and then got the ammonia and brought her around again.

The lashes of her eyes flicked several times, and she stared at me once more, and stared at the room.

"Hello," I said.

She lifted herself wearily and sat on the table and felt the side of her jaw where I'd smacked her.

"Sorry," I said. "It slipped."

"That's all right. I don't mind that. What gets me is your gag about him still being alive. A gag like that stinks of moth balls."

"It worked, didn't it?"

"Yes. And that's what gets me. It worked." She gave a loose shrug. "Well, what do we do now?"

"That explanation," I said. "We're back where we started from. Remember?"

"I remember."

"Will you talk?"

Her dark eyes had a shrewd look in them, like a Main Street business man driving a hard bargain. "If I talk, does it buy me out of here? A start?"

"It does," I agreed.

"A promise?"

"It's a deal."

"O.K.," she said, "what do you want to know—aside from the fact that I didn't hang Jelks?"

I went over to the roll-top desk and got the batch of dusty prescription blanks. I showed them to her. "He was peddling dope, wasn't he?"

She nodded, but her eyes remained on the papers. "Where'd you find those? He always kept them hidden."

"They were right out here on the desk. Maybe he got them out himself. Took one last look at them and hanged himself. The feds were after him. You mentioned something about G-men."

"Yes," she admitted. "They were after him. Before July first he could fill all the prescriptions he wanted, as long as he invented new names for the dope customers and sent them to different pharmacies. But since July a new law makes doctors use blanks provided by the Division of Narcotics. He had to be careful then. But his dope customers kept bothering him. And I guess he made out too many prescriptions. A federal man was in to see him yesterday afternoon. I'm telling you the truth. I'm his nurse."

I said I believed her and I did. But there was a lot more I wanted to know. "For instance," I said, "when did you find the doctor?" I pointed with my chin toward the dressing-closet.

She lowered her eyes. "I found him at nine this morning when I came to work. As soon as I found him . . . hanging like that—I left."

"Didn't want to get caught by the feds. That it?"

"Yes."

"Then you went home and thought it over. The feds might be able to trace you through the laundry marks in your uniforms. You came to get them. You didn't want to be nabbed on a narcotic rap, along with the doctor. Right?"

"Yes."

"Did he give you any hint about killing himself?"

"None at all," she said. "In fact we had a date last night. A treasure hunt."

"A what?" I guess I barked it at her, because her eyes widened at my question.

"Treasure hunt. A kind of party where you—"

I waved a hand at her. "I know, I know. That's why the doctor is wearing a tuxedo. Did you go on the date?"

"No. He called it off. He phoned me early last evening and said he couldn't make it. So I didn't see him again until I came in here this morning and found him—like that."

"Who was giving the party?"

Her eyes got shrewd again. She said: "You ask too many questions. I don't think you'll stick to your bargain."

"I'll stick to it," I promised.

She glanced at a watch upon her wrist. "Can I leave in five minutes?"

"Yes," I said. "Who gave the party?"

"A Mrs. Rufus La Farge. The party was at her house. At 1924 Alpine Way, in Beverly Crest. She's been very friendly with the doctor for a long time. That's about all I know. I didn't go to the party when he called the date off."

"O.K.," I said, "one more thing. Did you ever hear of a man named Walgreen? Lew Walgreen? Or Bugsy Walgreen?"

The name brought a glimmer into her dark eyes. "I think the doctor knew him. He came into the office a few times. But he wasn't a patient. That's all I know. Can I leave now?"

"You can."

Hurriedly she snatched up the gray handbag, the leather traveling-case. She took one last worried look at me, at the doctor's body swaying gently, and then she fled, leaving only a slam of doors behind her.

I gave her just about enough time to reach the sidewalk. Then I picked up the telephone and double-crossed her.

Captain Hollister was still out. A lieutenant of detectives answered the phone. He said: "The captain is in the morgue with the autopsy surgeon. He doesn't want to be disturbed."

"Well, here's something to disturb him anyhow," I said. "At the end of the trolley line in Playa del Rey there's a Doctor Otto C. Jelks. He's hanging by his neck in his office."

"You mean dead?" said the detective.

"That's what I mean. And he was supposed to go on a treasure hunt party last night. The one Lew Walgreen was on when he got killed near Valhalla."

"Say, wait a minute! Who's this talking?"

"Another thing," I said, ignoring his question. "Doctor Jelks has a nurse working for him. She was supposed to go on the party with Jelks last night. He called it off. The nurse knows he's dead and she's skipping town. She has a ticket for Train 49, Union Pacific, leaving L. A. Station at 3:45 this afternoon. You'd better cover the bus depots and the airports, too—in case she changes her mind about the train. Her name is Dorothy Tyler. Big husky gal in a gray suit tailored like a man's. The feds will want her for a witness against the doctor. He was peddling narcotics. You got all that?"

"Got it." And then the lieutenant gave a rasping cough to cover the sound of somebody at headquarters clicking into the line to trace my call. "Hold on a minute. Who shall I tell the captain is calling?"

"Steve Midnight," I said. "Tell him I'm still hot on the trail of my thirty bucks."

Six
Heaven With a Fence

It was an hour's trip from Playa del Rey to Beverly. On Sunday afternoon the trolleys ran infrequently, and I had to change twice on buses in order to get there at all. I began to wish I'd called one of our Red Owl Cabs and bargained with the driver to ride me on company rates—I. O. U.

At about 2 P.M. I found Alpine Way, and hiked up the steep winding road into the swank district known as Beverly Crest.

There were mansions clinging precariously to the hillside, steep gardens behind vine-covered brick walls, and all the private garages had space for at least half a dozen cars. In this retreat of luxury lived movie people, oil tycoons, and retired industrialists who had accumulated wealth outside of California. It was a district where even the trees seemed to be shaped like dollar signs and the raindrops clinging to their branches were fourteen carat diamonds.

I followed the road to the very top of a mountain and there found a dream-palace of rambling roof and sweeping glass, the house itself set back in a garden of terraced lily-pools. A pair of downy swans paddled blissfully in one of the pools, and birds chirped and scolded through the trees, conversing about the recent rain. All the place lacked was sunshine and the sudden appearance of a beautiful maiden riding a snow-crested steed. I felt like Ronald Colman discovering Shangri-La.

No wall surrounded this Heaven—just a steel fence which allowed you to enjoy the beauty inside but still guaranteed that you wouldn't try to touch it. I found a tall gate, locked, with the numbers 1924 made of bronze. I pushed the bell, and the birds stopped chirping and the swans craned their long graceful necks to give me the once-over through the fence.

There was a garage near the gate, built deeply into the side of the hill. Its roof was lawn and flowers. Only its gaping doorway opened out onto the road.

A man came out of this doorway and spoiled the serene picture by saying: "Hello. You want something?"

He wore a uniform of dark green whipcord, and flared trousers narrowing to a laced fit inside shiny black boots. His cap had a leather visor, was tall-fronted, like the cap of a German submarine commander. Under this, his face was square-jawed, freckled, and tough.

"I'd like to see Mrs. Rufus La Farge," I told him.

He looked me over carefully, from battered face to the slash across my coat, and I didn't let him think he worried me by the examination. I gave him the same thing, right back. I glanced down at his boots, then up at his cap. I studied the embroidered initials over the breast pocket of the uniform. The initials were *G. M.* Very fancy too. The *G.* interwoven with the *M.*

He said: "Mrs. La Farge ain't home. She's away at her Palm Springs estate. Did you have an appointment?"

"Not exactly an appointment. Since when did she leave for Palm Springs?"

"Day before yesterday," he said.

"Then she wasn't on hand for her own treasure hunt party last night?"

His eyes peered deep into mine and the set of his jaw didn't relax. He removed his cap and with the same hand scratched his head. He had red hair, thick, curling, and neatly combed.

"I don't know what you're talking about," he said. "She didn't have any party last night. The house is all closed up. Mr. La Farge is just back from Frisco and he's staying downtown at the church."

"Were you here last night?"

"No," he said. "Why?"

I began to wonder about Dorothy Tyler, the nurse. Maybe she'd tossed me a blind steer in the same neat way she'd slashed my coat with the scalpel.

I said to the chauffeur: "There was a treasure hunt party last night. A fellow named Lew Walgreen was on it and he got killed under a freight train down near Valhalla Cemetery. A Doctor Jelks was supposed to be on the party too. He didn't go. He's hanging by his neck down at his office in Playa del Rey."

The chauffeur put his cap back on, and his eyes never left me for a second. "You talk kind of funny. What's all this got to do with Mrs. La Farge?"

"It was Mrs. La Farge that held the party."

"Not here, she didn't."

My eyes wandered away from him, and over his shoulder I saw the terraces of lily-pools and the swans now out of the water and moving across the lawn under the trees. In the house itself, way up beyond, a venetian blind moved in one of the windows looking down at us. The slats of the blind tilted horizontal, then tilted to a steeper angle. My eyes came back to the chauffeur.

"And you say there's nobody home here at all?"

"Not a soul," he said. "They even sent the dogs to the boarding kennels. You must have the wrong house, mister. The wrong address. The wrong name."

"Maybe I have," I admitted. "Sorry to trouble you."

"That's all right. It's just some mistake. Mrs. La Farge wouldn't have any party where people got hurt."

"Not hurt," I corrected. "Dead."

He nodded solemnly. "That's what makes me know it's some mistake. You know who Mrs. La Farge is? Her husband is Saint Rufus of the Thou Shalt Society. That's a church."

"I know," I said.

"So it's just some mistake. What did you say your name was?"

"I didn't say."

His eyes dropped to my shoes, then shifted to the paved road that led up to this hilltop from Beverly Hills. He got out a package of cigarets and selected one and put it to his lips. "I don't see any car. You hike up?"

"No, I'm a parachutist. I came by air."

He flared a match on a thumbnail. "You don't have to get tough about it. I was only asking. If you want to clam up, then clam."

"You're pretty good on the clam-act youself," I told him.

He dropped the match and his jaw tightened. "You think I'm a liar? Well, you listen to *me*, short pants. Personally, I don't think you're just a liar. I think you're a fugitive from a booby hatch. I don't know what you're beefing about, all this treasure-stuff, and dead guys—and I don't like you hanging around here, so *scram*. I can call the cops to pick you up, or I can toss you down the hill."

"You'd better call the cops," I suggested. "If you try to toss me anywhere, you might get hurt."

"You think I can't?"

"You can try," I offered.

For a long moment he gave me a fighter's appraisal. Tiny muscles twitched along the line of his jaw. His hands worked and moved, started to become fists, then relaxed, and his facial expression changed from rage to disgust.

"Nuts," he said. "I can't be bothered."

He turned on his heel and strode back into the subterranean garage, a big handsome man whose uniform gave him swagger.

I started to hike on down the hill, but I only started. As I reached the far boundary of the estate, I took one last glimpse backward at the terraces, lily ponds and the swans. I saw the chauffeur emerge from a tunnel behind the garage and hurry through the garden. He was headed for the house itself, that palace of Shangri-La, and I saw him disappear through an arched doorway at the side.

I returned to the garage. It was a roomy place, with at least a five-car capacity, but now it had only two cars inside—one a long shiny limousine, a Rolls-Royce, and the other an inexpensive little coupe. I looked at the registrations on both cars. The Rolls, of course, belonged to the La Farge family—Rufus La Farge. The coupe was registered to George Manning, of 37 Seaside Way, Manhattan Beach. The initials *G. M.* made a faded muddy monogram on the left-hand door, the same interwoven fancy initials he had embroidered on his chauffeur's uniform.

While I was examining the cars, I heard quick hard footsteps coming through a tunnel at the back, so I slipped out of the garage and ducked into thick shrubbery beside the doorway.

I was just in time. The chauffeur came out briskly and looked up and down the road. He went to the edge of it, where he got a good view of the lower turn. He waited there for several minutes. He was looking for *me*, of course.

After a little more sentinel duty, he strolled to the big steel gate and unlocked it. He returned to the garage, gunned up the motor of the long limousine and backed it out. Then he drove it through the gateway and up to the mansion.

I came out of my shrubbery and looked up the terraces of lily-pools. The Rolls stood outside the main entrance, like a battleship tied to a wharf, and the chauffeur was stowing luggage. Then a woman appeared, a large buxom woman who wore about a thousand dollars worth of fur coat. She was pulling on gloves, and I saw a flash of diamond rings. She stepped into the limousine, seating herself alone in the rear compartment.

George Manning slammed the door and got up front, and the big car rolled smoothly down the private drive and through the gate. By that time I was back in the shrubbery again.

Manning stopped the long Rolls and went back to lock the gate. He stepped over to the edge of the road and looked down it again. He still didn't see me down there. He returned to the car and said something to the woman. She nodded, and then the big limousine was rolling again.

It didn't go down the hill. It went up over the crest on another route, a back road which would finally reach Mulholland Drive. Evidently they weren't taking any chances on meeting me along Alpine Way.

I watched the car disappear over the crest, and wished I could follow it, of course. But after all I'm not a Spartan runner.

Seven
The Saint in Silver

Around every corner in Southern California you find mystics, fortune tellers, old-age pensions, shrewd real estate schemes, fake oil companies, phoney gold mines, quack dental offices, and Swedish massage parlors where the massage is not particularly Swedish. Grifters, hustlers, promoters, swindlers . . . all of them making an unending source of trouble for the law. And if it wasn't for the fine operation of that law-enforcement machine, both state and local, you wouldn't be able to cross a street without having some smooth-speaking promoter take your shirt and necktie as down payment on the L. A. City Hall.

The Thou Shalt Society was one of the newer innovations. Not entirely new, of course, since for hundreds of years shady swindlers have hidden behind a mask of religion in order to ply their graft. Hallelujah, praise the Lord! Put fifty cents in the collection basket and save thy immortal soul! Dig down, brethren!

The Thou Shalt Society was one of those. A racket plied against lonely people, against the sick, against the worried, against the aged. The lousiest racket in the world, hiding behind a cloak of spiritual religion and defying you to prove it's just a cloak. The Thou Shalt Society preached a doctrine that "thou shalt soon die. Therefore, thou hast no need for thy earthly wealth." Dig down, brethren.

So the congregation dug down, shelled out. And Mr. Rufus La Farge—Saint Rufus—lived in a fine mansion in Beverly Crest and last year paid the federal government over ten thousand dollars for income tax.

Saint Rufus, like the poor members of his congregation, might soon die. But his own pessimistic doctrine didn't prevent him from enjoying a hell of a good time while he was living.

* * *

I took a bus down Sunset Boulevard to L. A. and reached the Temple of the Thou Shalt Society sometime late in the afternoon. It was a huge garish temple which might have been designed by a movie studio for use in a film depicting the future. Its walls were somber and gray with tall narrow windows of crimson glass. On the tremendous rounded dome was a colossal neon sign you could see across the roof-tops for miles—two words of brooding threat—

THOU SHALT!

There had been an afternoon service and people were just leaving. Most of them trudged along silently toward trolleys and buses. There were only a few automobiles—most of those battered and dilapidated, the cars of the poor. There were a few light delivery trucks loaded with families, and one ancient electric resembling a glass box set high on wheels. A pair of old ladies in lavender sat primly behind the glass.

I went up the broad steps to the doorway and spoke to a man who wore a cutaway frock coat and a full black tie. His face held the feigned sadness of an undertaker as he said good-bye here and there to the departing members of the congregation. He was the head usher, and he frowned at me with annoyance when I spoke.

"I'd like to see Mr. La Farge," I told him.

He shook his head. "Saint Rufus is resting. He has just given a service. His health is not good, and he never sees anyone until after he rests."

"This is a personal matter. Important. It's something about his wife."

The usher glanced around us worriedly, as if fearing some member of the congregation had overheard me. But no one had. They'd all left, even the stragglers, and we were alone on the steps. The usher put a thin hand to his lips and coughed into it politely.

"Perhaps he might see you. What name shall I give?"

"No name."

"None?"

"None," I said.

The usher bowed and left me, but he wasn't gone even a full minute. He returned with a sad, loose-jointed walk, announcing wearily: "Step this way, please."

I followed him down a side aisle in the hall, past countless rows of empty pews, and finally through a small door behind the pulpit from which Saint Rufus preached his doctrine of death and advised his brethren to shell out.

We went up a short flight of steps in a dark corridor, and the usher opened another door. "You may enter," he said, and promptly closed the door behind me, and departed with soft regular footsteps.

I was in the presence of Saint Rufus himself. He was alone in a somber consulting-room, but he was not resting. He sat behind a broad walnut table, smoking a cigar.

"You may be seated," he said, and I groped into a chair and looked at him across the table.

He was something to look at, an amazing spectacle of a man. Not young, maybe over sixty, with a stern but healthy face, almost without lines. His hair was a silvery gray, brows bushy and silver, and under them a pair of deep-set, appealing eyes. He wore a fine flannel suit that was more silver than white. Under the table, his shoes were silver, even his socks silver. The only things not silver about him were the healthy glow of his cheeks, the tan of his hands and a full black ascot scarf about his throat. Even his voice had a silvery ring when he asked: "What was it about my wife?"

"It's about a party she had last night."

"Party?" His features sagged a little, showing lines of weariness and age in a face that hadn't had them when I first came in. "I wouldn't know anything about that," he went on. "I've been out of the city. I haven't been home at all. Too busy with duties of the faith. What kind of a party did you say?"

"A treasure hunt party. They met at the home in Beverly Crest. Sent out in couples following notes. The first couple back was supposed to win prizes. Fur coat for the lady, gold watch for the man. You didn't know about it?"

He shook his head. "I wish she wouldn't hold these parties. She's promised me she wouldn't do this sort of thing. I think you understand." He cleared his throat and made his voice silver again. His eyes held worry far back in their depths. "There was some . . . some sort of trouble last night?"

"Plenty. A man named Lew Walgreen was on the party. He was killed during the course of it. His partner disappeared. And a Doctor Jelks was supposed to attend the party with his nurse. Now Jelks is dead, and the nurse tried to vanish."

Saint Rufus paled. His face got almost as silvery white as his flannel suit. He fished out a handkerchief and dabbed nervously at his lips. They were moist. His eyes became deep green glass.

"You—you're from the police?"

"Not exactly."

He sat for a moment in silence. His body seemed to wilt. Then he straightened up, and got out of the chair, bracing hands on the table-edge. "Oh. I think I understand. Excuse me a moment."

He turned and opened a cabinet behind the table. Inside it, on a broad shelf, I saw money. Stacks of nickels, dimes, quarters, pennies—stacks and stacks of them. And on a lower shelf more money, this in currency, neatly assorted. Bunches and bunches of currency. And all this probably consisted of his collections over the week-end services.

He selected a fat wad of currency, counting it over. I only saw his back, the shrug of his shoulders. Then he slammed the cabinet door and returned to his chair at the table, with enough money to plug a dike in Holland.

"Let's get this conference over with as quickly as possible," he said, in a flat weary voice. "How much do you want?"

"Want?" I guess I gave him a puzzled stare. "What are you paying for?"

"Silence, of course. Isn't that why you came here?"

"Not at all. I came for information."

His moist lips twitched a little, and a deeper sadness crept into his eyes. "I think you have all the information you require. How much shall I pay?"

I didn't answer that. I said: "Then you know about your wife's party."

"No. Certainly not. And I don't care to hear the sordid details." He counted out several hundred-dollar bills. "How much, please?"

I waved a hand. "Wait a minute. Who's this Lew Walgreen?"

"A friend of my wife. A rather unpleasant friend. You must know that. Probably Mr. Walgreen sent you here."

"No," I corrected, "he didn't. And Doctor Jelks didn't send me either. Is the doctor another friend of your wife's?"

"Yes," he said.

"Your wife has nice friends."

He frowned at that, became somehow pitiful in the way he rolled his eyes. "Please don't be sarcastic. I'm willing to pay your price, but I'd rather not listen to your comments." He shoved a cool thousand dollars across the table to me, and when I didn't touch it he peeled more off the roll and added another thousand dollars to the pile of money within reach of my hand.

I shook my head. "You don't seem to get the idea, Mr. La Farge. I'm not here to shake you down . . . though you're giving me a hell of a fight with temptation." I pushed the money back across the desk to him. "Information is still what I'm after. What kind of contact did your wife have with Walgreen and the doctor?"

"I don't know," he said. "And I don't care to learn. I'd rather not discuss it at all. My wife means a great deal to me, in spite of her unpleasant behavior. My temple, and the Thou Shalt Society, also mean a great deal to me. I'm willing to pay anything to preserve both. Will you take your money now and leave?"

He fingered the two grand, added more to it, built it into a pile that was like the jack-pot in a high caliber, Wall Street poker game. He pushed all that money toward me, and resisting it brought sweat to my forehead. I'd gotten into this thing to collect only thirty dollars for Pat Regan and the Red Owl Cab Company. I'd been working like hell to collect only thirty bucks. And now I was having about five thousand dollars shoved at me, by a Saint in Silver, and I was trying to be noble.

The saint said: "I can't see what difference it makes about the information, and there's nothing you can say that will surprise me. I know my wife had some sort of an affair with this Doctor Jelks, know she then switched to some man named Walgreen, just in the last six months. And I know she's paid him a lot of money. I guess he made love to her. I don't care. When she gets over these . . . er, incidents . . . she always comes back to me. So you can't tell me anything that will surprise me. I even know she has a new man now. I don't know who he is, but my lawyers found out she goes to Manhattan Beach. It's undoubtedly some man. But she'll tire of him, like she's tired of the others. She'll come back to me."

"Did you say Manhattan Beach?"

"Yes. Some kind of a love-nest down there. It doesn't matter. It doesn't surprise me. How much will you take for your silence? The Thou Shalt Society, as you must understand, can't afford scandals of this kind."

I stood up. I pushed the money back to him once more across the table. That amazed him.

"You won't take it?"

I shook my head, and a faint smile, bitter, flirted across his mouth. "You're a very unusual person," he said. "And if you're not a police officer, or a blackmailer, I can't understand you at all. It's something new. Will you have a cigar?"

It was a long thin smoke wrapped in silver foil, and the paper ring on it bore his name, Rufus La Farge, in crimson letters. The cigars were made especially for him, he said, by one of his flock in the tobacco business in Havana.

He got up and saw me to the door. "Are you going to wreck my temple and my reputation?"

"I'm not making a point of it," I said.

"And my wife," he went on, with almost a glimmer of tears in deep eyes. "Sheila grew out of a sinful environment, but her eventual reformation is as certain as early death is certain to all of us. We all die, and most of us die sooner than we expect."

The way he said that gave me an odd feeling. I wasn't sure whether it was a statement of his doctrine or a veiled threat. And I left him—not knowing.

Eight
Love Nest Feathered
With Lead

I got out to Manhattan Beach, via trolley, as the light began to fade. Back of the prosperous little beach town were scattered cottages on the bare dunes.

A paved street groped its way through the dunes, past fewer and fewer houses, finally lost its sidewalks in drifts of sand. I turned off the pavement when I saw a lonely sign reading *Seaside Way*, and I followed a muddy dirt road for about half a mile and then found another small stucco cottage built in the dunes. There was no garden in front of it, just a broken garden gate in a leaning picket fence, and a tin mail box on a rotting wooden post. The faded letters said: *37 Seaside Way*.

I opened the box and took out the letters. There were three of them, and they looked like bills. They were addressed to Mr. George Manning, which didn't surprise me, since I'd been guided there by the registration on his coupe—the one in the garage at Beverly Crest.

I looked up at the house. The shades were pulled at the windows, no light seeped out. The whole place looked like nobody had come near it in years. But, belying that idea, was the fact of mail in the box and the criss-cross of tire tracks in the muddy sand outside.

I bent down and examined the tracks in the fading light. The more recent tracks had been made by one car—since the last fall of rain this afternoon. Fat tires, with deep clear treads. You could see where the car parked, where it backed around to leave. And by the thickness of the tires, the long sweeping pattern they left as the car backed and turned, I had a picture of the great Rolls-Royce battleship which I'd last seen leaving Beverly Crest.

I limped through the broken gate, went up to the front stoop of the house and tried the bell. It didn't ring. The button was rusted, the whole electrical system out of commission. I knocked on the panels of the door, but nobody responded. I tried turning the knob. It wouldn't turn.

Rain began to fall now, in far-spaced, pattering drops. Night was closing in fast.

I went around to the back door, tried the knob, and it turned readily.

I entered a rear service porch in which there was a washtub full of empty gin bottles, a rusty water heater, a clothesline with a pair of socks pinned to it. I opened another door into a kitchen, and found more gin bottles, and empty highball glasses which hadn't been washed. I went over to the drainboard and examined the glasses. Two of them had cubes of ice in them—not quite melted.

I pushed open a swing door into the combination living-room-dining-room, and the place wasn't empty. There was a woman in the house, and the first glimpse of her caused me to stop in the swing door. I thought she might sit up and scream, or reach for the phone to call the police.

But she did none of those things. She just lay flat on her back on the sofa, a fur coat thrown carelessly over her body, her face as pallid as death.

I said softly: "Hello. Pardon me. . . ."

She didn't move.

I crossed the room and looked down at a smoothly beautiful face. It had no color at all, except rouge on cheek-bones, and on her lips.

A wisp of dyed dark hair had come down over her closed eyes, and she lay there on the sofa with no more motion than a hewn log.

I lifted the fur coat and placed the flat of my hand between her breasts. Holding it there, I could feel a little breathing. Soft, throbbing, not rhythmic.

I turned from her, and on a table found a pocket-size case containing a hypodermic needle, and a tiny vial with only a wad of cotton in it—no tablets. The glass cylinder of the needle was wet with moisture. There was a small enamel pan with warm water in it. The water had been boiling not so long ago. That's where the needle had been disinfected.

On the table also, I found a woman's suede handbag with a clasp of diamonds. I opened the bag, and it was full of money. There was also a check-book and club cards and a carbon copy of a voter's registration. But I really didn't have to use any of that stuff to identify her. I already knew who she was. The queen from Shangri-La. The big buxom woman who caused her husband so much trouble. The wife of Saint Rufus.

I explored the rest of the bungalow. In the bathroom a tube of shaving soap and a razor in the basin, a man's suit of silk pajamas tossed into the tub. In the bedroom, socks and shirts crumpled on the floor, the bed unmade, a pair of pants hanging flat from the picture molding—the kind of bedroom where a bachelor lived. A messy collection of clothes, but none of them revealing bloodstains.

I went outside into the backyard, through kitchen and service porch, and found a concrete incinerator.

I opened the steel door on the incinerator and put my hand inside. The ashes were cold in there, but not as wet as they should be. Unless George Manning was a fine housekeeper and only recently burned the last of his combustible rubbish. But having seen the inside of George Manning's bachelor quarters, I didn't think he was a fine housekeeper.

Inside the incinerator there was a smell of burned cloth. I reached my hand deep into the ashes, and pulled out the sole of a leather shoe. It was blackened, charred, and it smelled of gasoline.

I reached deeper and got out only ashes and some hard objects there were buttons. Everything was burned, charred. Everything had the smell of gasoline. A steel belt-buckle was almost warm.

I wiped my hands on my handkerchief, removing the blackness of the ashes, and I discovered that night had settled completely on the dunes.

I returned into the house through the service porch and kitchen. I flicked a switch and the electric lights came on. At the same instant there was a clap of thunder in the sky, and a downpour of rain.

In the living-room Mrs. Rufus La Farge still slept motionless on the sofa, under the fur coat. I found a towel in the bathroom, wet it under the cold-water tap, and returned to Mrs. La Farge and slapped it across her face. She rolled and groaned, turning the shape of her body away from me. But she didn't wake up.

"Come on," I said, "snap out of it . . ."

And another voice came sharply from the noise of rain. "Take your hands off her, you son-of-a———!"

The last time I'd been called that was in the crypt at Valhalla.

He was standing in the kitchen doorway with a Luger in his fist. He still wore the chauffeur's uniform, black boots, the tall-fronted cap with the stiff black visor. Behind him in the door, was a small worried little man carrying a doctor's satchel. His eyes blinked nervously through thick-lensed spectacles, and he didn't like the gun in the chauffeur's fist nor the way it pointed at me.

"If you'll excuse me a moment . . . my other case . . . I left it out in the car. . . ."

Manning reached back with his free hand and clutched the little man by the collar. "Take it easy, doc."

"But my other case?"

"Baloney," Manning said, "you didn't bring any other case. Just keep the ants out of your pants, doc. You won't get hurt. It's this other guy might get hurt."

I was standing beside the sofa and the sleeping woman. I had the wet towel in my hand, and against George Manning's Luger I felt about as capable of defense as a Boy Scout against the Dover artillery. My heart began to pound and my throat felt parched. I wanted to get away from Manning and the Luger as badly as the little doctor did. But it was the little doctor who acted first.

He swung up the satchel and hit Manning in the face with it. The Luger went off in one sharp explosion, like the hard slam of a door, and glass fell out of a window across the room from me.

The little doctor had a lot of guts—you had to hand him that. He almost hung suspended from the floor with Manning's firm grip still on his collar, but using that for a swinging pivot he kept slapping the satchel against Manning's face, against the Luger, against the fist that held it.

Mrs. Rufus La Farge sat up on the sofa and screamed thickly, like a person choking. She was trying to say something but the thickness of her tongue under the influence of drugs only allowed for choked screams and inhuman babblings.

I rushed across the room in a crouching run, tackled Manning, and went down under his kicking legs and the doctor's.

All three of us rolled and scrambled, and then the little doctor lurched to his feet, snatched up his satchel and his hat, and fled from the house like a rabbit.

That left me alone to fight Manning.

I had a grip on his wrist, and it took all my strength to keep the muzzle of the Luger away from me when it blasted again. The jerk of its firing, the jolt Manning gave me with his shoulder, almost tore my grip loose. Somehow we both struggled to our feet, and both of us were holding the Luger, as if it were some great weight which took both of us to lift.

We stood in the kitchen doorway then, chest to chest, and his face was sweating, inches from mine, his breath hot and panting. I suddenly let go of the wrist, let him have the Luger all to himself for a split instant. But in that split instant I braced my legs and slugged him.

The Luger brought down several pounds of crumbling plaster from the ceiling, and George Manning went backwards in a stumbling, falling run. His outflung arm knocked a dozen empty gin bottles off the kitchen drain, and he went to the floor amid breaking glass.

I landed on his belly with both feet, in a running broad jump. The force of my landing threw me across the kitchen and against the stove, but the force of it also put the finish on Manning's fight.

He doubled up on the floor, holding his stomach, gasping for breath like a beached shark. His face turned green and he began to vomit. The Luger fell forgotten from his fingers—he was in too much agony to be bothered with it any more. I got the gun and stowed it on my hip.

I took down the length of clothesline from the service porch and tied his ankles together and his wrists behind his back.

I stepped cautiously into the living-room to see what had happened to Mrs. Rufus La Farge, but nothing at all had happened to her. She was asleep again, under the fur coat, and she still slept there long after the neighbors phoned for Law.

Captain Hollister arrived in a squad car in time to prevent a pair of local radio officers from clamping steel bracelets on me.

"You been playing cop again, Steve?"

I told him, "I've done a pretty good job of it, at that," and pointed my chin toward the kitchen. "In there you'll find the guy who killed Lew Walgreen."

Hollister said: "Yeah?" He peeked briefly into the kitchen where an ambulance surgeon was using a pulmotor. "Who is he?"

"The name is George Manning."

He strolled across the living-room to the sofa and turned back the fur coat and frowned at the sleeping woman. "Who's this?"

"Mrs. Rufus La Farge. You've probably heard of her husband—the Silver Saint. Manning's the family chauffeur, but recently he's been spreading his duties over a wider area. This place is sort of a love nest."

"Oh. What's the matter with her?"

"Drugged. That's the whole story."

The captain flared a match to fire the soggy end of his cigar. "I'd like to hear it, Steve. If it's not too much trouble."

"Well, she uses dope. I don't know whether her husband knows it or not, but he knows she's always in a lot of trouble because he's been shelling out hush-money to blackmailers."

"You know that for a fact, Steve?"

"I know he tried to pay me five grand this afternoon—with no questions asked."

"Did you take it?" Then he grinned. "Forget that crack, Steve. So she used dope and she got it from that doctor in Playa del Rey—the one you called me about. Doctor Jelks. We found him lynched down there."

"She used to get the dope from Jelks," I said, "but recently she couldn't get enough. After July first there was a new federal law about doctors filling narcotic prescriptions. They couldn't use their old pads any more, they had to use certificates issued by the government. And of course if they filled too many prescriptions, the feds would want to know why, and how, and who. So that left Jelks in a tough spot. The patients that patronized his dope-concession couldn't get enough of it from him now, and the doctor was blackmailed into giving out too many prescriptions."

"Mrs. La Farge?"

I shook my head. "Not her. I don't think so. When Doctor Jelks began to fail her she had enough money to find somebody else. She found Lew Walgreen. Maybe Jelks himself steered her to Walgreen, because Jelks' nurse said she used to see Walgreen hanging around the office and Walgreen once served a federal narcotic rap—you told me that yourself."

"Correct," the captain said.

"And you told me Walgreen was financed into a night club. The answer is Mrs. La Farge. He was supplying the dope the doctor couldn't supply and more. And making it pay."

"Blackmail?"

"I think so. You don't get a night club and a nice car just peddling dope. Not when you've served a rap for it in the past and you're watched closely by parole officers and the feds. So he must've been getting all his financing just from Mrs. La Farge. He demanded too much from her. She decided to get rid of him."

"Shoved him under a freight train?"

I shook my head. "It's a little more complicated than that. She was having this treasure hunt party. You know what that is. Notes hidden at out-of-the-way spots. She wouldn't plant those notes herself. I can't see her climbing into tombs to hide notes. The chauffeur is the logical one for that task. And Manning went around planting them.

"When he was down at Valhalla, the day before the party, he saw it was a good spot for a bump-off. He was the boy-friend of Mrs. La Farge, and he went back home and told her how nice it would be if Lew Walgreen happened to get killed on the treasure hunt. A lot of railroad bums use Valhalla as a hide-out from yard dicks, and it would be just swell if Walgreen met up with one of these bums and got polished off. With robbery as the motive. And very little police investigation. See what I mean?"

"I see," the captain said. "So they framed the party so Walgreen and his blonde would get the series of notes leading to Valhalla. And Manning hid out there, with gloves and a pick-handle. To finish Walgreen."

"Exactly," I said. "Manning propped a heavy statue against the door of the tomb. That was to keep the blonde from coming in with Walgreen. One murder was all he wanted. He knew the blonde wouldn't climb in the tomb with Walgreen through a skylight.

"It was a nice scheme, except Walgreen got drunk, and the

blonde hired a cab for the rest of the treasure hunt. It was me that climbed into the tomb, instead of Walgreen. Manning saw the mistake and robbed me. That was just to make it still look like some bum had been in the tomb.

"Then Manning left the tomb, and there was no blonde around. She had fled. He went down to the cab and found Walgreen. Passed out. Drunk. So Manning got a swell idea. The murder scheme hadn't soured after all. Walgreen would get robbed and shoved under a train down in the yards. He had to take Walgreen out of the cab in a hurry, because he didn't know when the blonde would come back to the cab. Or the driver would come back. So the train idea seemed fine."

"I get it. And he was already wearing gloves to conceal his prints."

"Sure. But he got blood all over him down there in the freight yards. He had to get rid of his clothes. I found where he burned them. In the incinerator back of this shack."

"How about Jelks? Did Manning lynch the doctor?"

"No," I said. "That was a real suicide, and it gummed up the works. Doctor Jelks was supposed to be on the party himself. Escorting his nurse. Dorothy Tyler. By the way, did you nab her?"

"The feds did," Hollister told me. "They had a tail on her and they picked her up as she was boarding the train. They want her on the same narcotic rap. So Jelks hanged himself, huh?"

"He did. He couldn't face federal prosecution, so he decided to die. Mrs. La Farge couldn't understand why Jelks didn't show up for the party. Either she, or Manning, or both of them, went to the office in Playa del Rey. There he was, dead. And they couldn't have two deaths on the same treasure hunt party, not without a lot of investigation. So they decided to switch plans and wash their hands completely of both deaths. . . ."

"It seemed easy with the doctor. Mrs. La Farge's name didn't appear on any of the prescriptions, of course. Any narcotics she bought would be under assumed names. But she and Manning searched the doctor's place anyhow, just to be sure, and they discovered a lot of hidden, dusty prescription copies, her name not on any of them. So they placed all the papers on the desk. They left them there so the police would be sure to see the motive for the suicide and not dig too deep on an investigation. And to wash their hands of any connection with Walgreen's death, they just called off the treasure hunt."

The captain frowned darkly. "It was too late for that. The party had started."

"Sure, but you can guess the kind of people who attended it. Probably persons who worked in her husband's racket, those could be bargained with. Any others, like the missing blonde and Dorothy Tyler, could be reached with the La Farge money. So as they filed back to the house from the hunt she made it clear to them that *there hadn't been any party*. She broke it up in a hurry. She even worked out a story whereby she was supposed to be in Palm Springs for the last couple of days—if the police happened to check. Maybe she was even really headed for Palm Springs when she and Manning stopped off here."

"The love nest, huh?"

"Yeah, but I don't think that's why they stopped. Mrs. La Farge needed a bang in the arm, and this is where she took it, along with some of Manning's gin. The combination knocked her cold. That scared Manning. He went out for a doctor, and brought back one."

"A quack," said the captain.

"Yeah, but don't malign him. If the little guy hadn't slapped Manning with a satchel, I wouldn't be here. And you wouldn't have to loan me eighteen bucks."

Hollister scowled. "What for?"

"Meter receipts," I said. "I took twelve dollars and my watch back from Manning. But I'm still shy the fare to Valhalla that the blonde and Lew Walgreen didn't pay me. You wouldn't want me to lose my job, would you, captain? After all I've done for you, what's a little matter of eighteen bucks? You can get it back as soon as you find that blonde."

"You're a funny kind of blackmailer, Steve. In one afternoon you turn down five grand from a guy that can afford it, and you hook a poor police captain for eighteen fish." He reached for his wallet.

The way it turned out, George Manning pleaded guilty to dodge the death penalty and get life at Folsom. The court handed Mrs. Rufus La Farge ten years in the State Women's Pen.

Saint Rufus sadly informed the press: "I shall fight on alone, without Sheila, and in my great loneliness I shall continue to preach the doctrine of the Unavoidable, Unalterable, Inescapable— Death."

So it worked out fine. Just the blonde on the treasure hunt was still missing—and the eighteen bucks I owed Hollister.

The blonde, Maybelle Knapp, former torch singer for Lew Walgreen's club, had dropped out of sight completely.

One afternoon in early spring I was covering Olie Greenberg's run and I picked up a fare at a swank apartment house in Westwood. The fare was a blonde, and dressed in about a thousand dollars' worth of fur. Diamonds sparkled on her fingers and the scent of high-priced perfume almost wafted me to sleep.

I said, "Hello, Mabel. I see you won the mink coat after all.

Her red mouth sagged wide. Her lips trembled. "Come upstairs," she said.

So we went up to her apartment, a beautiful place with carpet like fine lawn and soft ivory walls and furnishings showing the touch of an expensive decorator. She slammed the door and faced me.

"All right. How much do you want?"

"Just the eighteen bucks you owe me."

"You mean only eighteen dollars?"

"That's all," I said.

She got a roll of bills out of her purse, peeled off a twenty, and said: "Keep the change. The rest is a tip."

"Thanks," I said.

"Are you sure that's all you want?"

I glanced down at a crystal glass ashtray on a carved walnut table. In it were the stubs of several cigars—cigars that had been long, thin, and costly, from Havana. And there were crumpled foil wrappings with bands bearing the name Rufus La Farge.

I said to the blonde: "One other thing, lady. When you see the Silver Saint, tell him a sucker who refused five grand sends regards. And hopes he won't be too lonely in his womanless world of remorse."

John Jakes spent years writing for the pulps and the paperback original markets. He was always good but he got even better as he went along. He became a breakout bestseller with his historical novels that began with *The Bastard*. In the process, however, his crime fiction was overlooked. He wrote a good dozen stunning crime pieces in the fifties and early sixties, of which the following is a good example.

The Man Who Wanted to Be in the Movies

John Jakes

George Rollo stepped away from the mirror and surveyed his scrupulous grooming. His hair was neatly brushed back, his suit freshly pressed, and his maroon tie with the white polka dots was artfully knotted. His face was almost eclipsed by the carefully planned sartorial perfection.

George Rollo was in love. He happened to be in love with a young woman who received his attention with reserve. But he went right on pursuing her, doing anything within his power to win her affections. Because of her, he dressed carefully.

He picked up the expensive box of candy secured from the drug store. He was able to afford a large box because he was a pharmacist in the drug store and could get the candy wholesale.

He locked the door of his room soundly behind him and clattered down the stairs. On the second landing a young and rather pretty woman with big amber eyes stood leaning on the doorjamb, next to a sign that announced, *Yolanda Fox, Licensed Thaumaturgist, Helpful and Benevolent Spells of All Types.*

"Hello, George," she said warmly as he came banging down the stairway.

"Oh. Hello, Yolanda, how are you?" His voice was strained, absent.

A large furry white thing rushed past the girl's legs and began lapping affectionately at the young man's shoes.

"Down, Faust," Yolanda said sharply. "Come here."

The familiar, who resembled a large and pugnacious bull dog with amber eyes quite like the girl's, crept back to a position at the side of his mistress, whining helplessly.

"Going out?" Yolanda asked yearningly.

"Yes," George replied in a nervous tone, "with Mabel."

"Oh." Sadness dropped like a curtain across her face.

"Well," he said nervously, "well, I guess I'd better be going."

He hurried off down the stairs. Yolanda caught a glimpse of the candy box and her amber eyes narrowed with faint jealous anger.

Faust growled, displaying bulldog teeth.

She shrugged then, as if winning out against an impulse to injure George, who shot a hasty glance at her from the bottom of the stairs just as she returned to her apartment.

Out in the street, George shivered. He knew Yolanda liked him, even though he had a distinct fear of witches. Even white witches licensed by the State Thaumaturgy Board. They could only conjure helpful spirits or make hexes to ward off illness. The law said they could do no more, but George was certain many of them had darker, half-forgotten powers.

He put Yolanda from his thoughts and hurried on down the street.

Miss Mabel Fry sat in her dirty armchair, surrounded by piles of magazines. Their glazed covers blanketed the rugs, made colorful landscapes even in the small dinette. The walls of the apartment were covered with pictures of male movie idols, wearing hound's tooth jackets or holding a golf club or smiling at starlets.

The doorbell clacked with a noise of sad disrepair.

Mabel reached for another peppermint, shoved it into her red mouth and went on reading her magazine: *It's the Simple Home Girl For Me, by Rodney de Cord, Rising Young Parafilm Star.*

The doorbell clacked a seond time.

Mabel lifted her large body and moved disconsolately to the alcove. She opened the door and said in a bored manner, "Oh. George."

"Hello . . . uh . . . Mabel."

He burst eagerly into the room, presenting his candy. She accepted it with mumbled thanks. She was a perfume clerk in a local department store, but she didn't much like the idea of accepting candy from an ordinary druggist.

"Where are we going tonight?" she asked, slipping into her coat.

"Anyplace," George replied casually. "There's a fine concert at the Music Hall. . . ."

She ignored him. "The Royal has a wonderful new picture, *I'll Slay My Love*, with Todd St. Bartholomew. He's *so* masculine. When he played a private detective and slapped Lona Lawndale in *Bodies to Burn*, I just couldn't stand it, it was so thrilling."

George didn't argue. "Anything you say," he mumbled.

As they walked to the theatre she babbled about the latest gossip from Hollywood. Who was marrying whom. Who was divorcing whom. Who was in bed with whom when who came home with who's perfume all over him. George listened with resignation.

Mabel waited under the glaring lights of the marquee while he bought the tickets. She rolled her eyes ecstatically at Todd St. Bartholomew staring belligerently from the poster, gun in hand. A caption balloon from his lithographed lips announced, *I'll Slay My Love*.

As they passed through the door, Terry Silver, the aging owner of the theatre, waved to Mabel.

"Evening," he called affably. "Next week we're showing *Husbands and Paramours* with Michale Yarven."

"Ooooooo," Mabel exclaimed loudly. "How wonderful!"

She allowed George to take her hand as they approached the main aisle. Just then a young man in a bright red sport coat sauntered over.

" 'Lo, Mabel," said Bertie Wallen.

George swore in a whisper. Bertie Wallen was a bit actor on local television shows. He dressed and looked like a movie actor.

"Thought I might find you here," Bertie said to Mabel. "Got big news. Friend of mine in Hollywood just wired me that I should fly out there right away. Metropole wants to test me."

Mabel squealed with delight.

George stood by impotently, glaring at Bertie as if he were a liar.

"Like to see the wire?" Bertie asked in broadly humorous tones.

"Sure, Bertie," Mabel cooed.

"Come on out to my car. Only take a minute."

Mabel started away, then turned to George. "Be a sweetie and go inside and wait for me. I'll be right in. The usual seats."

He started to protest feebly, hesitated, and stumbled into the auditorium. He found the customary seats, saving the adjacent chair for Mabel.

For two hours he sat woodenly, alone, watching Todd St. Bartholomew consuming quarts of alcohol and being pounded by assorted mobsters. George rather enjoyed the picture. One of Hollywood's better character actors, a man named Tab something or other, played a kindly old judge. George liked Tab whatever-it-was, although he doddered a bit. He must have been at least seventy-five. He had a sympathetic rugged face. He did not impress George as a professional lover.

George tapped on Yolanda Fox's door at eleven-thirty that evening. The door opened after a moment and she invited him in, surprised and pleased. Slipping out of a black robe and erasing a chalk pentagram from the floor, she turned up the lights.

"Just practicing a hay fever prevention spell," she explained. "Pollen season coming on."

He sank down on her sofa, staring moodily at the floor. Faust nuzzled his leg.

"Yolanda," he said at last as she bustled out of the kitchen with two steaming cups of tea, "you're the one for me."

She almost dropped the cups. Quickly she set them down and hurried to his side. "Oh, George. . . ."

"Yes sir," he added gloomily, "you're the one to help me get Mabel."

"Oh."

Her face smoothed out. She seemed quite calm. She served the tea and inquired in a helpful tone, "What can I do?"

"I love Mabel Fry. I'll do anything to make her love me. But she . . . well . . . she likes movie stars. Isn't there any kind of a spell to make me lucky?" He paused, deliberated and plunged on. "Can't you get me into the movies?"

"I don't know," she answered, thinking.

"I'll pay anything," he offered. "That is, anything I can."

"It won't be necessary to pay me," she replied carefully. "I'll be glad to help you. In fact, I think I can get you into the movies tonight."

"You . . . can?" He was startled.

"Certainly." She picked up a valise, began to stuff it with the paraphernalia of demonology. "But we must have the right atmosphere."

"Atmosphere?"

"A theatre. The Royal is near. I guarantee that before morning you'll be in the movies. Come, Faust."

They hurried through the dark streets.

The Royal was a mound of shadow, closed for the night. The street was relatively deserted. Only a drunk reeled from a cocktail lounge opposite the theatre.

"Sssssh," Yolanda cautioned, finger to lips. "We've got to get inside."

They crept through the vacant lot adjoining the theatre. Before the brick wall, Yolanda halted and made several passes in the air, murmuring something about Asmodeus, and a cold wind shoved George forward through grey fog.

He looked about. They were in the middle of the darkened theatre lobby.

Faust yipped with satanic glee. His large amber eyes glowed with strange delight. Yolanda's eyes glowed in the same fashion. George didn't notice.

They made their way down one aisle of the auditorium. Above them, the screen was a formless patch of silver-white.

Yolanda opened her valise, pulling forth her black robe. She lit two small braziers that gave off pungent fumes. She drew circles on the rug, remembering all of the bits of black magic the law had forced her to forget.

George watched the screen in fascination, because if Yolanda proved successful, he would be up there, and soon!

Yolanda moaned and waved her hands in the air and chanted. The braziers smouldered with oily bronze fire. Faust capered up and down the aisle, barking. And then Yolanda tapped George on the shoulder. Her face was illuminated by some unholy light.

"All right, George," she whispered. "Here you go."

He was strangely lifted.

Yolanda erased her marks, put out her braziers, repacked her valise and departed. Faust cavorted behind her, bulldog face aglow with strange humor.

For a long time George Rollo didn't know what had happened, or where he was. If this was the way to get into the movies, it was certainly a peculiar way.

When he tried to move his hands or feet he found it was impossible. In fact, he was unable even to feel them at the ends of his arms or legs. That is, he amended in his thoughts, he would have been, if he could have felt his arms or legs.

Everything was strangely dark. Then suddenly it was as though a curtain had been swept away from his eyes.

He saw rows of white staring faces. Two of them belonged to Mabel Fry and Bertie Wallen. Suddenly it began to dawn on him just what Yolanda had done. Blinding lights hit him. He screamed.

The only sound that came out was a ruffle of drums and a snatch of vaguely familiar music.

He wasn't George Rollo. *God in heaven!* . . . he wasn't even a *man! He was flat . . . and from one end of him to the other, in gigantic letters, he said* IN CINEMASCOPE. . . .